久保帯人

The cat that became the model for Mr. Yoruichi. The thing next to it that looks like a bicycle wheel is the author.

I don't know why but I've been super busy lately getting, like, two hours of sleep, not leaving the house even once the whole week. Sounds like the life of a manga artist.
Tite Kubo

BLEACH is author Tite Kubo's second title. Kubo made his debut with *ZOMBIE POWDER*, a four-volume series for *WEEKLY SHONEN JUMP*. To date, *BLEACH* has been translated into numerous languages and has also inspired an animated TV series that began airing in Japan in 2004. Beginning its serialization in 2001, Bleach is still a mainstay in the pages of *WEEKLY SHONEN JUMP*.

BLEACH
Vol. 6: THE DEATH TRILOGY OVERTURE
The SHONEN JUMP Graphic Novel Edition

STORY AND ART BY TITE KUBO

English Adaptation/Lance Caselman
Translation/Joe Yamazaki
Touch-Up Art & Lettering/Dave Lanphear
Design/Sean Lee
Editor/Kit Fox

Managing Editor/Elizabeth Kawasaki
Director of Production/Noboru Watanabe
Editorial Director/Alvin Lu
Executive Vice President & Editor in Chief/Hyoe Narita
Sr. Director of Acquisitions/Rika Inouye
Vice President of Sales & Marketing/Liza Coppola
Vice President of Strategic Development/Yumi Hoashi
Publisher/Seiji Horibuchi

Printed in the U.S.A.

Published by VIZ, LLC
P.O. Box 77010
San Francisco, CA 94107

SHONEN JUMP Graphic Novel Edition
10 9 8 7 6 5 4 3 2 1
First printing, March 2005

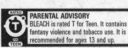

PARENTAL ADVISORY
BLEACH is rated T for Teen. It contains
fantasy violence and tobacco use. It is
recommended for ages 13 and up.

THE WORLD'S
MOST POPULAR MANGA

SHONEN JUMP
GRAPHIC NOVEL

www.viz.com

www.shonenjump.com

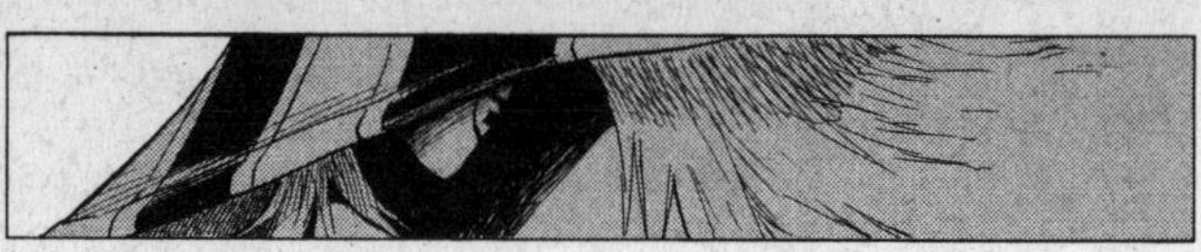

Yes, there is no Fate for us
Only those who are swallowed by
Ignorance and fear and miss a step
Fall into the rapid river called Fate

BLEACH 6 THE DEATH TRILOGY OVERTURE

Shonen Jump Graphic Novel

STARS AND

Rukia Kuchiki

Orihime Inoue

Ichigo Kurosaki

★ plot ★

Fifteen-year-old Ichigo "Strawberry" Kurosaki can see ghosts. Otherwise, he was a typical (?) high school student until the day a Hollow—a malevolent lost soul—came to eat him, and the Soul Reaper Rukia Kuchiki stepped into his life. To defeat the Hollow and save his family, Ichigo let Rukia transfer some of her Soul Reaper powers to him. But when Rukia was left powerless, she recruited Ichigo for her war against the murderous, soul-gobbling Hollows.

Now Ichigo finds himself in a deadly contest with Uryû Ishida, a "Quincy" who hates Soul Reapers—whoever defeats the most Hollows wins! But in no time the neighborhood of Karakura is swarming with ravenous Hollows!!

BLEACH ALL

Uryû Ishida

Chad Yasutora

Kisuke Urahara

STORIES

BLEACH6

THE DEATH TRILOGY OVERTURE

Contents

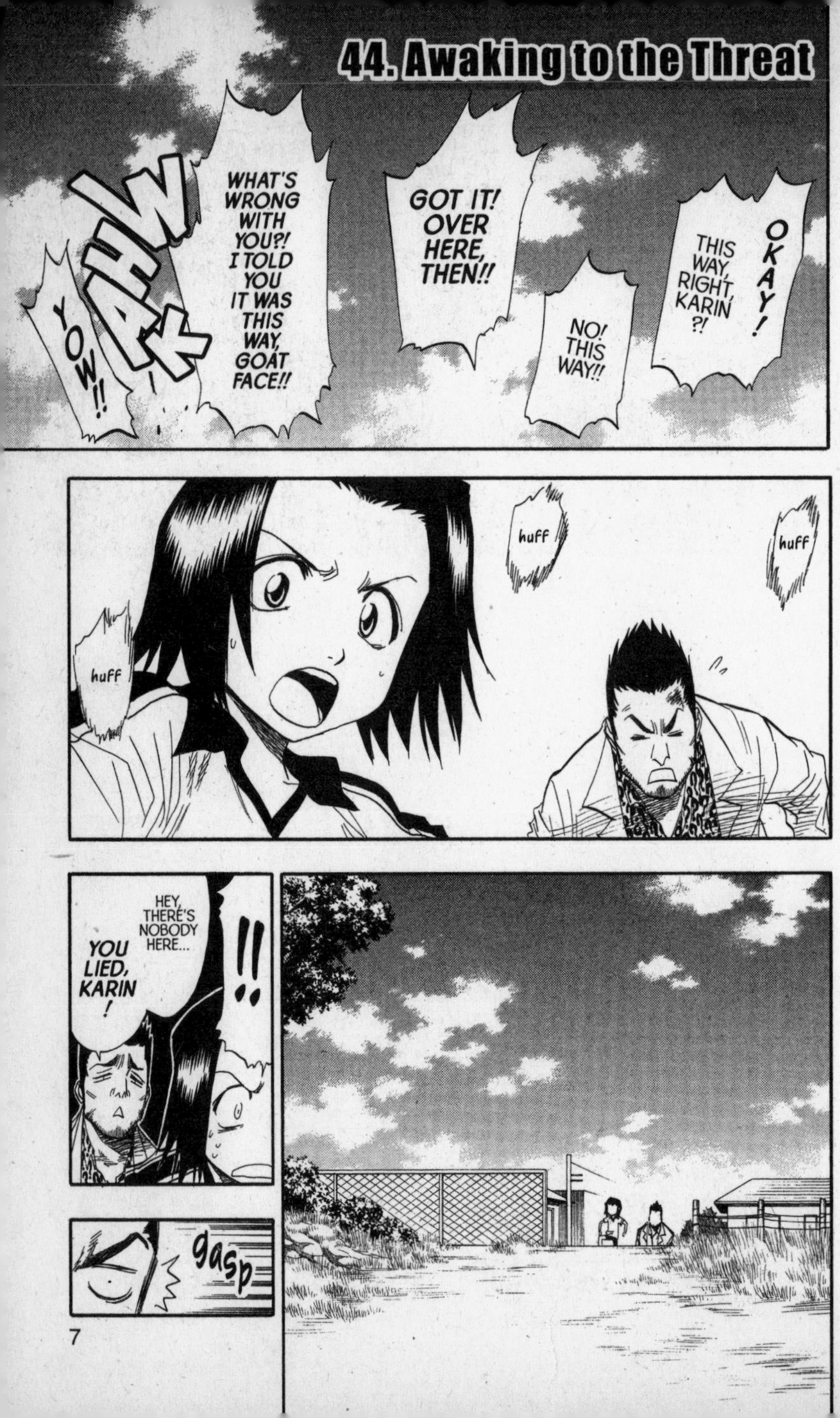
44. Awaking to the Threat
OKAY!
THIS WAY, RIGHT, KARIN?!
NO! THIS WAY!!
GOT IT! OVER HERE, THEN!!
WHAT'S WRONG WITH YOU?! I TOLD YOU IT WAS THIS WAY, GOAT FACE!!
WHAK
YOW!!
huff
huff
huff
!!
HEY, THERE'S NOBODY HERE...
YOU LIED, KARIN!
gasp

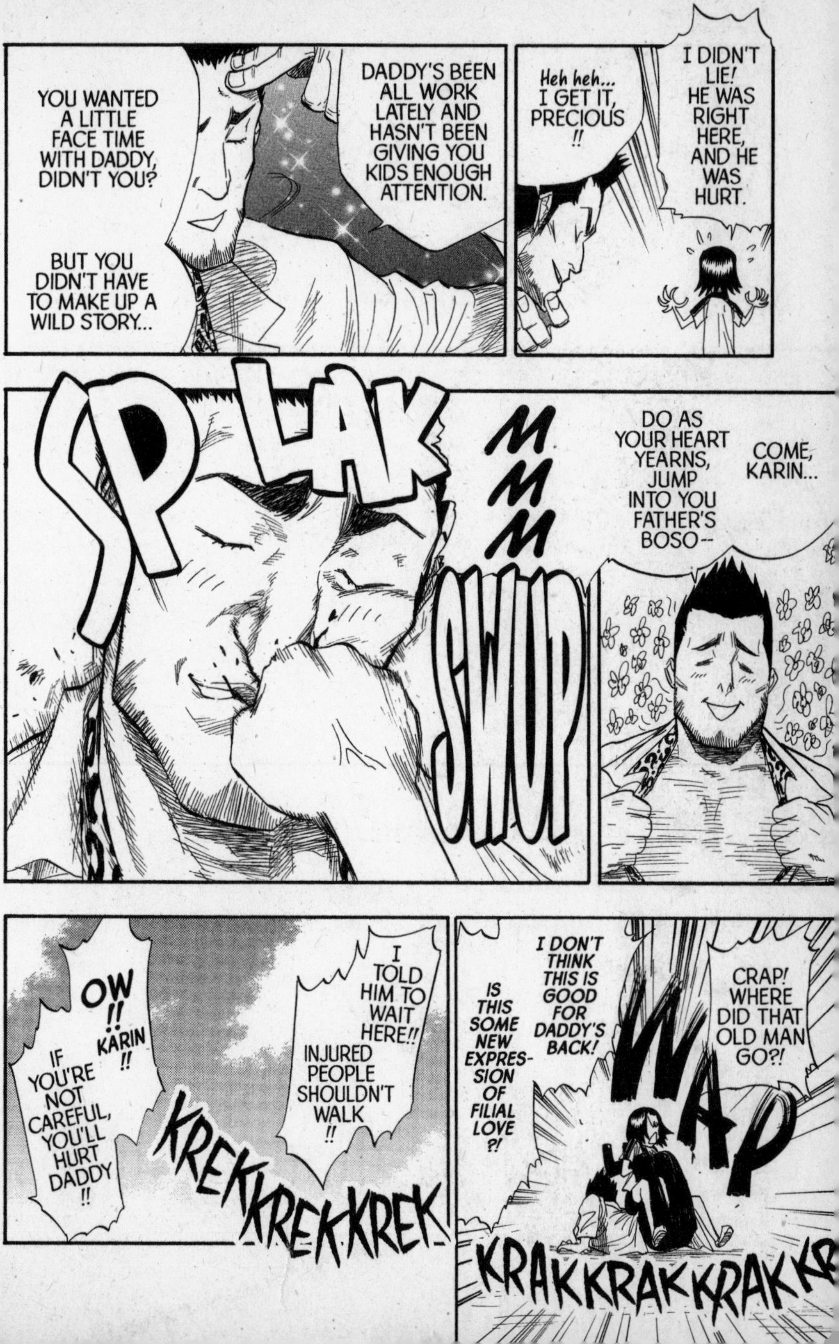
I DIDN'T LIE! HE WAS RIGHT HERE, AND HE WAS HURT.
Heh heh... I GET IT, PRECIOUS!!
DADDY'S BEEN ALL WORK LATELY AND HASN'T BEEN GIVING YOU KIDS ENOUGH ATTENTION.
YOU WANTED A LITTLE FACE TIME WITH DADDY, DIDN'T YOU?
BUT YOU DIDN'T HAVE TO MAKE UP A WILD STORY...
COME, KARIN...
DO AS YOUR HEART YEARNS, JUMP INTO YOU FATHER'S BOSO--
SPLAK
MMM
SWUP
CRAP! WHERE DID THAT OLD MAN GO?!
I DON'T THINK THIS IS GOOD FOR DADDY'S BACK!
IS THIS SOME NEW EXPRESSION OF FILIAL LOVE?!
WAP
KRAKKRAKKRAKKR
I TOLD HIM TO WAIT HERE!!
INJURED PEOPLE SHOULDN'T WALK!!
OW!! KARIN!!
IF YOU'RE NOT CAREFUL, YOU'LL HURT DADDY!!
KREKKREKKREK

READ THIS WAY

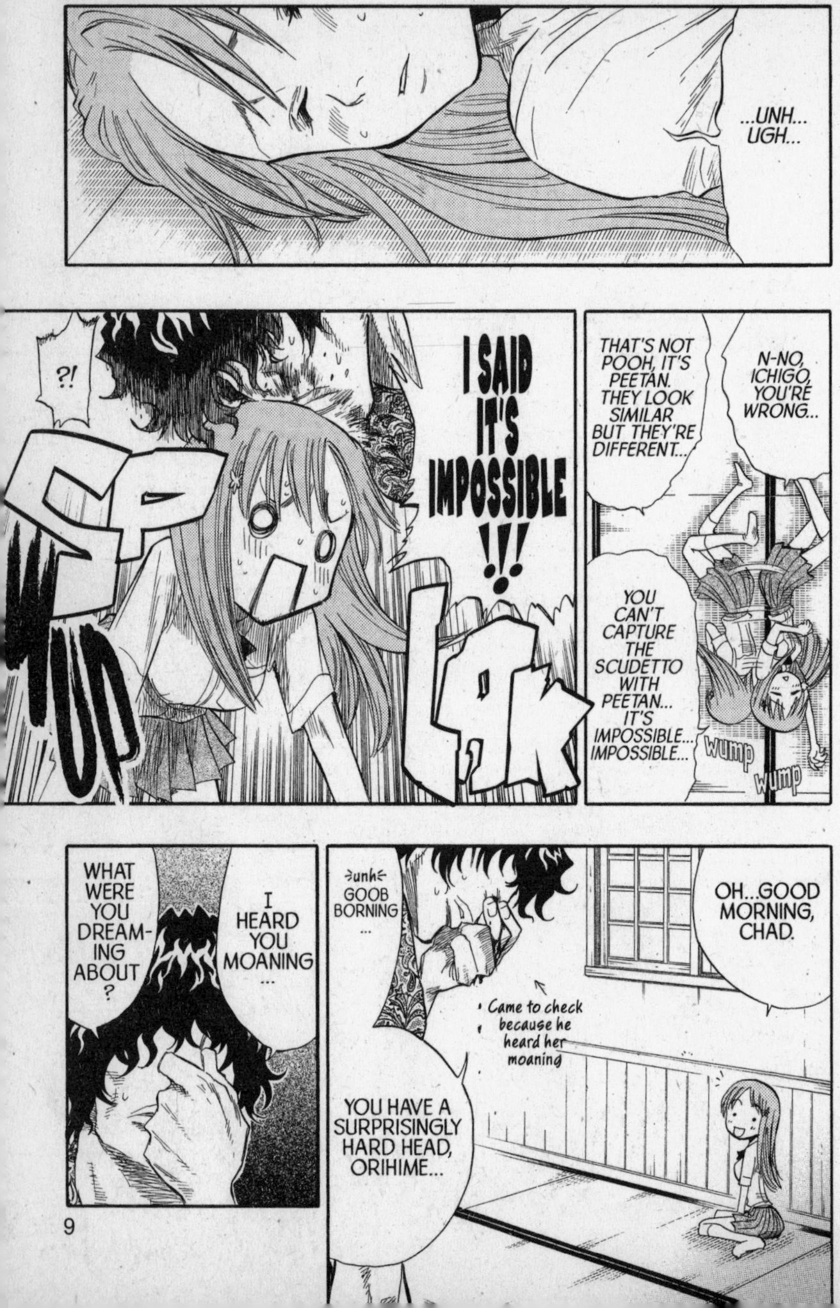
...UNH... UGH...
N-NO, ICHIGO, YOU'RE WRONG...
THAT'S NOT POOH, IT'S PEETAN. THEY LOOK SIMILAR BUT THEY'RE DIFFERENT...
YOU CAN'T CAPTURE THE SCUDETTO WITH PEETAN... IT'S IMPOSSIBLE... IMPOSSIBLE...
wump
wump
I SAID IT'S IMPOSSIBLE!!
?!
OH...GOOD MORNING, CHAD.
unh GOOB BORNING...
Came to check because he heard her moaning
YOU HAVE A SURPRISINGLY HARD HEAD, ORIHIME...
I HEARD YOU MOANING...
WHAT WERE YOU DREAMING ABOUT?

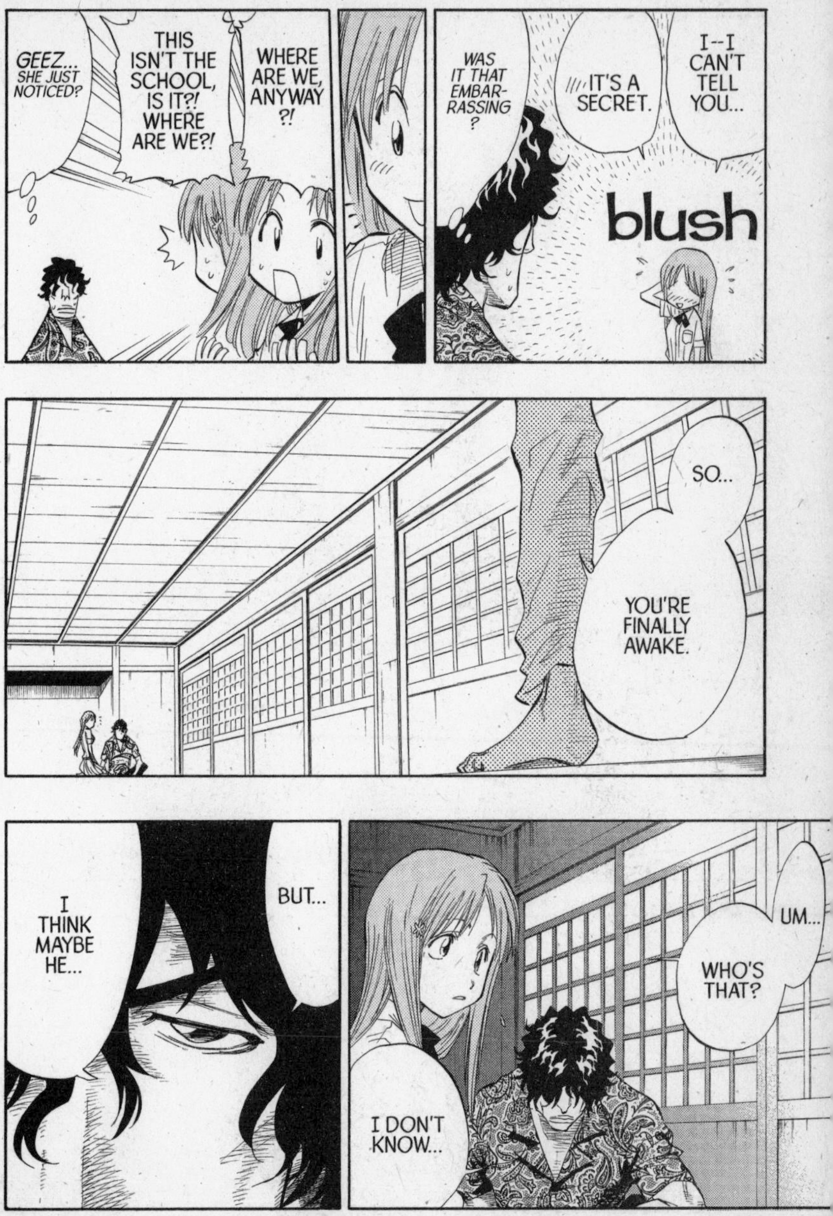
I--I CAN'T TELL YOU...
IT'S A SECRET.
WAS IT THAT EMBARRASSING?
blush
WHERE ARE WE, ANYWAY?!
THIS ISN'T THE SCHOOL, IS IT?! WHERE ARE WE?!
GEEZ... SHE JUST NOTICED?
SO...
YOU'RE FINALLY AWAKE.
UM...
WHO'S THAT?
I DON'T KNOW...
BUT...
I THINK MAYBE HE...

READ THIS WAY

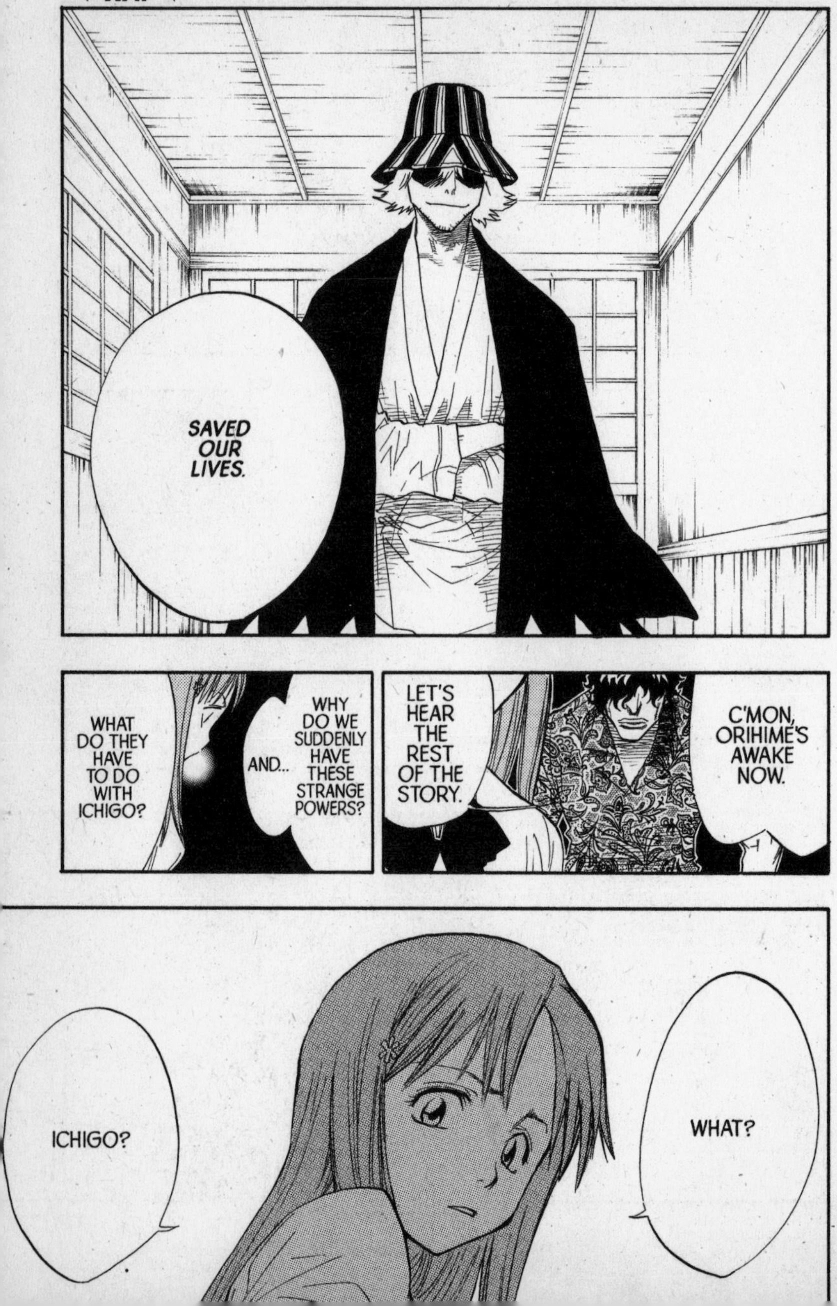
SAVED OUR LIVES.
C'MON, ORIHIME'S AWAKE NOW.
LET'S HEAR THE REST OF THE STORY.
WHY DO WE SUDDENLY HAVE THESE STRANGE POWERS?
AND...
WHAT DO THEY HAVE TO DO WITH ICHIGO?
WHAT?
ICHIGO?

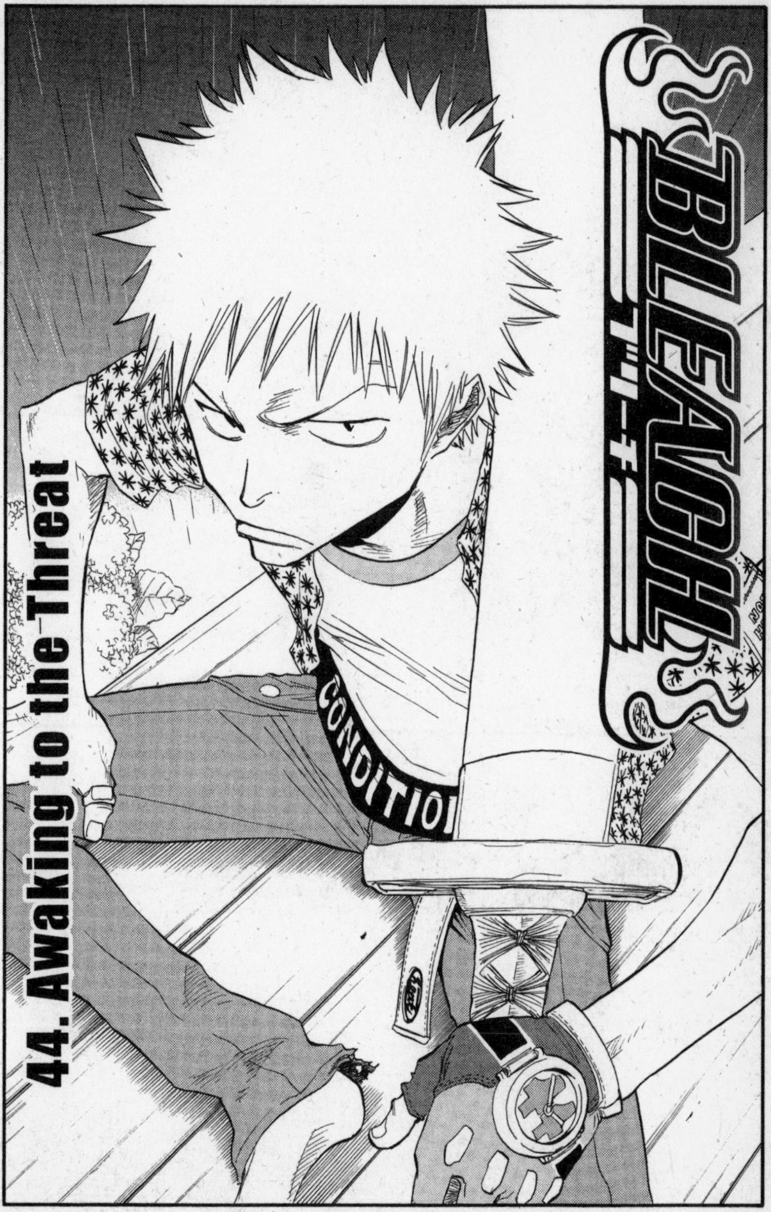
BLEACH
44. Awaking to the Threat

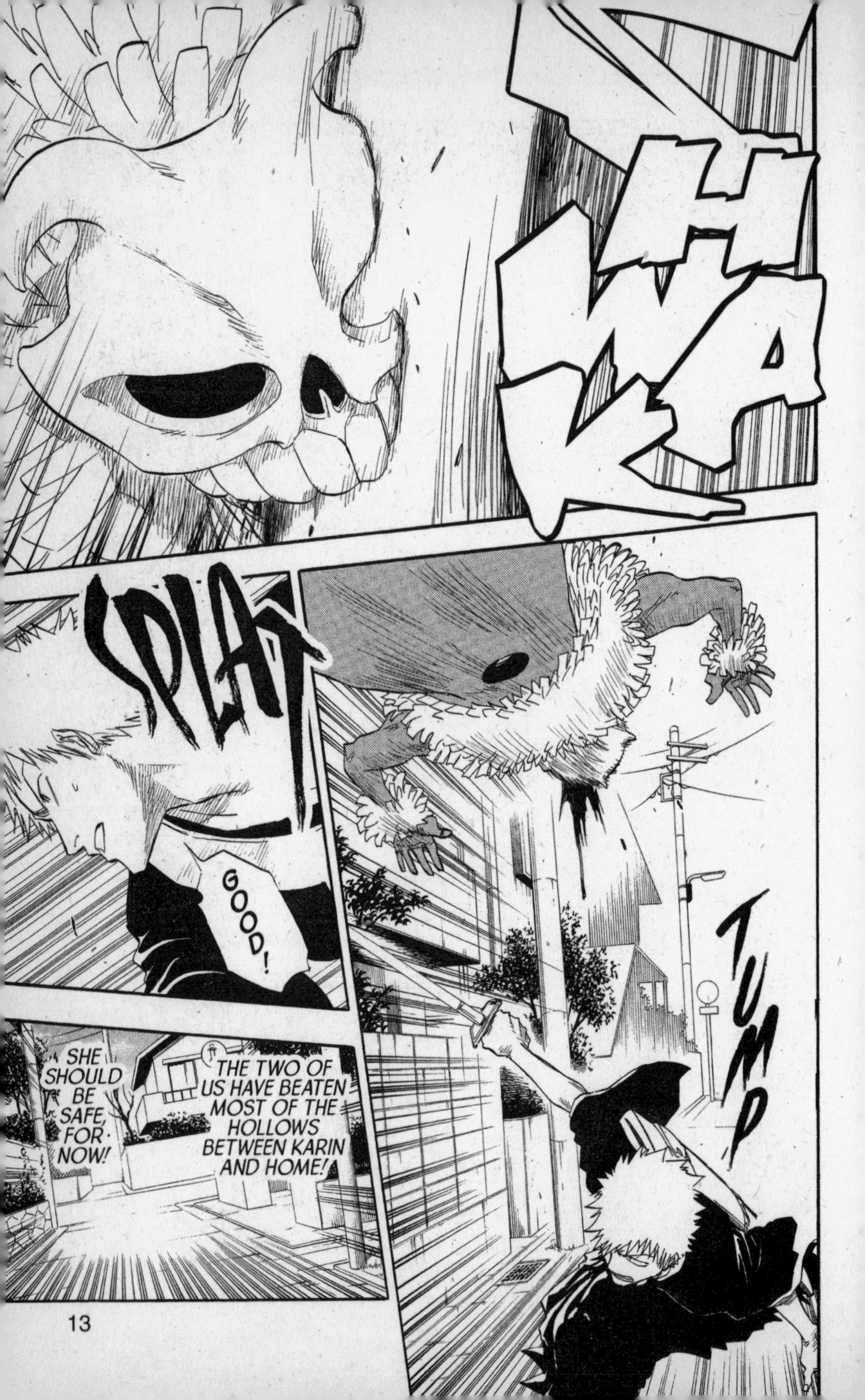

SHWAK
SPLAT
GOOD!
TUMP
THE TWO OF US HAVE BEATEN MOST OF THE HOLLOWS BETWEEN KARIN AND HOME!
SHE SHOULD BE SAFE, FOR NOW!

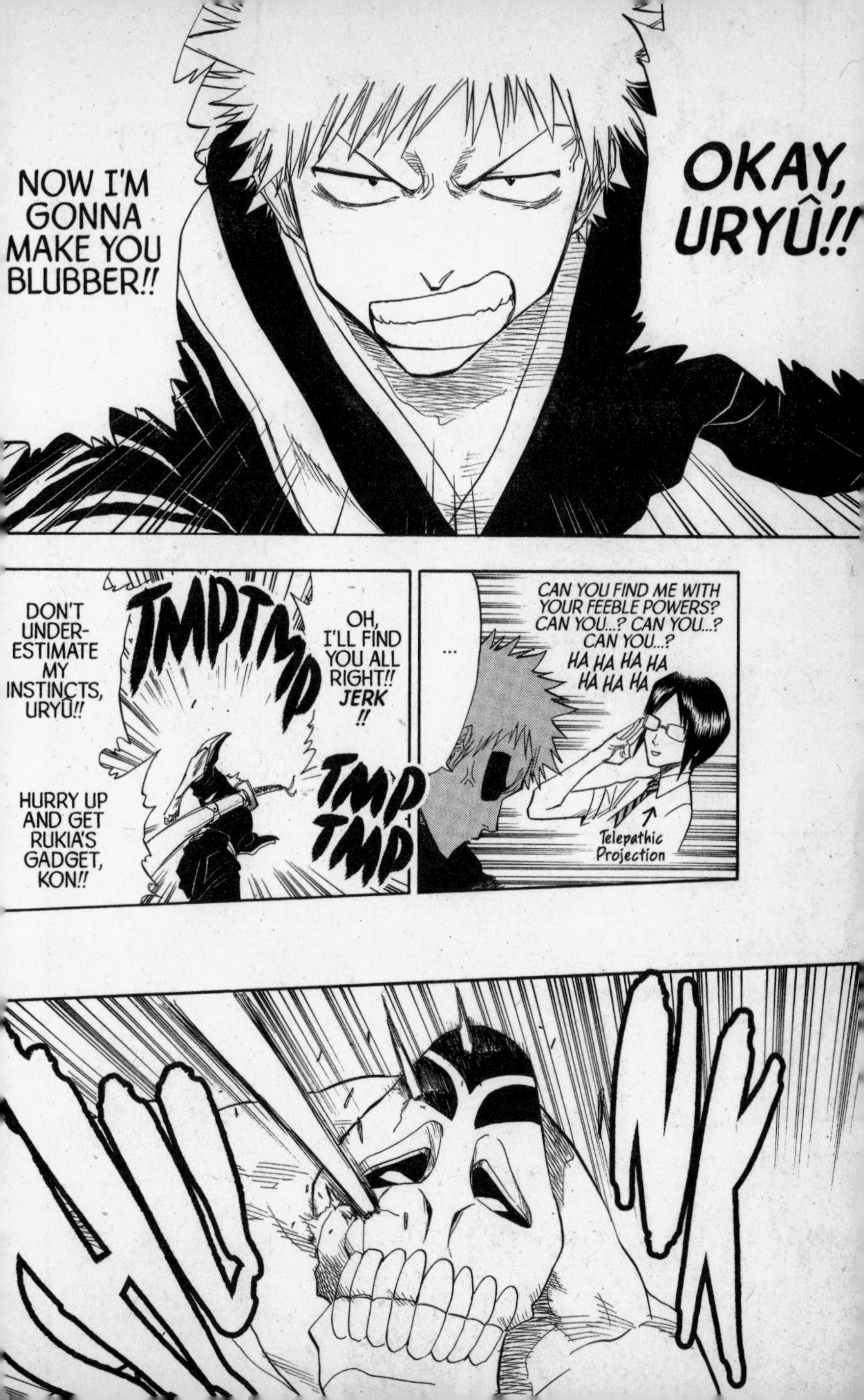
OKAY, URYÛ!!
NOW I'M GONNA MAKE YOU BLUBBER!!
CAN YOU FIND ME WITH YOUR FEEBLE POWERS? CAN YOU...? CAN YOU...? CAN YOU...?
HA HA HA HA HA HA HA
Telepathic Projection
...
OH, I'LL FIND YOU ALL RIGHT!! JERK!!
TMP TMP
TMPTMP
DON'T UNDER-ESTIMATE MY INSTINCTS, URYÛ!!
HURRY UP AND GET RUKIA'S GADGET, KON!!

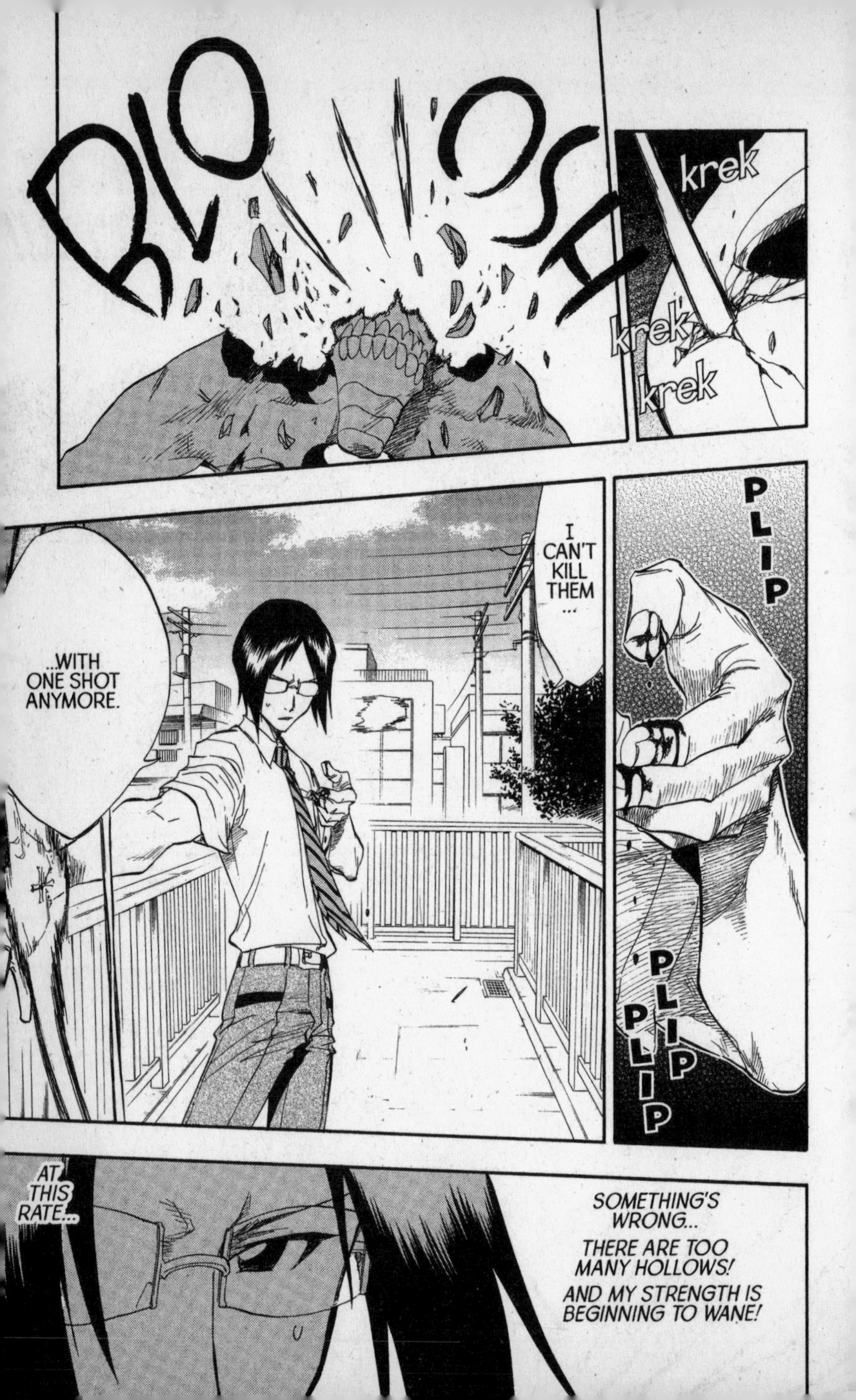
krek
krek
krek
BLOOSH
PLIP
PLIP
PLIP
I CAN'T KILL THEM...
...WITH ONE SHOT ANYMORE.
SOMETHING'S WRONG...
THERE ARE TOO MANY HOLLOWS!
AND MY STRENGTH IS BEGINNING TO WANE!
AT THIS RATE...

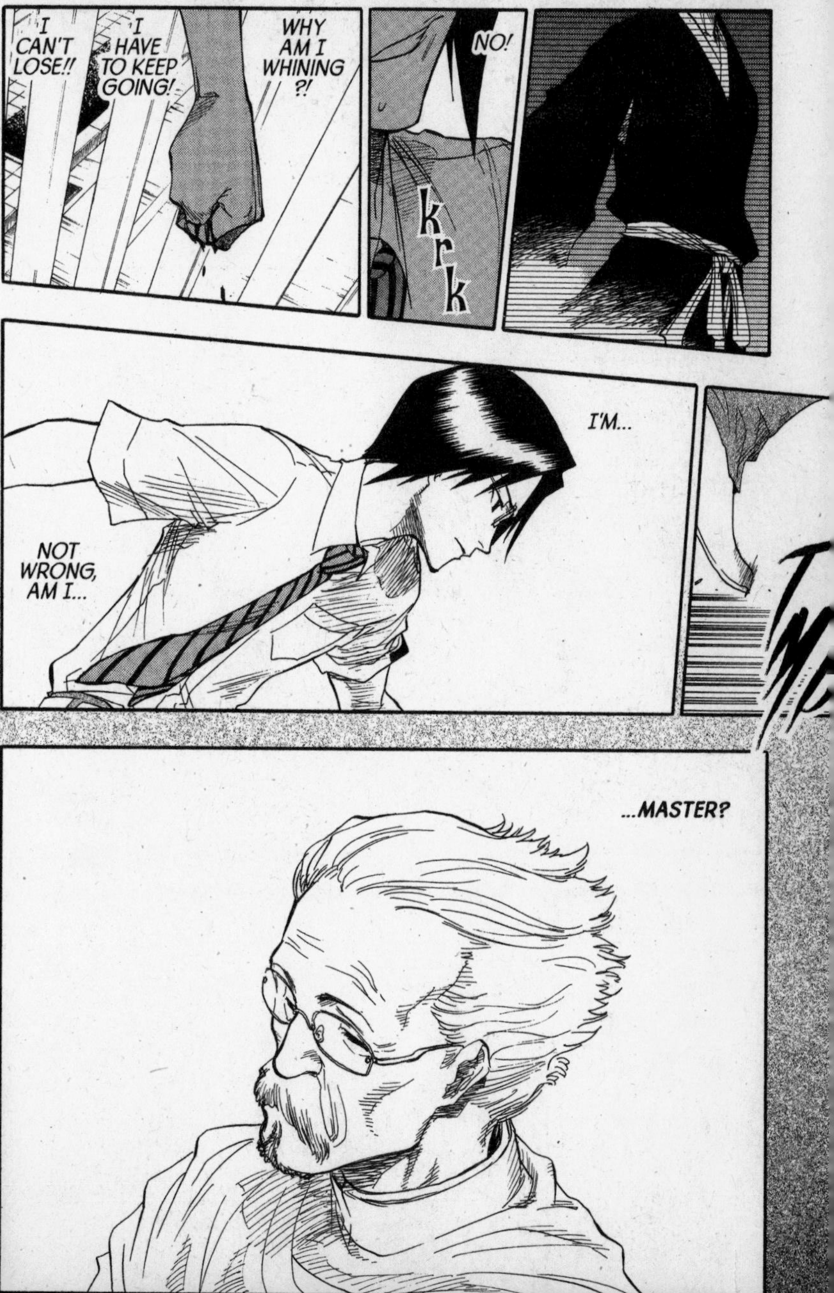
NO!
krk
WHY AM I WHINING ?!
I HAVE TO KEEP GOING!
I CAN'T LOSE!!
I'M...
NOT WRONG, AM I...
...MASTER?

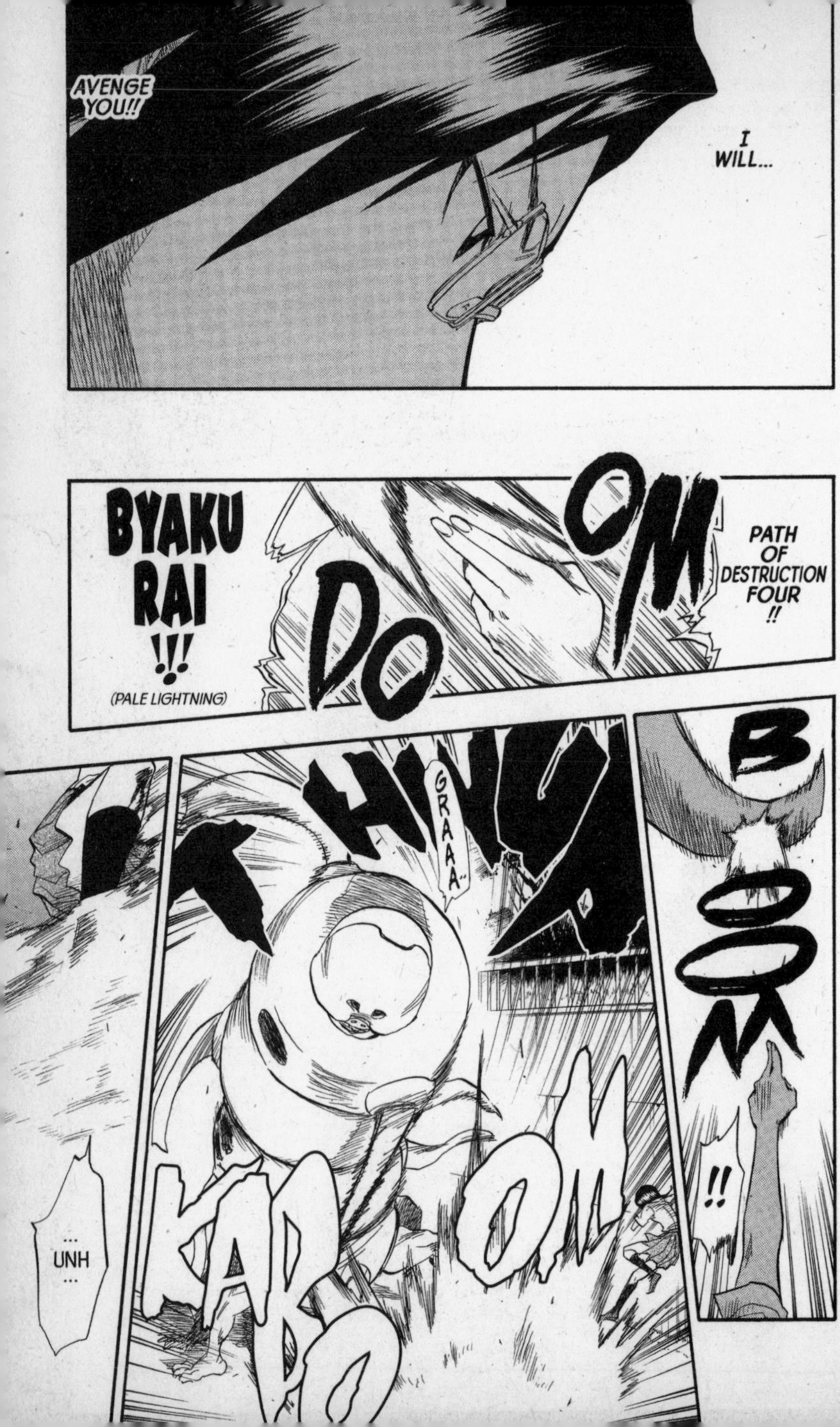
I WILL...
AVENGE YOU!!
PATH OF DESTRUCTION FOUR!!
DOOM
BYAKU RAI!!!
(PALE LIGHTNING)
BOOOM
!!
THWA
GRAAA...
KABOOM
...UNH...

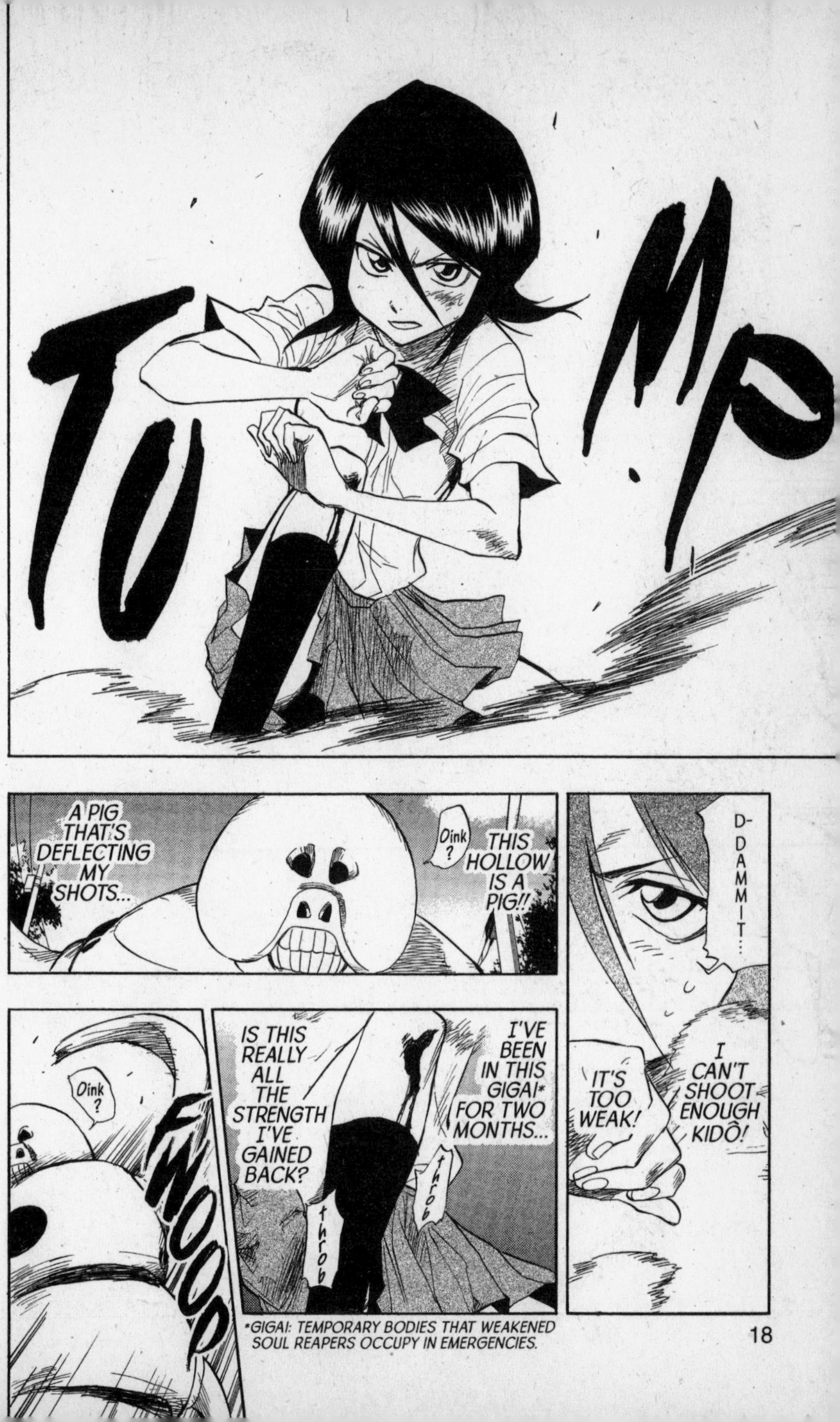
TOMP
D-DAMMIT...
I CAN'T SHOOT ENOUGH KIDÔ!
IT'S TOO WEAK!
THIS HOLLOW IS A PIG!!
Oink?
A PIG THAT'S DEFLECTING MY SHOTS...
I'VE BEEN IN THIS GIGAI* FOR TWO MONTHS...
IS THIS REALLY ALL THE STRENGTH I'VE GAINED BACK?
throb
throb
Oink?
FWOOO

*GIGAI: TEMPORARY BODIES THAT WEAKENED SOUL REAPERS OCCUPY IN EMERGENCIES.

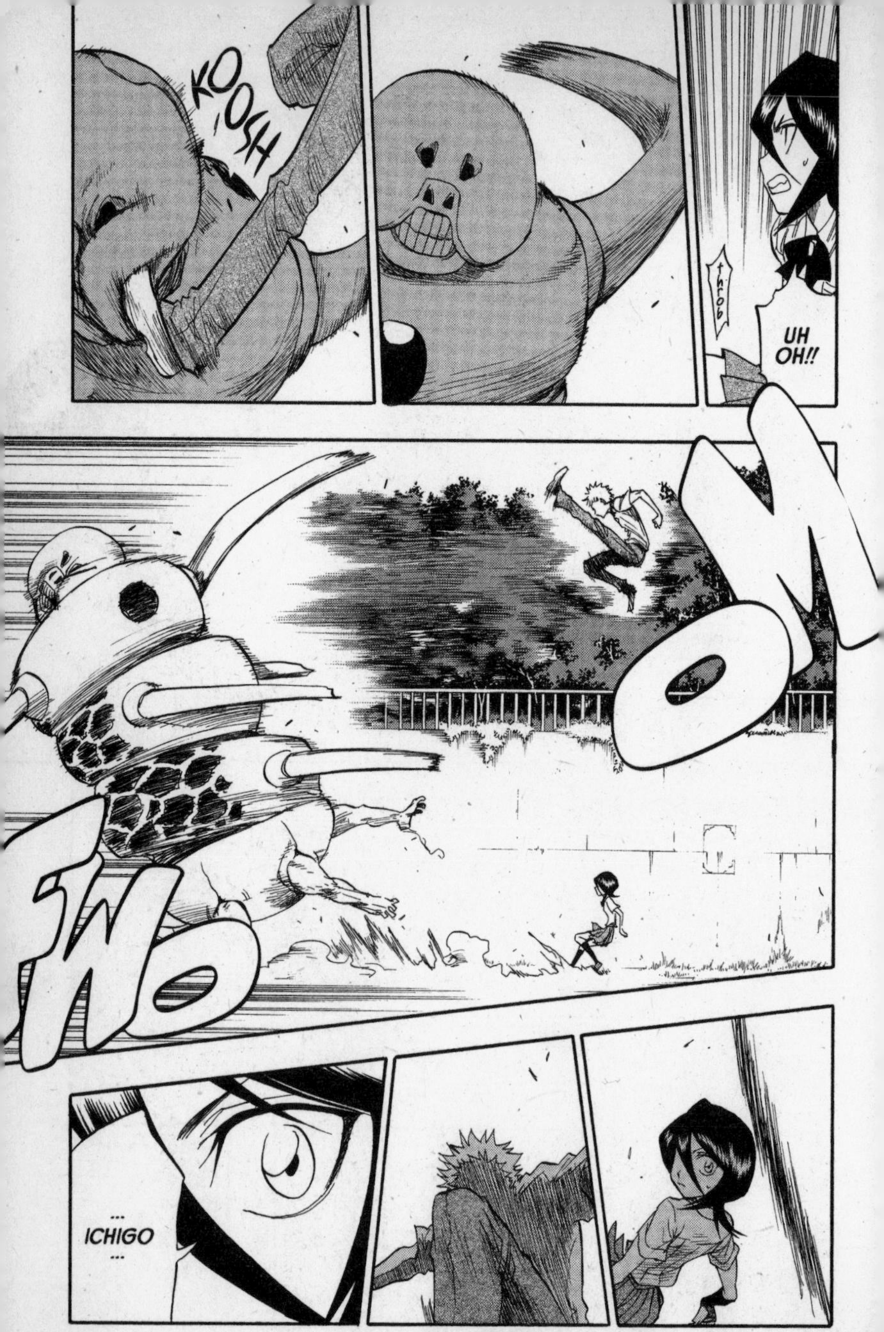
throb
UH OH!!
KOOSH
WOOM
... ICHIGO ...

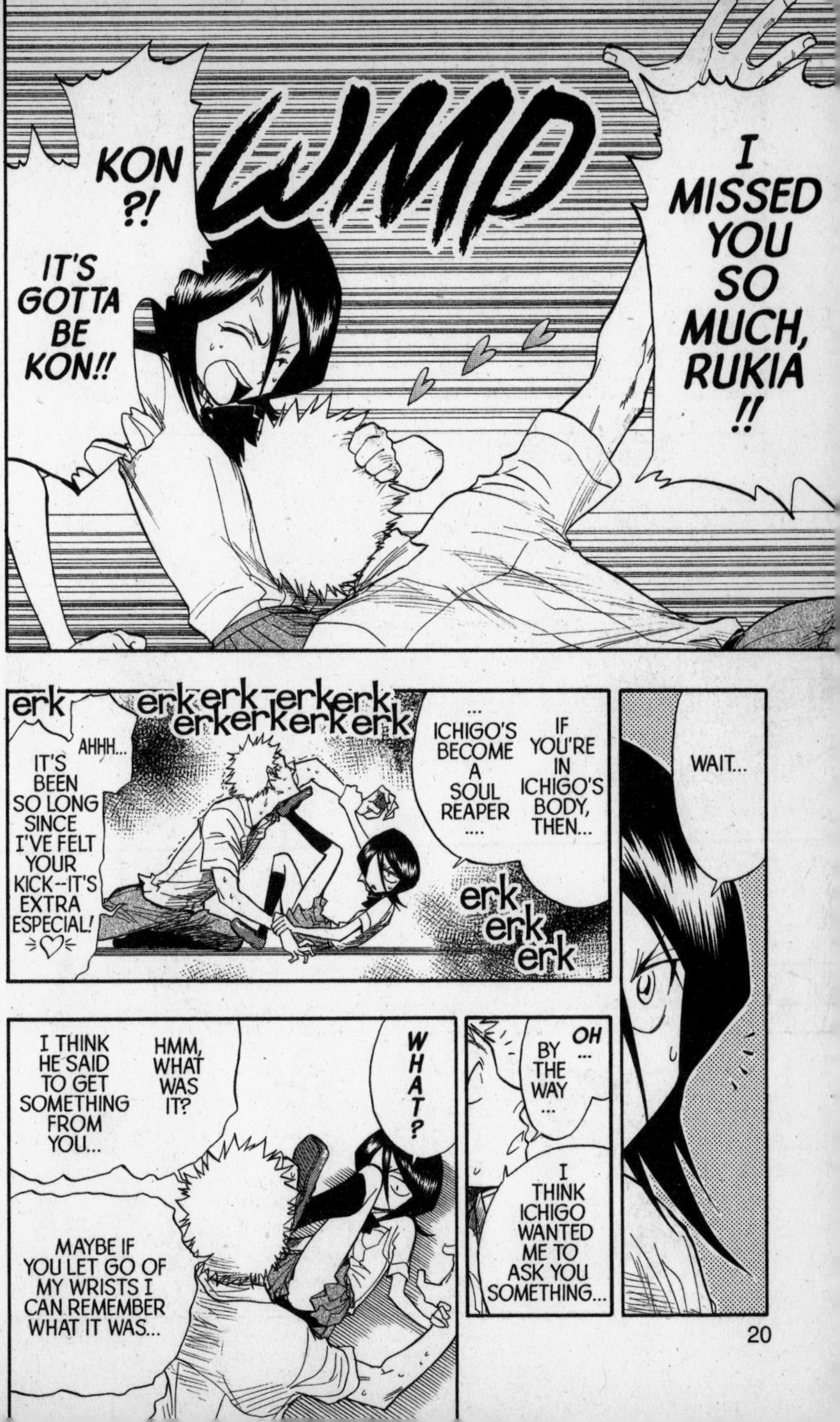
I MISSED YOU SO MUCH, RUKIA!!
WMP
KON?!
IT'S GOTTA BE KON!!
WAIT...
IF YOU'RE IN ICHIGO'S BODY, THEN...
...ICHIGO'S BECOME A SOUL REAPER....
erk erk erk-erk erk erk erk erk erk erk erk
erk
AHHH... IT'S BEEN SO LONG SINCE I'VE FELT YOUR KICK--IT'S EXTRA ESPECIAL! ♡
erk erk erk
OH...
BY THE WAY...
I THINK ICHIGO WANTED ME TO ASK YOU SOMETHING...
WHAT?
HMM, WHAT WAS IT?
I THINK HE SAID TO GET SOMETHING FROM YOU...
MAYBE IF YOU LET GO OF MY WRISTS I CAN REMEMBER WHAT IT WAS...

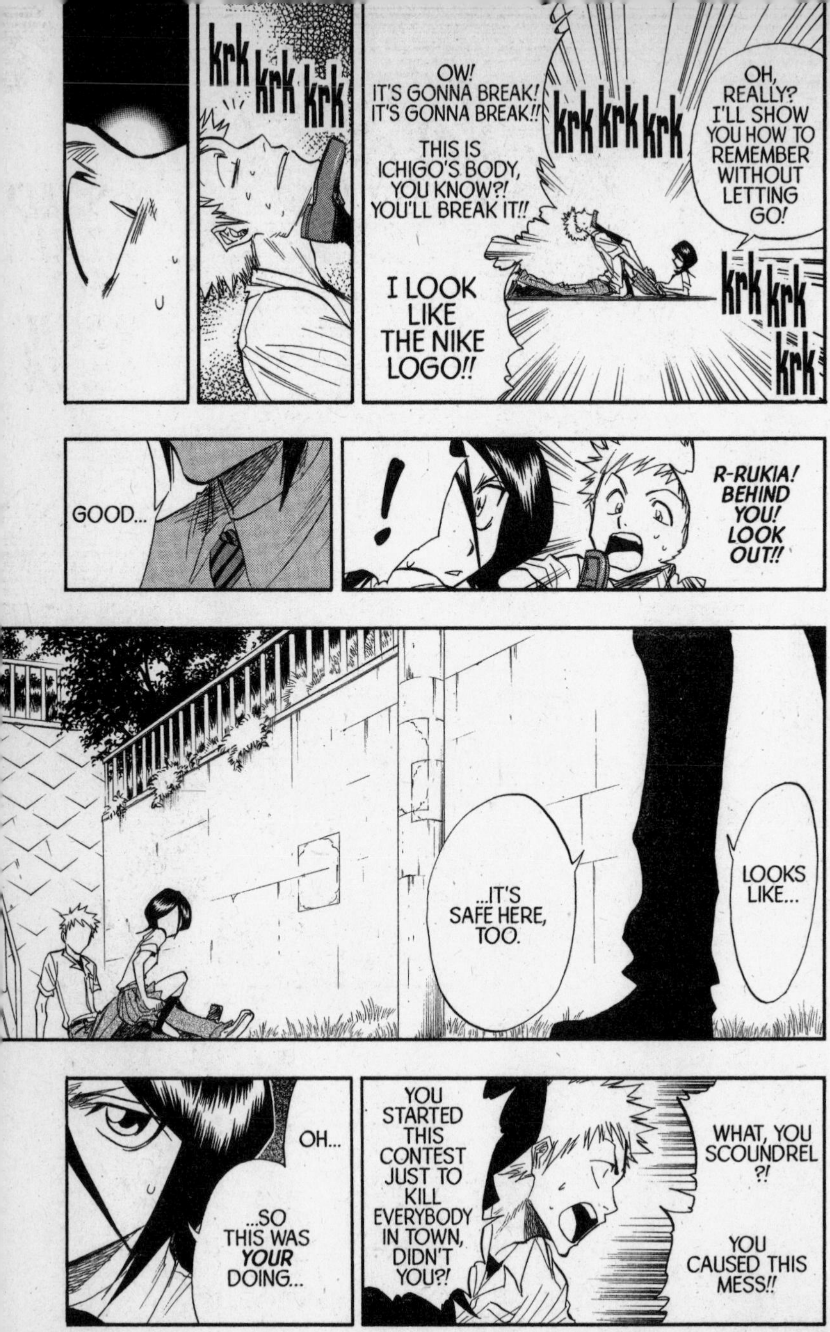
OH, REALLY? I'LL SHOW YOU HOW TO REMEMBER WITHOUT LETTING GO!
krk krk krk
krk krk krk
OW! IT'S GONNA BREAK! IT'S GONNA BREAK!!
THIS IS ICHIGO'S BODY, YOU KNOW?! YOU'LL BREAK IT!!
I LOOK LIKE THE NIKE LOGO!!
krk krk krk
R-RUKIA! BEHIND YOU! LOOK OUT!!
!
GOOD...
LOOKS LIKE...
...IT'S SAFE HERE, TOO.
WHAT, YOU SCOUNDREL?!
YOU CAUSED THIS MESS!!
YOU STARTED THIS CONTEST JUST TO KILL EVERYBODY IN TOWN, DIDN'T YOU?!
OH...
...SO THIS WAS *YOUR* DOING...

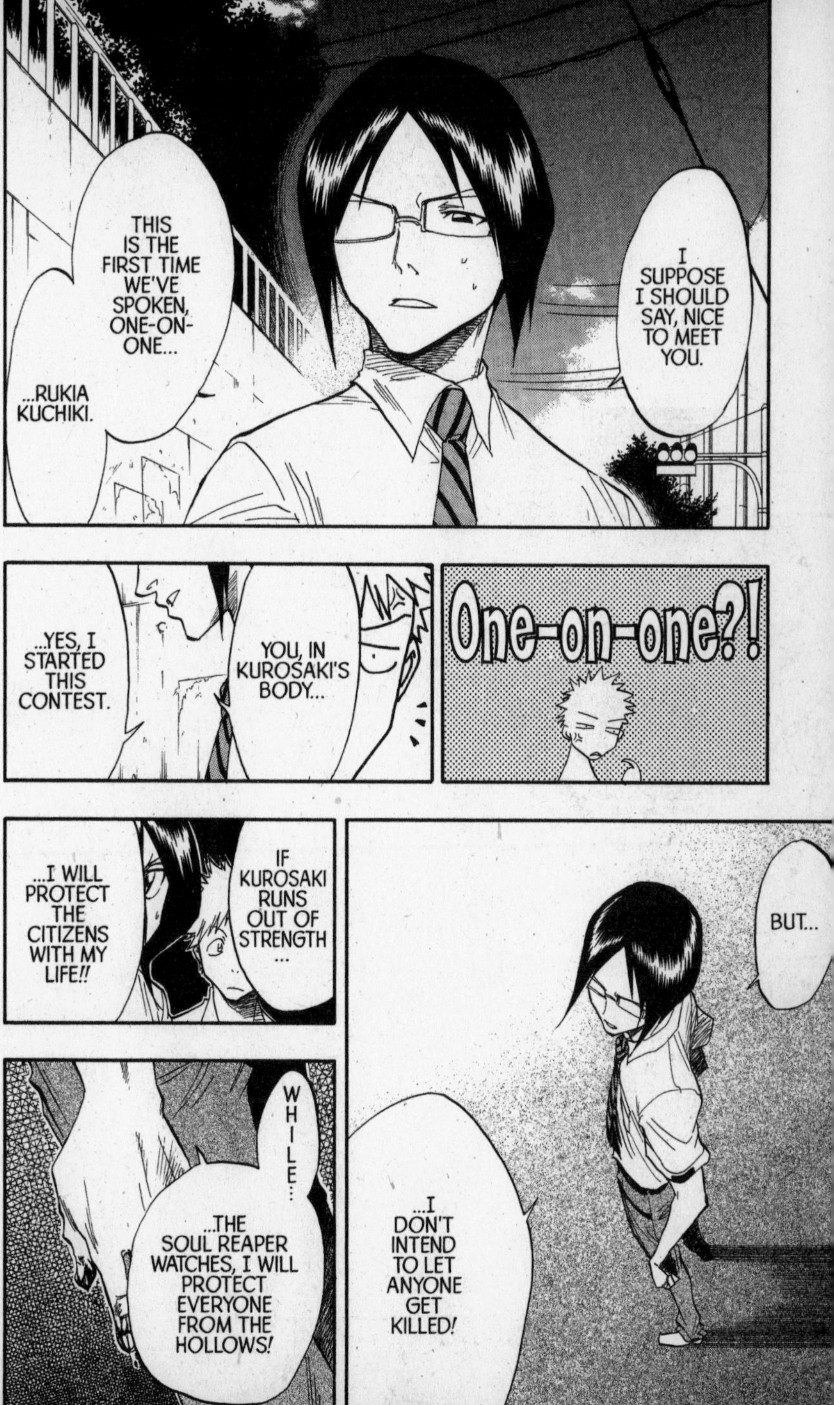
I SUPPOSE I SHOULD SAY, NICE TO MEET YOU.
THIS IS THE FIRST TIME WE'VE SPOKEN, ONE-ON-ONE...
...RUKIA KUCHIKI.
One-on-one?!
YOU, IN KUROSAKI'S BODY...
...YES, I STARTED THIS CONTEST.
BUT...
...I DON'T INTEND TO LET ANYONE GET KILLED!
IF KUROSAKI RUNS OUT OF STRENGTH...
...I WILL PROTECT THE CITIZENS WITH MY LIFE!!
WHILE...
...THE SOUL REAPER WATCHES, I WILL PROTECT EVERYONE FROM THE HOLLOWS!

READ THIS WAY

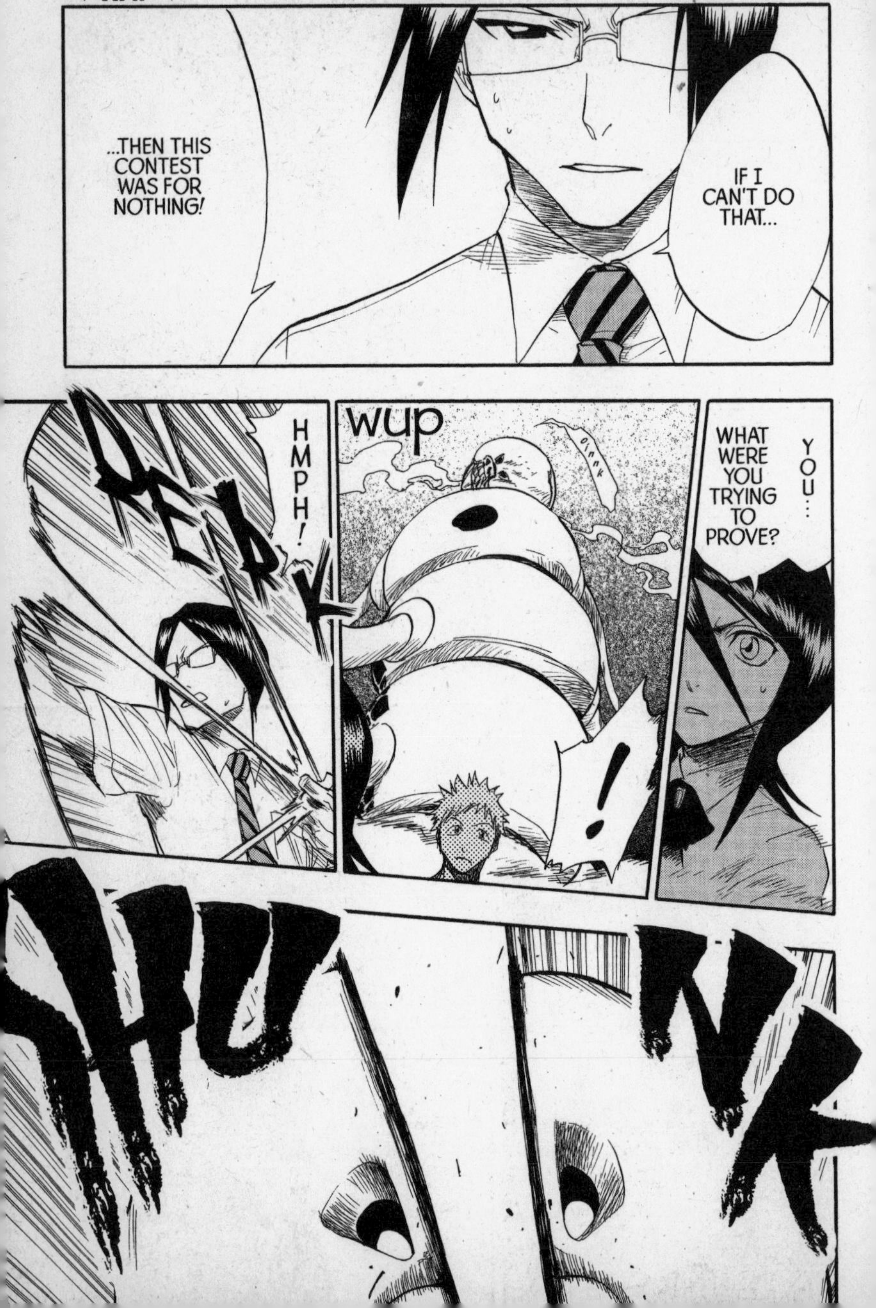
IF I CAN'T DO THAT...
...THEN THIS CONTEST WAS FOR NOTHING!
YOU...
WHAT WERE YOU TRYING TO PROVE?
wup
!
HMPH!

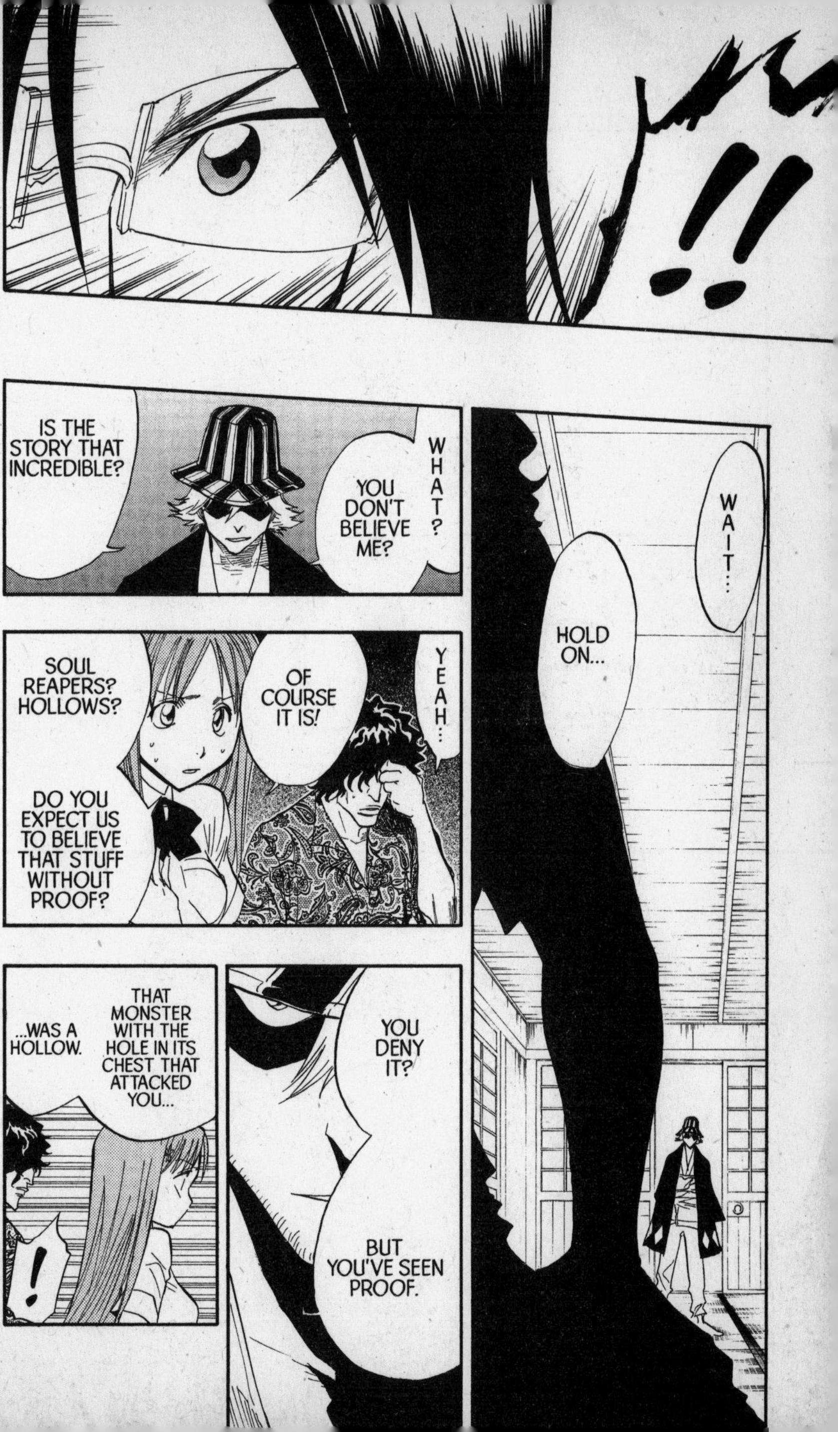
!!
WAIT...
HOLD ON...
WHAT?
YOU DON'T BELIEVE ME?
IS THE STORY THAT INCREDIBLE?
YEAH...
OF COURSE IT IS!
SOUL REAPERS? HOLLOWS?
DO YOU EXPECT US TO BELIEVE THAT STUFF WITHOUT PROOF?
YOU DENY IT?
BUT YOU'VE SEEN PROOF.
THAT MONSTER WITH THE HOLE IN ITS CHEST THAT ATTACKED YOU...
...WAS A HOLLOW.
!

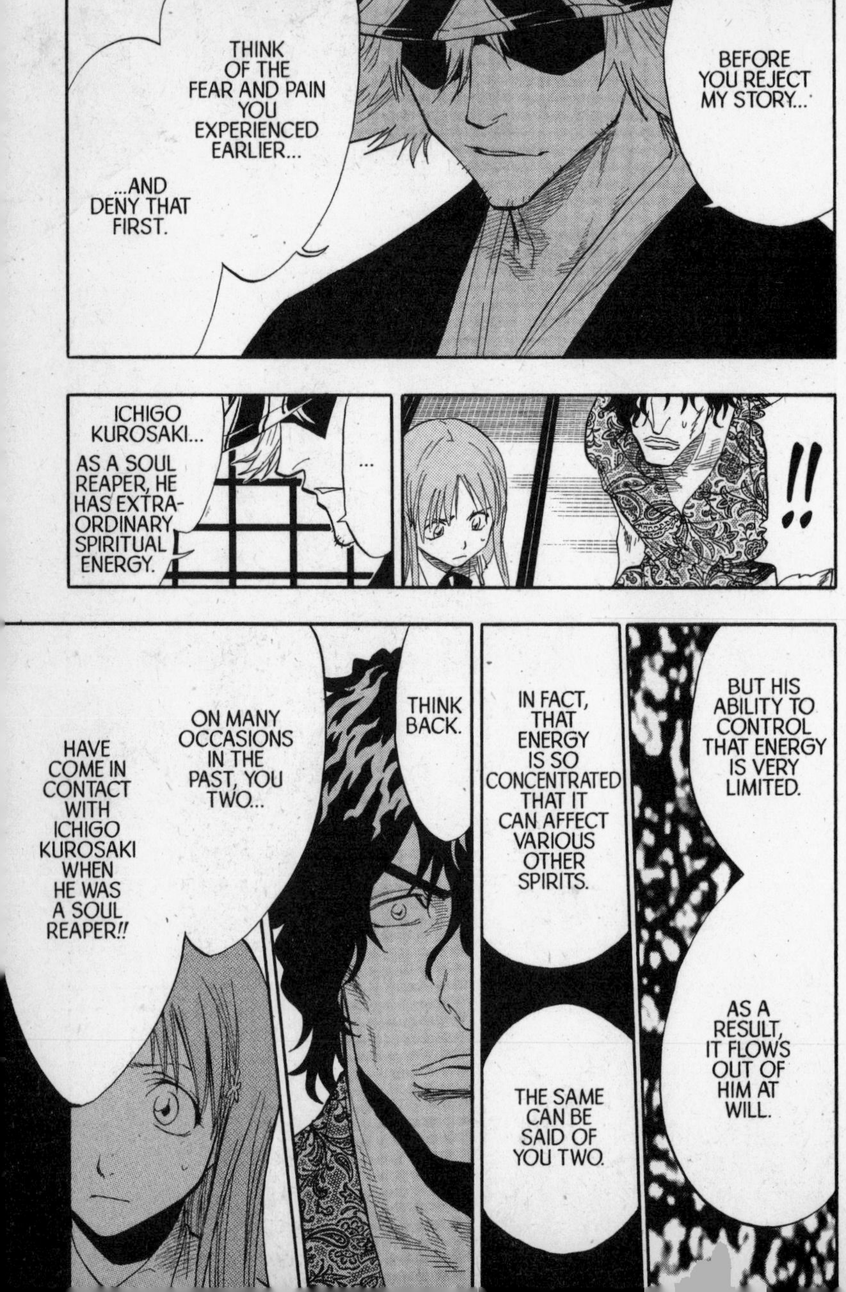
BEFORE YOU REJECT MY STORY...
THINK OF THE FEAR AND PAIN YOU EXPERIENCED EARLIER...
...AND DENY THAT FIRST.
!!
...
ICHIGO KUROSAKI...
AS A SOUL REAPER, HE HAS EXTRA-ORDINARY SPIRITUAL ENERGY.
BUT HIS ABILITY TO CONTROL THAT ENERGY IS VERY LIMITED.
AS A RESULT, IT FLOWS OUT OF HIM AT WILL.
IN FACT, THAT ENERGY IS SO CONCENTRATED THAT IT CAN AFFECT VARIOUS OTHER SPIRITS.
THE SAME CAN BE SAID OF YOU TWO.
THINK BACK.
ON MANY OCCASIONS IN THE PAST, YOU TWO...
HAVE COME IN CONTACT WITH ICHIGO KUROSAKI WHEN HE WAS A SOUL REAPER!!

I FINALLY FOUND YOU...

KUROSAKI!

URYŪ!

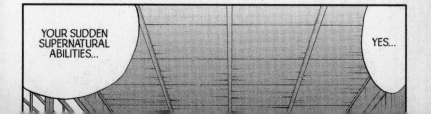

YOUR SUDDEN SUPERNATURAL ABILITIES...

YES...

READ THIS WAY

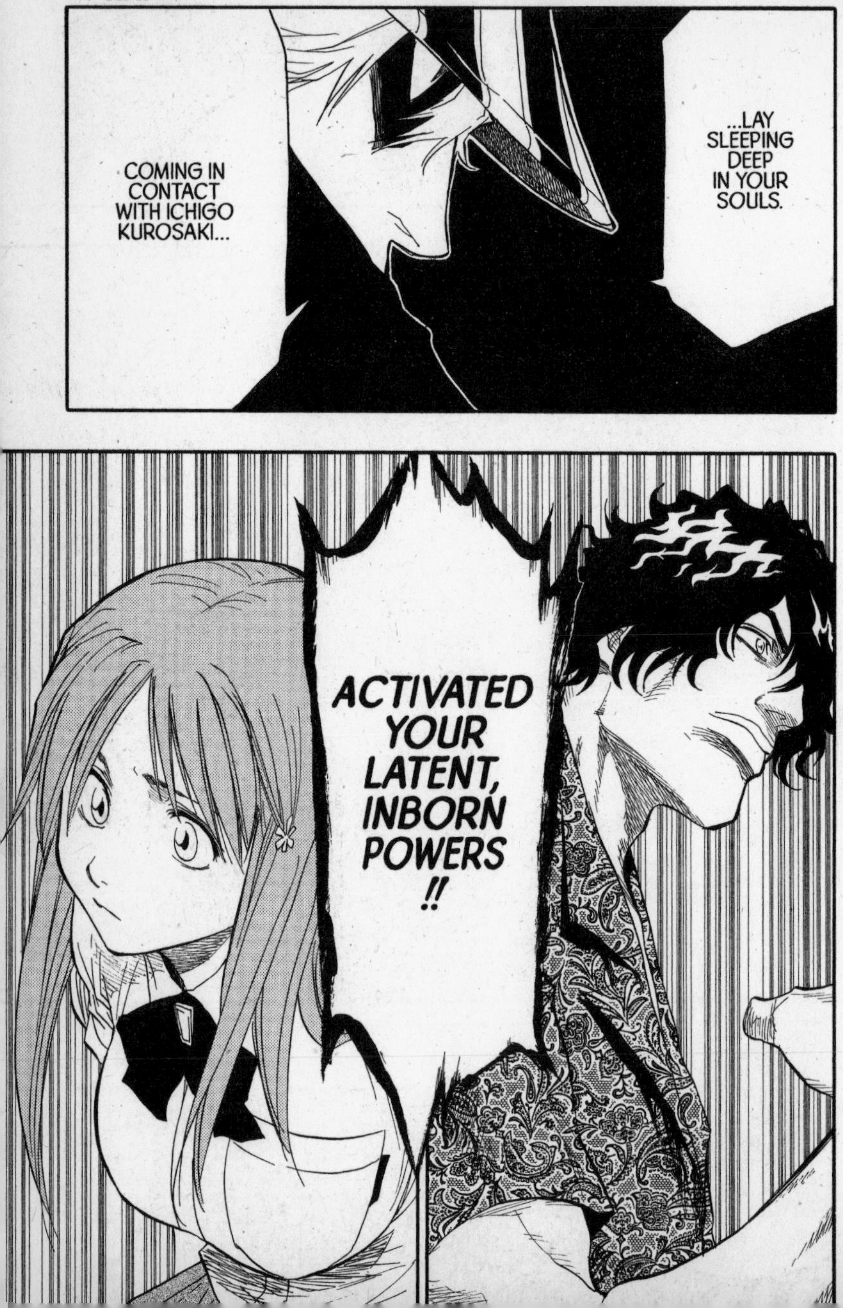

...LAY SLEEPING DEEP IN YOUR SOULS.
COMING IN CONTACT WITH ICHIGO KUROSAKI...
ACTIVATED YOUR LATENT, INBORN POWERS !!

Meanwhile, Karin and her father have
managed to forget their original objective.

Isshin X~O Karin
TKO~Round 8

45. Point of Purpose

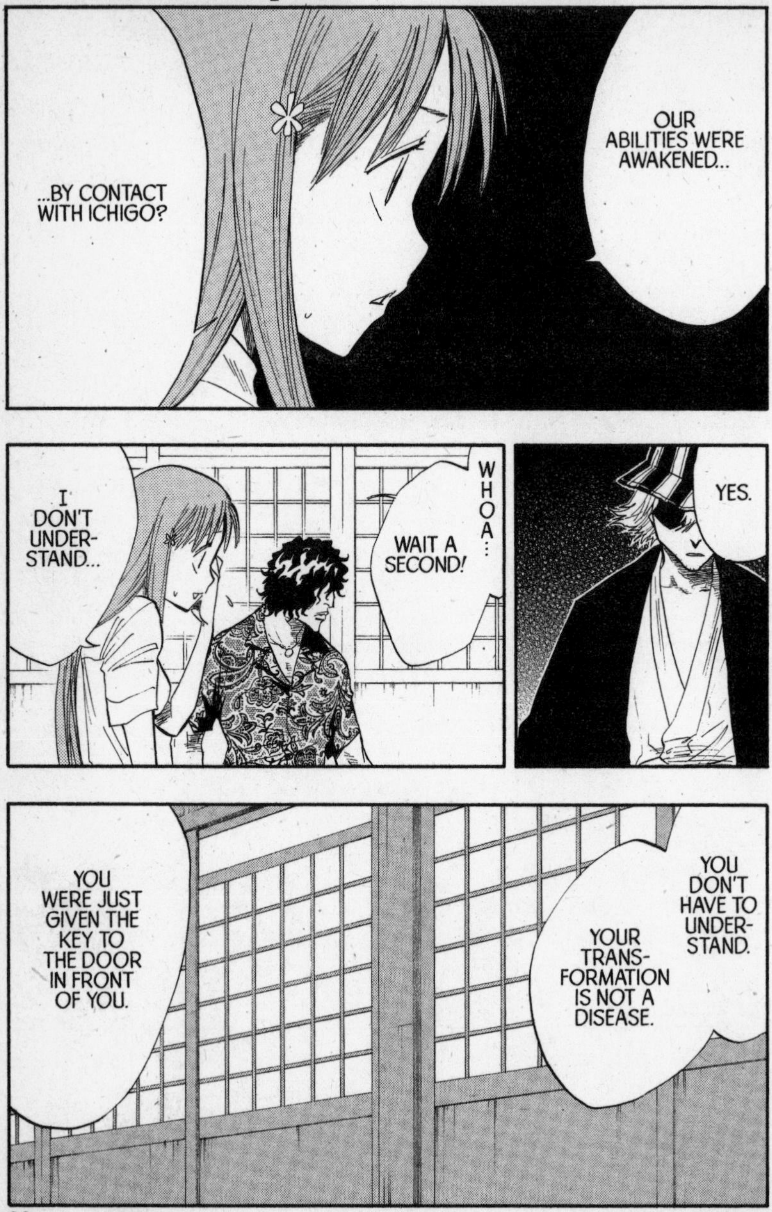
OUR ABILITIES WERE AWAKENED...
...BY CONTACT WITH ICHIGO?
YES.
WHOA...
WAIT A SECOND!
I DON'T UNDERSTAND...
YOU DON'T HAVE TO UNDERSTAND.
YOUR TRANSFORMATION IS NOT A DISEASE.
YOU WERE JUST GIVEN THE KEY TO THE DOOR IN FRONT OF YOU.

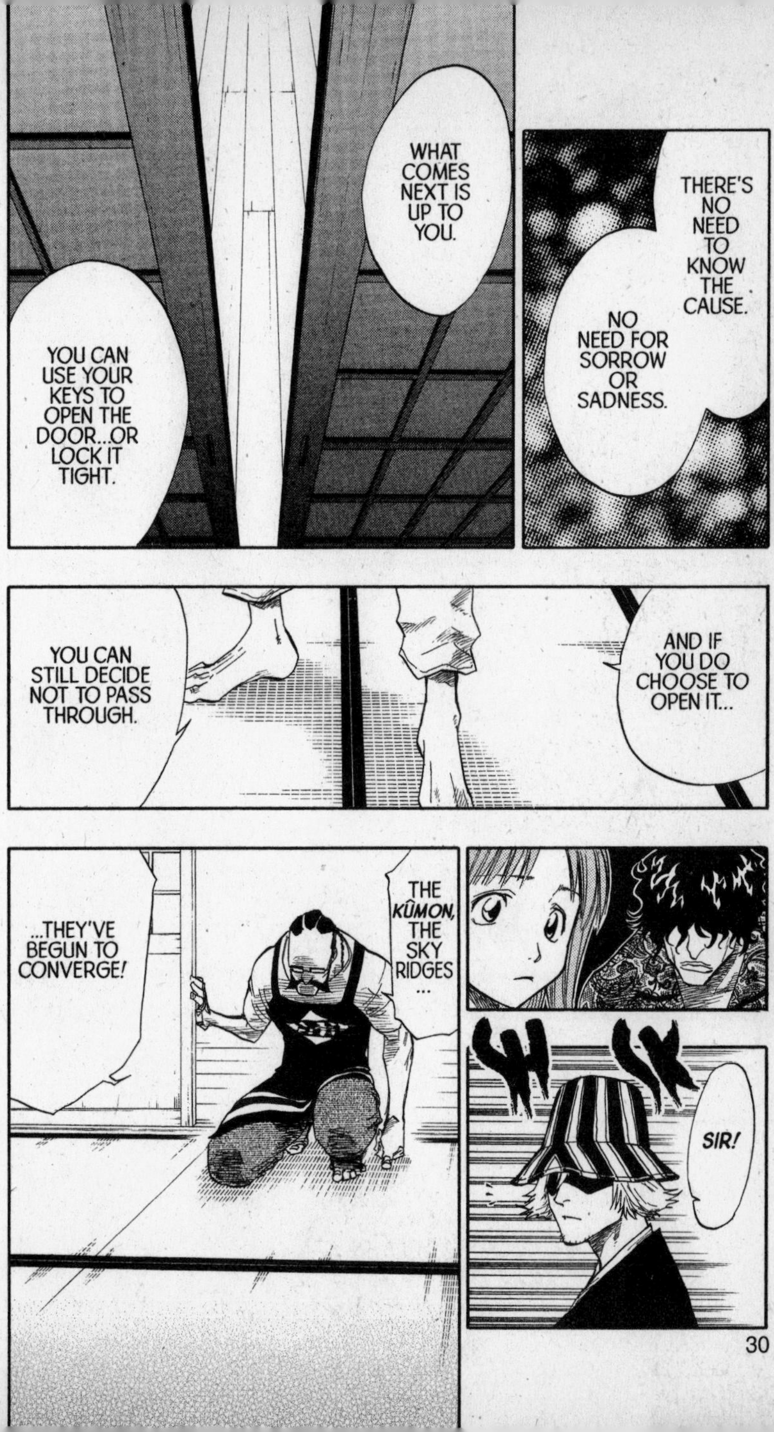
THERE'S NO NEED TO KNOW THE CAUSE.
NO NEED FOR SORROW OR SADNESS.
WHAT COMES NEXT IS UP TO YOU.
YOU CAN USE YOUR KEYS TO OPEN THE DOOR...OR LOCK IT TIGHT.
AND IF YOU DO CHOOSE TO OPEN IT...
YOU CAN STILL DECIDE NOT TO PASS THROUGH.
SIR!
THE *KÛMON*, THE SKY RIDGES ...
...THEY'VE BEGUN TO CONVERGE!

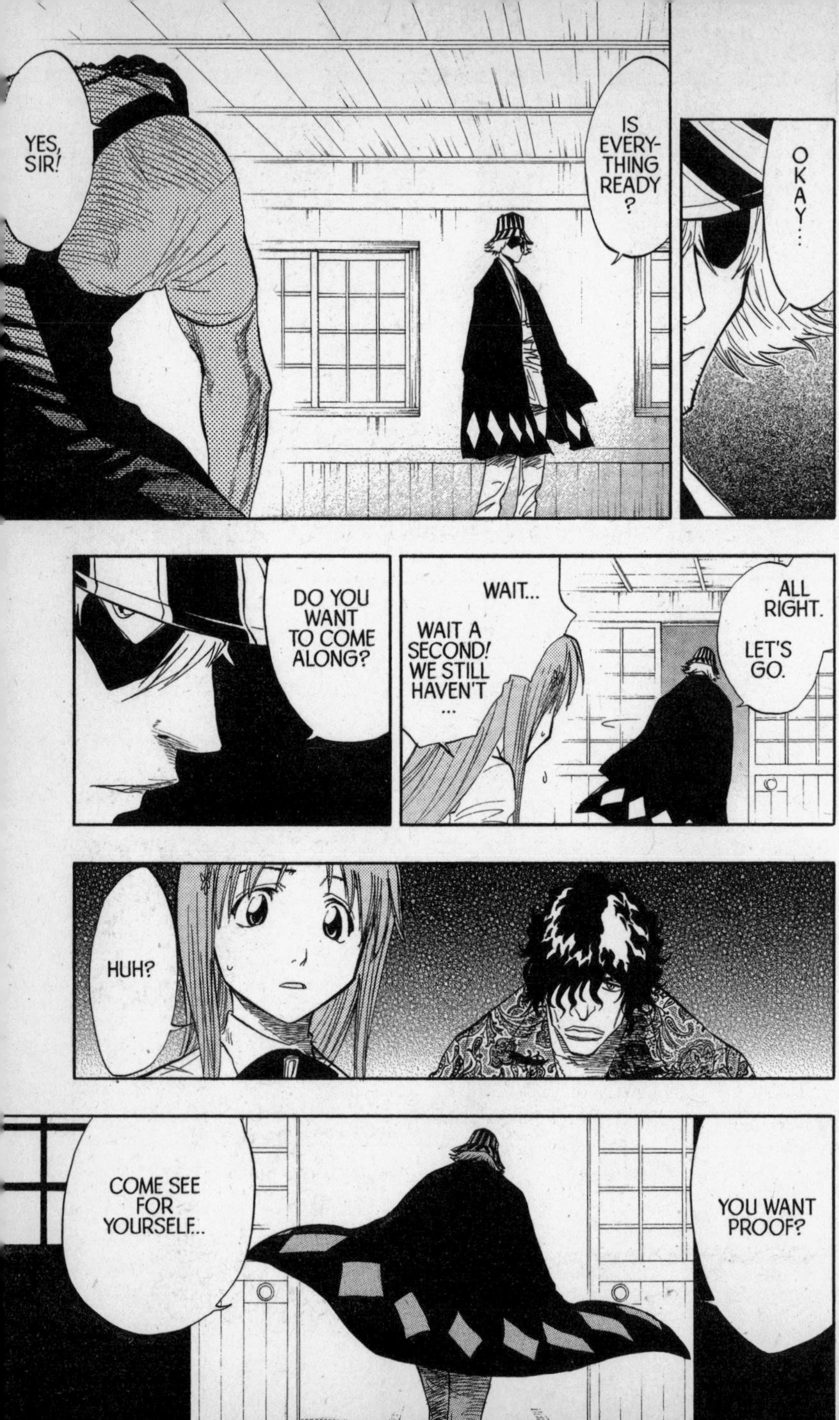
OKAY...
IS EVERYTHING READY?
YES, SIR!
ALL RIGHT.
LET'S GO.
WAIT...
WAIT A SECOND! WE STILL HAVEN'T...
DO YOU WANT TO COME ALONG?
HUH?
YOU WANT PROOF?
COME SEE FOR YOURSELF...

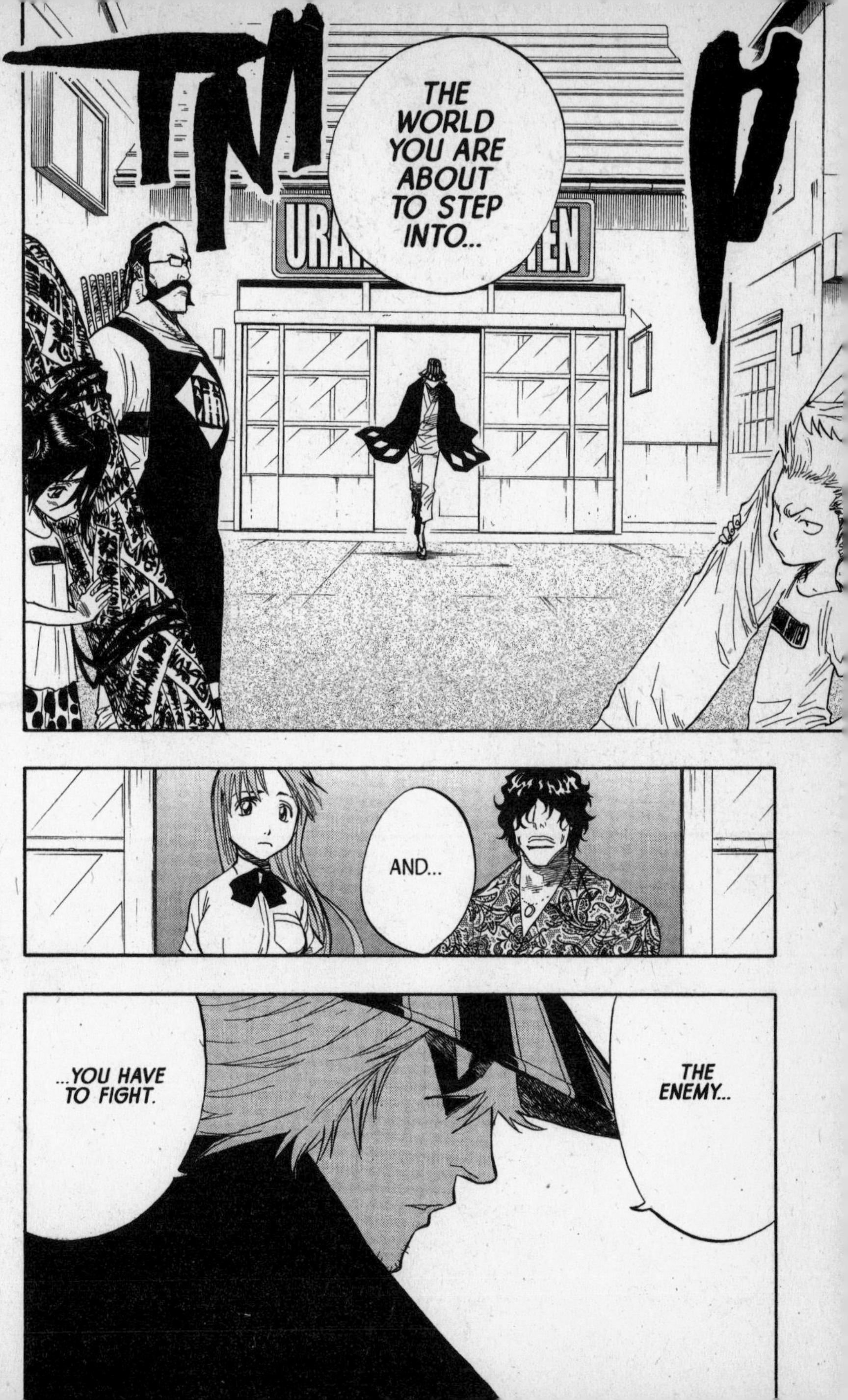
THE WORLD YOU ARE ABOUT TO STEP INTO...
AND...
THE ENEMY...
...YOU HAVE TO FIGHT.

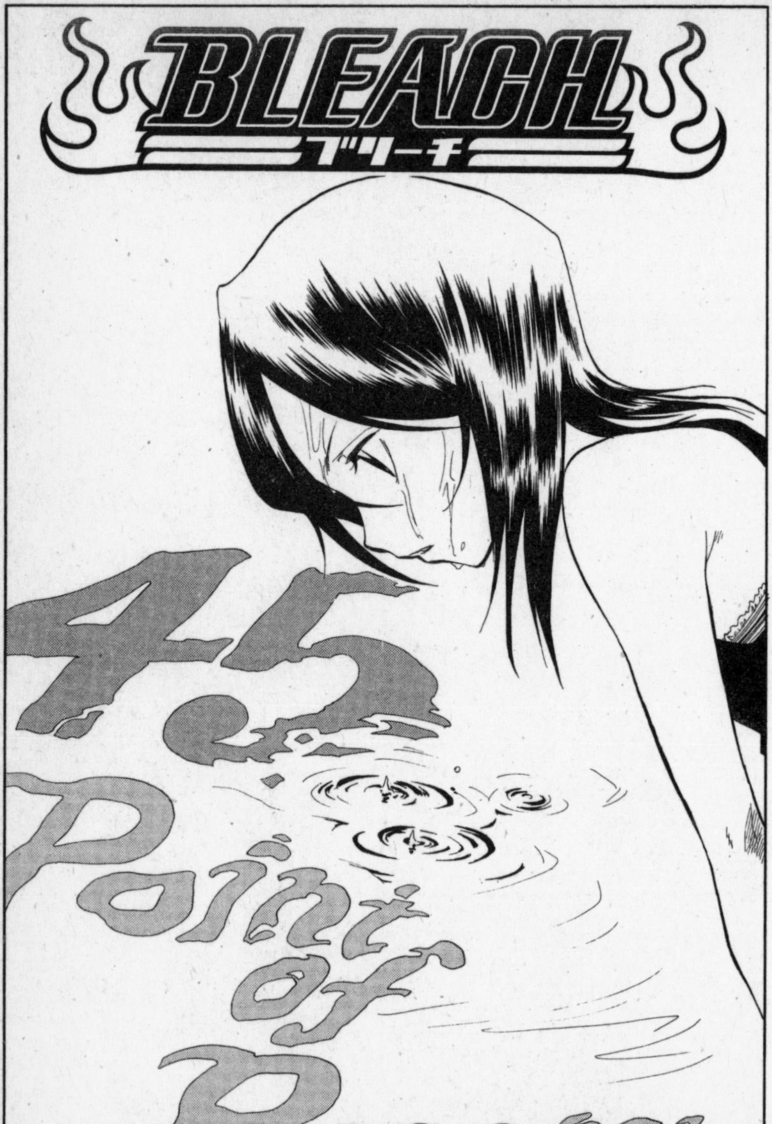
BLEACH
ブリーチ
45 Point of Purpose

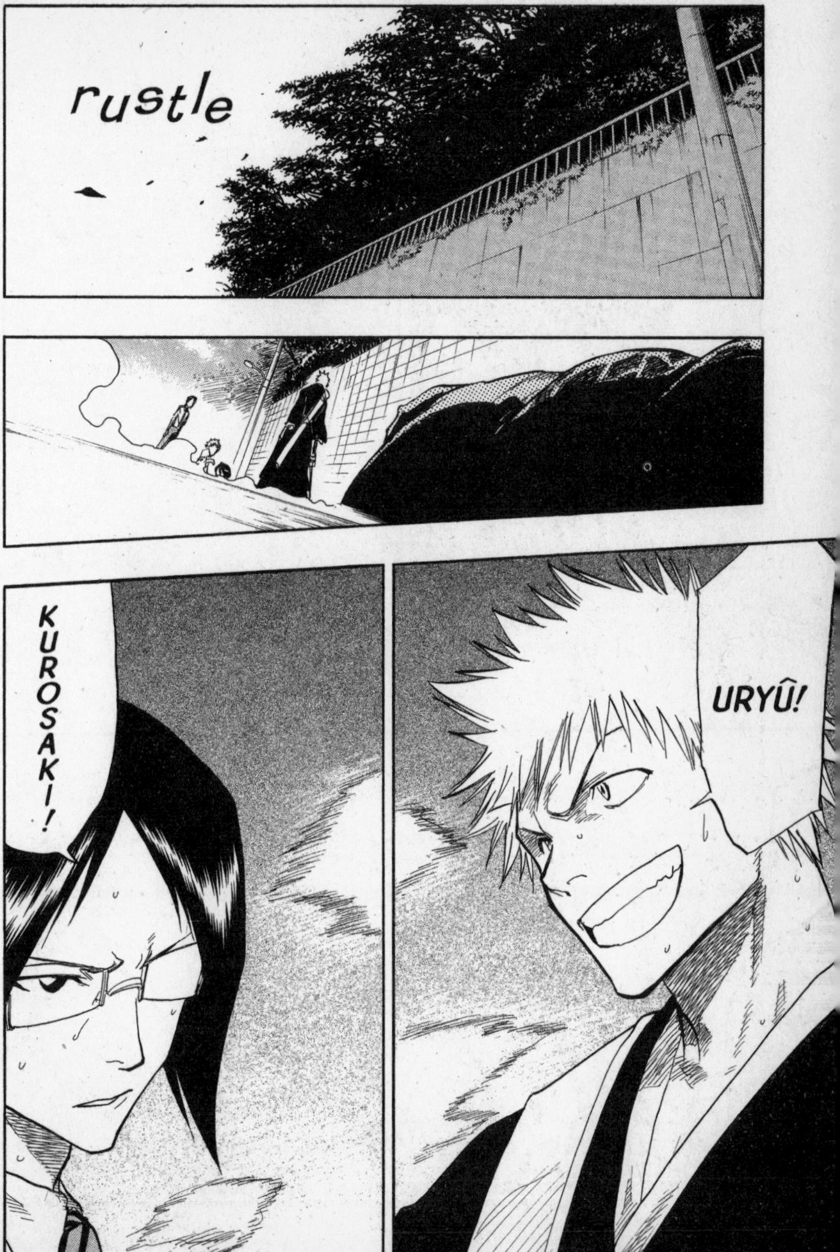
rustle
URYÛ!
KUROSAKI!

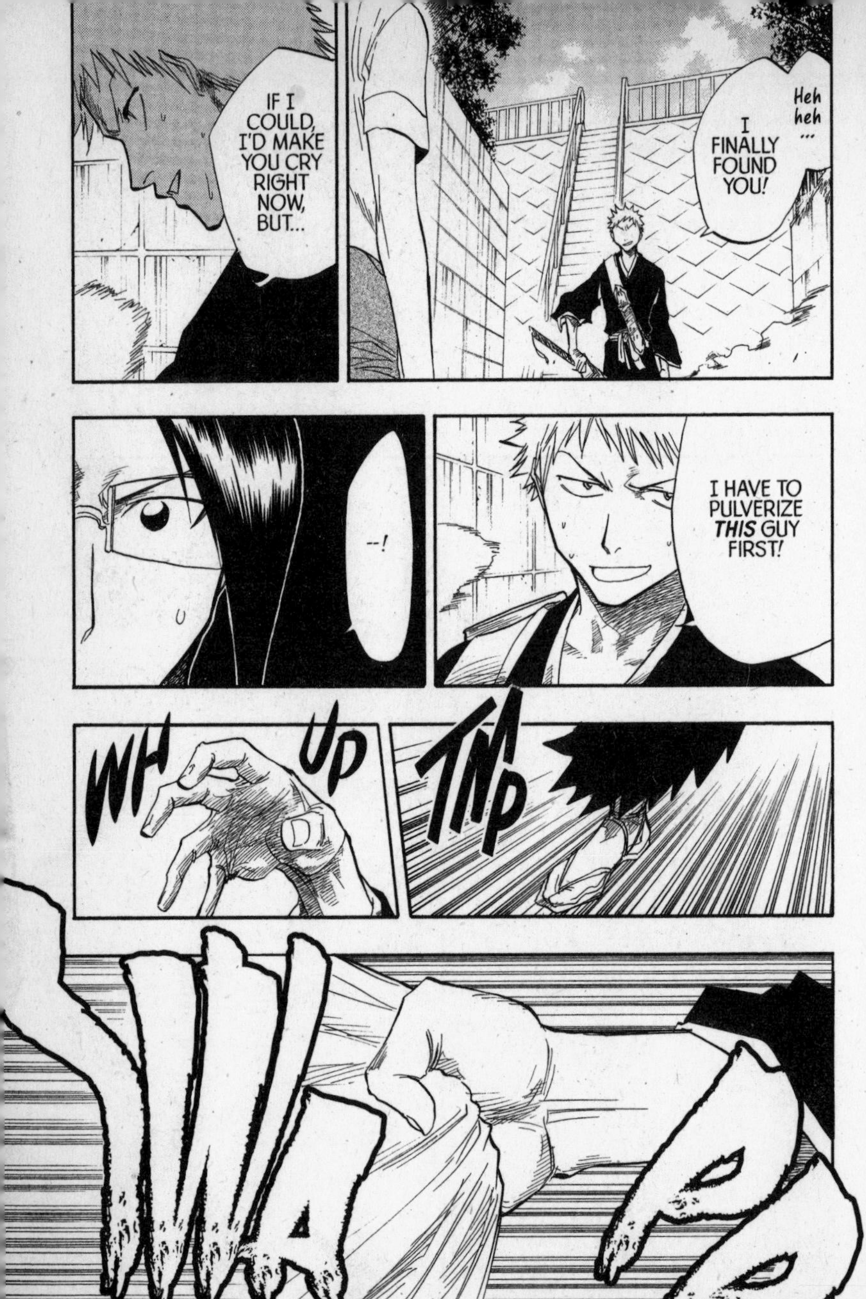
Heh heh...
I FINALLY FOUND YOU!
IF I COULD, I'D MAKE YOU CRY RIGHT NOW, BUT...
I HAVE TO PULVERIZE THIS GUY FIRST!
--!
TMP
WHUP

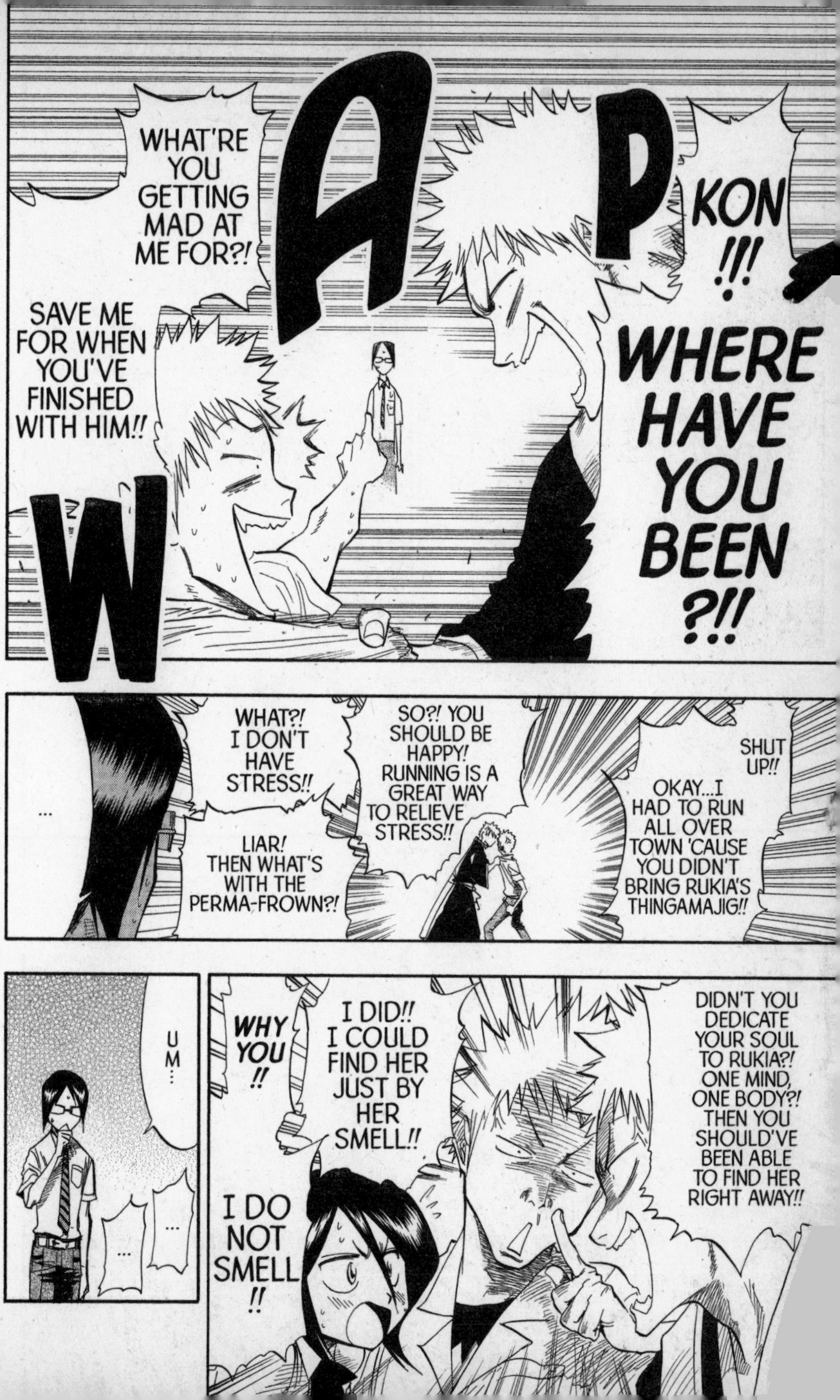

KON!!!
WHERE HAVE YOU BEEN?!!
WAP
WHAT'RE YOU GETTING MAD AT ME FOR?!
SAVE ME FOR WHEN YOU'VE FINISHED WITH HIM!!
SHUT UP!!
OKAY...I HAD TO RUN ALL OVER TOWN 'CAUSE YOU DIDN'T BRING RUKIA'S THINGAMAJIG!!
SO?! YOU SHOULD BE HAPPY! RUNNING IS A GREAT WAY TO RELIEVE STRESS!!
WHAT?! I DON'T HAVE STRESS!!
LIAR! THEN WHAT'S WITH THE PERMA-FROWN?!
...
DIDN'T YOU DEDICATE YOUR SOUL TO RUKIA?! ONE MIND, ONE BODY?! THEN YOU SHOULD'VE BEEN ABLE TO FIND HER RIGHT AWAY!!
I DID!! I COULD FIND HER JUST BY HER SMELL!!
WHY YOU!!
I DO NOT SMELL!!
UM...
...
...

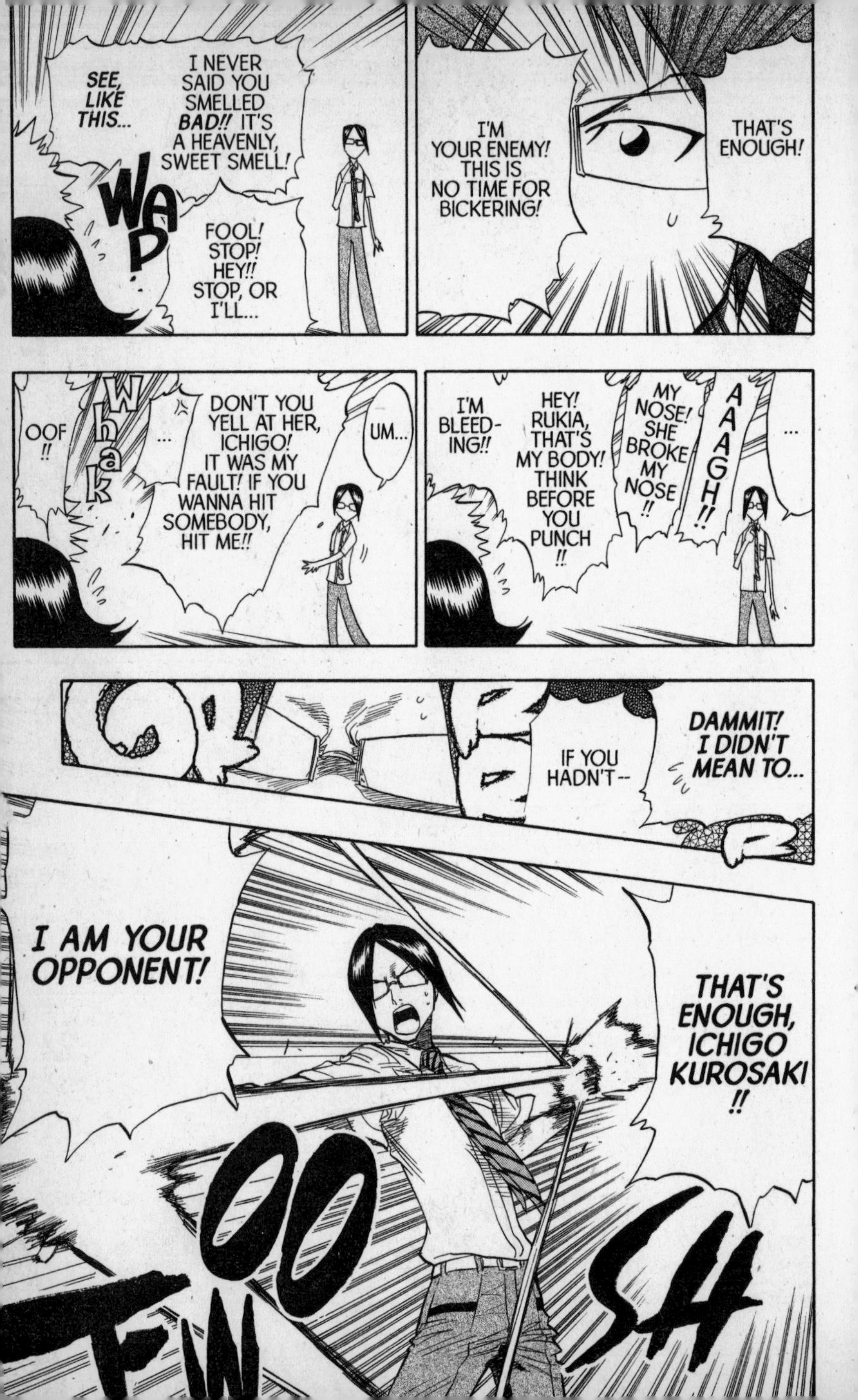
THAT'S ENOUGH!
I'M YOUR ENEMY! THIS IS NO TIME FOR BICKERING!
I NEVER SAID YOU SMELLED *BAD!!* IT'S A HEAVENLY, SWEET SMELL!
SEE, LIKE THIS...
WAP
FOOL! STOP! HEY!! STOP, OR I'LL...
...
AAAGH!!
MY NOSE! SHE BROKE MY NOSE!!
HEY! RUKIA, THAT'S MY BODY! THINK BEFORE YOU PUNCH!!
I'M BLEEDING!!
UM...
DON'T YOU YELL AT HER, ICHIGO! IT WAS MY FAULT! IF YOU WANNA HIT SOMEBODY, HIT ME!!
...
Whak
OOF!!
DAMMIT! I DIDN'T MEAN TO...
IF YOU HADN'T--
THAT'S ENOUGH, ICHIGO KUROSAKI!!
I AM YOUR OPPONENT!
FWOOSH

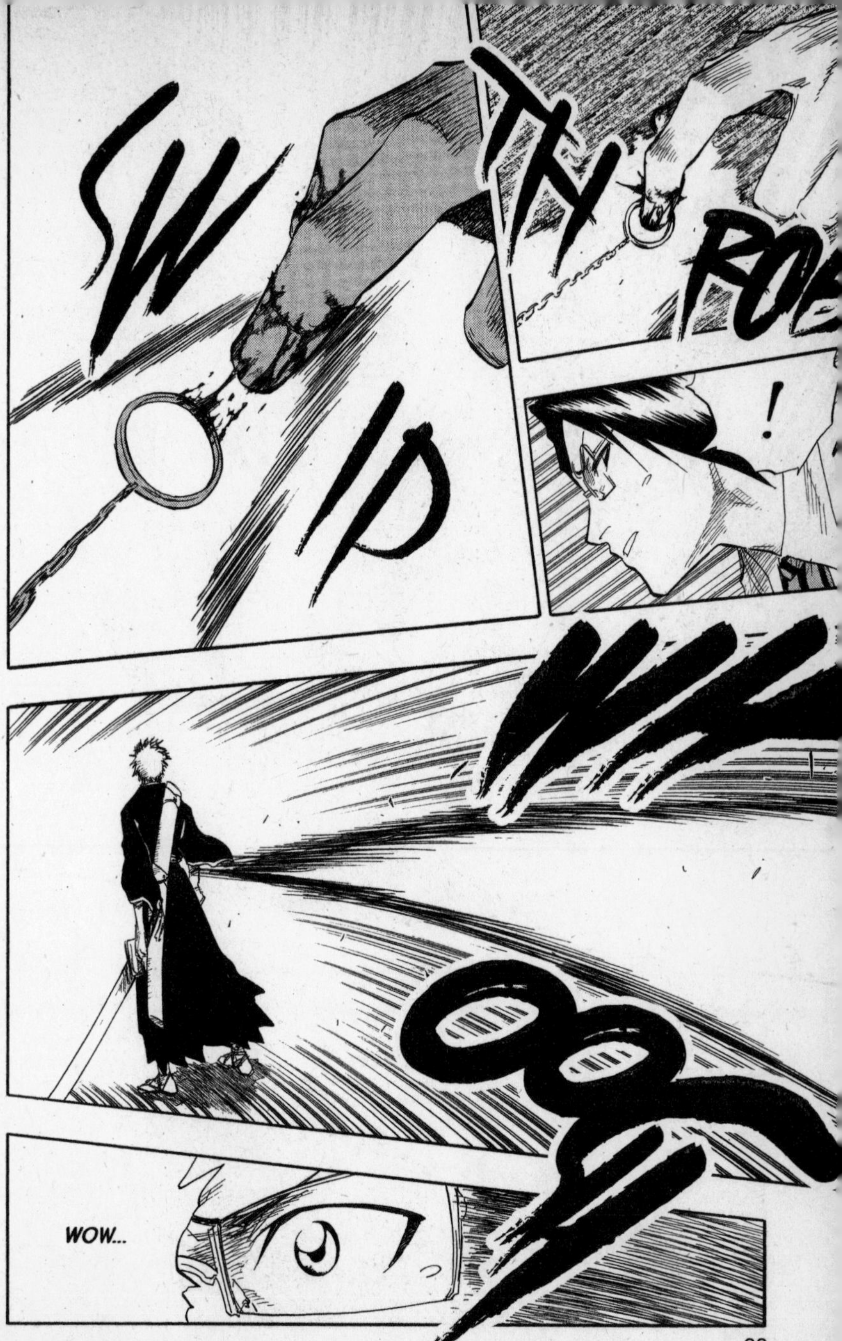
TH
ROB
!
SW
IP
WH
WOW...

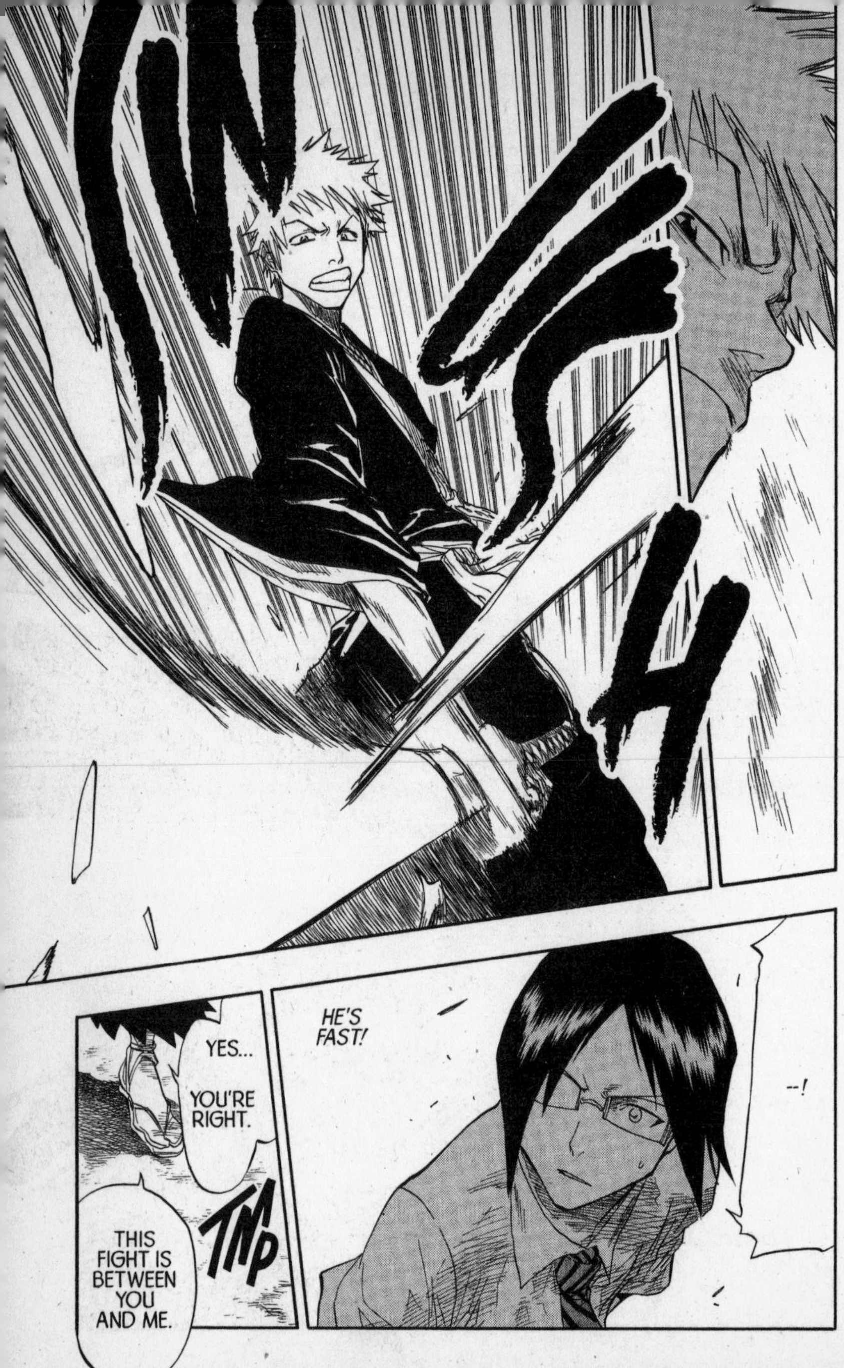
--!
HE'S FAST!
YES...
YOU'RE RIGHT.
TMP
THIS FIGHT IS BETWEEN YOU AND ME.

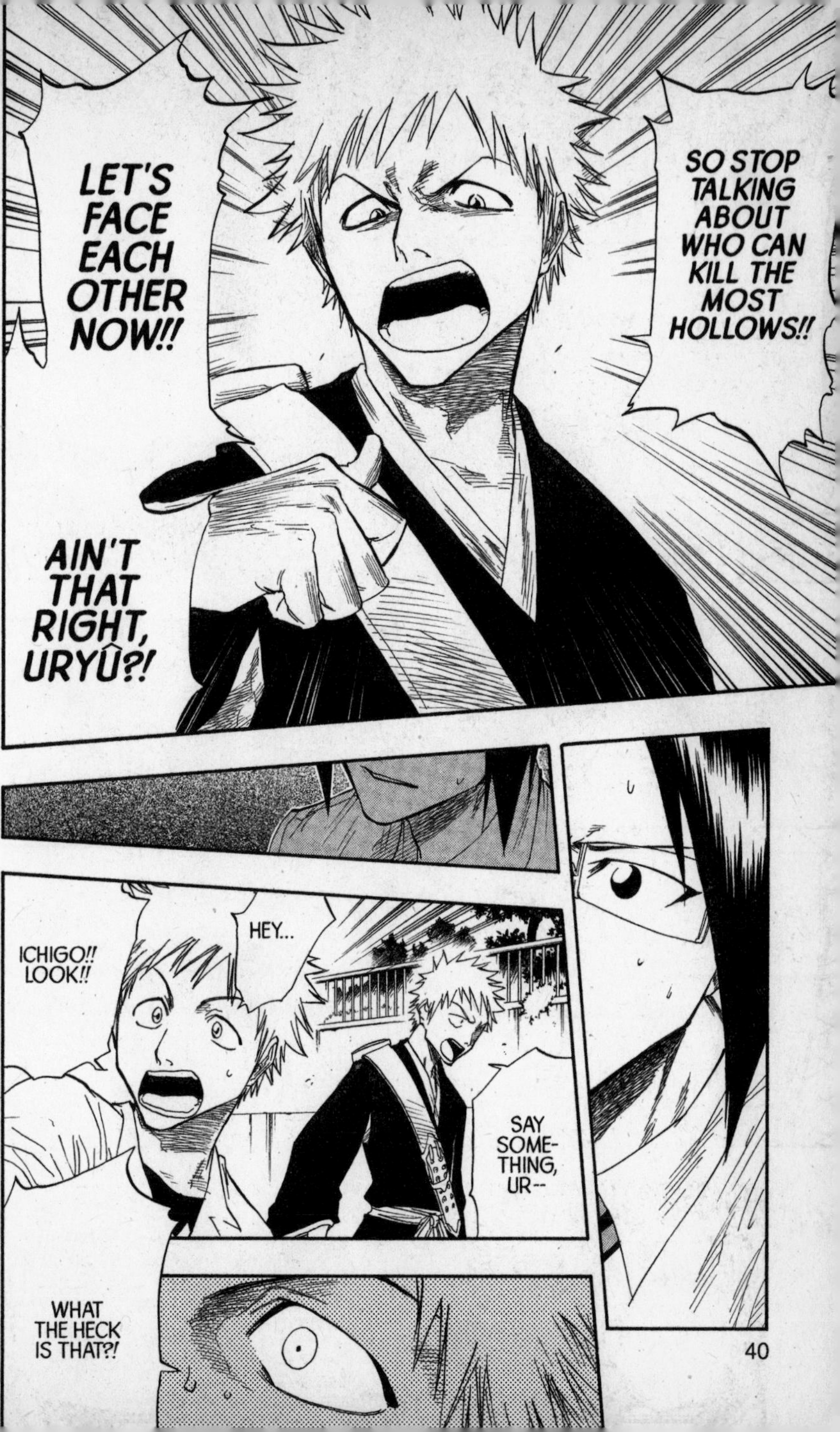
SO STOP TALKING ABOUT WHO CAN KILL THE MOST HOLLOWS!!
LET'S FACE EACH OTHER NOW!!
AIN'T THAT RIGHT, URYÛ?!
HEY...
SAY SOME-THING, UR--
ICHIGO!! LOOK!!
WHAT THE HECK IS THAT?!

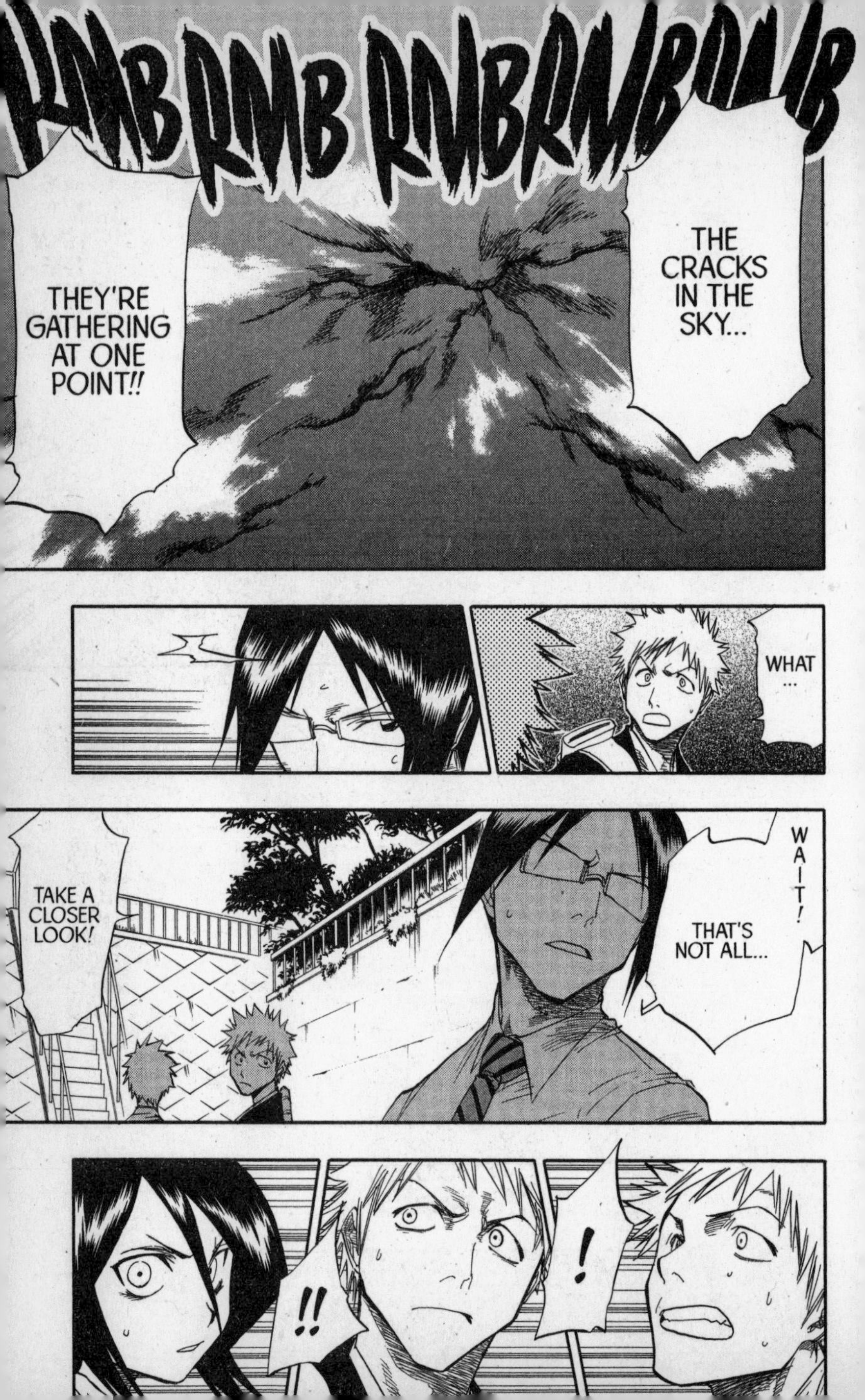
THE CRACKS IN THE SKY...
THEY'RE GATHERING AT ONE POINT!!
WHAT ...
WAIT!
THAT'S NOT ALL...
TAKE A CLOSER LOOK!
!
!!

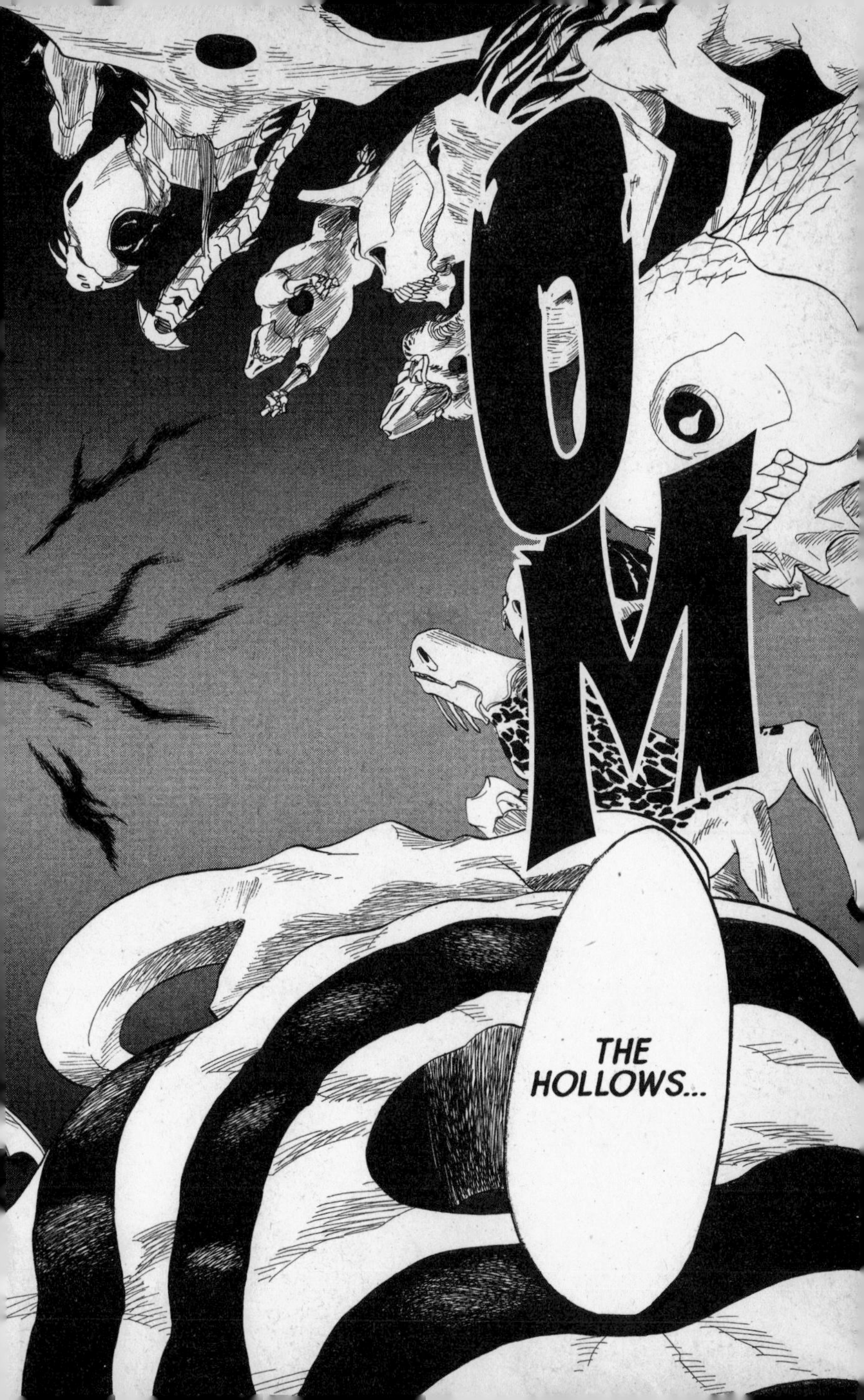
OM
THE HOLLOWS...

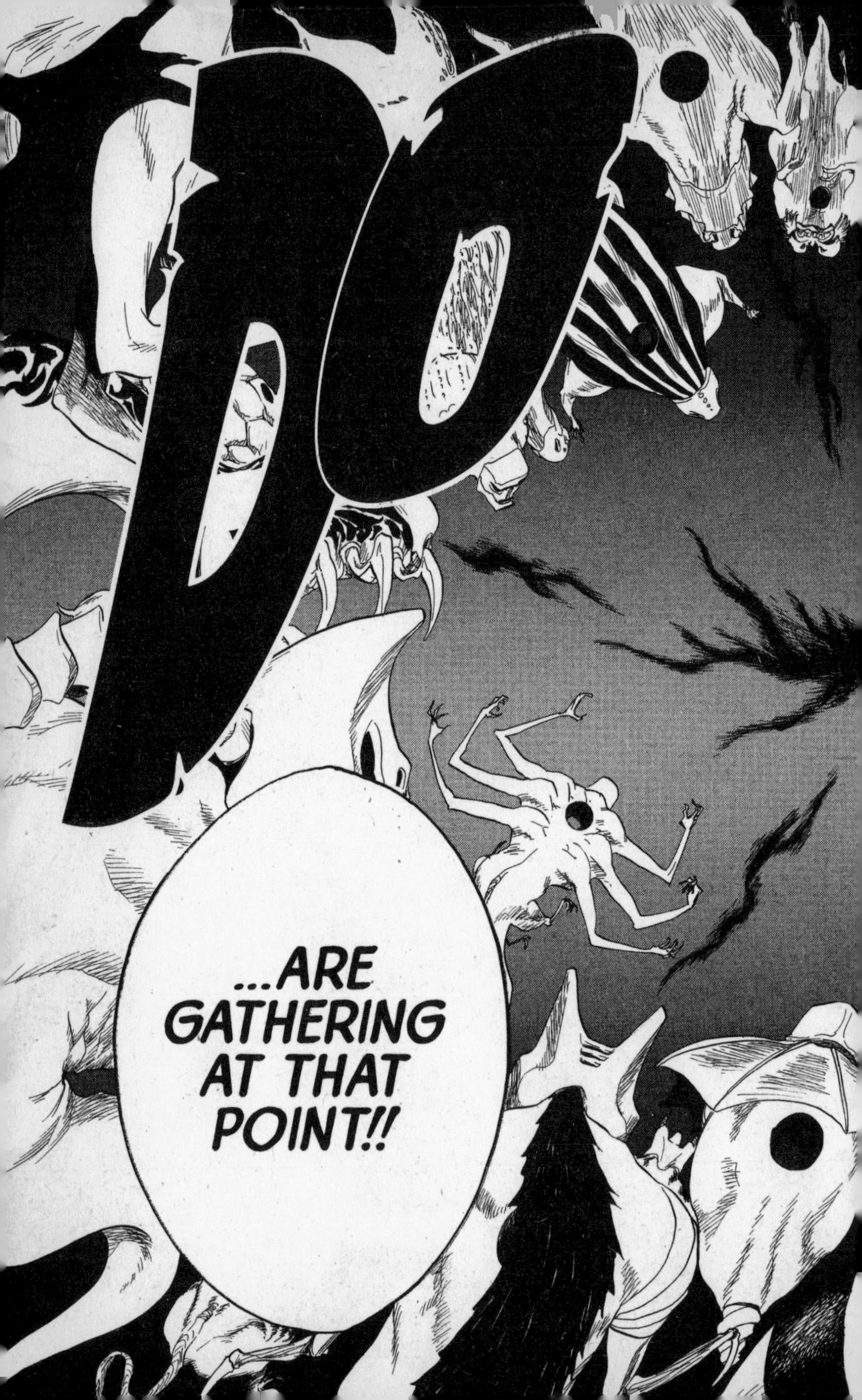
DO
...ARE GATHERING AT THAT POINT!!

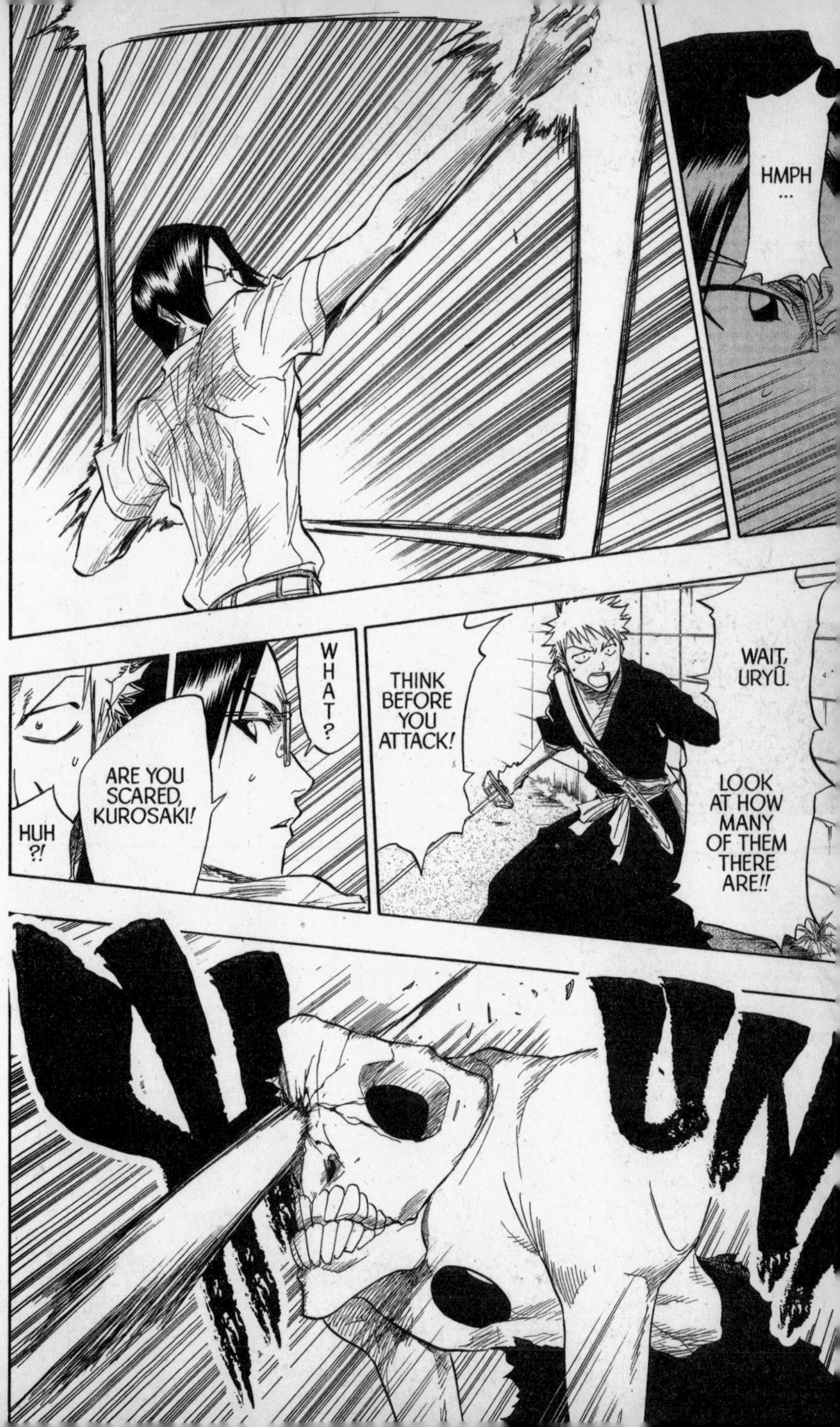
HMPH ...
WAIT, URYŪ.
LOOK AT HOW MANY OF THEM THERE ARE!!
THINK BEFORE YOU ATTACK!
WHAT?
ARE YOU SCARED, KUROSAKI!
HUH ?!

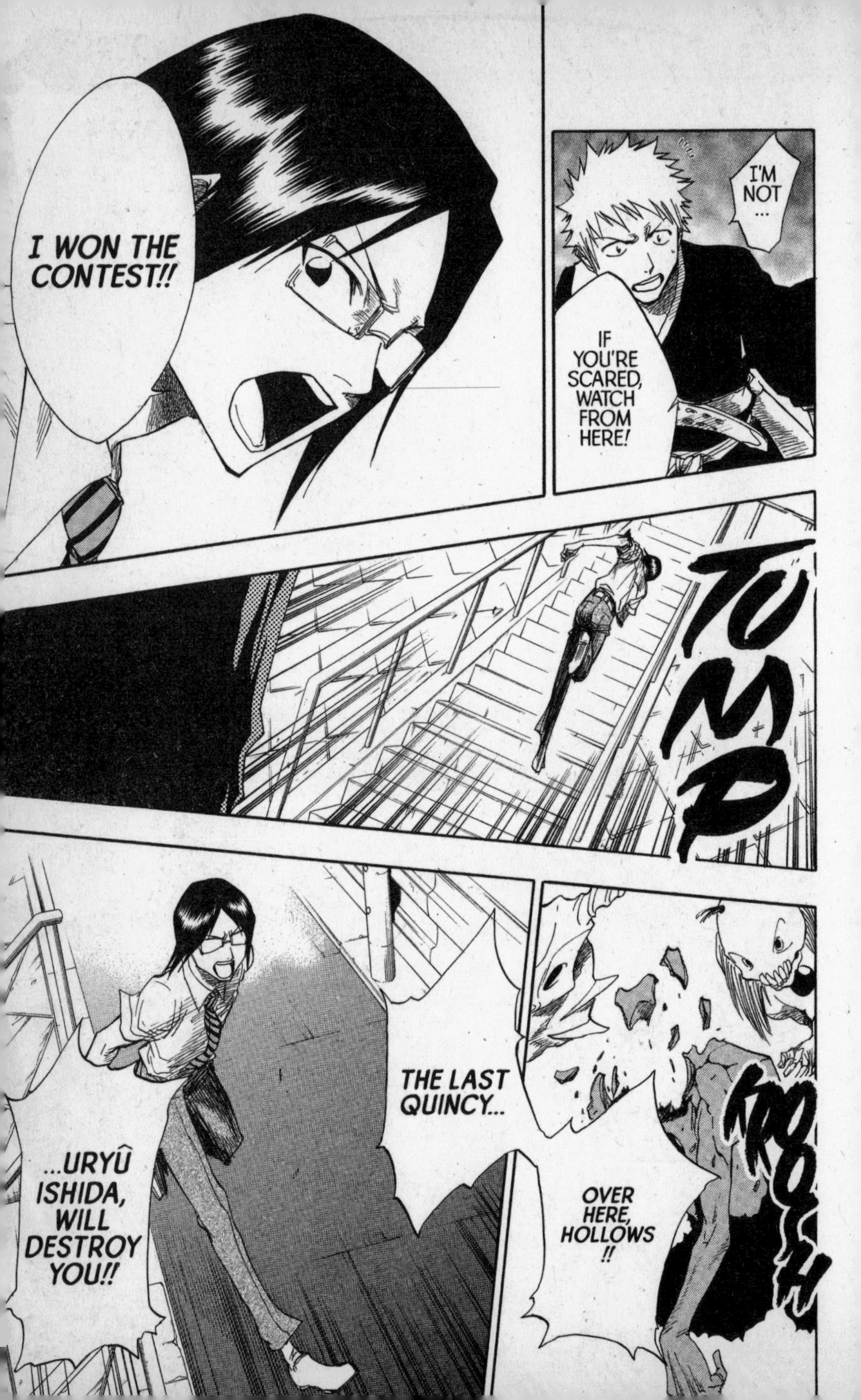
I'M NOT ...
IF YOU'RE SCARED, WATCH FROM HERE!
I WON THE CONTEST!!
TOMP
OVER HERE, HOLLOWS!!
THE LAST QUINCY...
...URYÛ ISHIDA, WILL DESTROY YOU!!

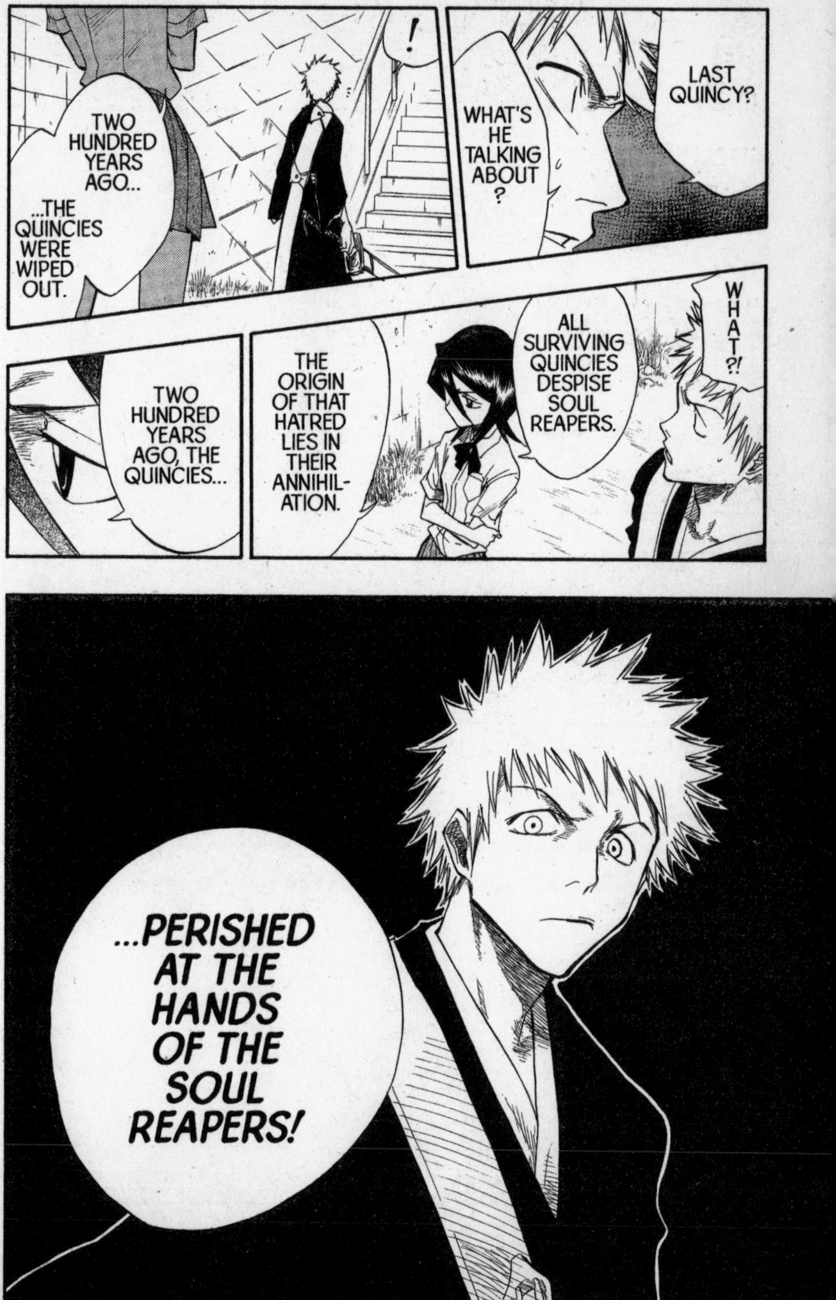
LAST QUINCY?
WHAT'S HE TALKING ABOUT?
!
TWO HUNDRED YEARS AGO...
...THE QUINCIES WERE WIPED OUT.
WHAT?!
ALL SURVIVING QUINCIES DESPISE SOUL REAPERS.
THE ORIGIN OF THAT HATRED LIES IN THEIR ANNIHILATION.
TWO HUNDRED YEARS AGO, THE QUINCIES...
...PERISHED AT THE HANDS OF THE SOUL REAPERS!

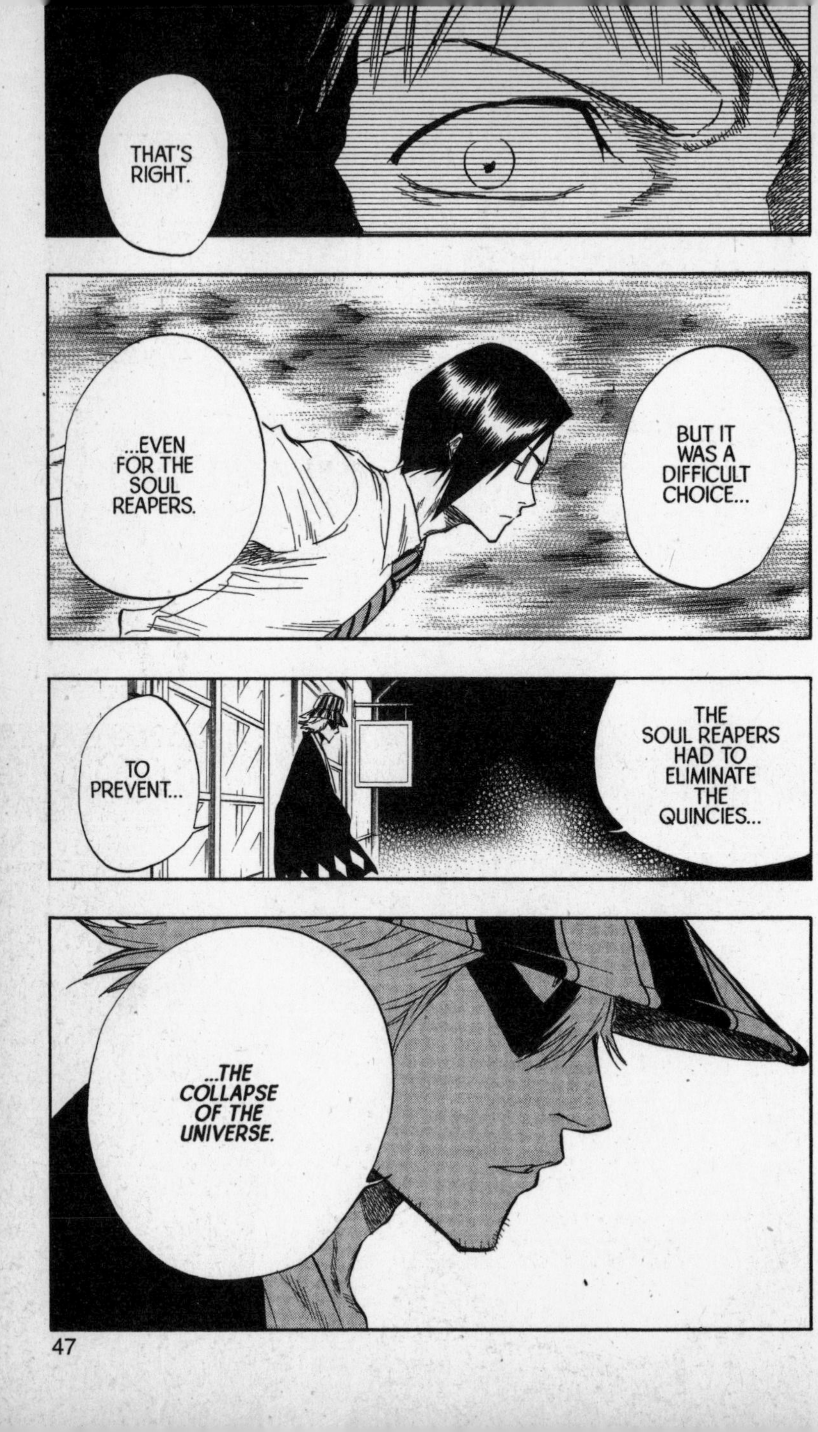
THAT'S RIGHT.
BUT IT WAS A DIFFICULT CHOICE...
...EVEN FOR THE SOUL REAPERS.
THE SOUL REAPERS HAD TO ELIMINATE THE QUINCIES...
TO PREVENT...
...THE COLLAPSE OF THE UNIVERSE.

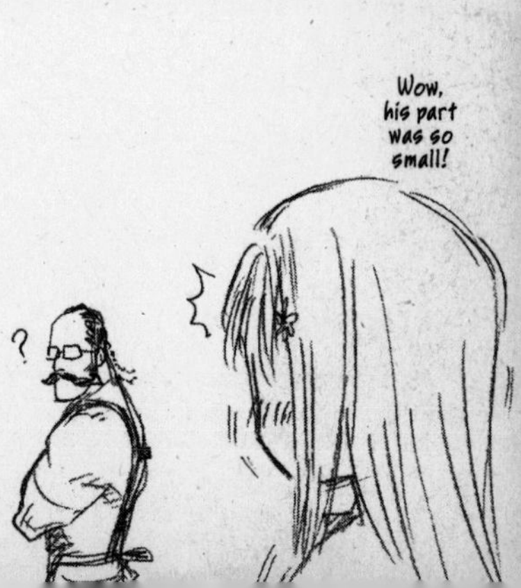
Wow, his part was so small!

46. Karneades ~ Back-to-Back

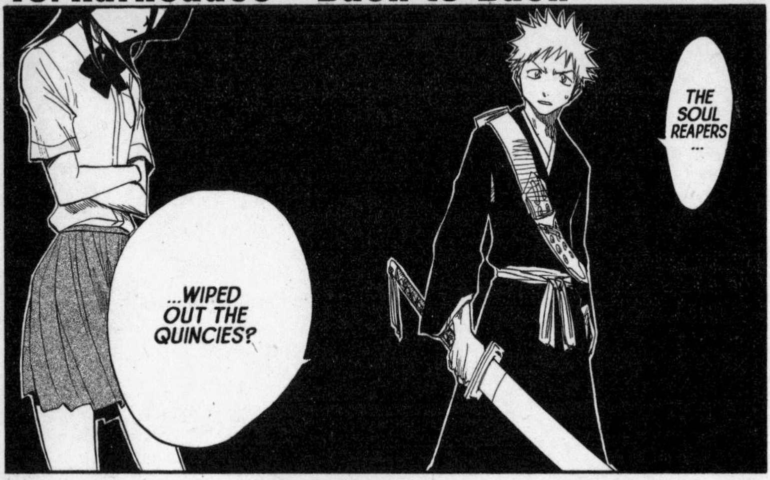
THE SOUL REAPERS...
...WIPED OUT THE QUINCIES?

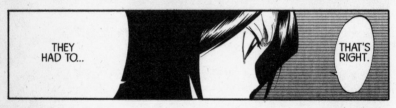

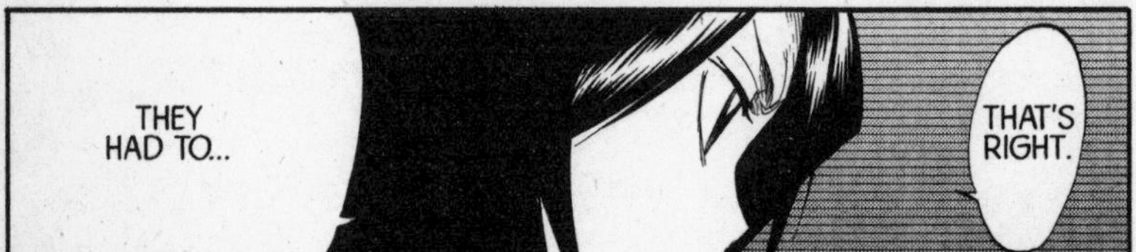
THAT'S RIGHT.
THEY HAD TO...

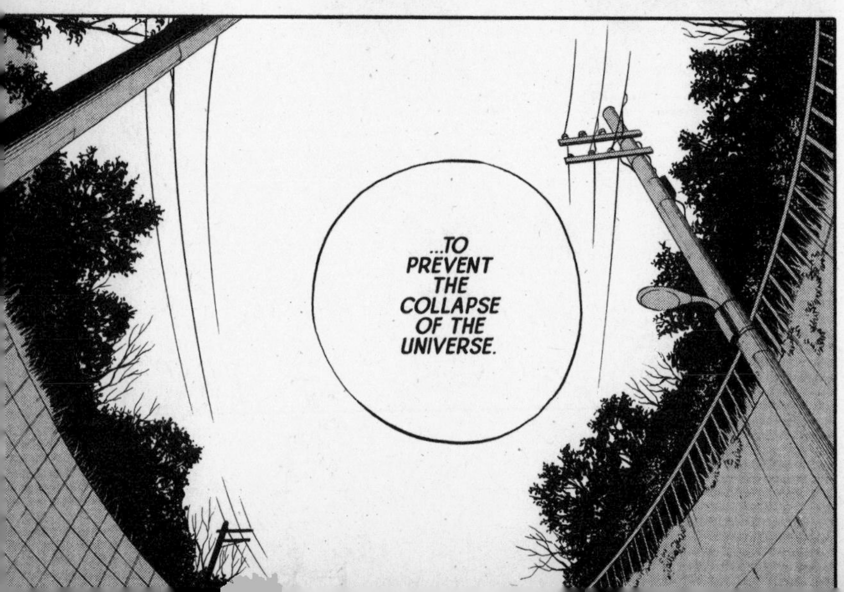
...TO PREVENT THE COLLAPSE OF THE UNIVERSE.

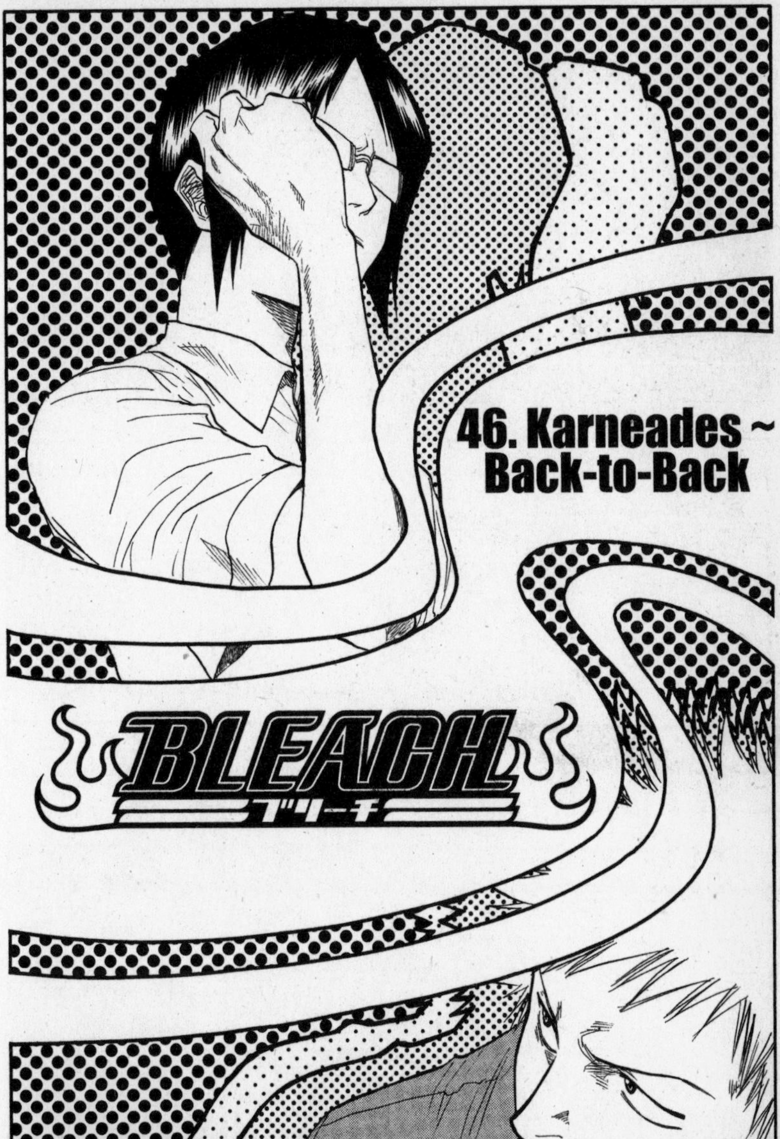

46. Karneades ~
Back-to-Back
BLEACH
ブリーチ

READ THIS WAY

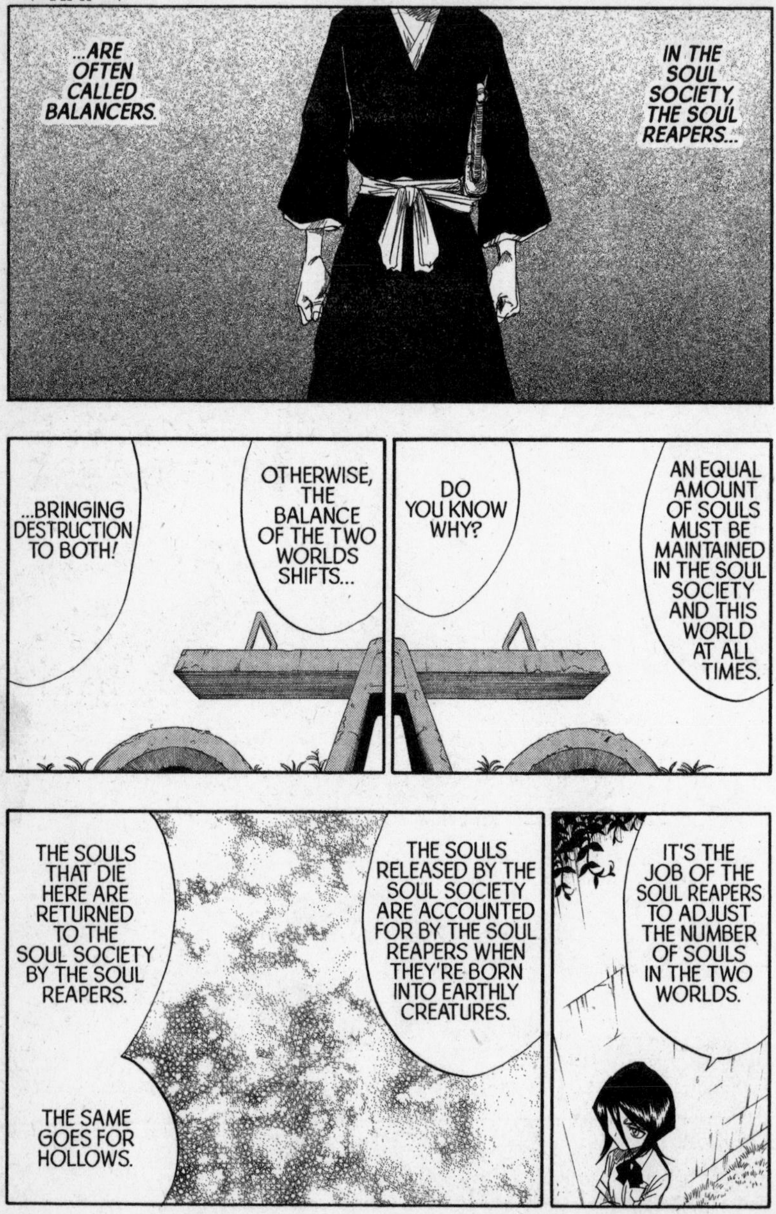
IN THE SOUL SOCIETY, THE SOUL REAPERS...
...ARE OFTEN CALLED BALANCERS.
AN EQUAL AMOUNT OF SOULS MUST BE MAINTAINED IN THE SOUL SOCIETY AND THIS WORLD AT ALL TIMES.
DO YOU KNOW WHY?
OTHERWISE, THE BALANCE OF THE TWO WORLDS SHIFTS...
...BRINGING DESTRUCTION TO BOTH!
IT'S THE JOB OF THE SOUL REAPERS TO ADJUST THE NUMBER OF SOULS IN THE TWO WORLDS.
THE SOULS RELEASED BY THE SOUL SOCIETY ARE ACCOUNTED FOR BY THE SOUL REAPERS WHEN THEY'RE BORN INTO EARTHLY CREATURES.
THE SOULS THAT DIE HERE ARE RETURNED TO THE SOUL SOCIETY BY THE SOUL REAPERS.
THE SAME GOES FOR HOLLOWS.

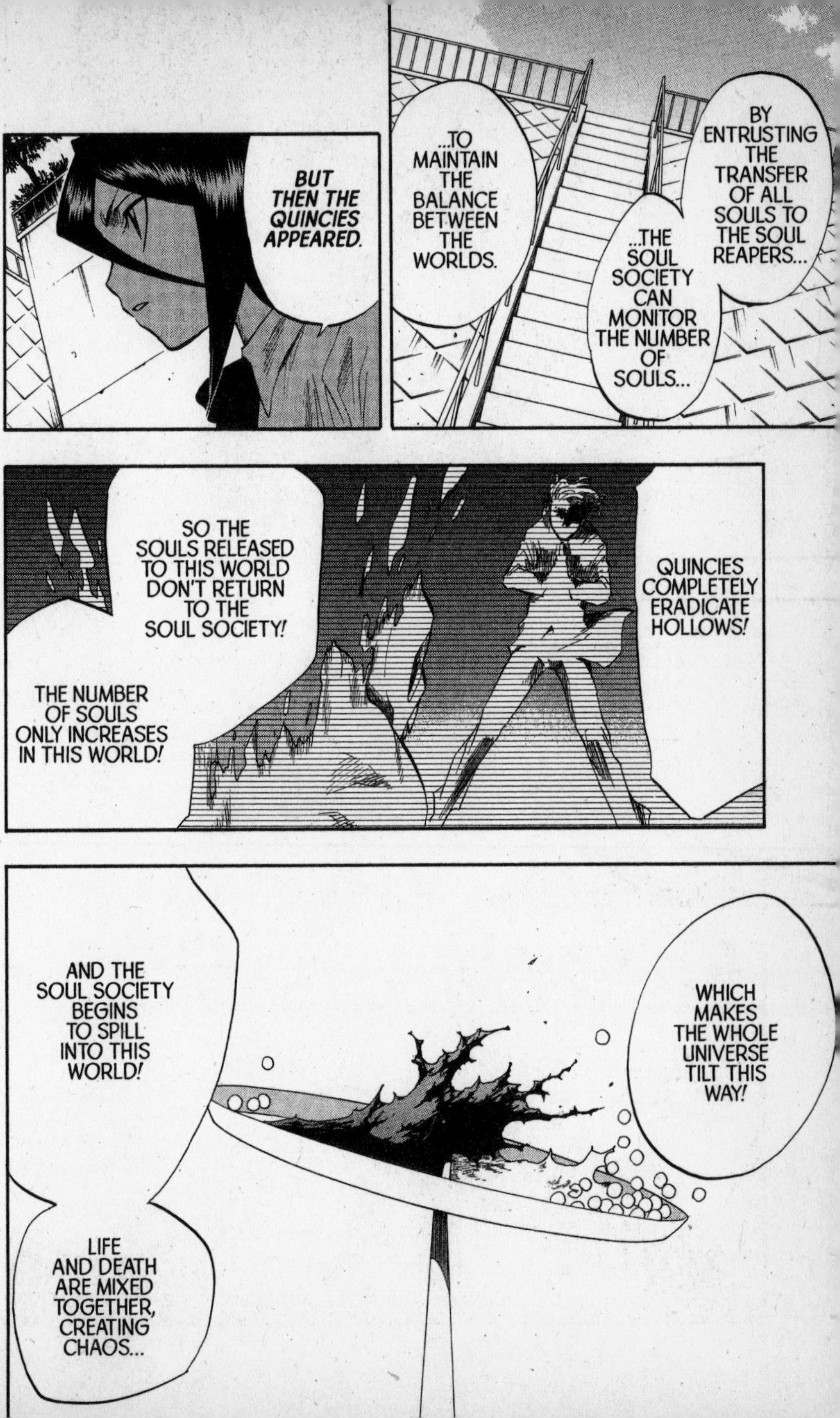
BY ENTRUSTING THE TRANSFER OF ALL SOULS TO THE SOUL REAPERS...
...THE SOUL SOCIETY CAN MONITOR THE NUMBER OF SOULS...
...TO MAINTAIN THE BALANCE BETWEEN THE WORLDS.
BUT THEN THE QUINCIES APPEARED.
QUINCIES COMPLETELY ERADICATE HOLLOWS!
SO THE SOULS RELEASED TO THIS WORLD DON'T RETURN TO THE SOUL SOCIETY!
THE NUMBER OF SOULS ONLY INCREASES IN THIS WORLD!
WHICH MAKES THE WHOLE UNIVERSE TILT THIS WAY!
AND THE SOUL SOCIETY BEGINS TO SPILL INTO THIS WORLD!
LIFE AND DEATH ARE MIXED TOGETHER, CREATING CHAOS...

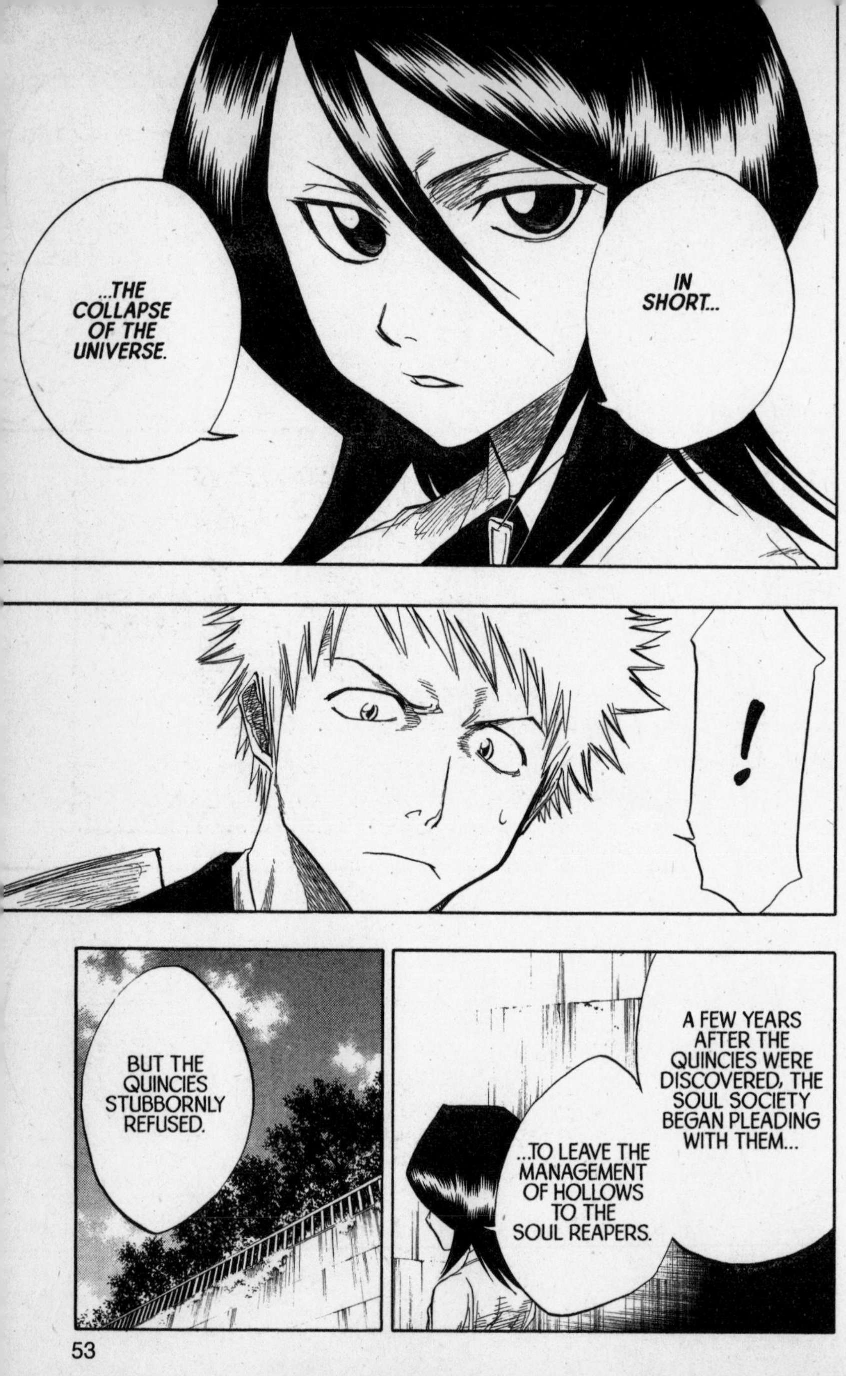
IN SHORT...
...THE COLLAPSE OF THE UNIVERSE.
!
A FEW YEARS AFTER THE QUINCIES WERE DISCOVERED, THE SOUL SOCIETY BEGAN PLEADING WITH THEM...
...TO LEAVE THE MANAGEMENT OF HOLLOWS TO THE SOUL REAPERS.
BUT THE QUINCIES STUBBORNLY REFUSED.

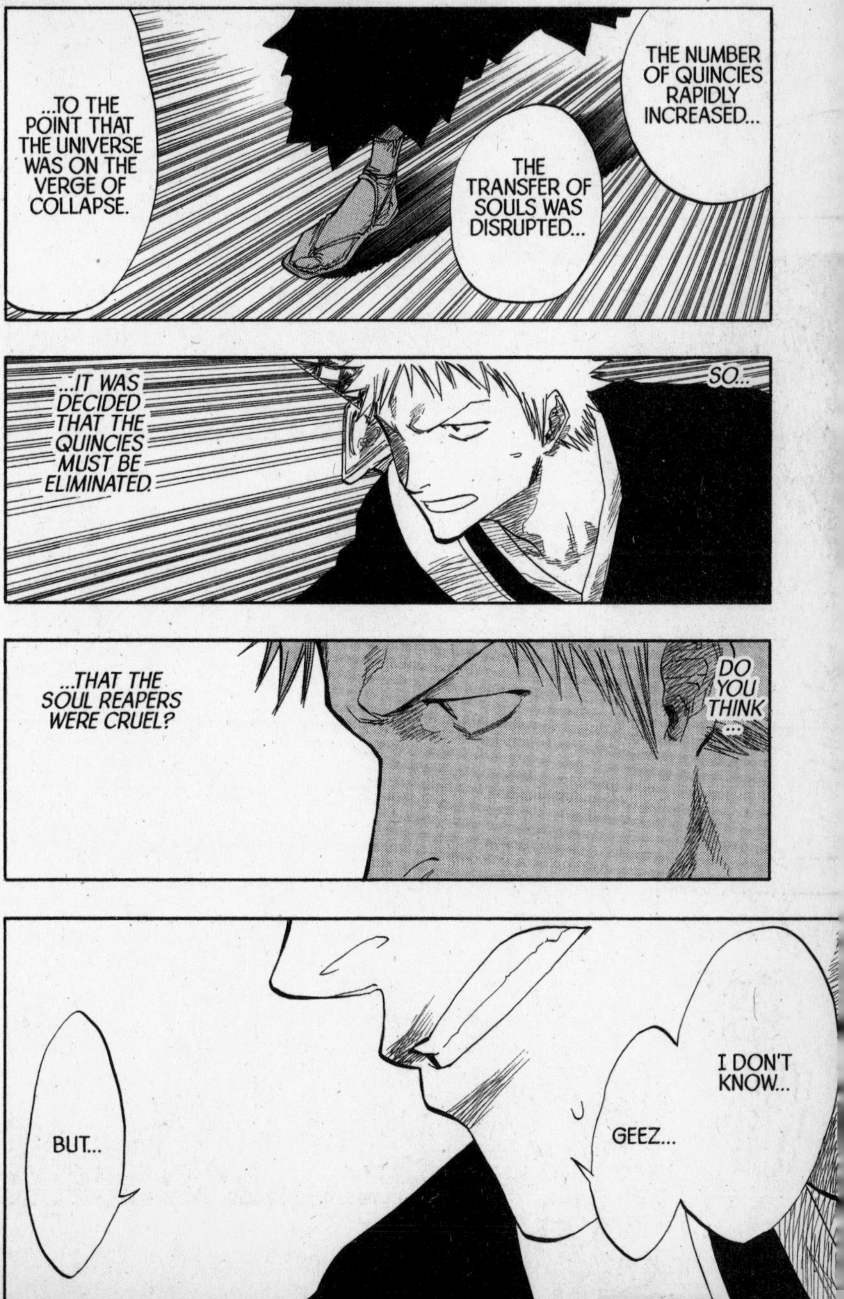
THE NUMBER OF QUINCIES RAPIDLY INCREASED...
THE TRANSFER OF SOULS WAS DISRUPTED...
...TO THE POINT THAT THE UNIVERSE WAS ON THE VERGE OF COLLAPSE.
SO...
...IT WAS DECIDED THAT THE QUINCIES MUST BE ELIMINATED.
DO YOU THINK...
...THAT THE SOUL REAPERS WERE CRUEL?
I DON'T KNOW...
GEEZ...
BUT...

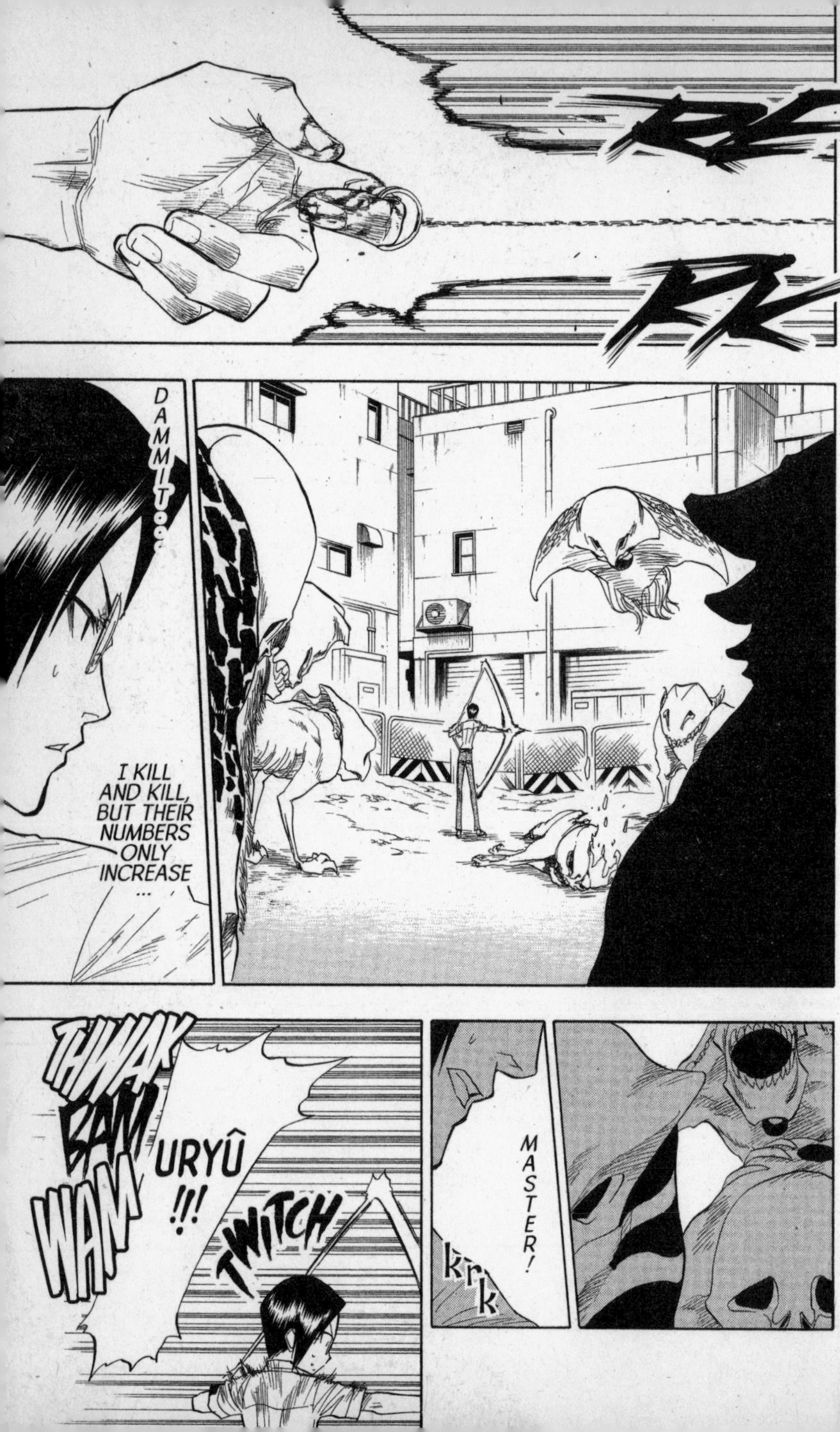
RRK
DAMMIT...
I KILL AND KILL, BUT THEIR NUMBERS ONLY INCREASE ...
MASTER!
krk
URYÛ!!!
THWAK
BAM
WAM
TWITCH

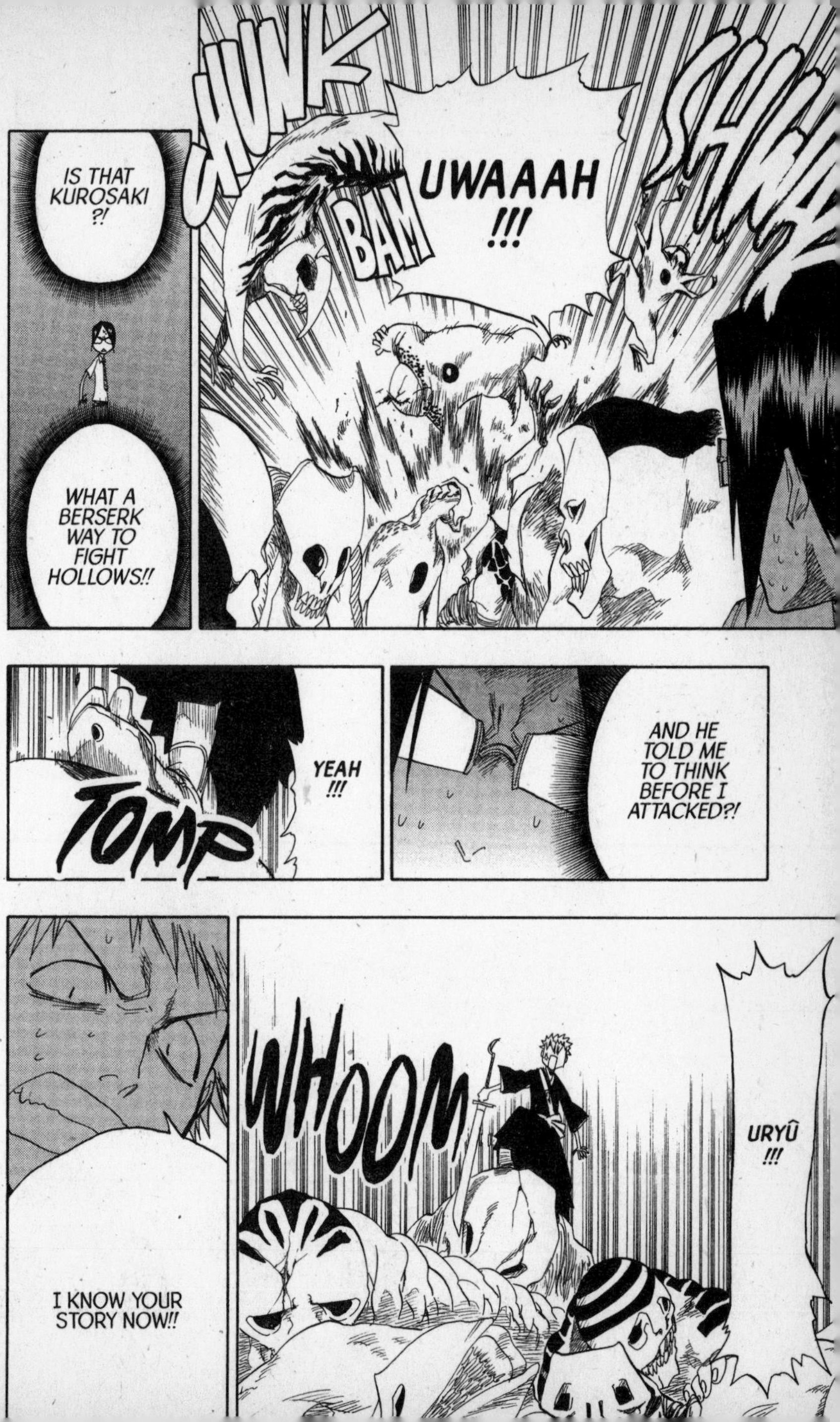
UWAAAH !!!
BAM
CHUNK
IS THAT KUROSAKI ?!
WHAT A BERSERK WAY TO FIGHT HOLLOWS!!
AND HE TOLD ME TO THINK BEFORE I ATTACKED?!
YEAH !!!
TOMP
URYÛ !!!
WHOOM
I KNOW YOUR STORY NOW!!

READ THIS WAY

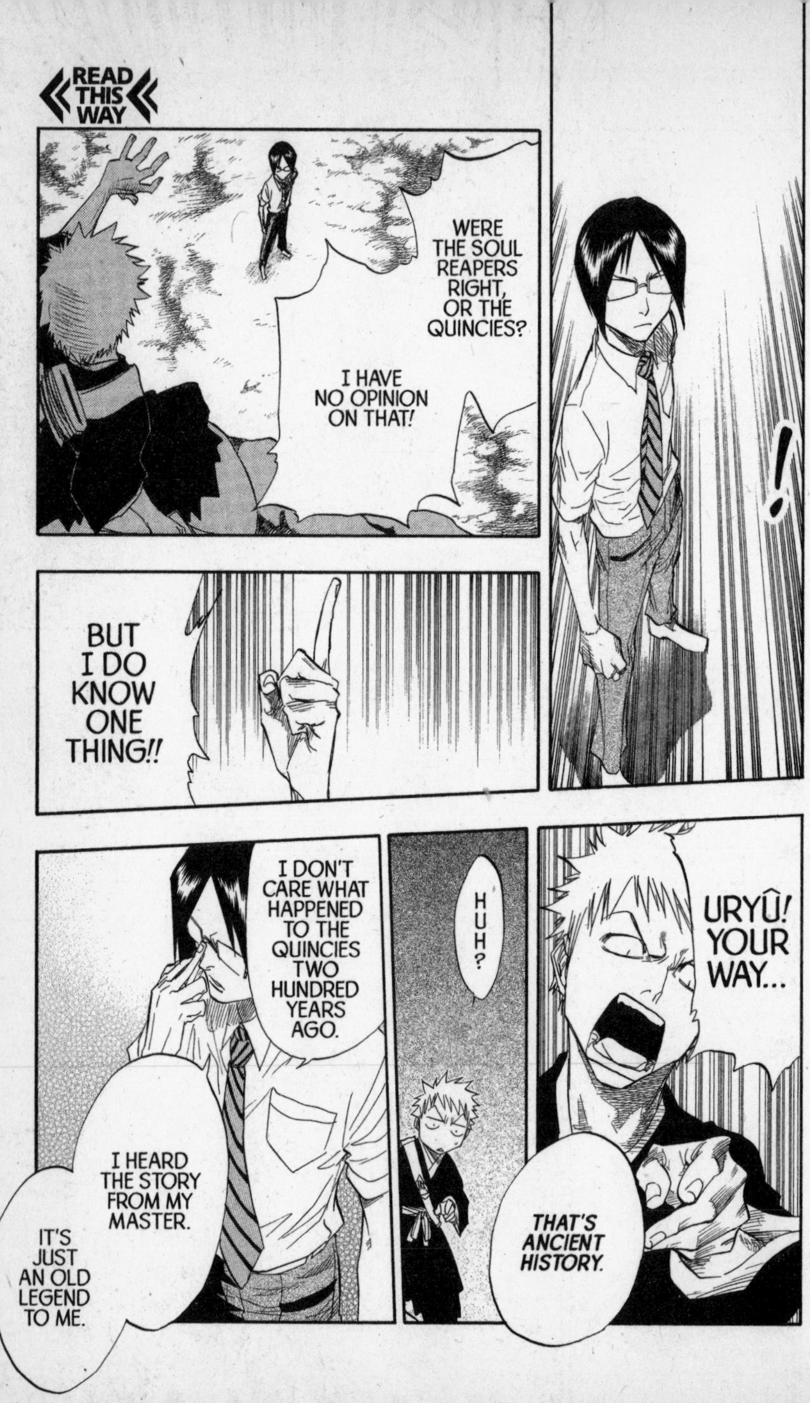
!
WERE THE SOUL REAPERS RIGHT, OR THE QUINCIES?
I HAVE NO OPINION ON THAT!
BUT I DO KNOW ONE THING!!
URYÛ! YOUR WAY...
THAT'S ANCIENT HISTORY.
HUH?
I DON'T CARE WHAT HAPPENED TO THE QUINCIES TWO HUNDRED YEARS AGO.
I HEARD THE STORY FROM MY MASTER.
IT'S JUST AN OLD LEGEND TO ME.

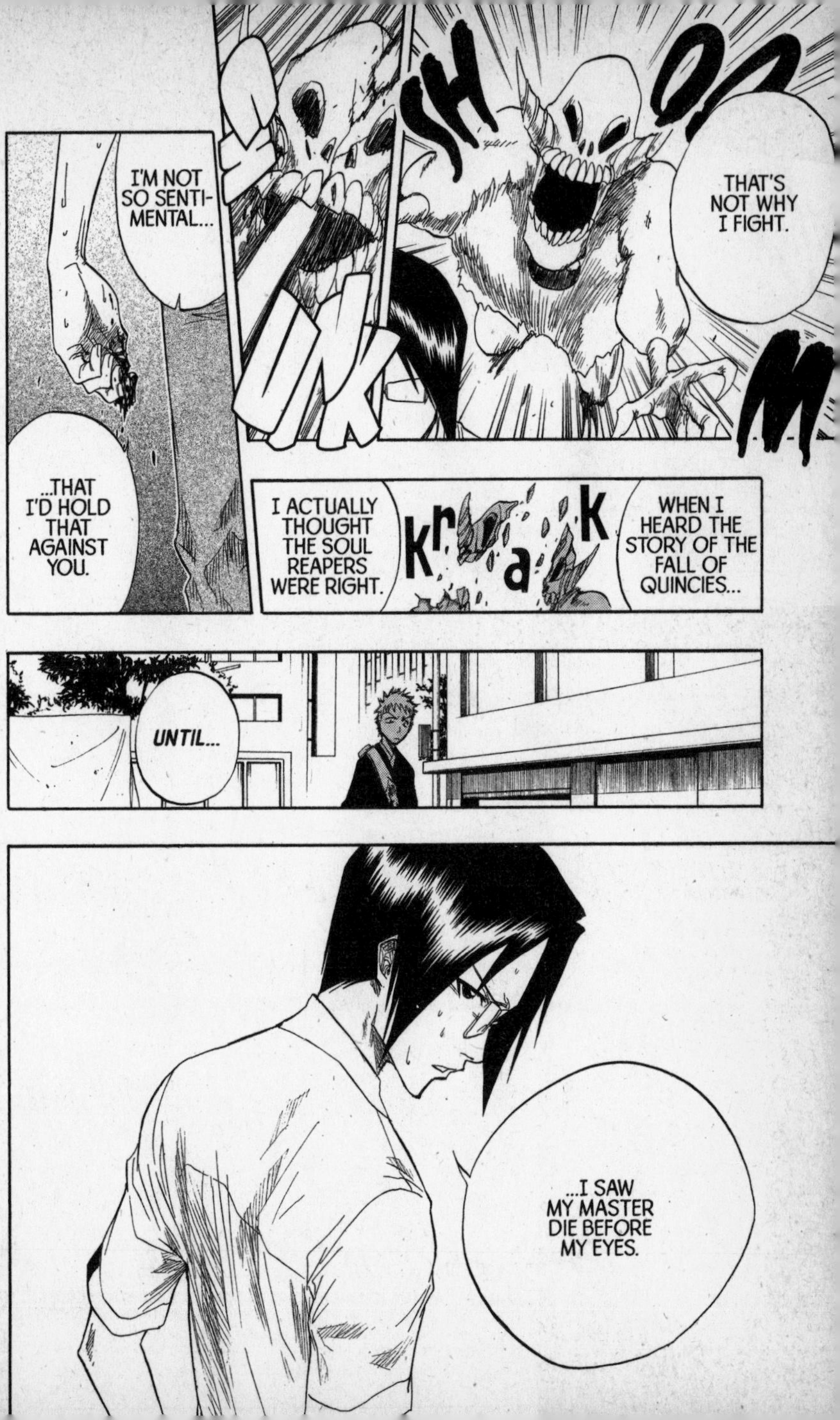
THAT'S NOT WHY I FIGHT.
WHEN I HEARD THE STORY OF THE FALL OF QUINCIES...
I ACTUALLY THOUGHT THE SOUL REAPERS WERE RIGHT.
I'M NOT SO SENTI-MENTAL...
...THAT I'D HOLD THAT AGAINST YOU.
UNTIL...
...I SAW MY MASTER DIE BEFORE MY EYES.

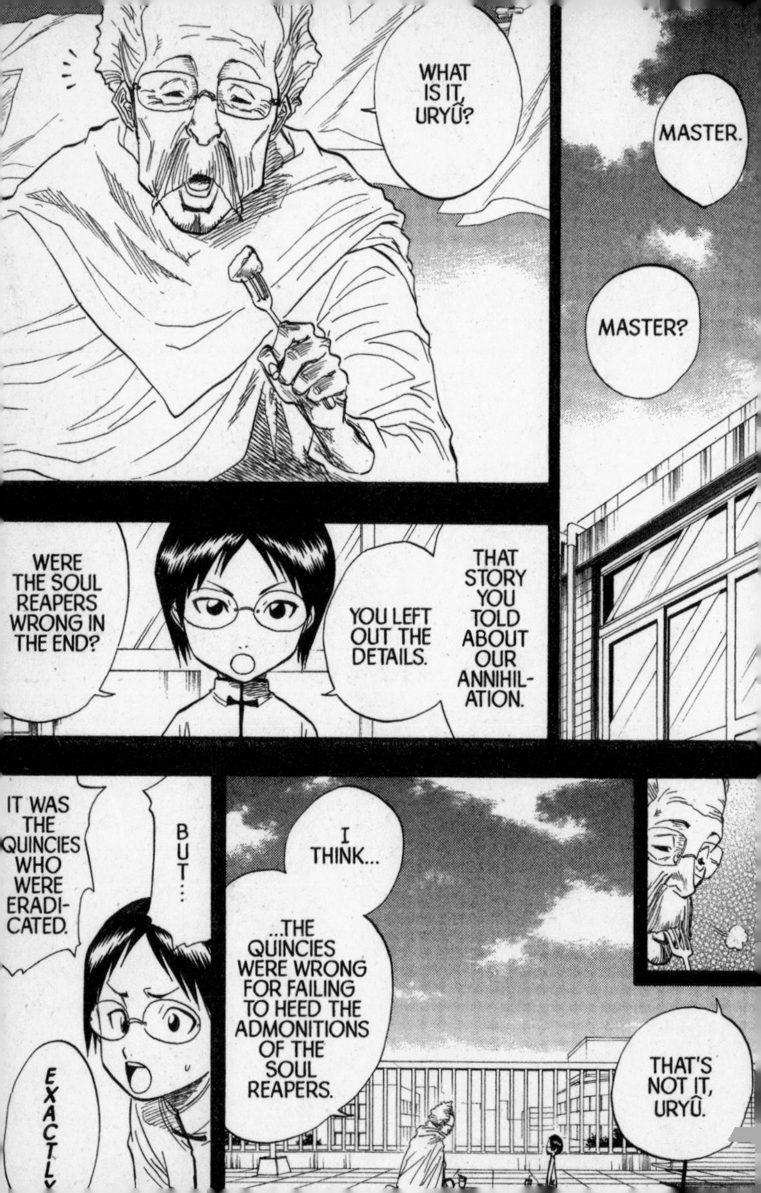
MASTER.
MASTER?
WHAT IS IT, URYŪ?
THAT STORY YOU TOLD ABOUT OUR ANNIHILATION.
YOU LEFT OUT THE DETAILS.
WERE THE SOUL REAPERS WRONG IN THE END?
I THINK...
...THE QUINCIES WERE WRONG FOR FAILING TO HEED THE ADMONITIONS OF THE SOUL REAPERS.
THAT'S NOT IT, URYŪ.
BUT...
IT WAS THE QUINCIES WHO WERE ERADICATED.
EXACTLY

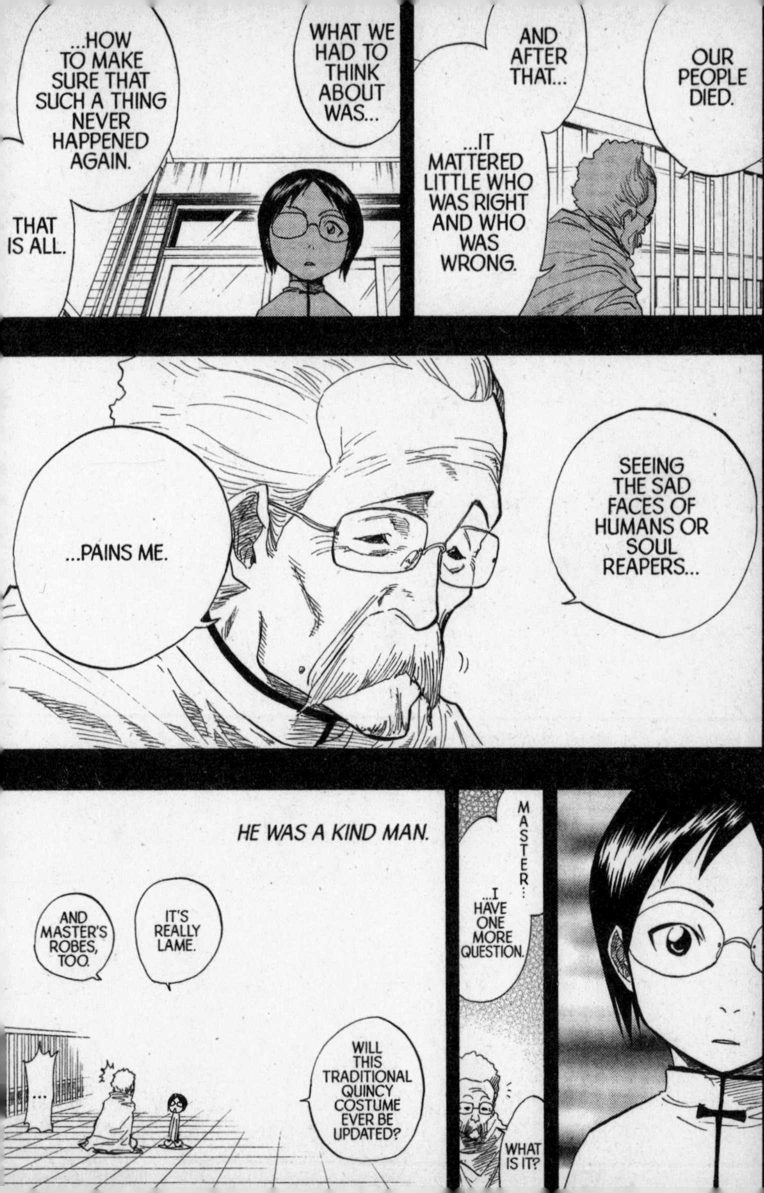
OUR PEOPLE DIED.
AND AFTER THAT...
...IT MATTERED LITTLE WHO WAS RIGHT AND WHO WAS WRONG.
WHAT WE HAD TO THINK ABOUT WAS...
...HOW TO MAKE SURE THAT SUCH A THING NEVER HAPPENED AGAIN.
THAT IS ALL.
SEEING THE SAD FACES OF HUMANS OR SOUL REAPERS...
...PAINS ME.
MASTER...
...I HAVE ONE MORE QUESTION.
WHAT IS IT?
HE WAS A KIND MAN.
WILL THIS TRADITIONAL QUINCY COSTUME EVER BE UPDATED?
...
IT'S REALLY LAME.
AND MASTER'S ROBES, TOO.

READ THIS WAY

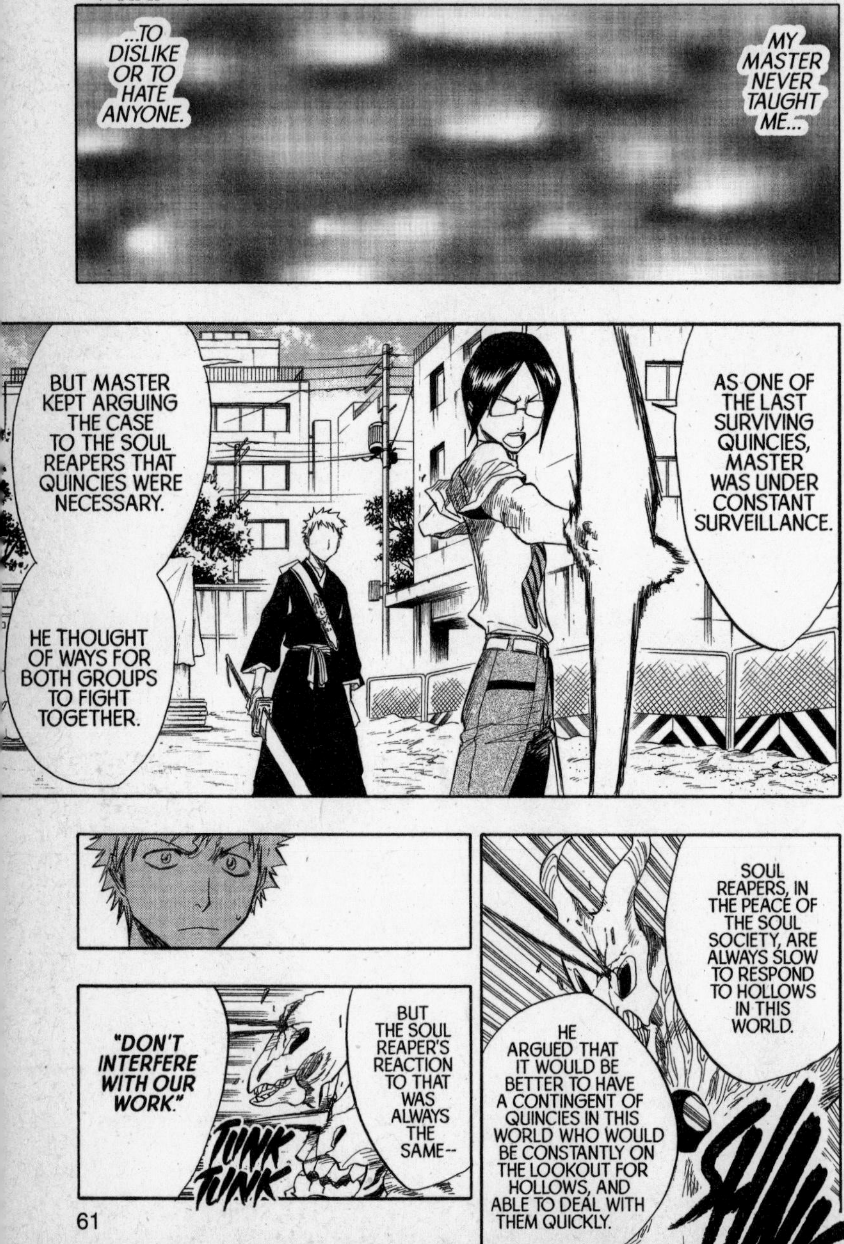

MY MASTER NEVER TAUGHT ME...
...TO DISLIKE OR TO HATE ANYONE.
AS ONE OF THE LAST SURVIVING QUINCIES, MASTER WAS UNDER CONSTANT SURVEILLANCE.
BUT MASTER KEPT ARGUING THE CASE TO THE SOUL REAPERS THAT QUINCIES WERE NECESSARY.
HE THOUGHT OF WAYS FOR BOTH GROUPS TO FIGHT TOGETHER.
SOUL REAPERS, IN THE PEACE OF THE SOUL SOCIETY, ARE ALWAYS SLOW TO RESPOND TO HOLLOWS IN THIS WORLD.
HE ARGUED THAT IT WOULD BE BETTER TO HAVE A CONTINGENT OF QUINCIES IN THIS WORLD WHO WOULD BE CONSTANTLY ON THE LOOKOUT FOR HOLLOWS, AND ABLE TO DEAL WITH THEM QUICKLY.
BUT THE SOUL REAPER'S REACTION TO THAT WAS ALWAYS THE SAME--
"DON'T INTERFERE WITH OUR WORK."
TUNK TUNK

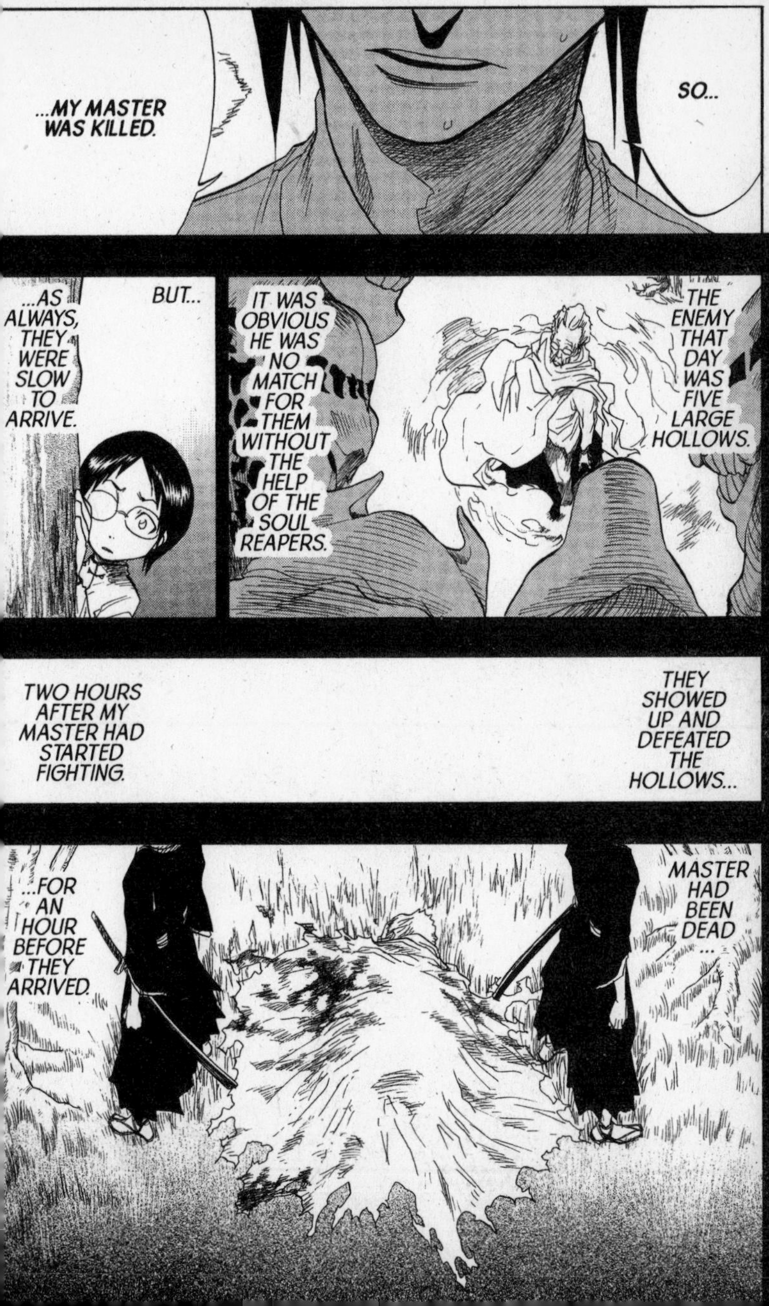
SO...
...MY MASTER WAS KILLED.
THE ENEMY THAT DAY WAS FIVE LARGE HOLLOWS.
IT WAS OBVIOUS HE WAS NO MATCH FOR THEM WITHOUT THE HELP OF THE SOUL REAPERS.
BUT...
...AS ALWAYS, THEY WERE SLOW TO ARRIVE.
THEY SHOWED UP AND DEFEATED THE HOLLOWS...
TWO HOURS AFTER MY MASTER HAD STARTED FIGHTING.
MASTER HAD BEEN DEAD...
...FOR AN HOUR BEFORE THEY ARRIVED.

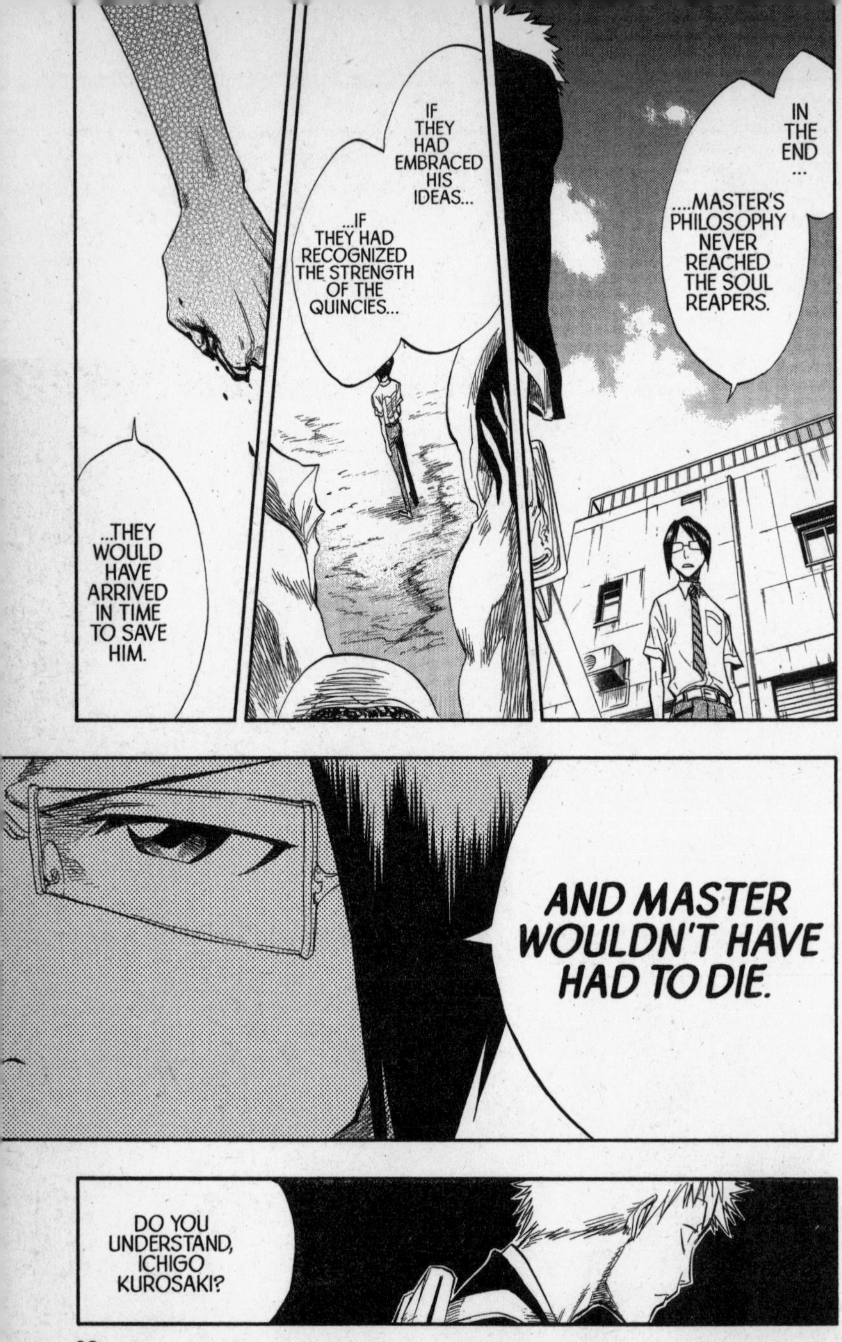
IN THE END ...
....MASTER'S PHILOSOPHY NEVER REACHED THE SOUL REAPERS.
IF THEY HAD EMBRACED HIS IDEAS...
...IF THEY HAD RECOGNIZED THE STRENGTH OF THE QUINCIES...
...THEY WOULD HAVE ARRIVED IN TIME TO SAVE HIM.
AND MASTER WOULDN'T HAVE HAD TO DIE.
DO YOU UNDERSTAND, ICHIGO KUROSAKI?

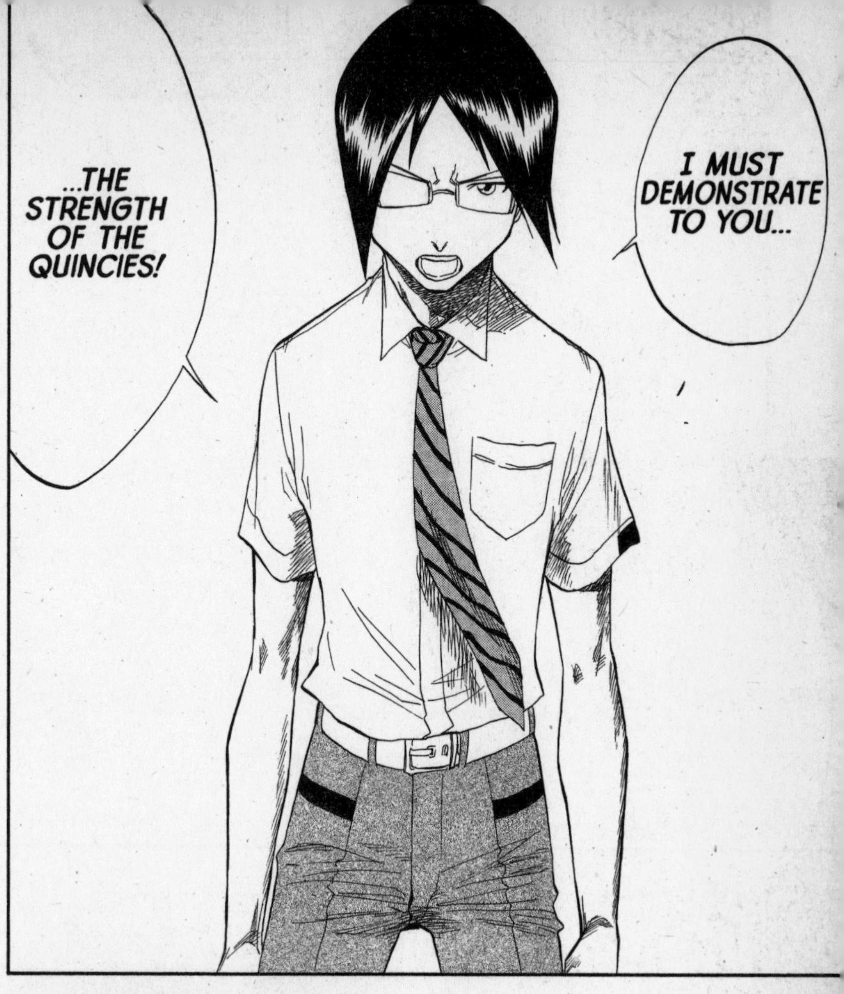
I MUST DEMONSTRATE TO YOU...
...THE STRENGTH OF THE QUINCIES!
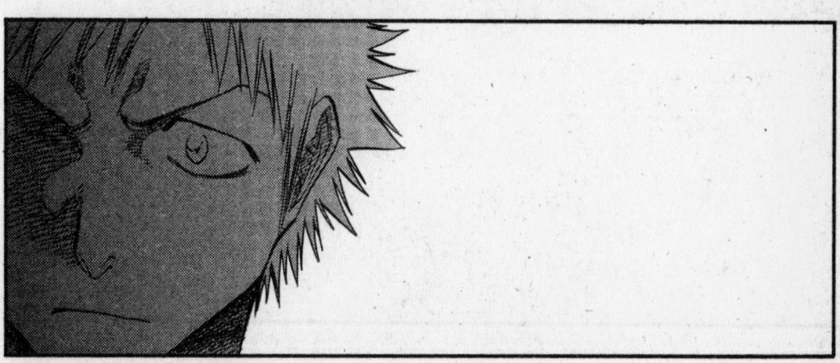

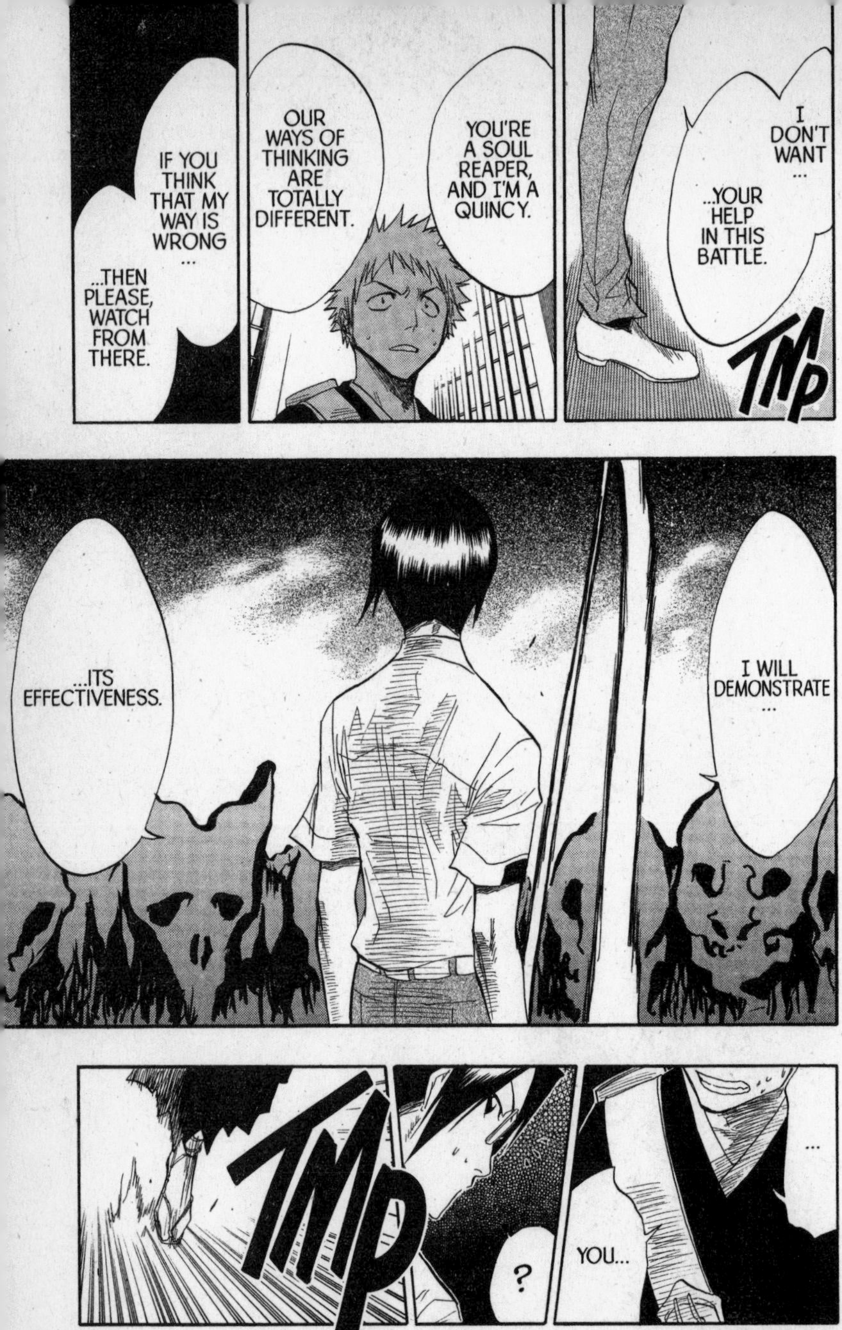
I DON'T WANT ...
...YOUR HELP IN THIS BATTLE.
TMP
YOU'RE A SOUL REAPER, AND I'M A QUINCY.
OUR WAYS OF THINKING ARE TOTALLY DIFFERENT.
IF YOU THINK THAT MY WAY IS WRONG ...
...THEN PLEASE, WATCH FROM THERE.
I WILL DEMONSTRATE ...
...ITS EFFECTIVENESS.
...
YOU...
?
TMP

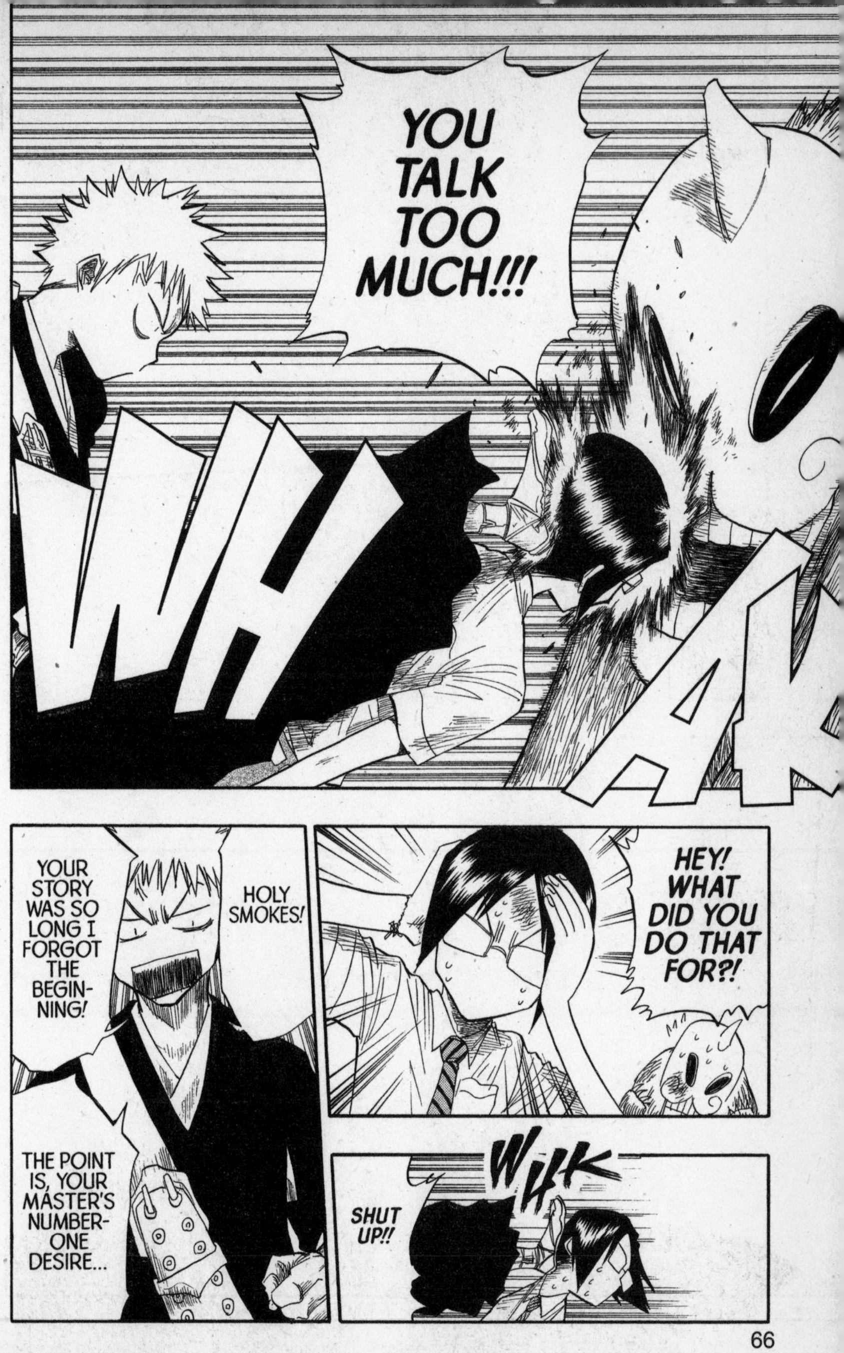
YOU TALK TOO MUCH!!!
WHAK
HEY! WHAT DID YOU DO THAT FOR?!
WHK
SHUT UP!!
HOLY SMOKES!
YOUR STORY WAS SO LONG I FORGOT THE BEGIN-NING!
THE POINT IS, YOUR MASTER'S NUMBER-ONE DESIRE...

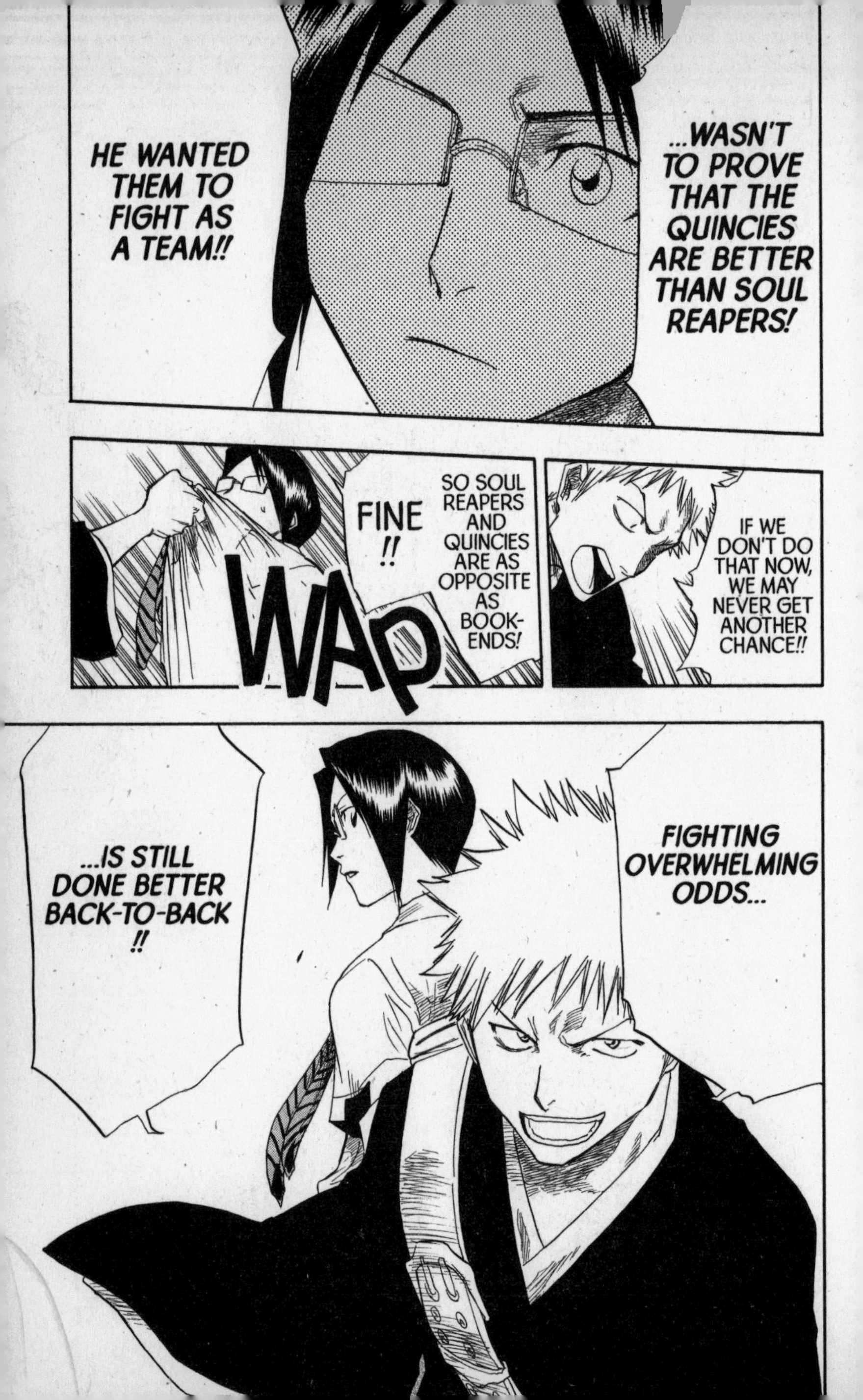
...WASN'T TO PROVE THAT THE QUINCIES ARE BETTER THAN SOUL REAPERS!
HE WANTED THEM TO FIGHT AS A TEAM!!
IF WE DON'T DO THAT NOW, WE MAY NEVER GET ANOTHER CHANCE!!
SO SOUL REAPERS AND QUINCIES ARE AS OPPOSITE AS BOOK-ENDS!
FINE!!
WAP
FIGHTING OVERWHELMING ODDS...
...IS STILL DONE BETTER BACK-TO-BACK!!

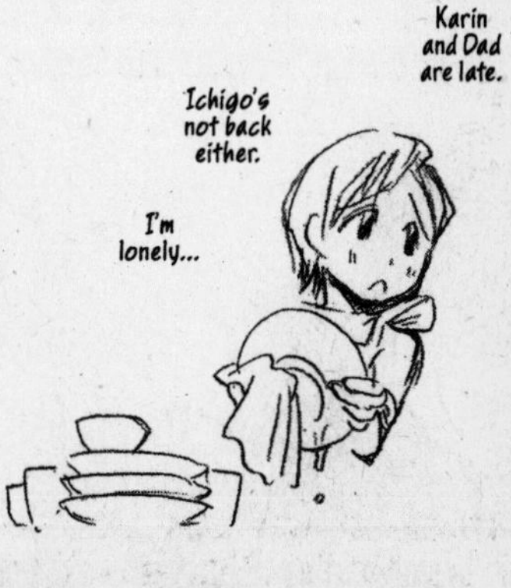
Karin and Dad are late.
Ichigo's not back either.
I'm lonely...

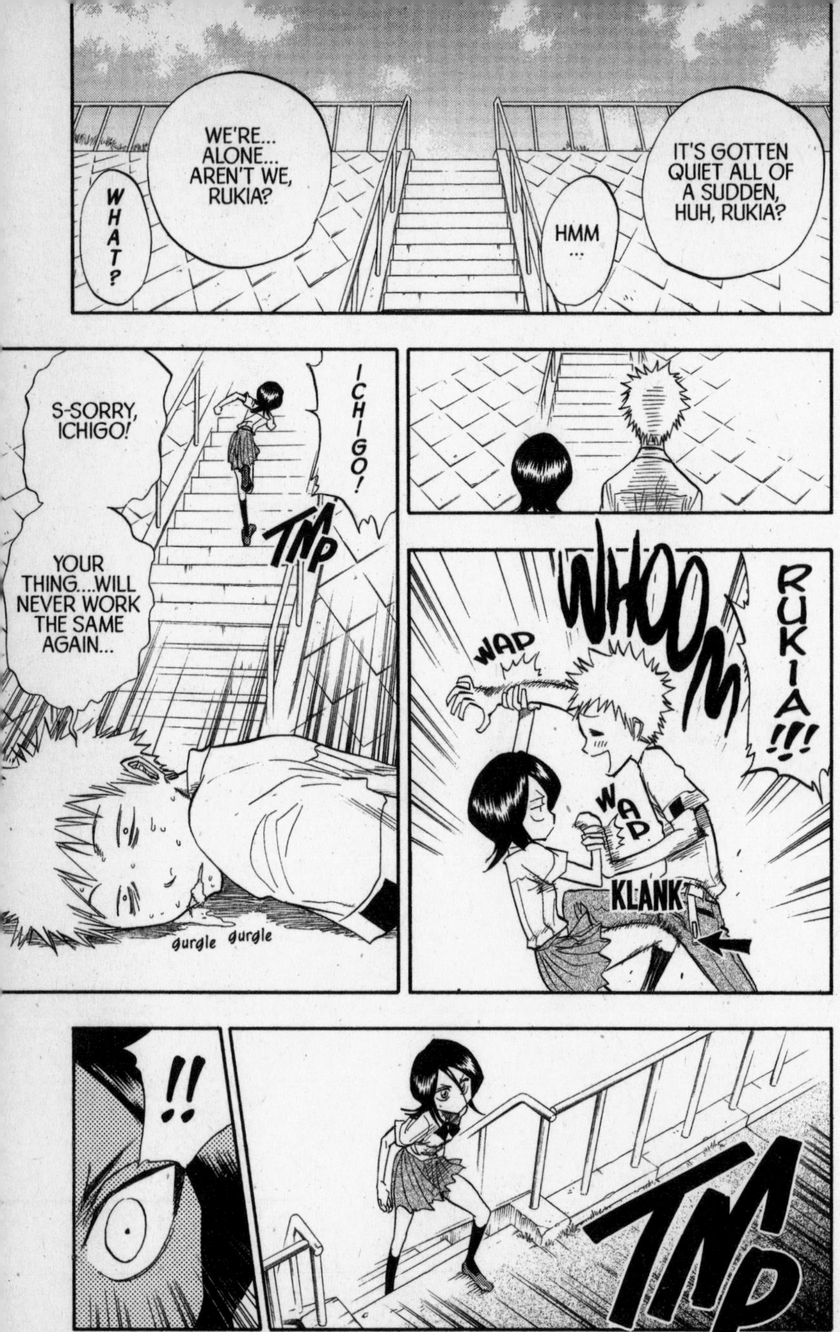
IT'S GOTTEN QUIET ALL OF A SUDDEN, HUH, RUKIA?
HMM...
WE'RE... ALONE... AREN'T WE, RUKIA?
WHAT?
RUKIA!!!
WHOOM
WAD
WAD
KLANK
ICHIGO!
TMP
S-SORRY, ICHIGO!
YOUR THING....WILL NEVER WORK THE SAME AGAIN...
gurgle gurgle
TMP
!!

47. Back-to-Back ~ Tearing Sky

BLEACH
ブリーチ

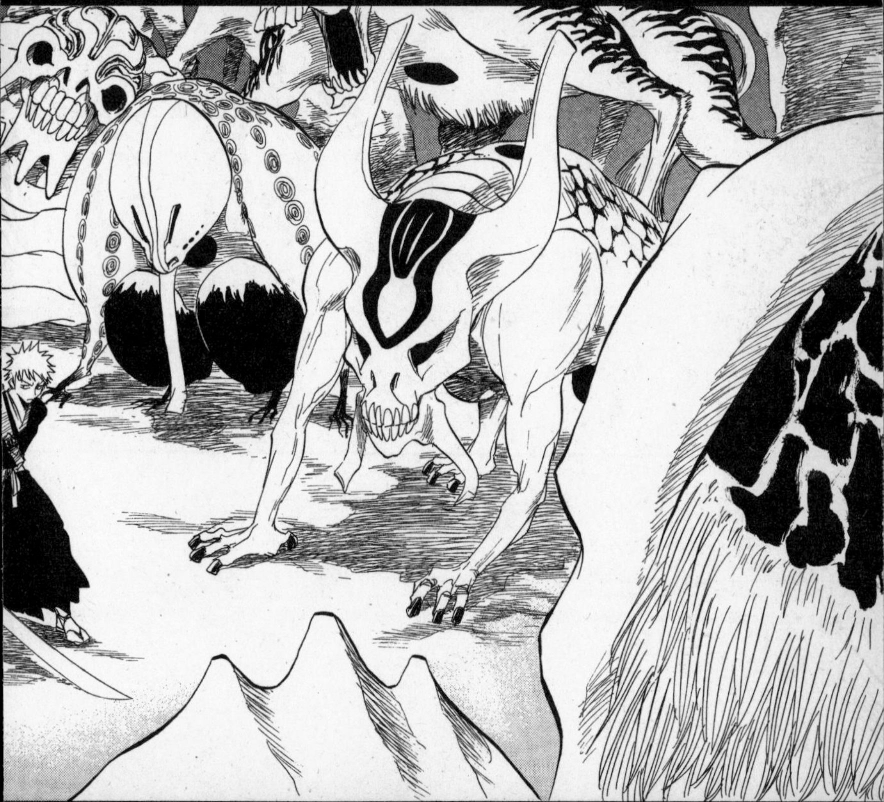

47. Back-to-Back
~ Tearing Sky

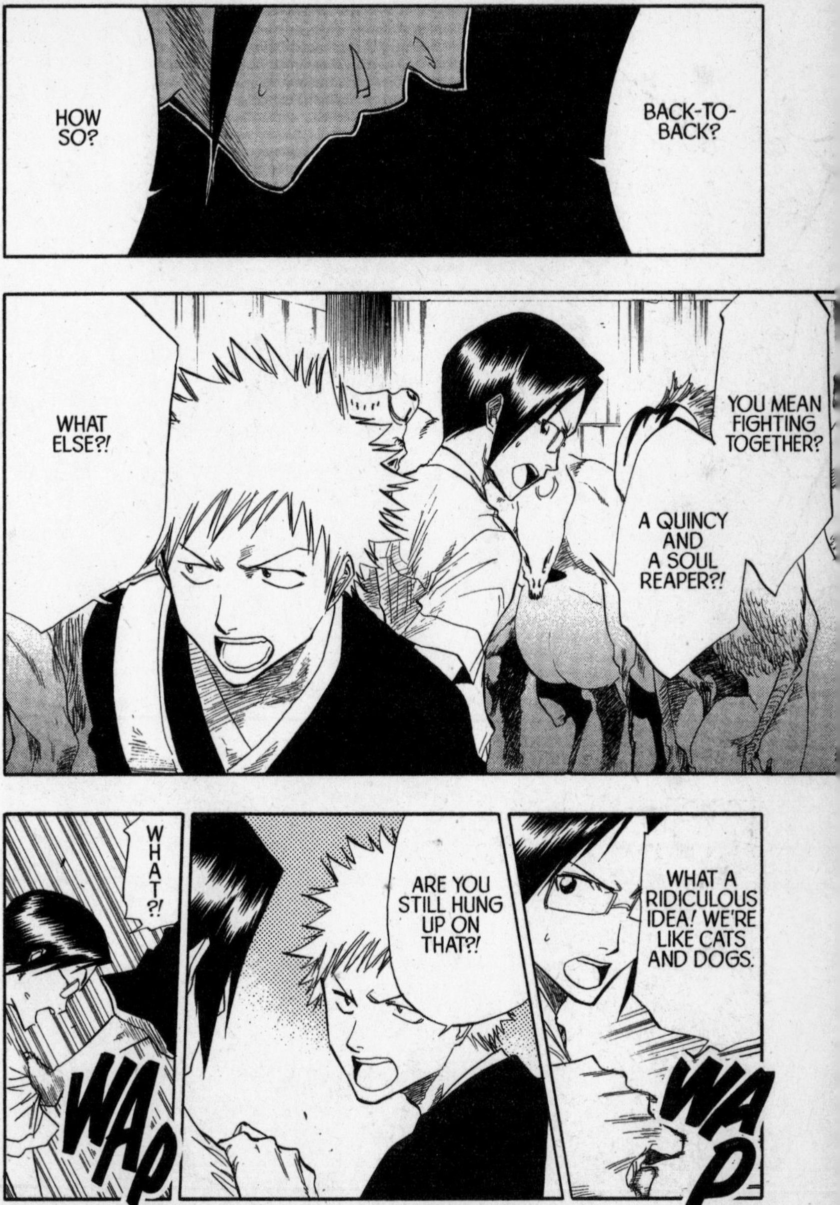
BACK-TO-BACK?
HOW SO?
YOU MEAN FIGHTING TOGETHER?
A QUINCY AND A SOUL REAPER?!
WHAT ELSE?!
WHAT A RIDICULOUS IDEA! WE'RE LIKE CATS AND DOGS.
WAP
ARE YOU STILL HUNG UP ON THAT?!
WHAT?!
WAP

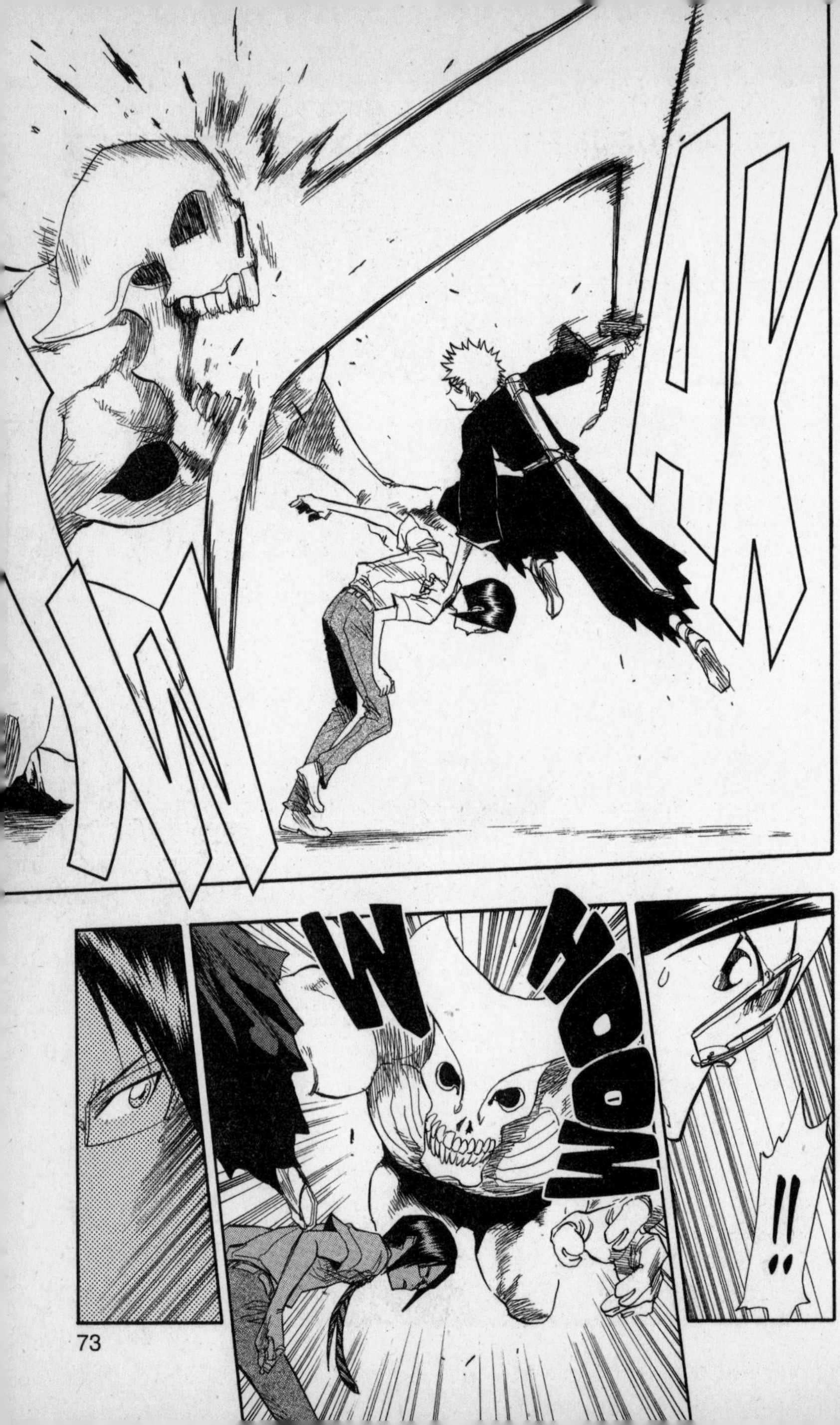
!!
WHOOM

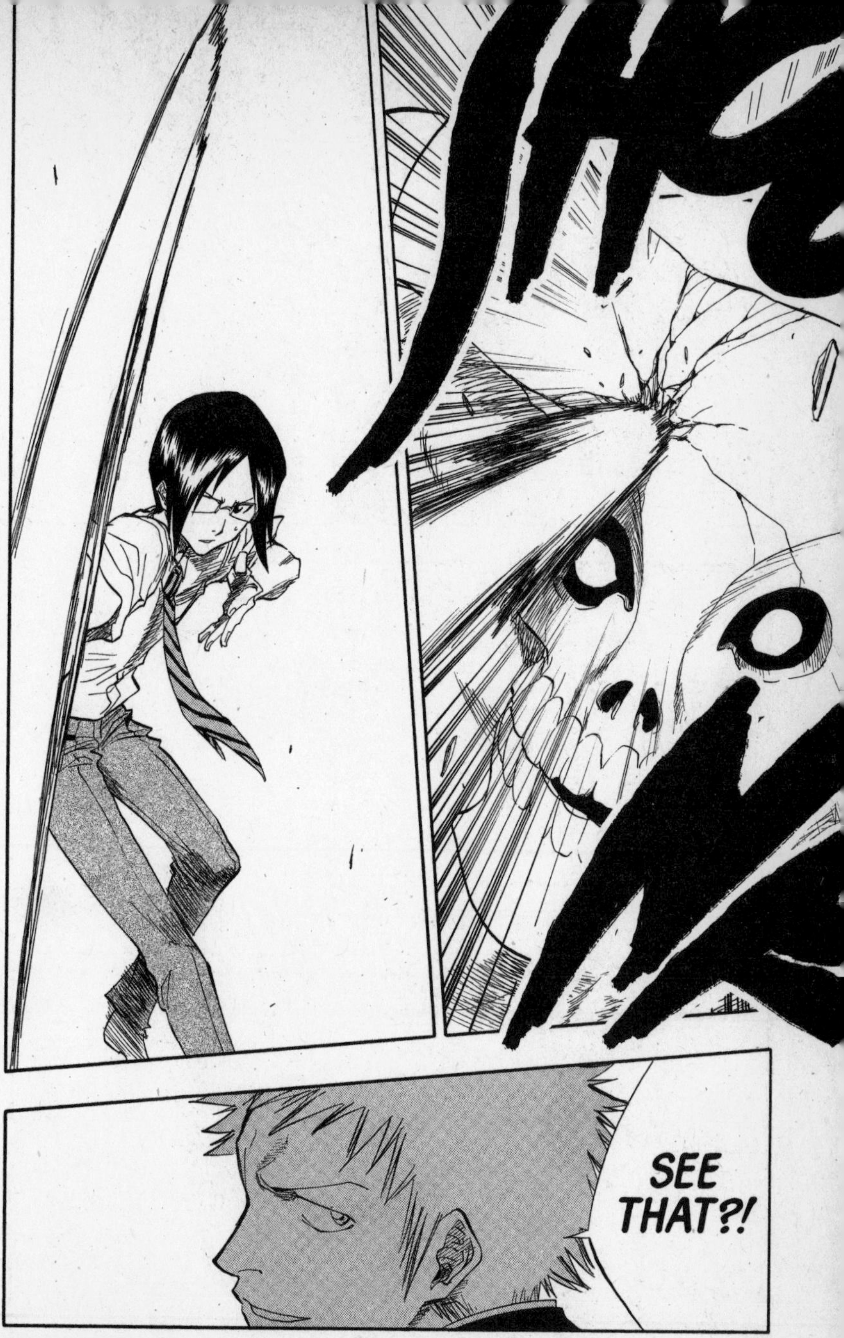
SEE THAT?!

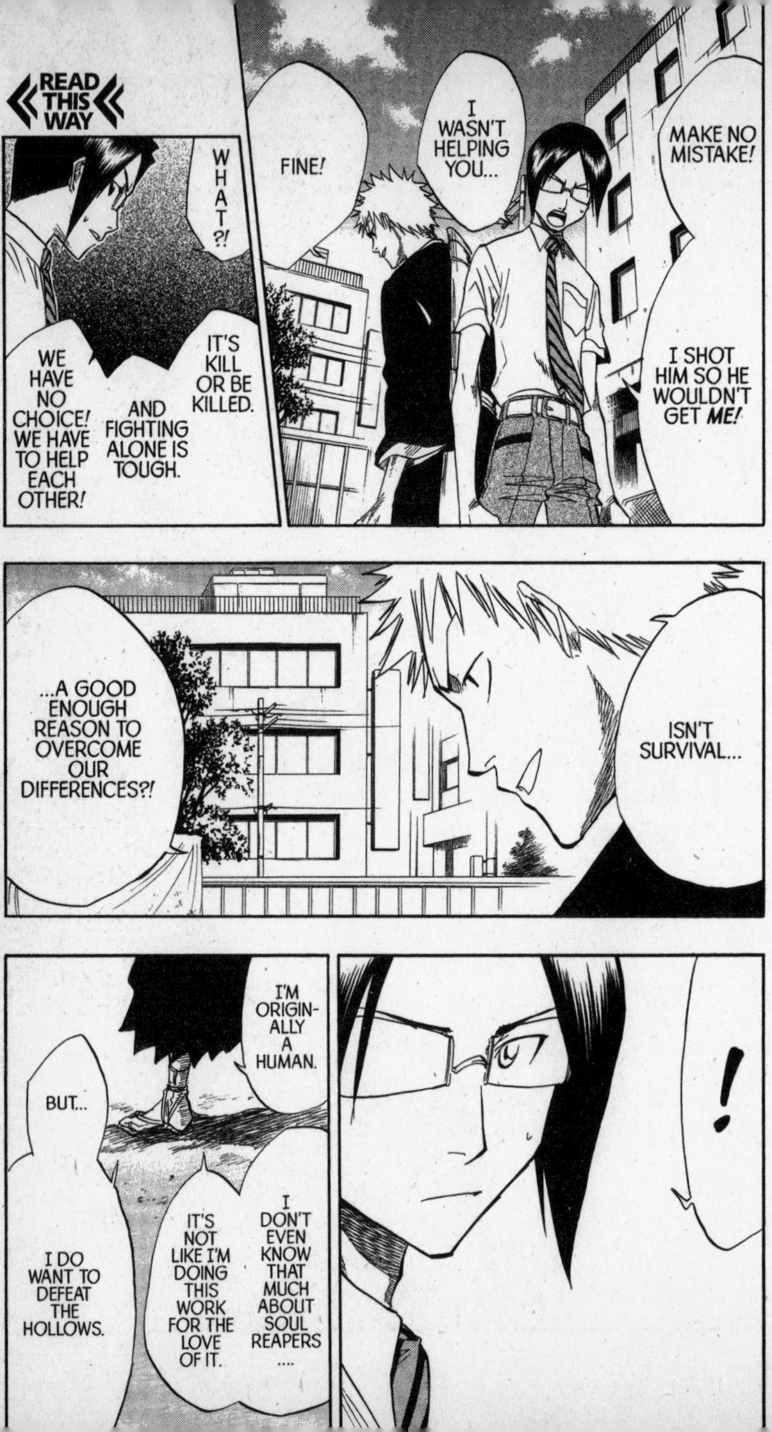
READ THIS WAY
MAKE NO MISTAKE!
I SHOT HIM SO HE WOULDN'T GET ME!
I WASN'T HELPING YOU...
FINE!
WHAT?!
IT'S KILL OR BE KILLED.
AND FIGHTING ALONE IS TOUGH.
WE HAVE NO CHOICE! WE HAVE TO HELP EACH OTHER!
ISN'T SURVIVAL...
...A GOOD ENOUGH REASON TO OVERCOME OUR DIFFERENCES?!
!
I'M ORIGINALLY A HUMAN.
I DON'T EVEN KNOW THAT MUCH ABOUT SOUL REAPERS....
IT'S NOT LIKE I'M DOING THIS WORK FOR THE LOVE OF IT.
BUT...
I DO WANT TO DEFEAT THE HOLLOWS.

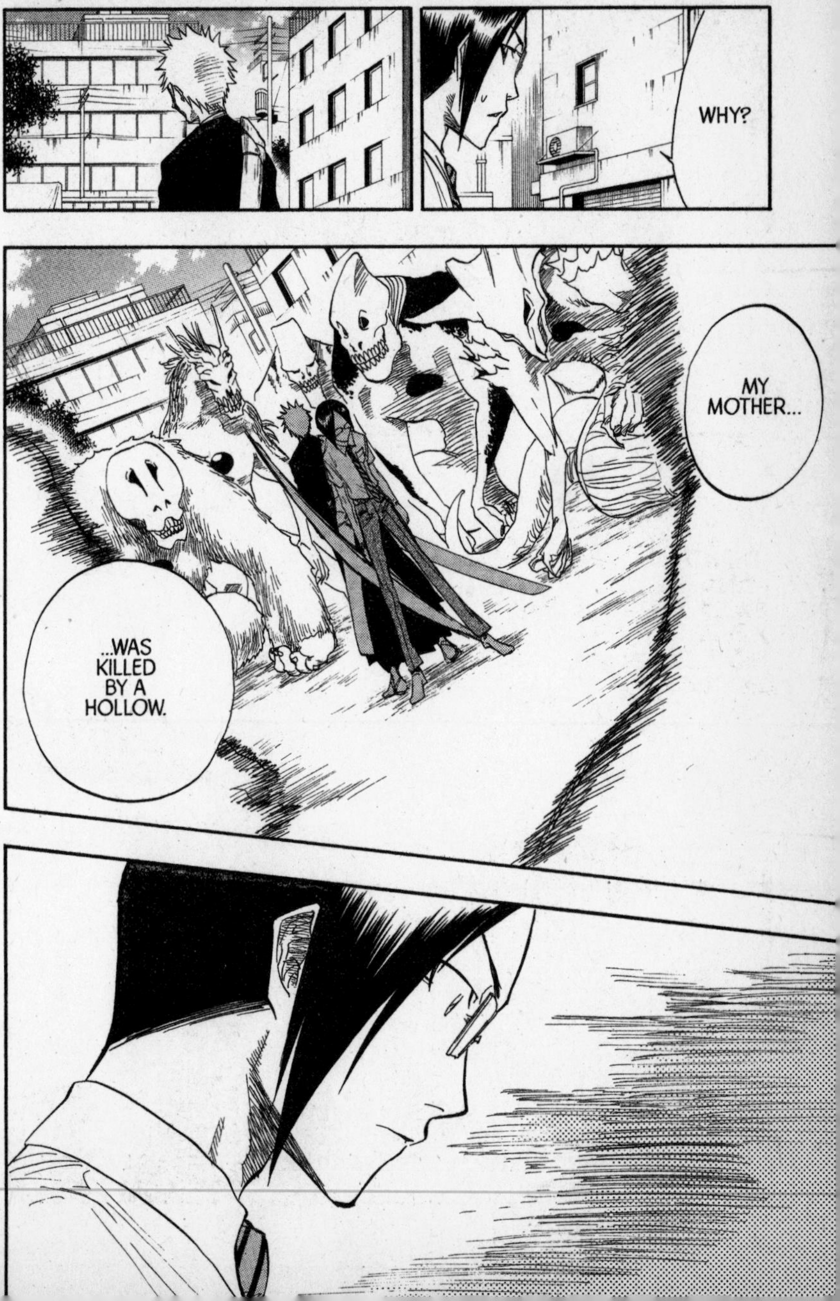
WHY?
MY MOTHER...
...WAS KILLED BY A HOLLOW.

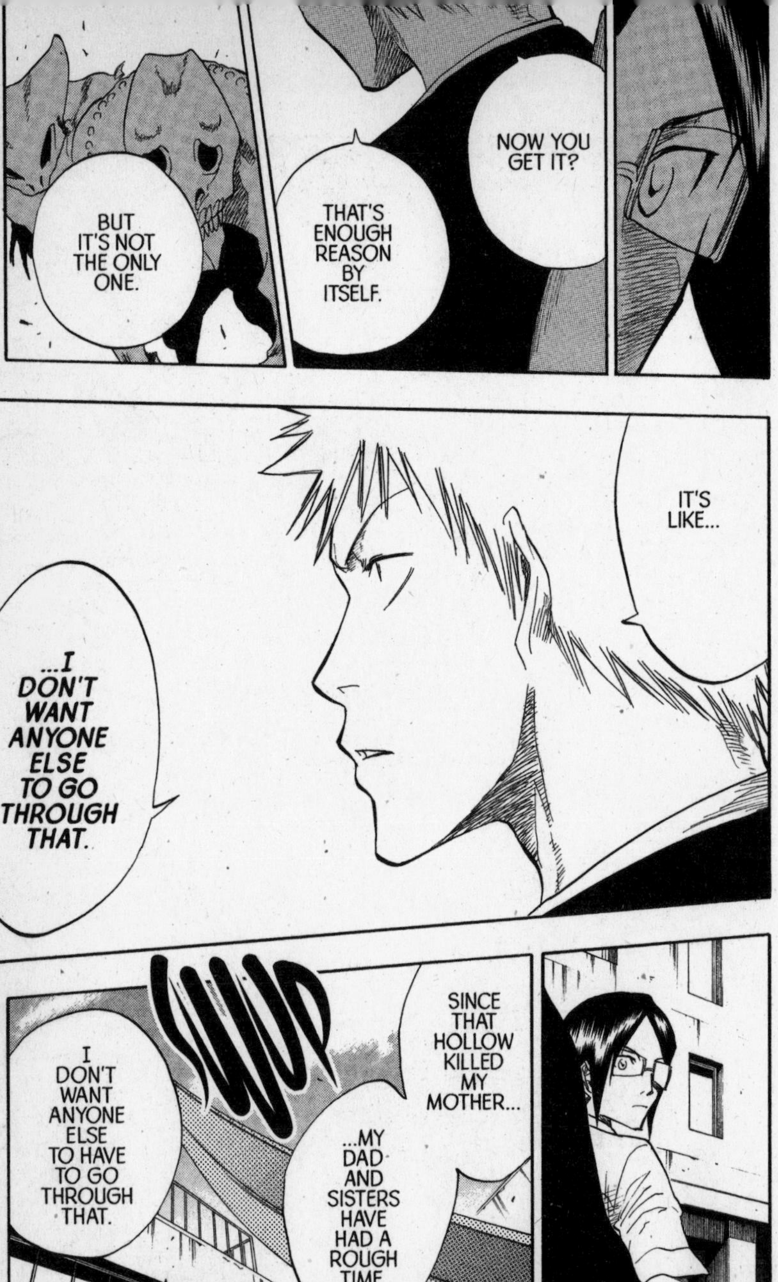
NOW YOU GET IT?
THAT'S ENOUGH REASON BY ITSELF.
BUT IT'S NOT THE ONLY ONE.
IT'S LIKE...
...I DON'T WANT ANYONE ELSE TO GO THROUGH THAT.
SINCE THAT HOLLOW KILLED MY MOTHER...
...MY DAD AND SISTERS HAVE HAD A ROUGH TIME.
I DON'T WANT ANYONE ELSE TO HAVE TO GO THROUGH THAT.

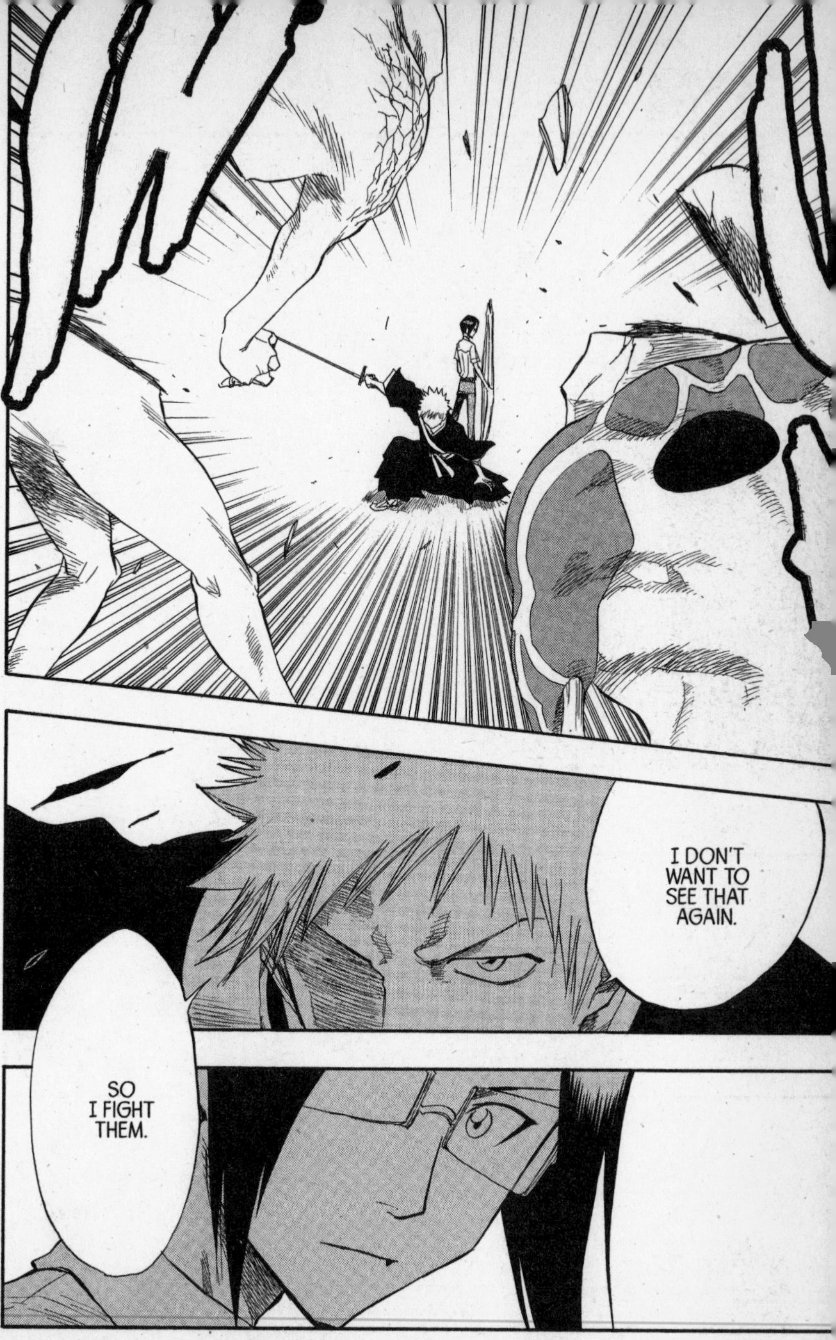
I DON'T WANT TO SEE THAT AGAIN.
SO I FIGHT THEM.

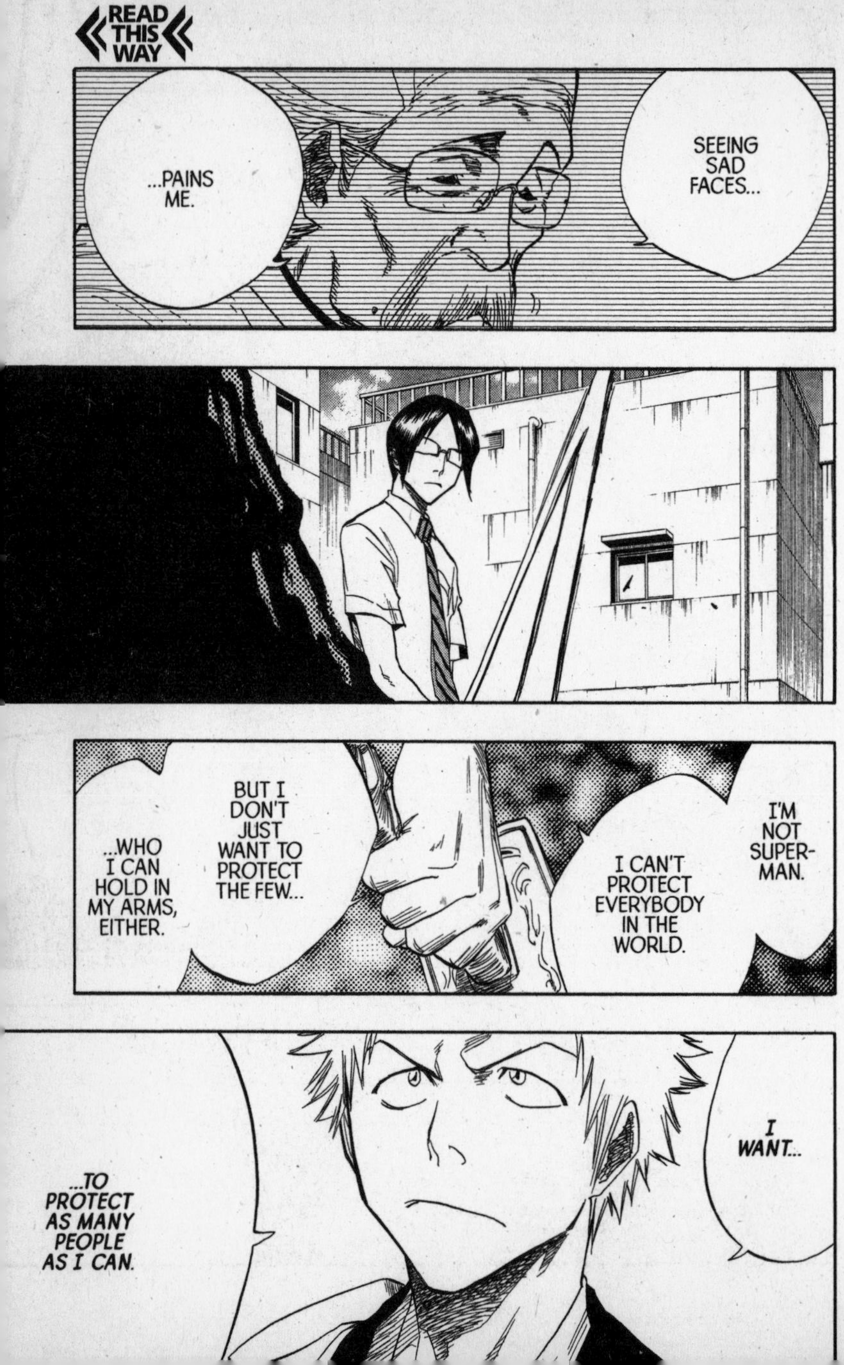
READ THIS WAY
SEEING SAD FACES...
...PAINS ME.
I'M NOT SUPER-MAN.
I CAN'T PROTECT EVERYBODY IN THE WORLD.
BUT I DON'T JUST WANT TO PROTECT THE FEW...
...WHO I CAN HOLD IN MY ARMS, EITHER.
I WANT...
...TO PROTECT AS MANY PEOPLE AS I CAN.

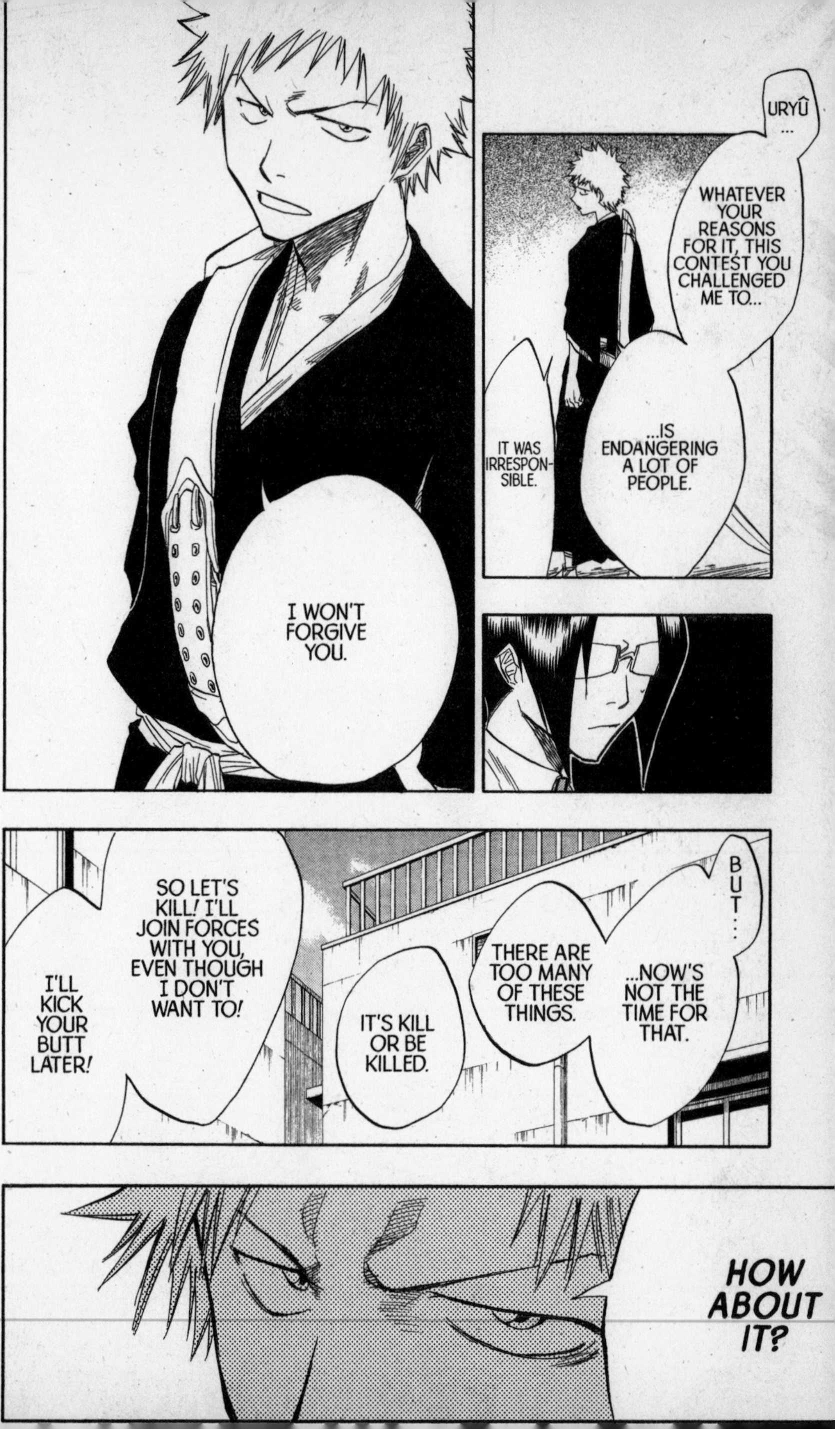
URYÛ ...
WHATEVER YOUR REASONS FOR IT, THIS CONTEST YOU CHALLENGED ME TO...
...IS ENDANGERING A LOT OF PEOPLE.
IT WAS IRRESPONSIBLE.
I WON'T FORGIVE YOU.
BUT...
...NOW'S NOT THE TIME FOR THAT.
THERE ARE TOO MANY OF THESE THINGS.
IT'S KILL OR BE KILLED.
SO LET'S KILL! I'LL JOIN FORCES WITH YOU, EVEN THOUGH I DON'T WANT TO!
I'LL KICK YOUR BUTT LATER!
HOW ABOUT IT?

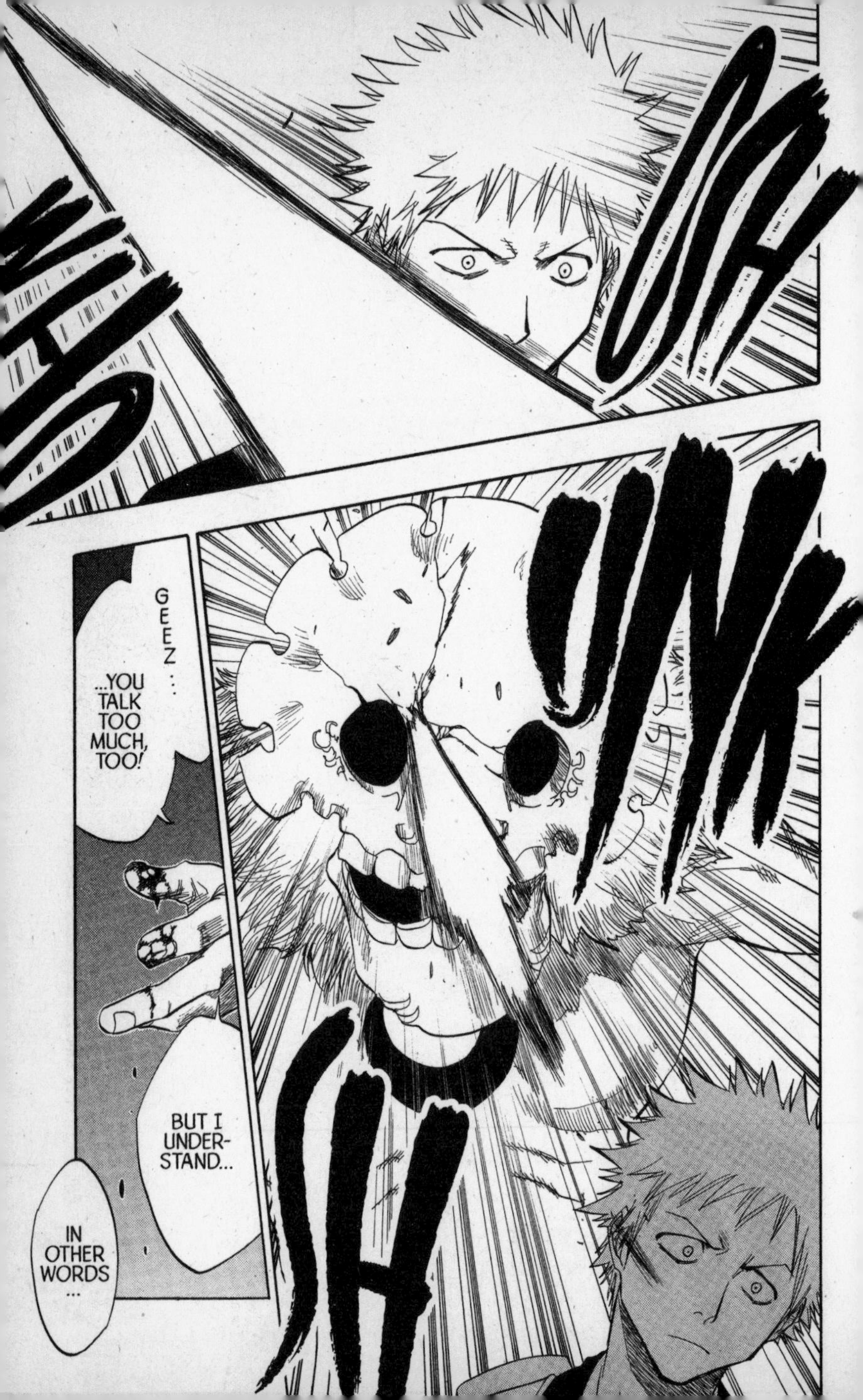
GEEZ...
...YOU TALK TOO MUCH, TOO!
BUT I UNDERSTAND...
IN OTHER WORDS...

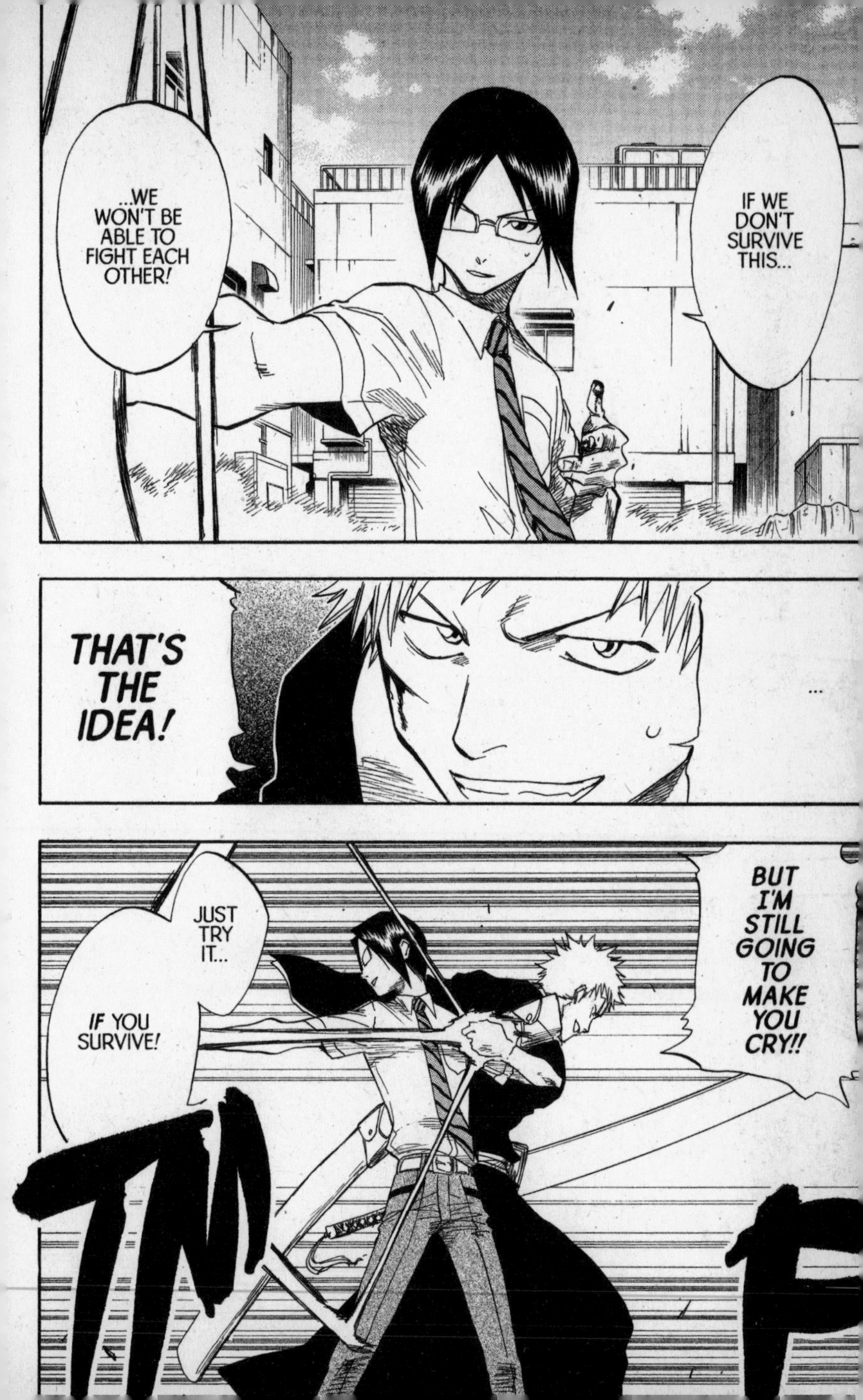
IF WE DON'T SURVIVE THIS...
...WE WON'T BE ABLE TO FIGHT EACH OTHER!
...
THAT'S THE IDEA!
BUT I'M STILL GOING TO MAKE YOU CRY!!
JUST TRY IT...
IF YOU SURVIVE!

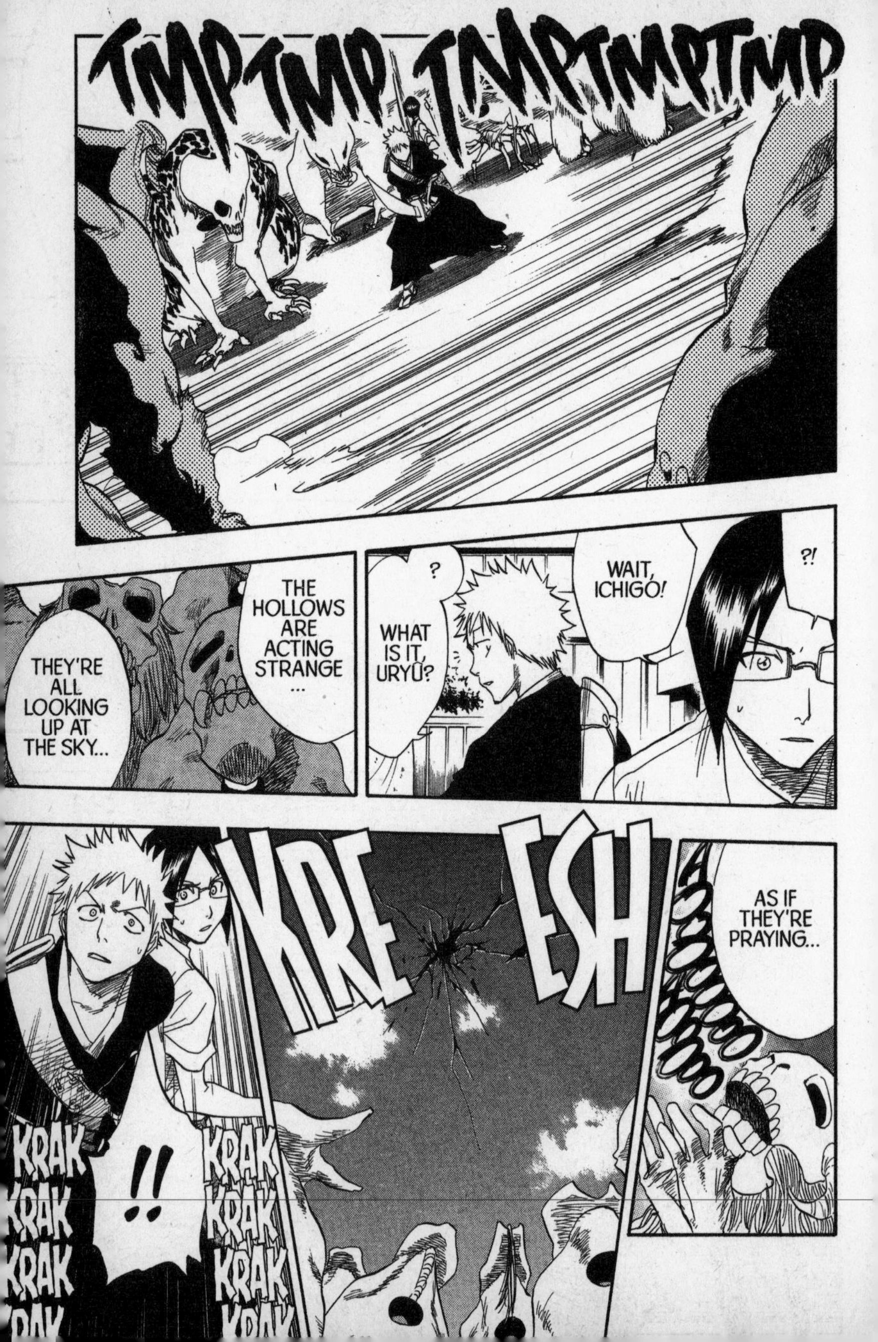

TMPTMP TMPTMPTMP
?!
WAIT, ICHIGO!
?
WHAT IS IT, URYŪ?
THE HOLLOWS ARE ACTING STRANGE...
THEY'RE ALL LOOKING UP AT THE SKY...
AS IF THEY'RE PRAYING...
KREESH
KRAK KRAK KRAK
!!
KRAK KRAK KRAK KRAK

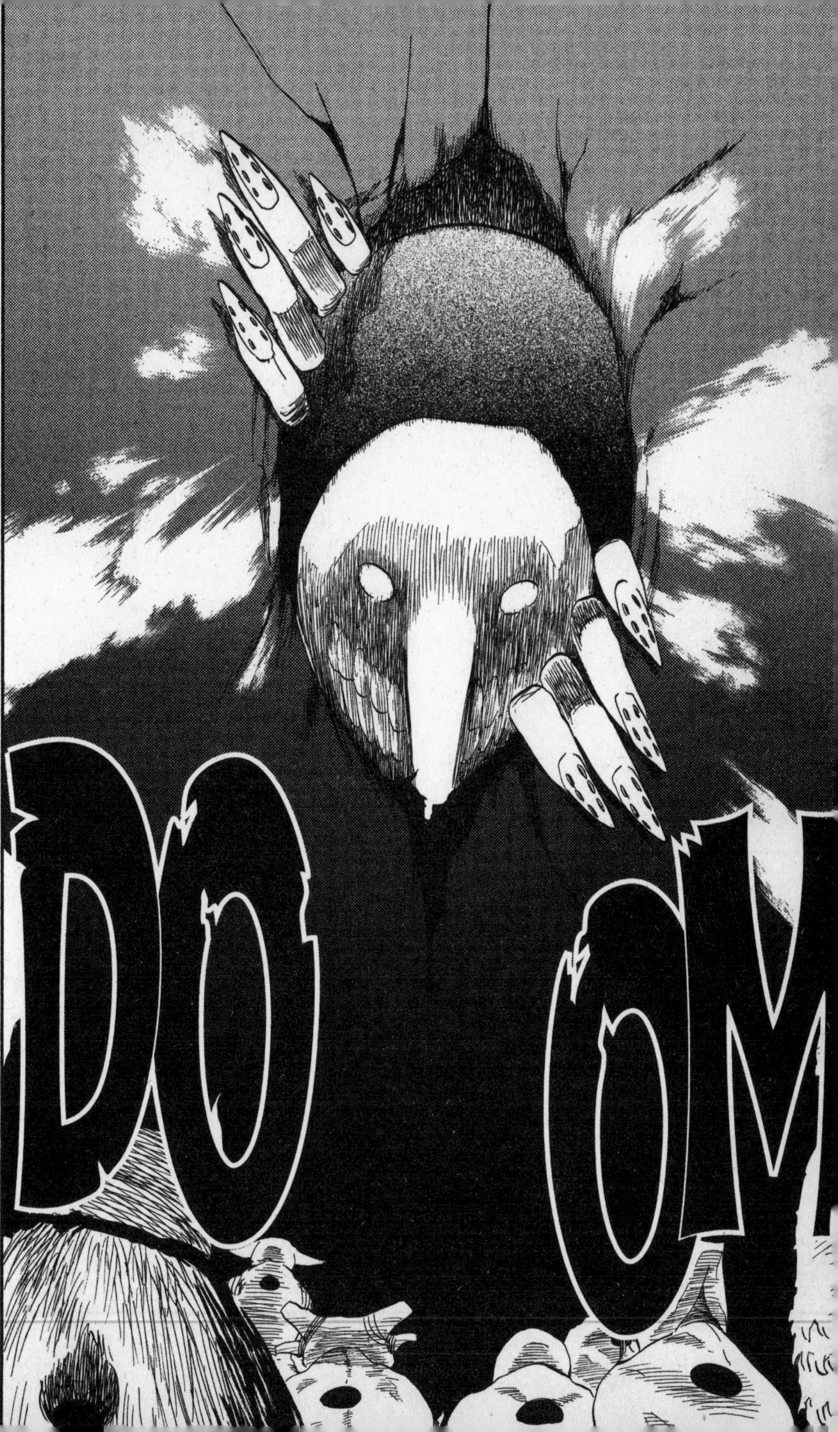
DO OM

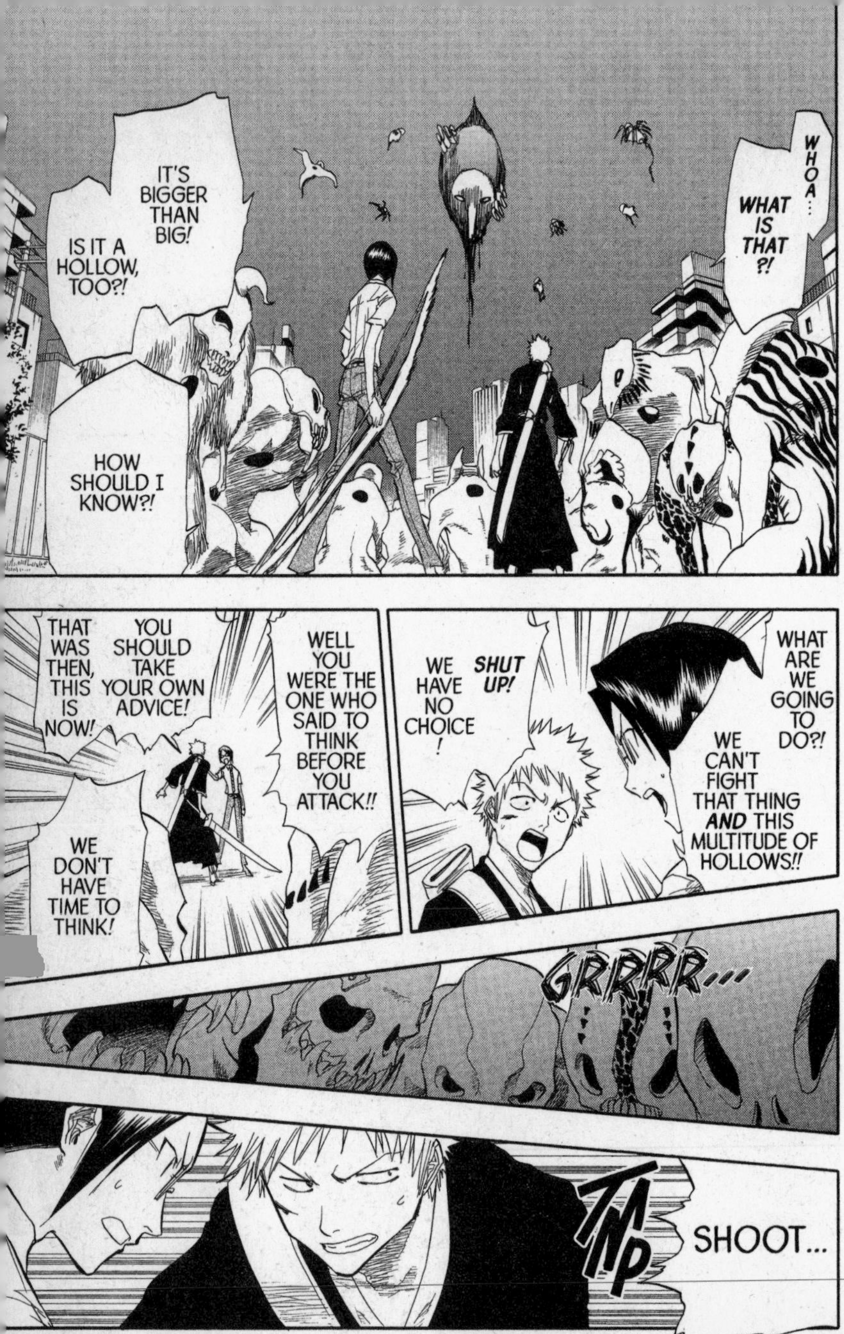
WHOA... WHAT IS THAT?!
IT'S BIGGER THAN BIG!
IS IT A HOLLOW, TOO?!
HOW SHOULD I KNOW?!
WHAT ARE WE GOING TO DO?!
WE CAN'T FIGHT THAT THING AND THIS MULTITUDE OF HOLLOWS!!
SHUT UP!
WE HAVE NO CHOICE!
WELL YOU WERE THE ONE WHO SAID TO THINK BEFORE YOU ATTACK!!
YOU SHOULD TAKE YOUR OWN ADVICE!
THAT WAS THEN, THIS IS NOW!
WE DON'T HAVE TIME TO THINK!
GRRRR...
TMP
SHOOT...

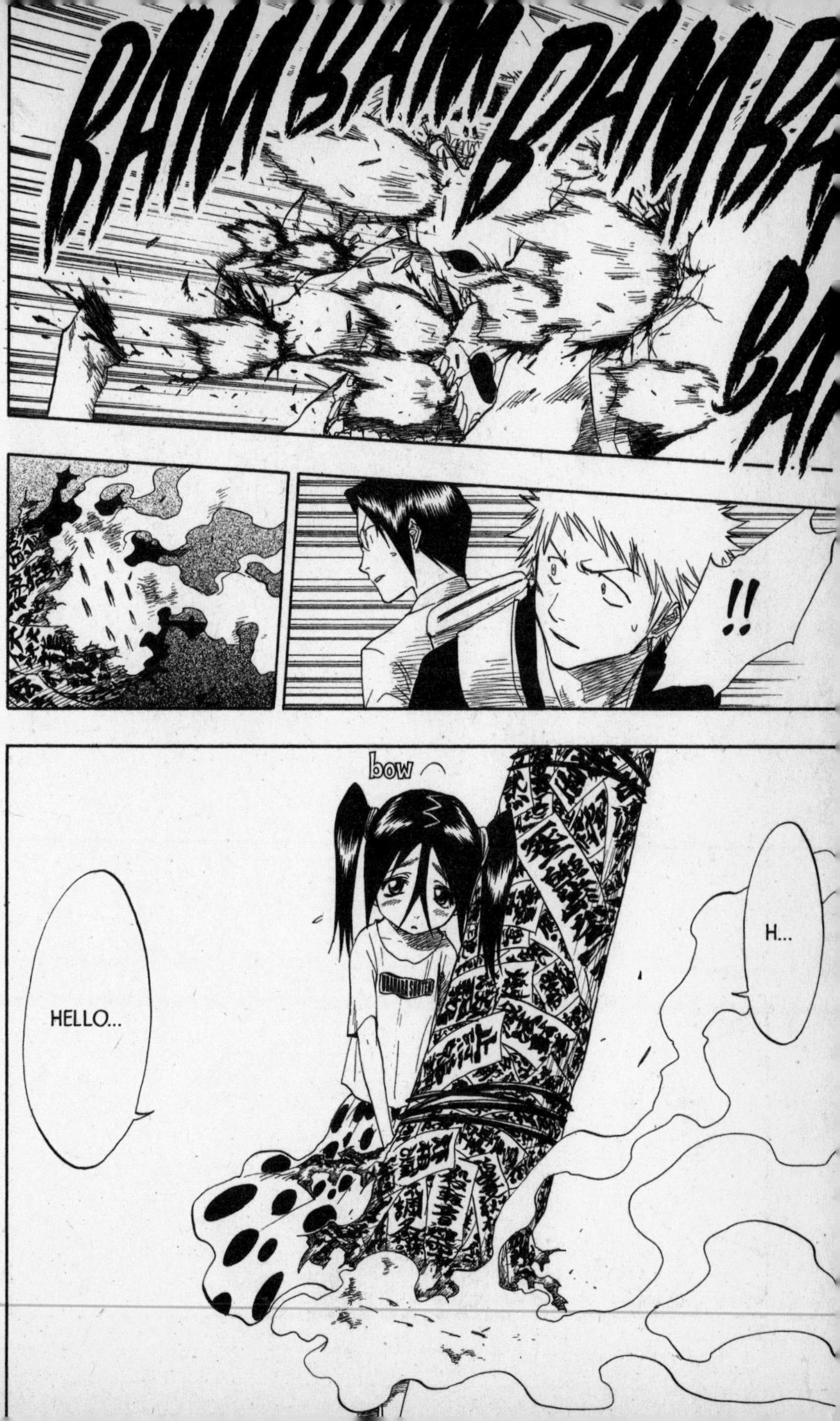
BAM BAM BAM BA
BA BA
!!
bow
H...
URAHARA SHOTEN
HELLO...

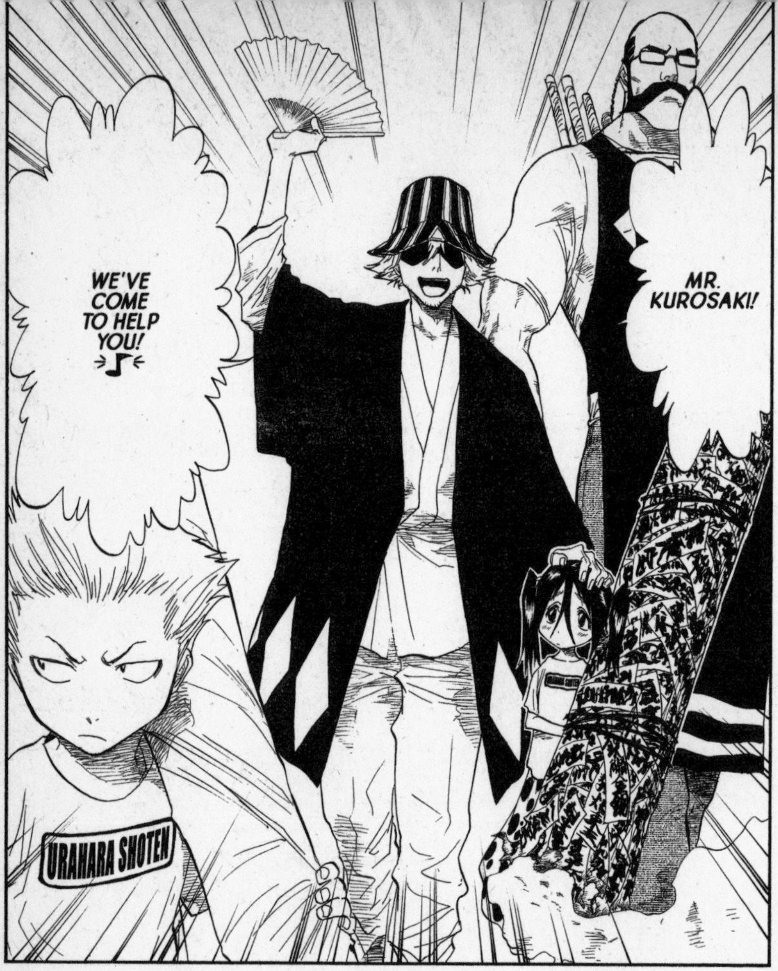
MR. KUROSAKI!
WE'VE COME TO HELP YOU! ♪
URAHARA SHOTEN

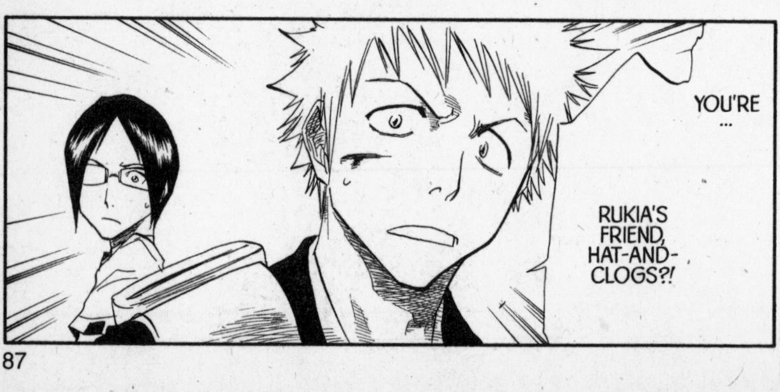
YOU'RE ...
RUKIA'S FRIEND, HAT-AND-CLOGS?!

Oh...

I can
breathe a
little
now...

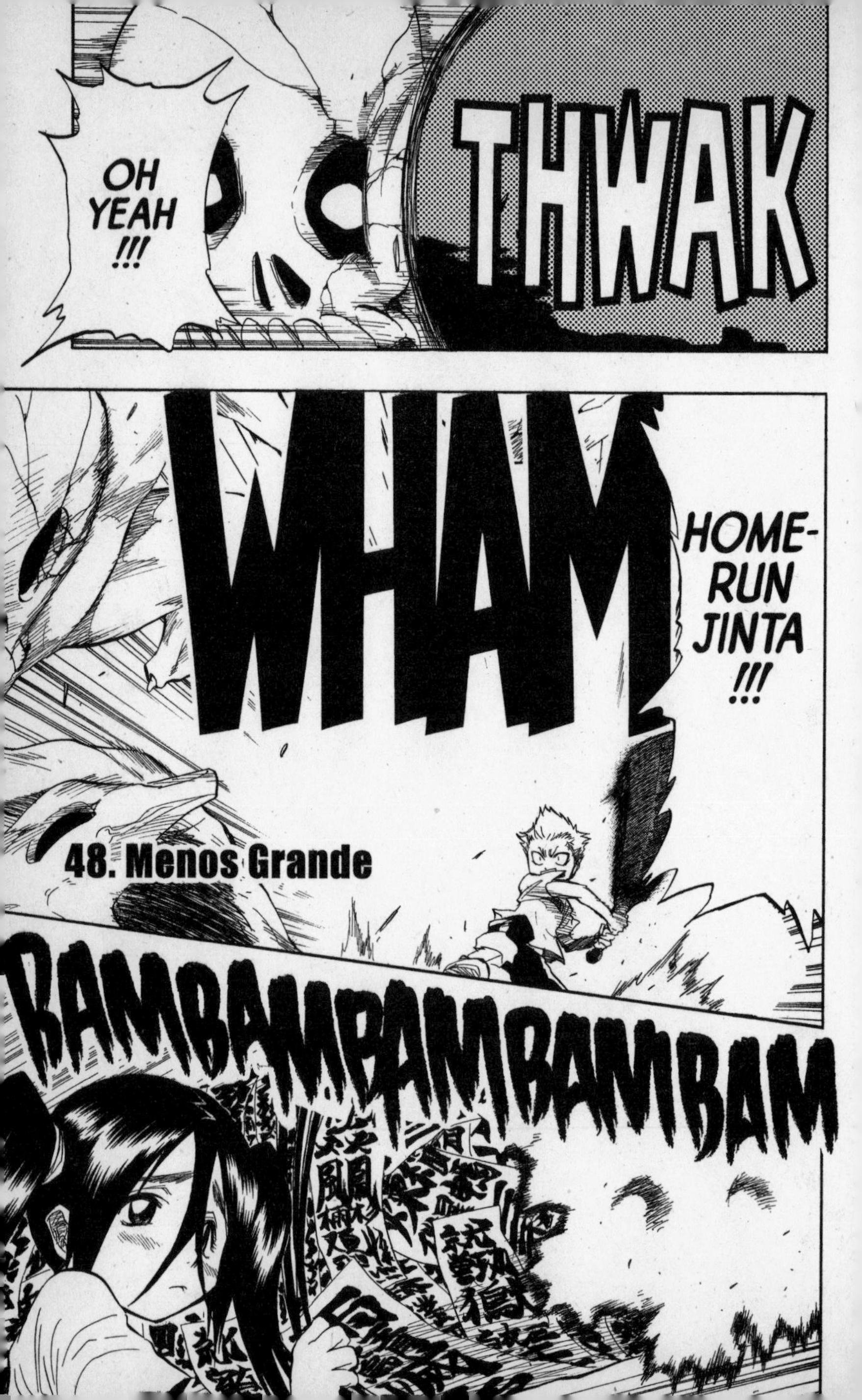
THWAK
OH YEAH !!!
HOME-RUN JINTA !!!
WHAM
48. Menos Grande
BAMBAMBAMBAMBAM

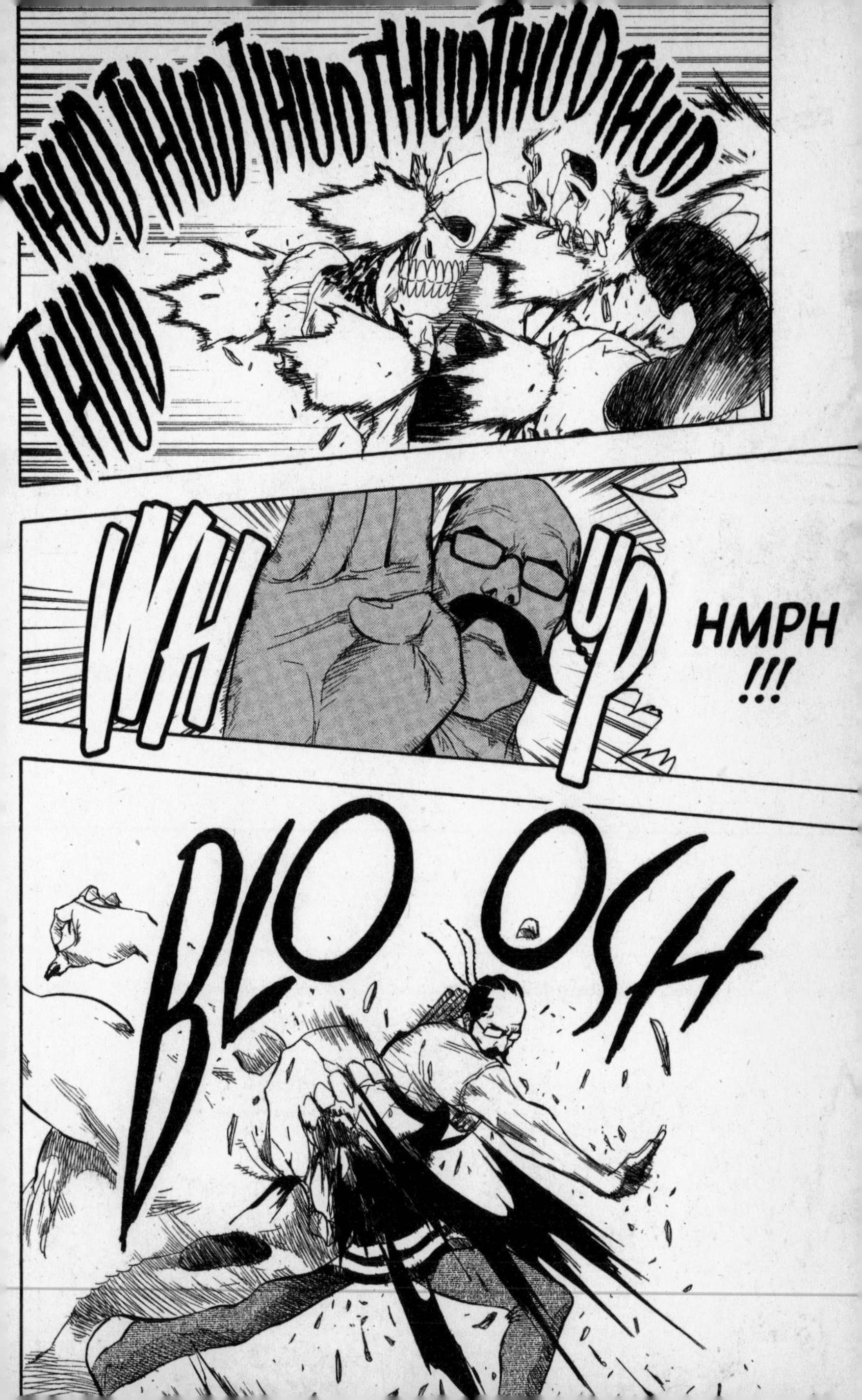
THUD THUD THUD THUD THUD THUD THUD
WHUP
WH
HMPH
!!!
BLOOSH

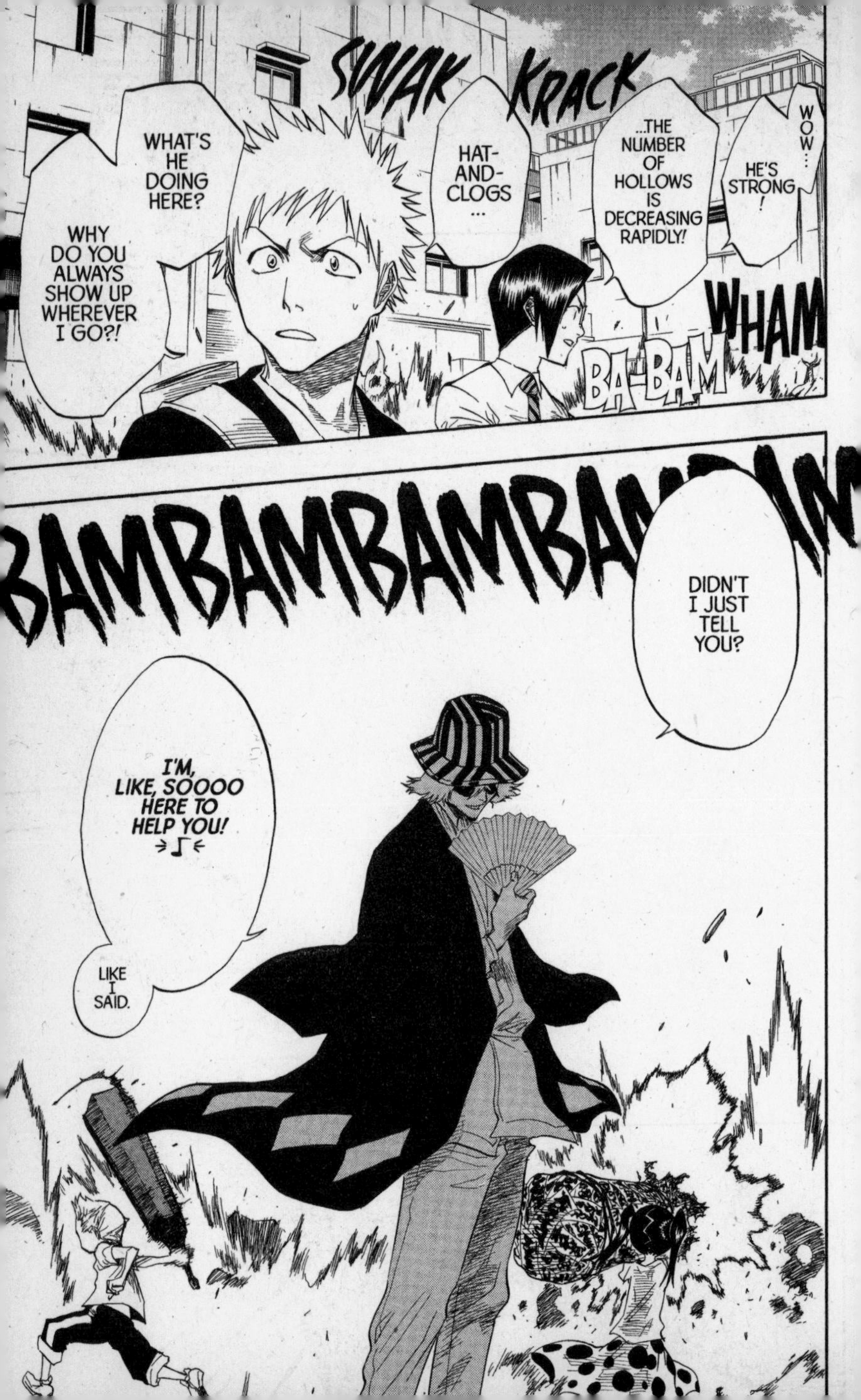
KRACK
SWAK
WOW...
HE'S STRONG!
...THE NUMBER OF HOLLOWS IS DECREASING RAPIDLY!
WHAM
BA-BAM
HAT-AND-CLOGS...
WHAT'S HE DOING HERE?
WHY DO YOU ALWAYS SHOW UP WHEREVER I GO?!
BAMBAMBAMBAM
DIDN'T I JUST TELL YOU?
I'M, LIKE, SOOOO HERE TO HELP YOU! ♪
LIKE I SAID.

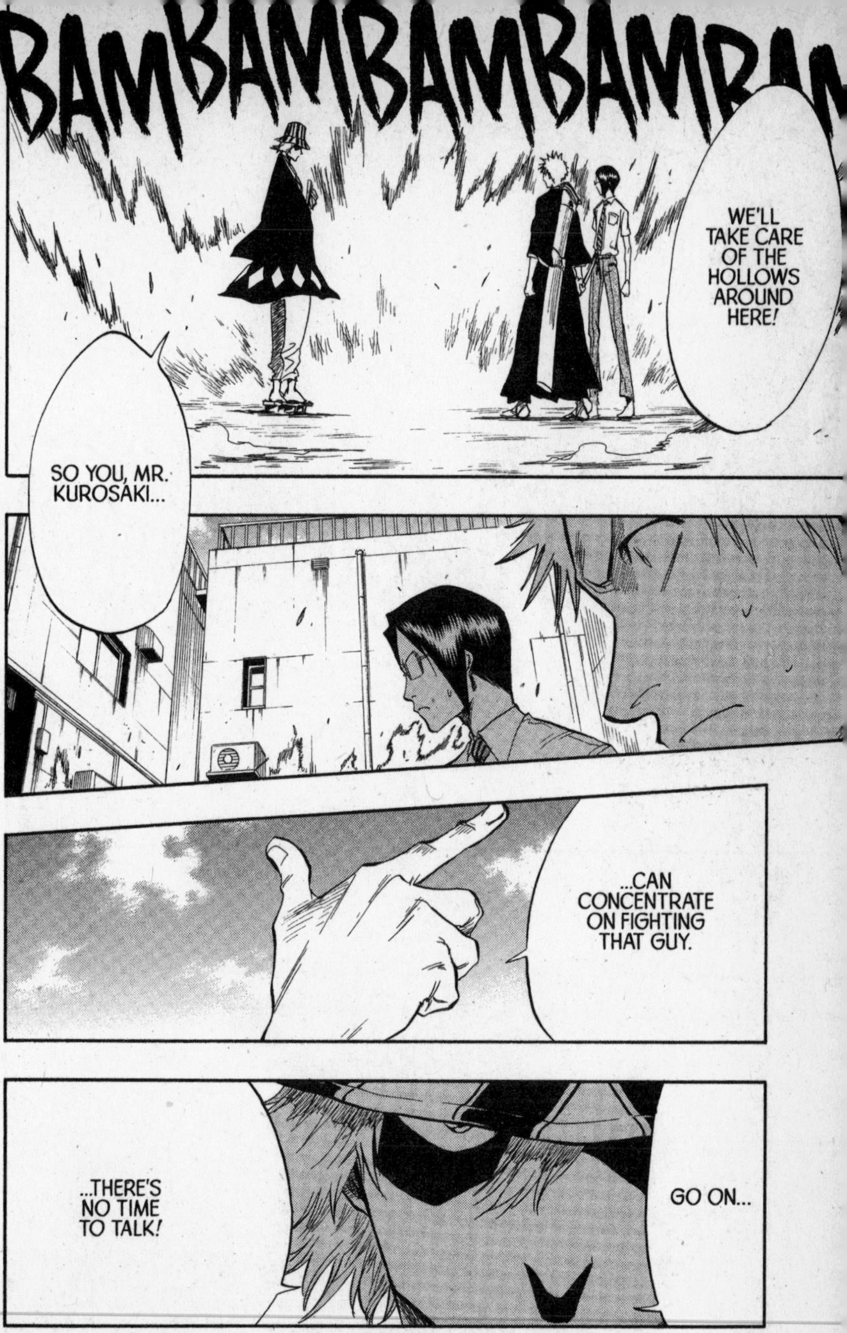
BAMBAMBAMBAM
WE'LL TAKE CARE OF THE HOLLOWS AROUND HERE!
SO YOU, MR. KUROSAKI...
...CAN CONCENTRATE ON FIGHTING THAT GUY.
GO ON...
...THERE'S NO TIME TO TALK!

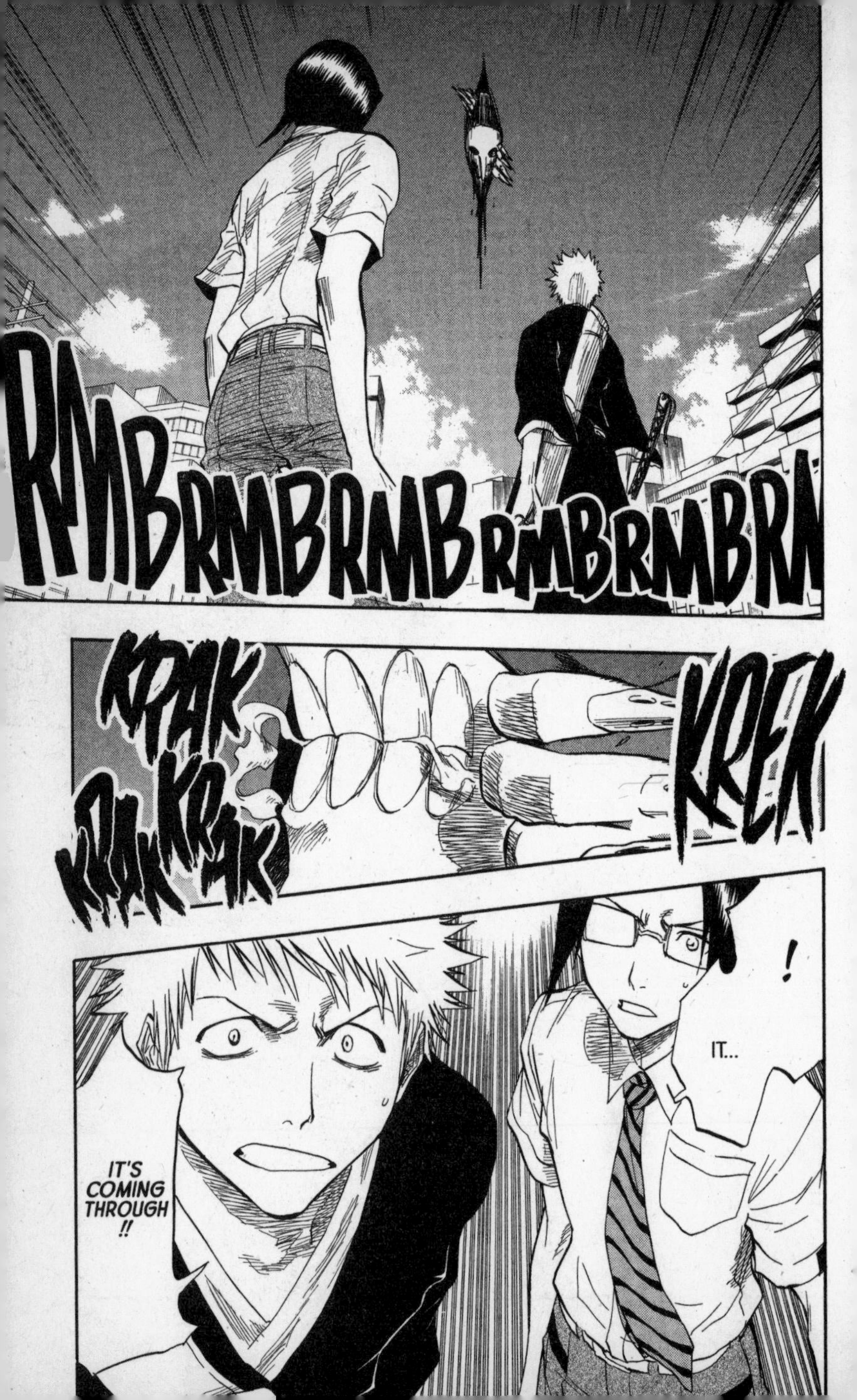
RMBRMBRMBRMBRMBRMBRM
KREK
KRAK
KRAK KRAK
!
IT...
IT'S COMING THROUGH!!

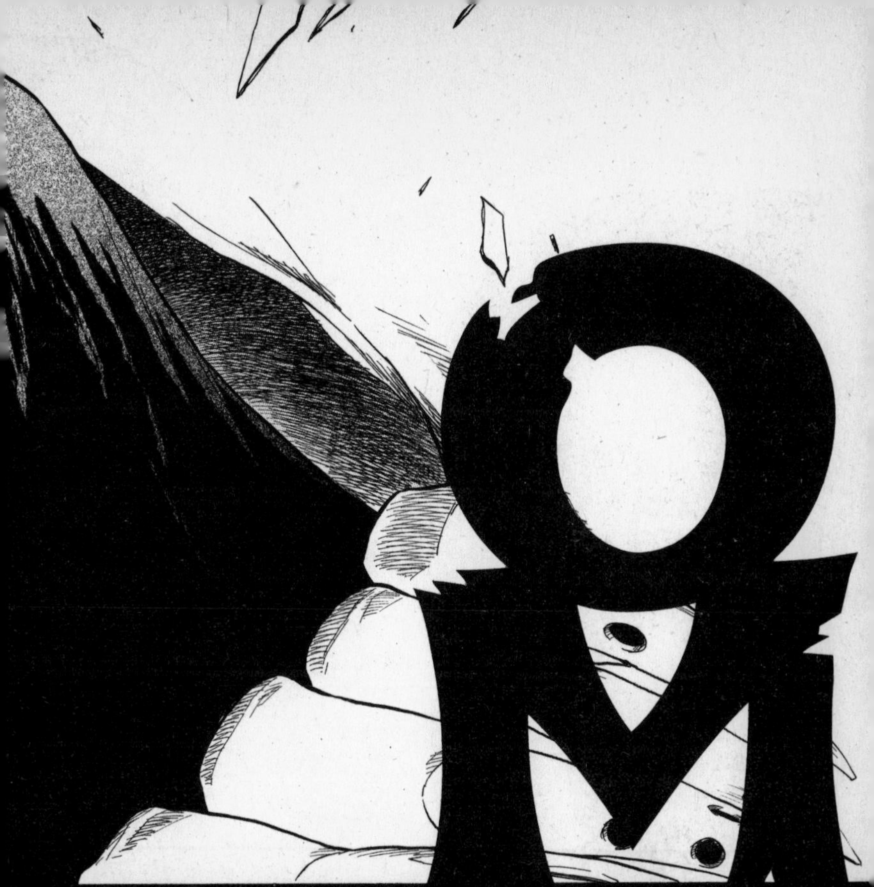

48. Menos Grande

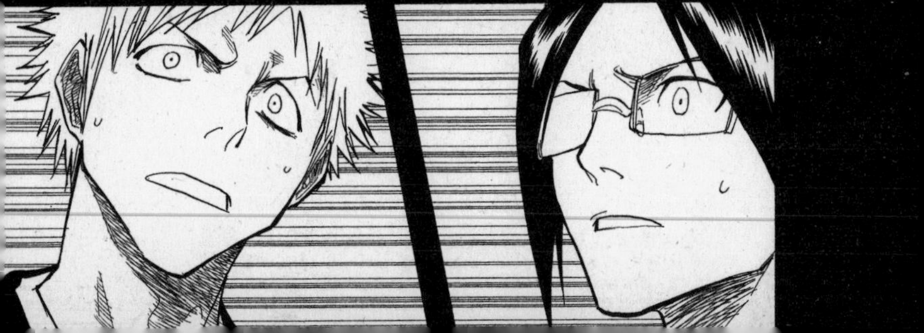

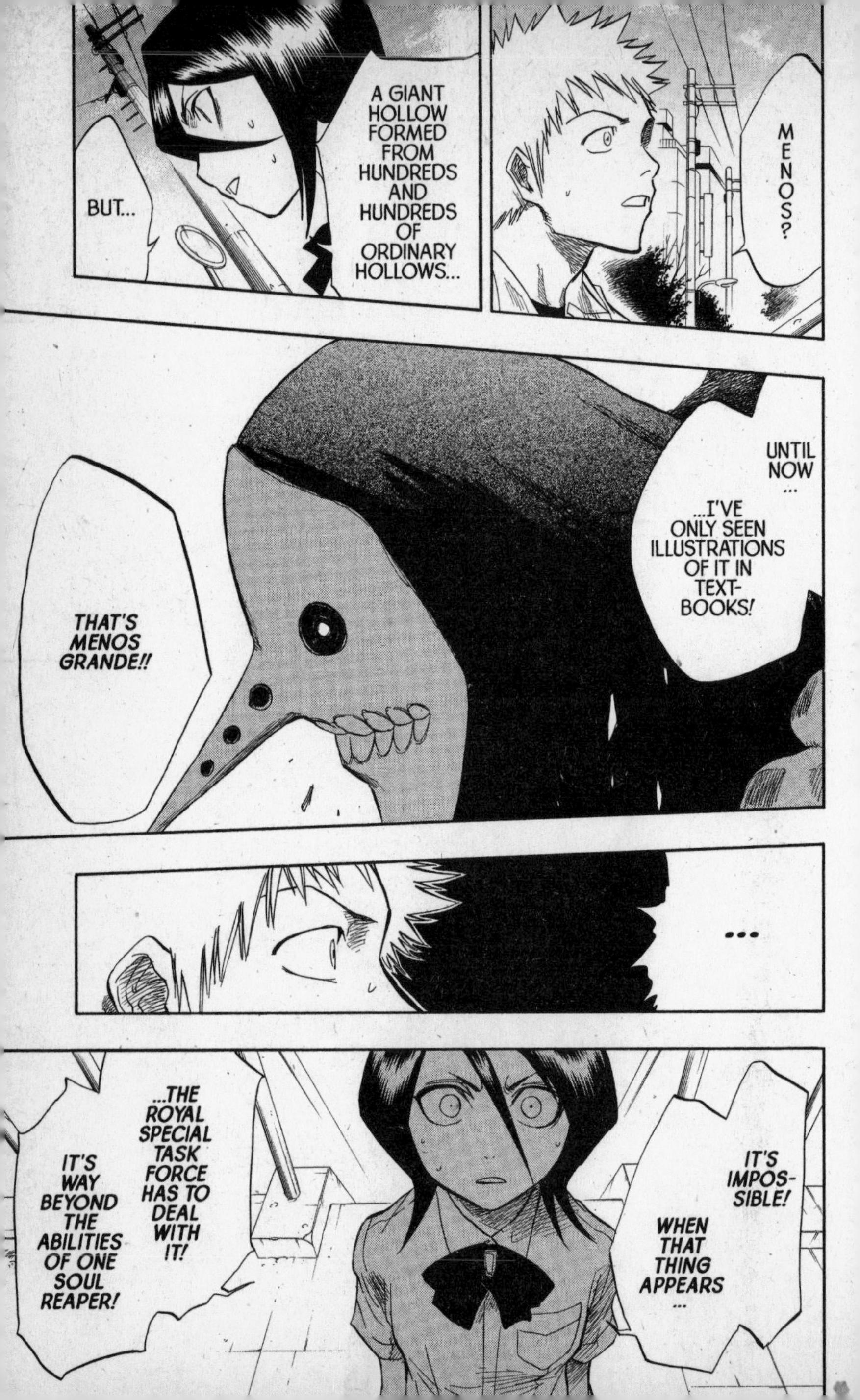
MENOS?
A GIANT HOLLOW FORMED FROM HUNDREDS AND HUNDREDS OF ORDINARY HOLLOWS...
BUT...
UNTIL NOW...
...I'VE ONLY SEEN ILLUSTRATIONS OF IT IN TEXT-BOOKS!
THAT'S MENOS GRANDE!!
...
IT'S IMPOS-SIBLE!
WHEN THAT THING APPEARS...
...THE ROYAL SPECIAL TASK FORCE HAS TO DEAL WITH IT!
IT'S WAY BEYOND THE ABILITIES OF ONE SOUL REAPER!

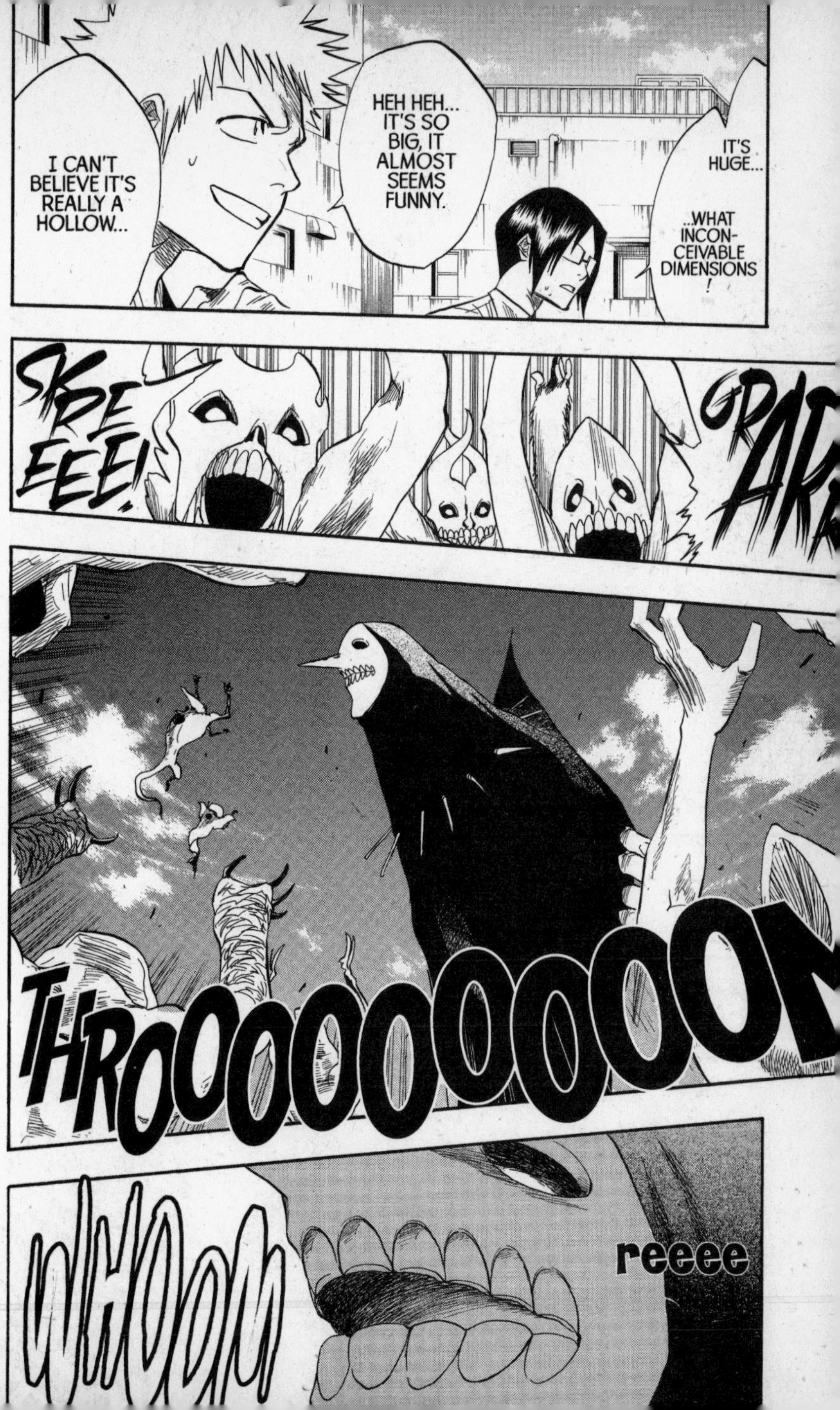
IT'S HUGE...
...WHAT INCONCEIVABLE DIMENSIONS!
HEH HEH... IT'S SO BIG, IT ALMOST SEEMS FUNNY.
I CAN'T BELIEVE IT'S REALLY A HOLLOW...
GRAR
SKREEEE!
THROOOOOOOOO
reeee
whoaa

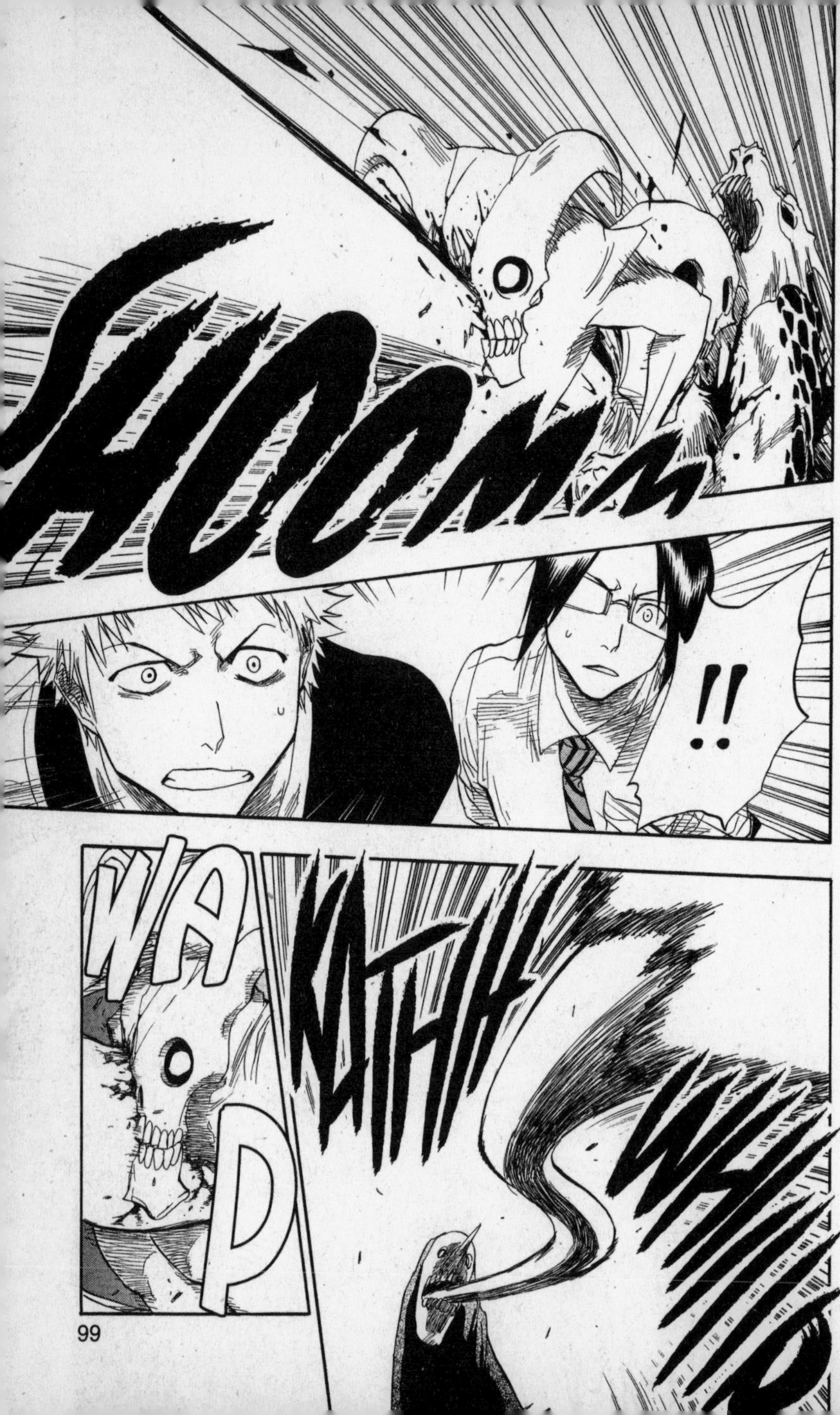
!!

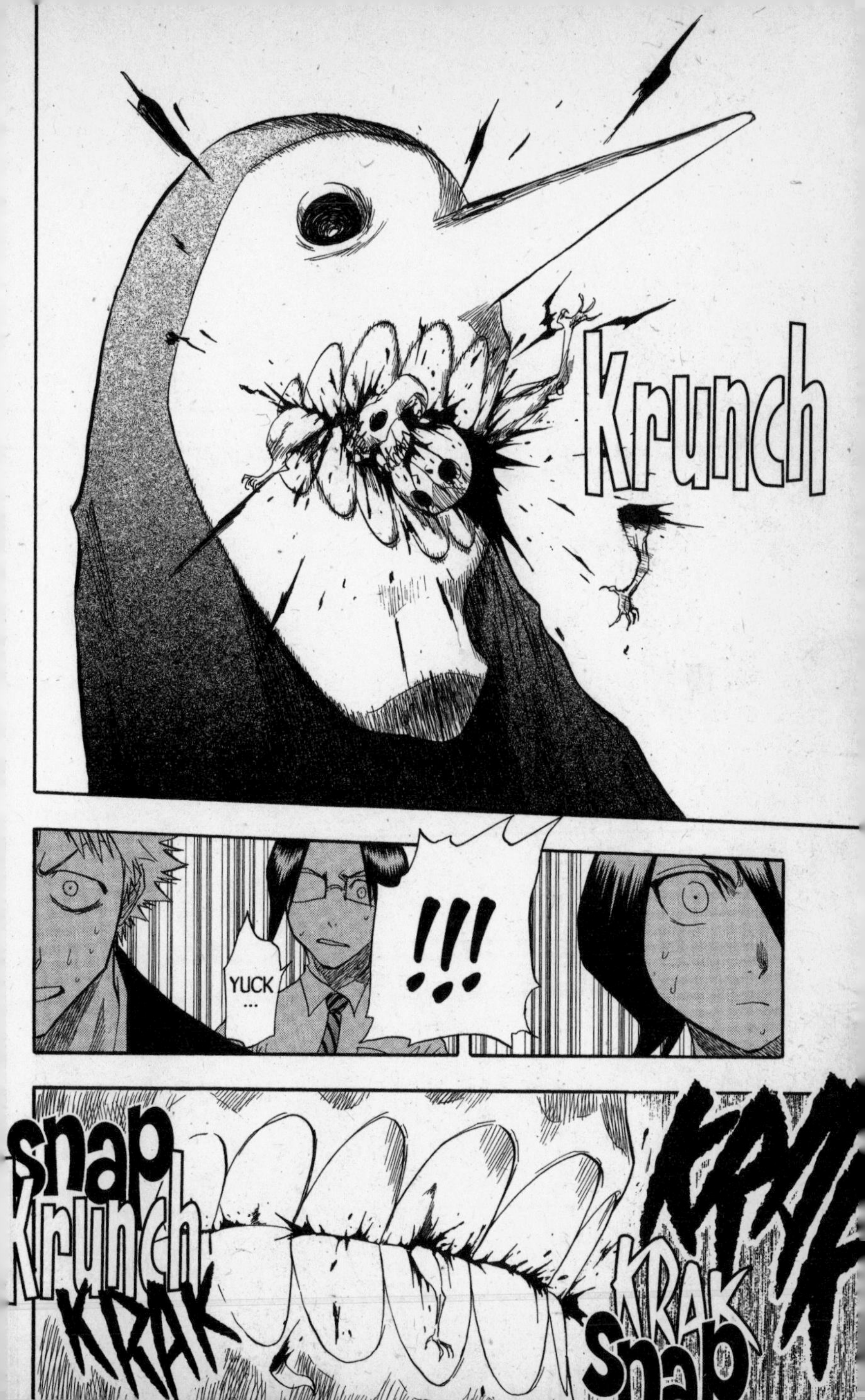
Krunch
!!!
YUCK
...
KRAK
Snap
snap
krunch
KRAK

READ THIS WAY

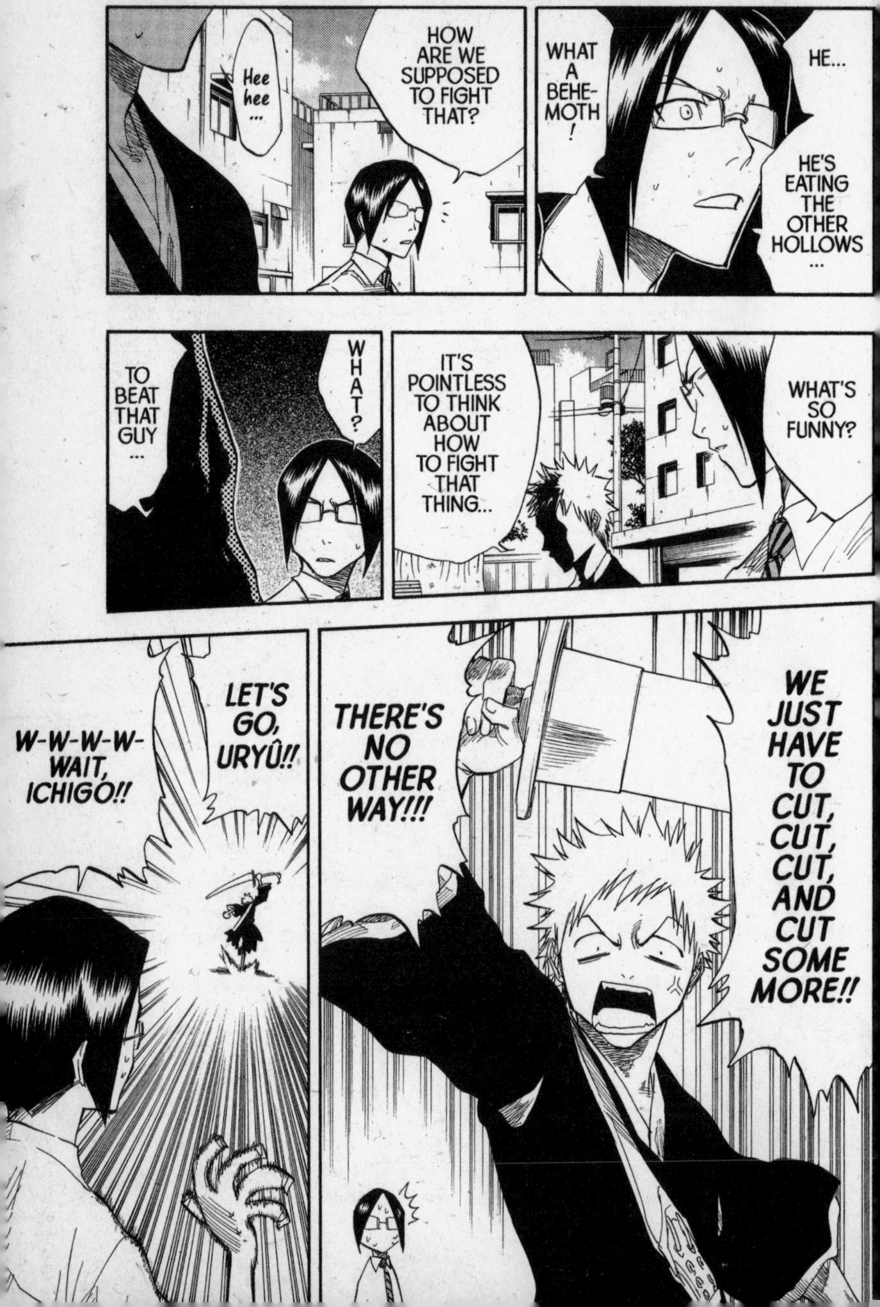
HE...
WHAT A BEHEMOTH!
HE'S EATING THE OTHER HOLLOWS...
HOW ARE WE SUPPOSED TO FIGHT THAT?
Hee hee...
WHAT'S SO FUNNY?
IT'S POINTLESS TO THINK ABOUT HOW TO FIGHT THAT THING...
WHAT?
TO BEAT THAT GUY...
WE JUST HAVE TO CUT, CUT, CUT, AND CUT SOME MORE!!
THERE'S NO OTHER WAY!!!
LET'S GO, URYÛ!!
W-W-W-W-WAIT, ICHIGO!!

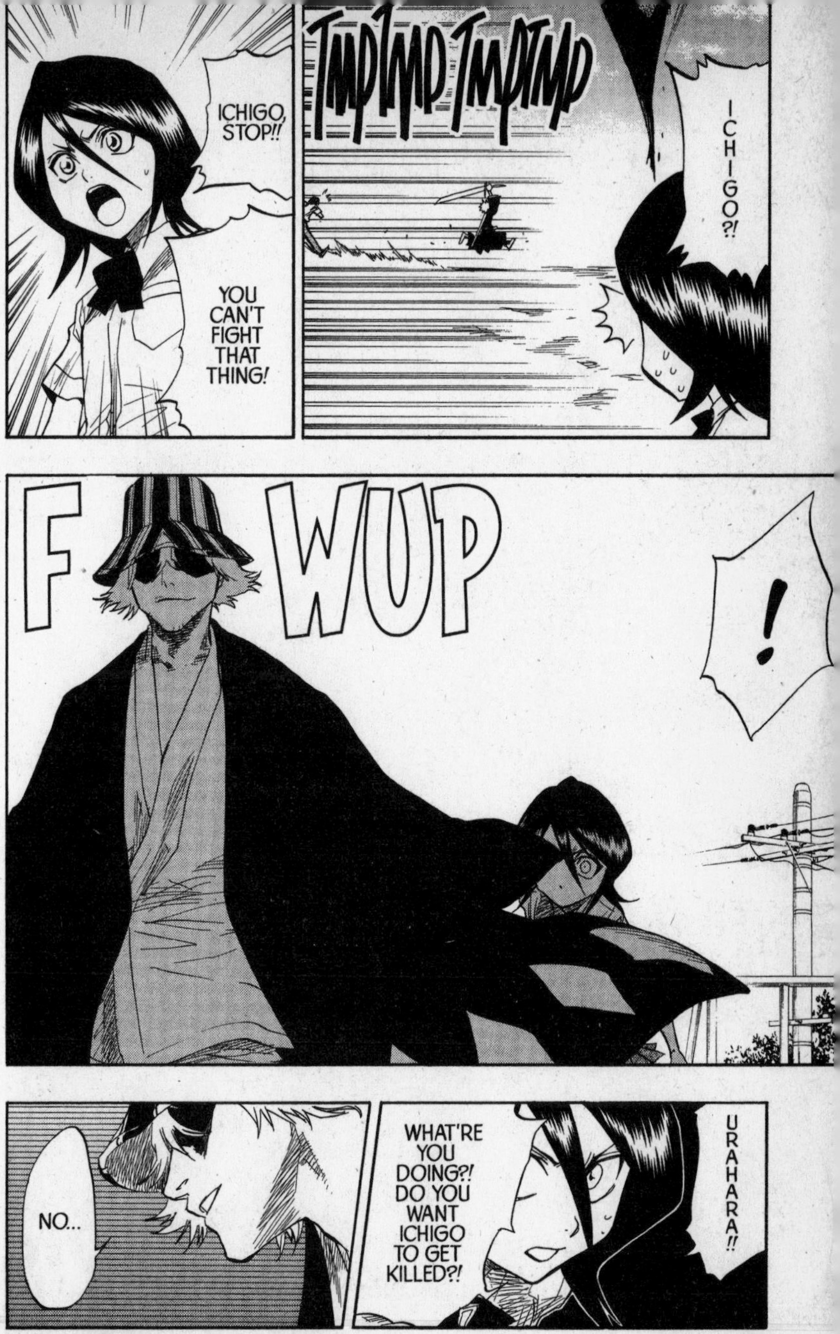
ICHIGO?!
TMPTMP TMPTMP
ICHIGO, STOP!!
YOU CAN'T FIGHT THAT THING!
!
FWUP
URAHARA!!
WHAT'RE YOU DOING?! DO YOU WANT ICHIGO TO GET KILLED?!
NO...

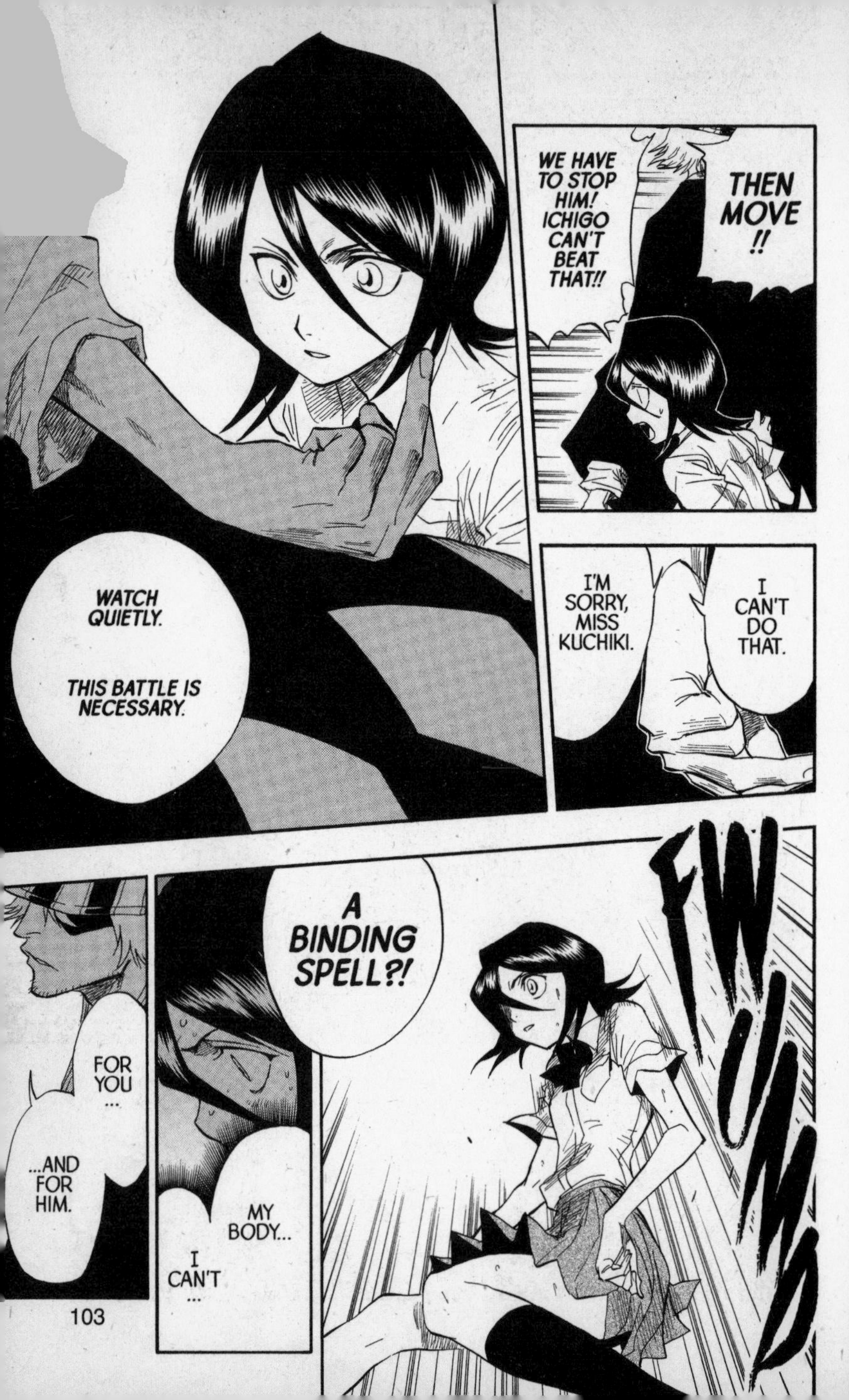
WE HAVE TO STOP HIM! ICHIGO CAN'T BEAT THAT!!
THEN MOVE!!
I'M SORRY, MISS KUCHIKI.
I CAN'T DO THAT.
WATCH QUIETLY.
THIS BATTLE IS NECESSARY.
FWUMS
A BINDING SPELL?!
MY BODY...
I CAN'T...
FOR YOU...
...AND FOR HIM.

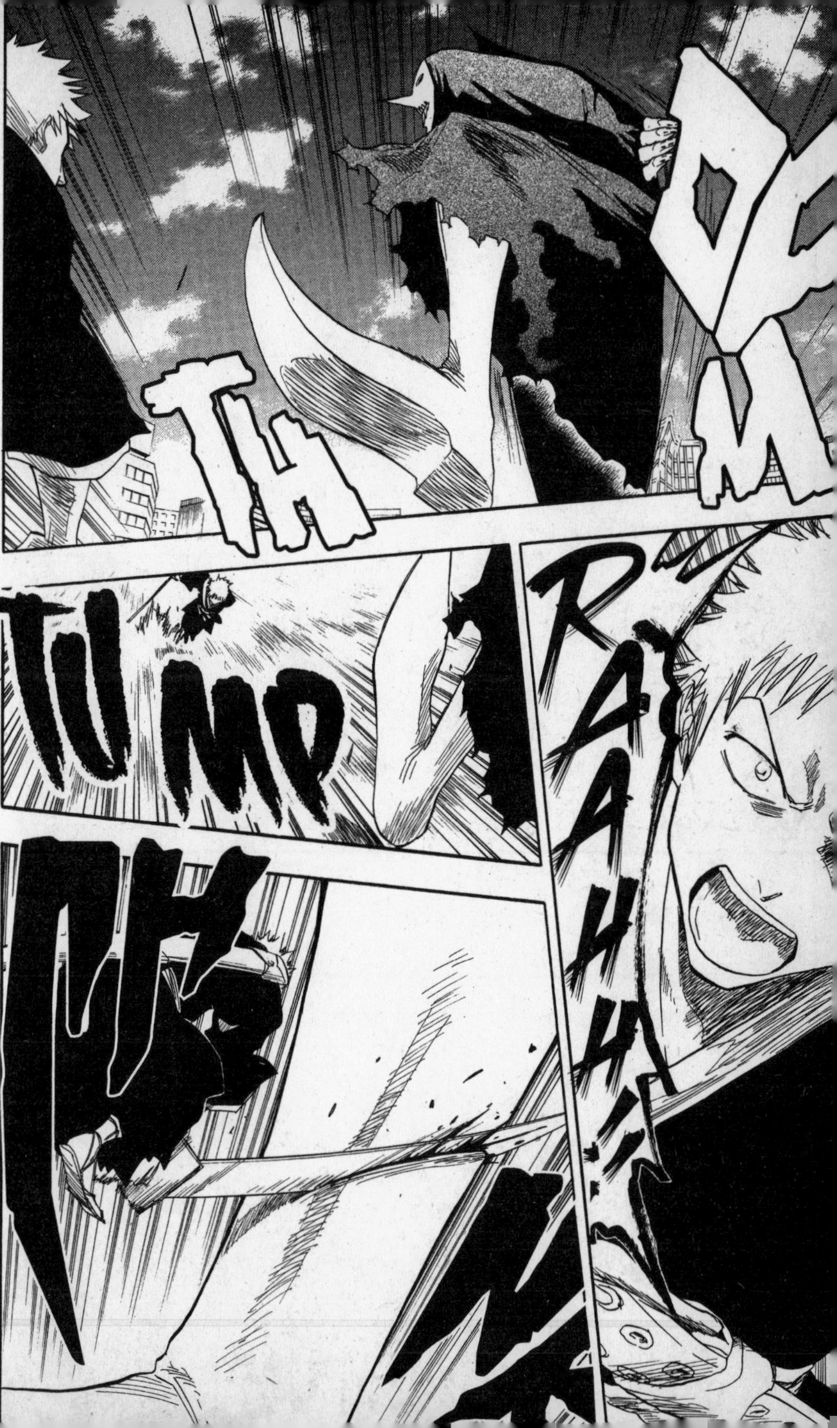
TH
RAAHH
THUMP

READ THIS WAY

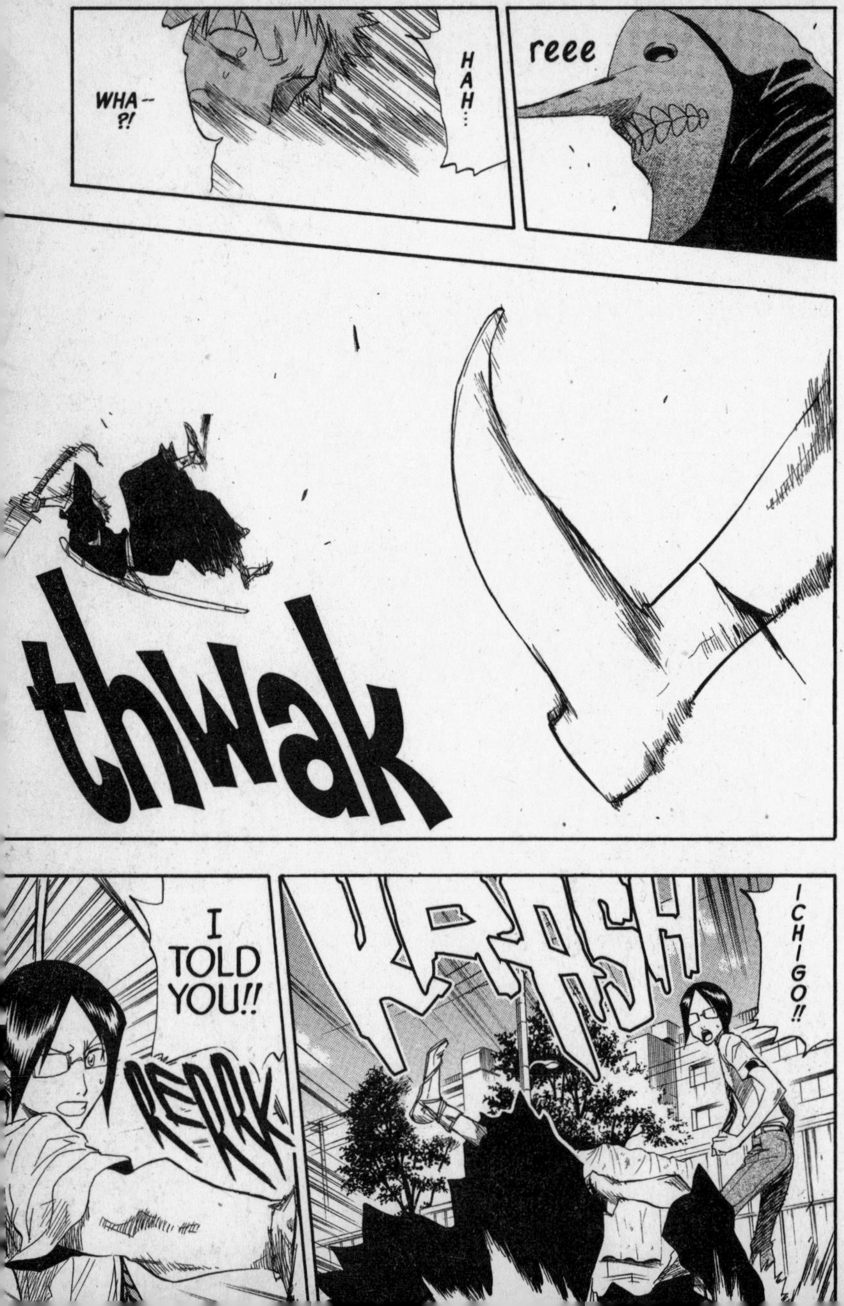
reee
HAH...
WHA-- ?!
thwak
ICHIGO!!
I TOLD YOU!!

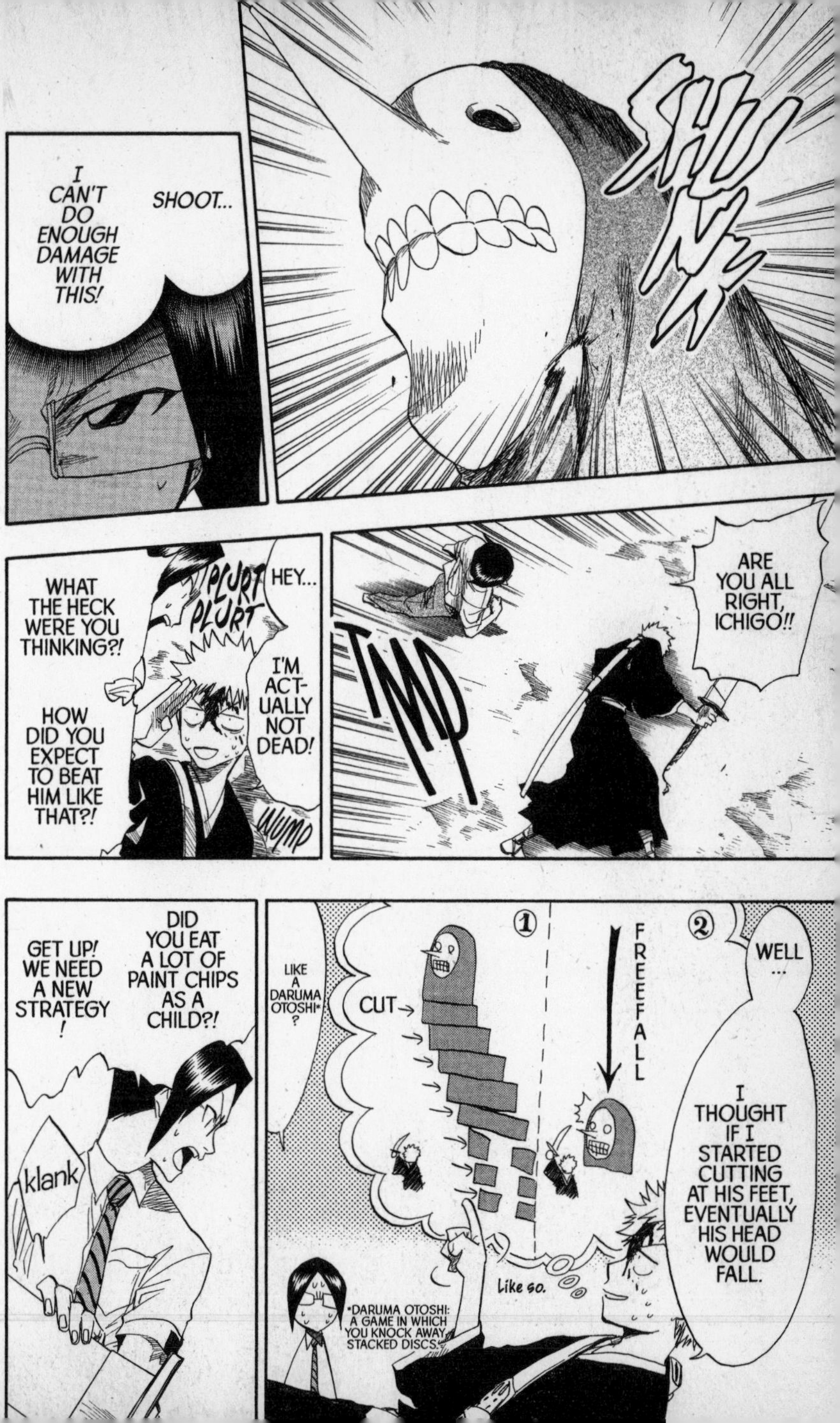
SHUNK
SHOOT...
I CAN'T DO ENOUGH DAMAGE WITH THIS!
ARE YOU ALL RIGHT, ICHIGO!!
TMP
HEY...
I'M ACTUALLY NOT DEAD!
PLURT PLURT
WHAT THE HECK WERE YOU THINKING?!
HOW DID YOU EXPECT TO BEAT HIM LIKE THAT?!
WUMP
WELL...
I THOUGHT IF I STARTED CUTTING AT HIS FEET, EVENTUALLY HIS HEAD WOULD FALL.
②
FREEFALL
①
CUT
LIKE A DARUMA OTOSHI*?
Like so.
*DARUMA OTOSHI: A GAME IN WHICH YOU KNOCK AWAY STACKED DISCS.
DID YOU EAT A LOT OF PAINT CHIPS AS A CHILD?!
GET UP! WE NEED A NEW STRATEGY!
klank

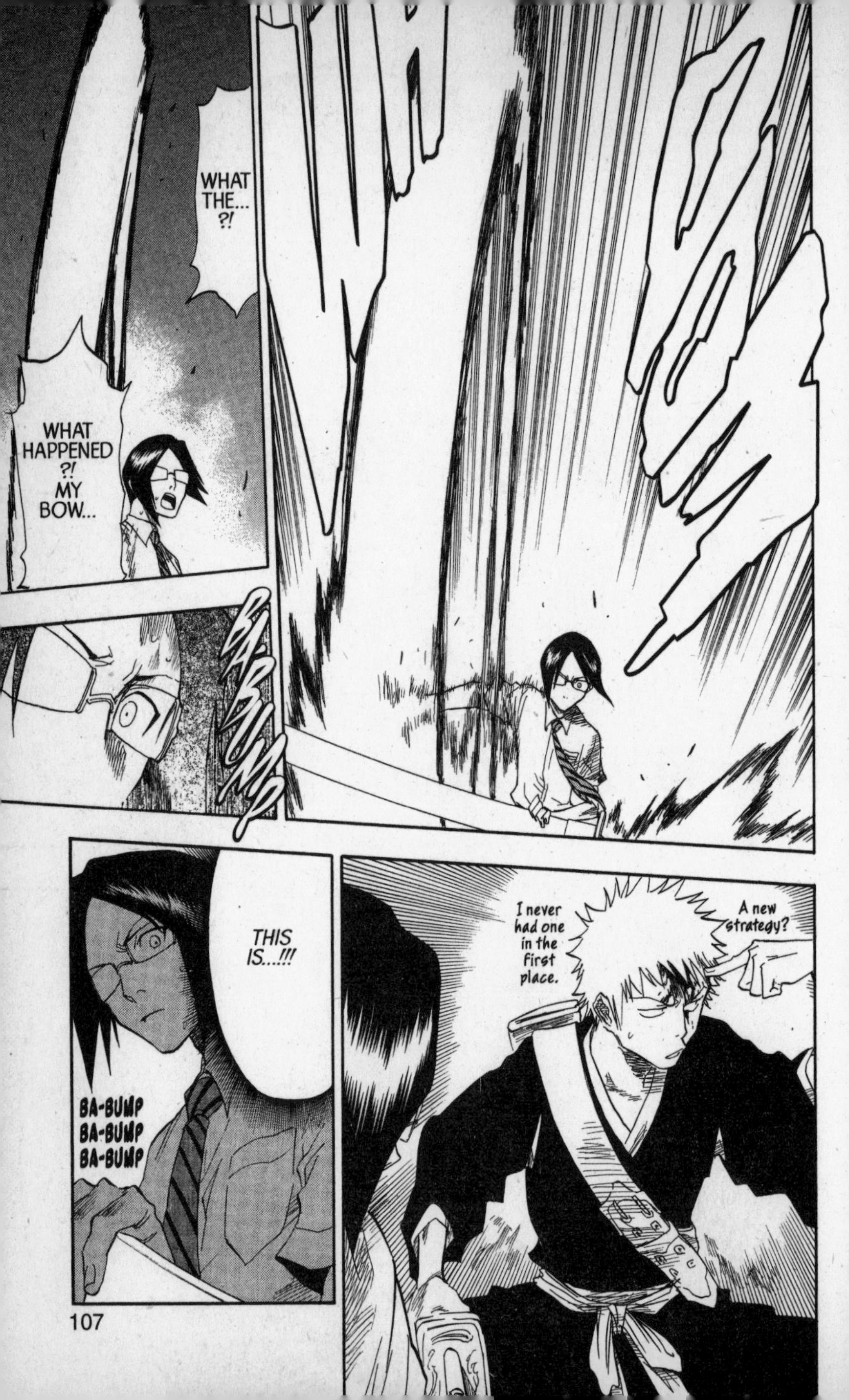
WHAT THE... ?!
WHAT HAPPENED ?! MY BOW...
A new strategy?
I never had one in the first place.
THIS IS...!!!
BA-BUMP BA-BUMP BA-BUMP

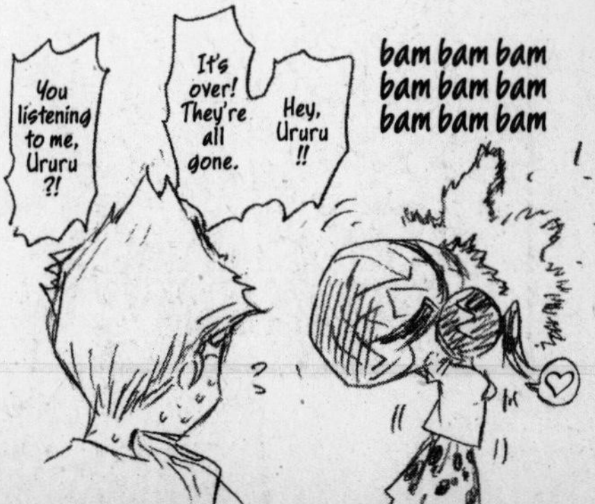
bam bam bam bam bam bam bam bam bam
Hey, Ururu!!
It's over! They're all gone.
You listening to me, Ururu?!

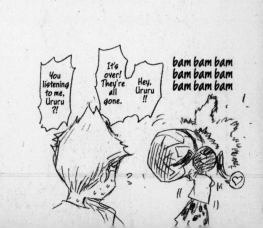

RMBRMBRMBRMB

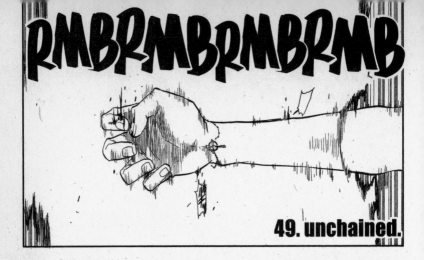

49. unchained.

IT'S...!!

THUMP

zak

zak

KrakKrak

Krek

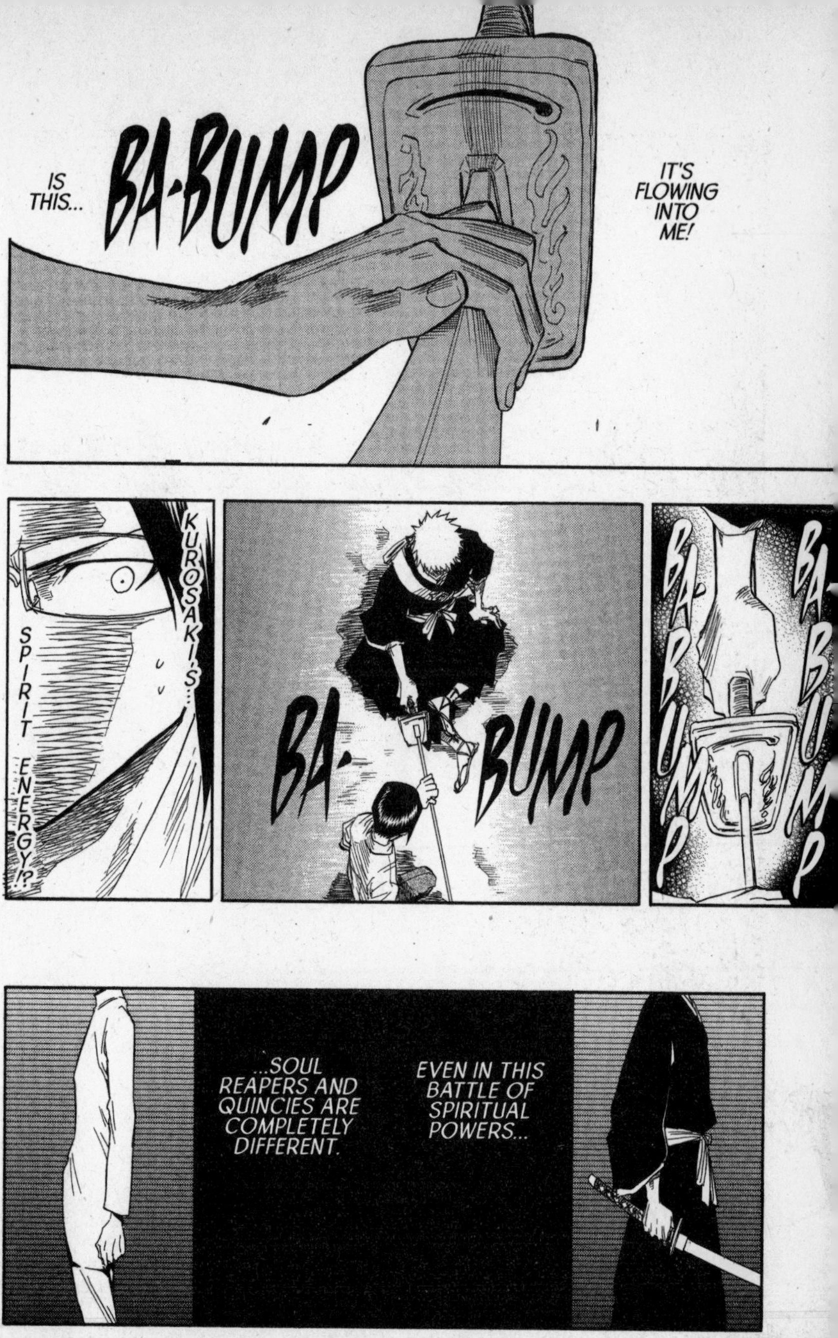
IT'S FLOWING INTO ME!
BA-BUMP
IS THIS...
BA-BUMP
BA-BUMP
BA-BUMP
KUROSAKI'S...
SPIRIT ENERGY!?
EVEN IN THIS BATTLE OF SPIRITUAL POWERS...
...SOUL REAPERS AND QUINCIES ARE COMPLETELY DIFFERENT.

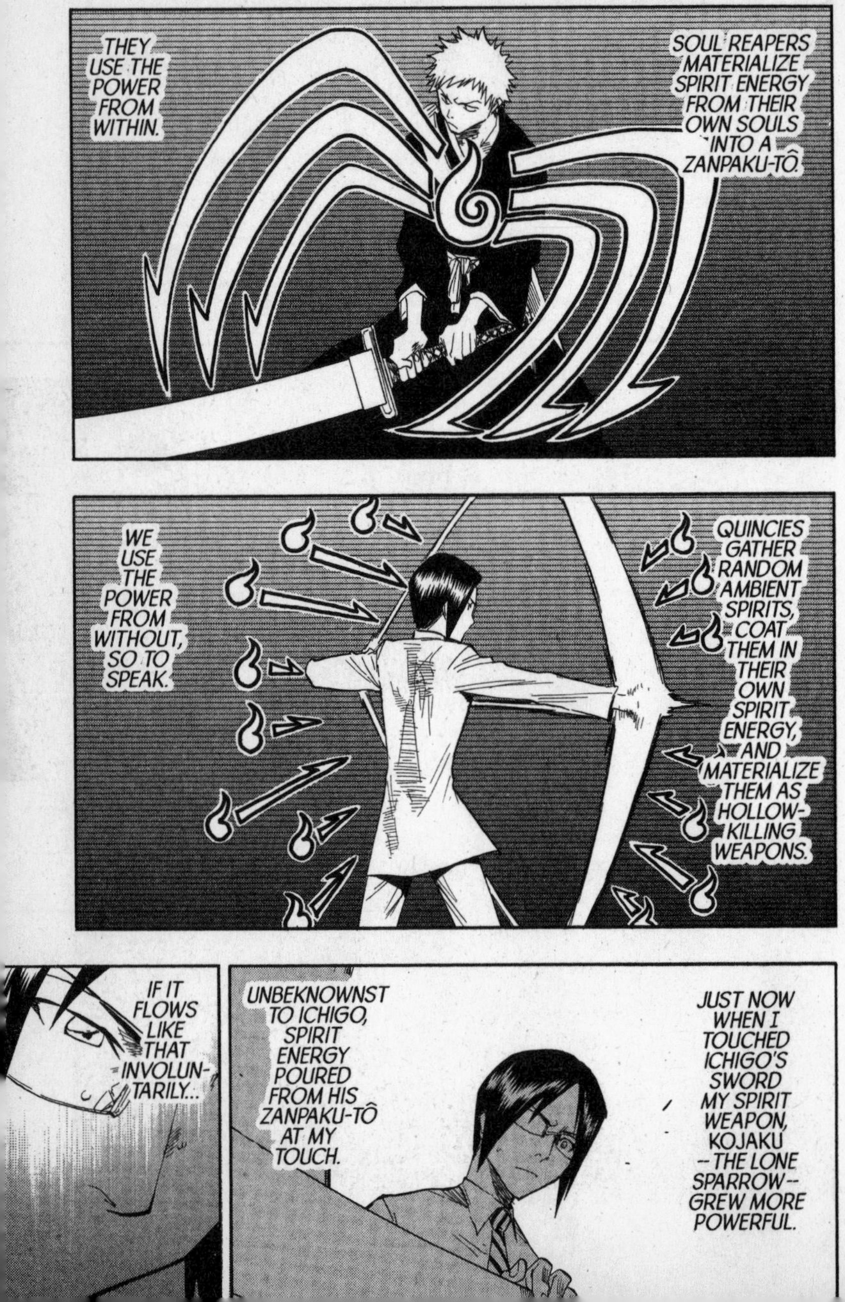
SOUL REAPERS MATERIALIZE SPIRIT ENERGY FROM THEIR OWN SOULS INTO A ZANPAKU-TÔ.
THEY USE THE POWER FROM WITHIN.
QUINCIES GATHER RANDOM AMBIENT SPIRITS, COAT THEM IN THEIR OWN SPIRIT ENERGY, AND MATERIALIZE THEM AS HOLLOW-KILLING WEAPONS.
WE USE THE POWER FROM WITHOUT, SO TO SPEAK.
JUST NOW WHEN I TOUCHED ICHIGO'S SWORD MY SPIRIT WEAPON, KOJAKU --THE LONE SPARROW-- GREW MORE POWERFUL.
UNBEKNOWNST TO ICHIGO, SPIRIT ENERGY POURED FROM HIS ZANPAKU-TÔ AT MY TOUCH.
IF IT FLOWS LIKE THAT INVOLUNTARILY...

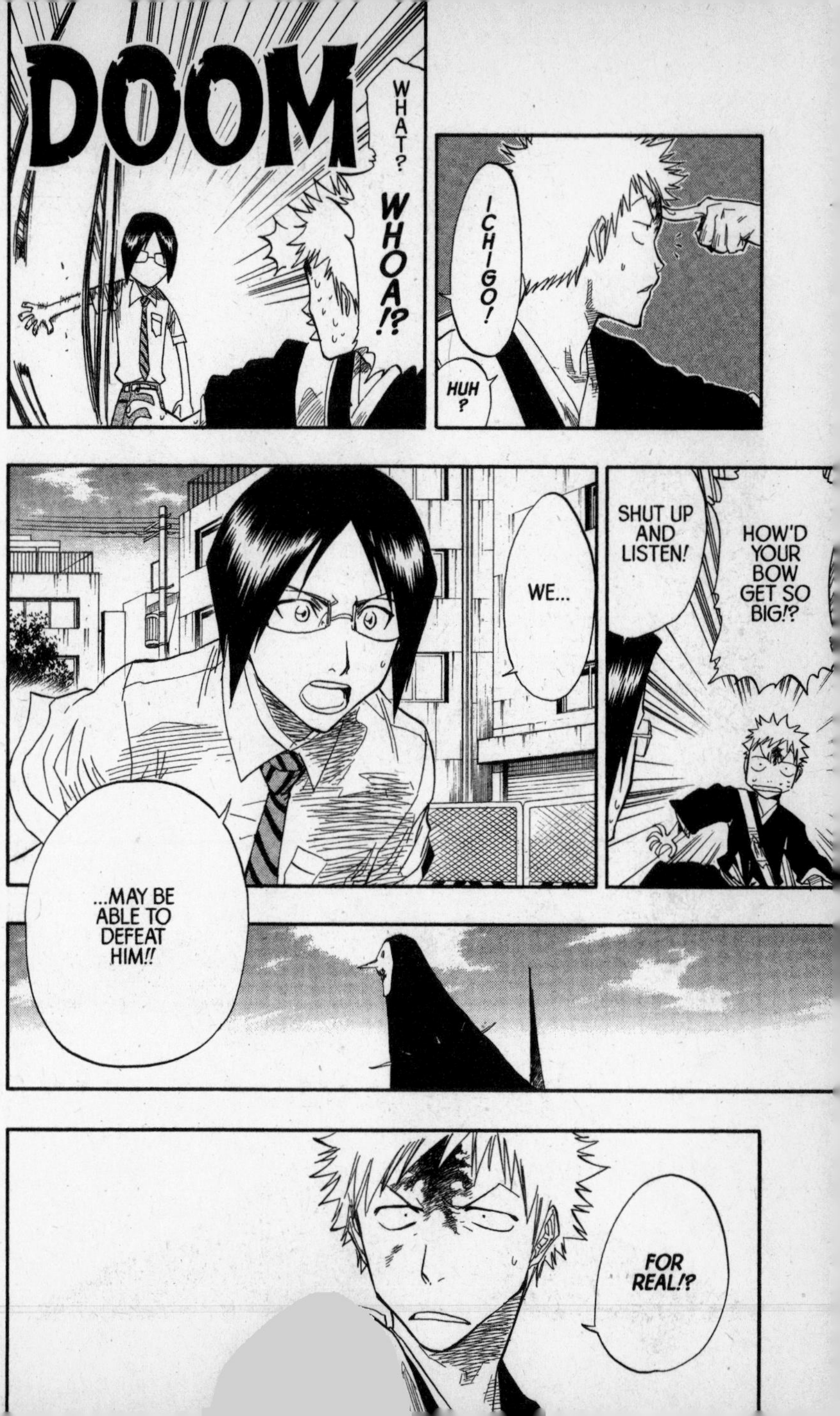
ICHIGO!
HUH?
DOOM
WHAT?
WHOA!?
HOW'D YOUR BOW GET SO BIG!?
SHUT UP AND LISTEN!
WE...
...MAY BE ABLE TO DEFEAT HIM!!
FOR REAL!?

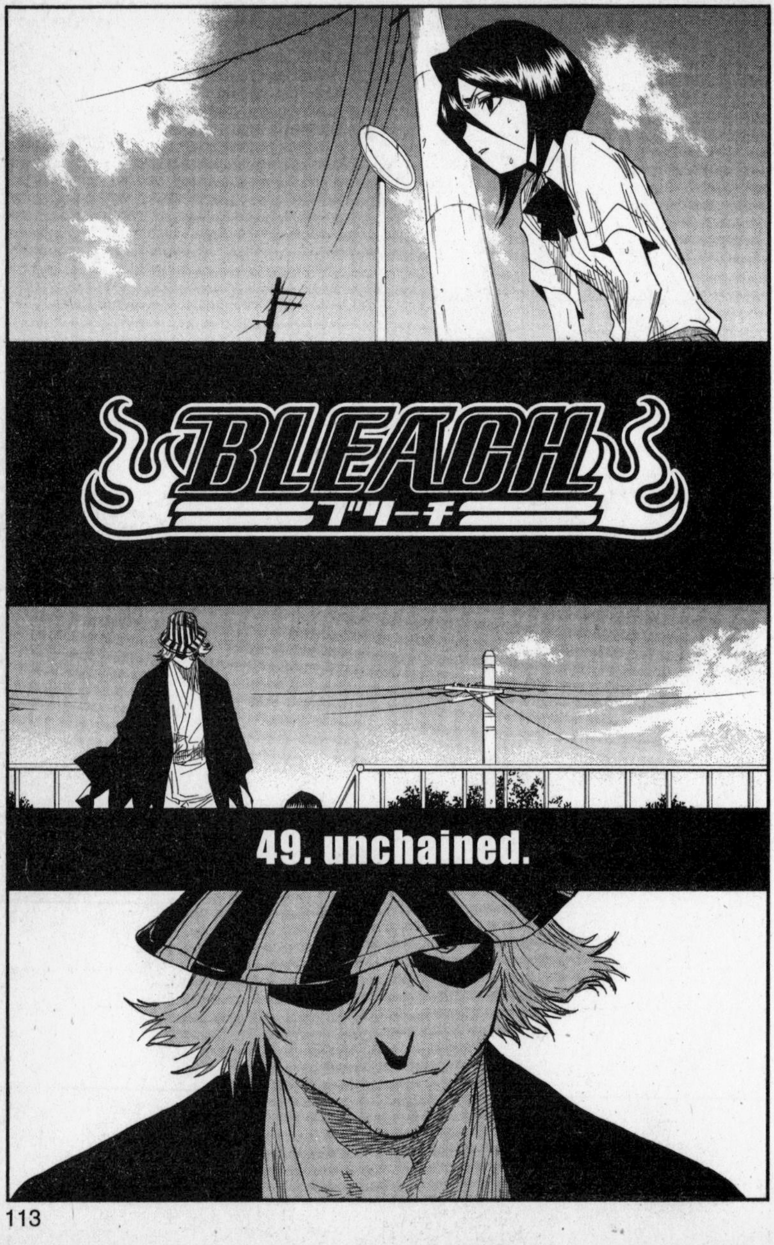
BLEACH
ブリーチ

49. unchained.

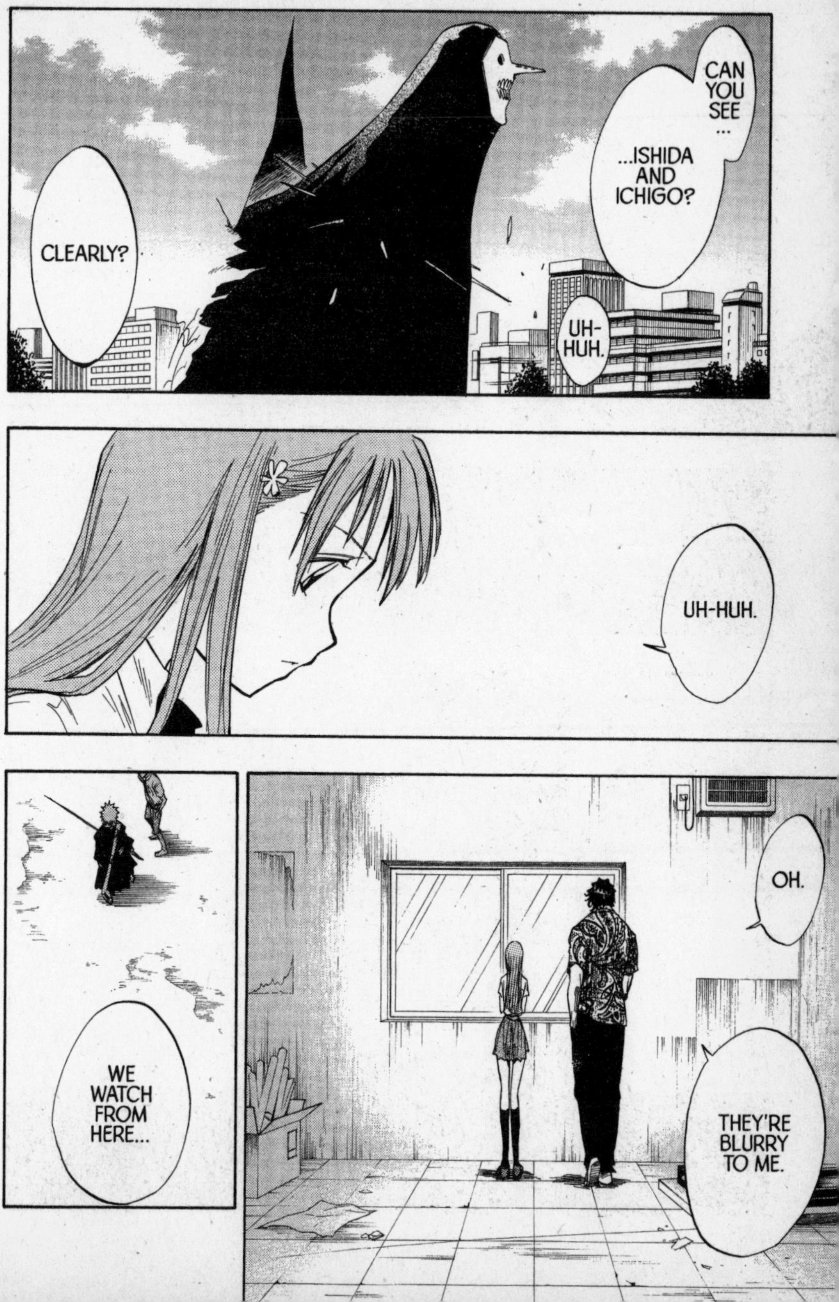
CAN YOU SEE ...
...ISHIDA AND ICHIGO?
UH-HUH.
CLEARLY?
UH-HUH.
OH.
THEY'RE BLURRY TO ME.
WE WATCH FROM HERE...

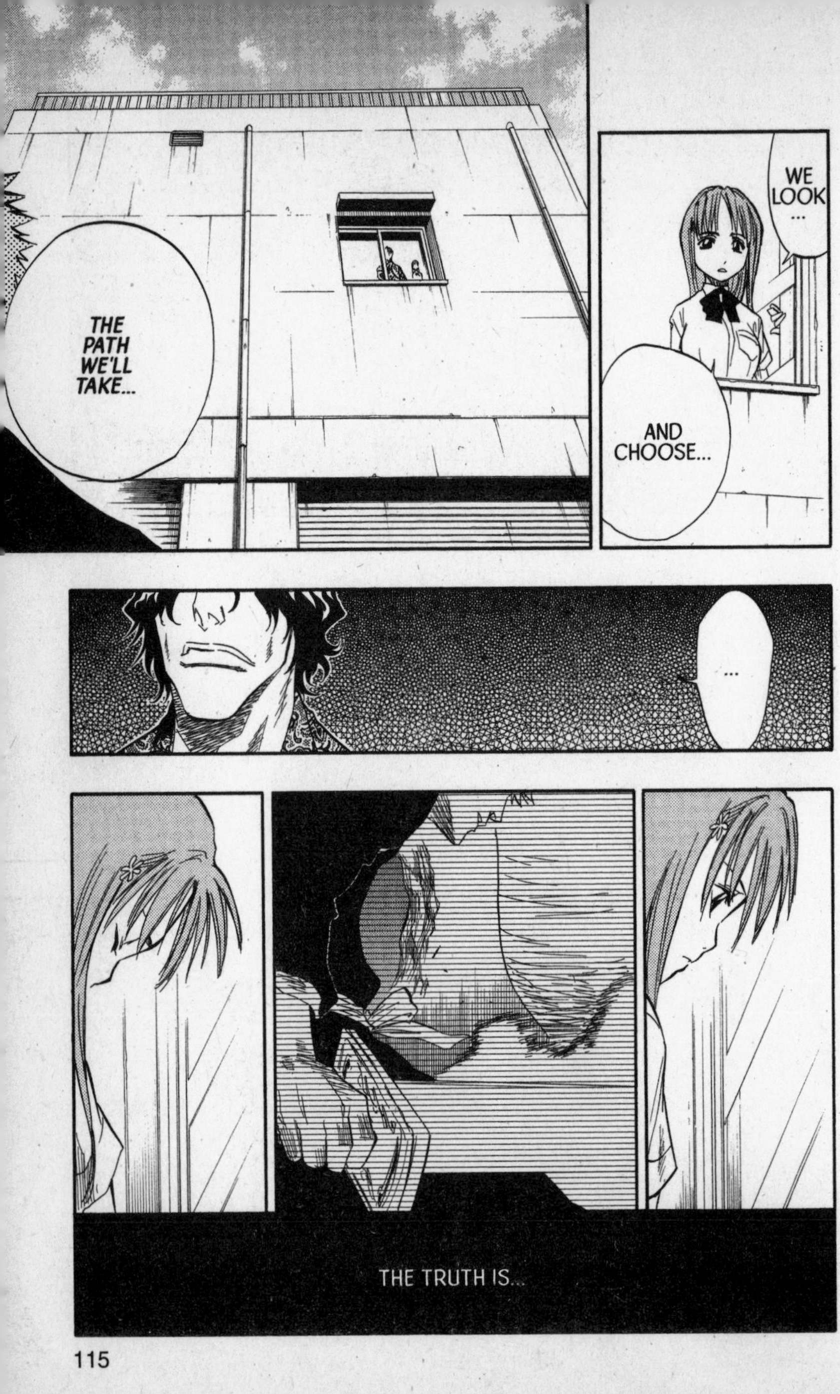
WE LOOK...
AND CHOOSE...
THE PATH WE'LL TAKE...
...
THE TRUTH IS...

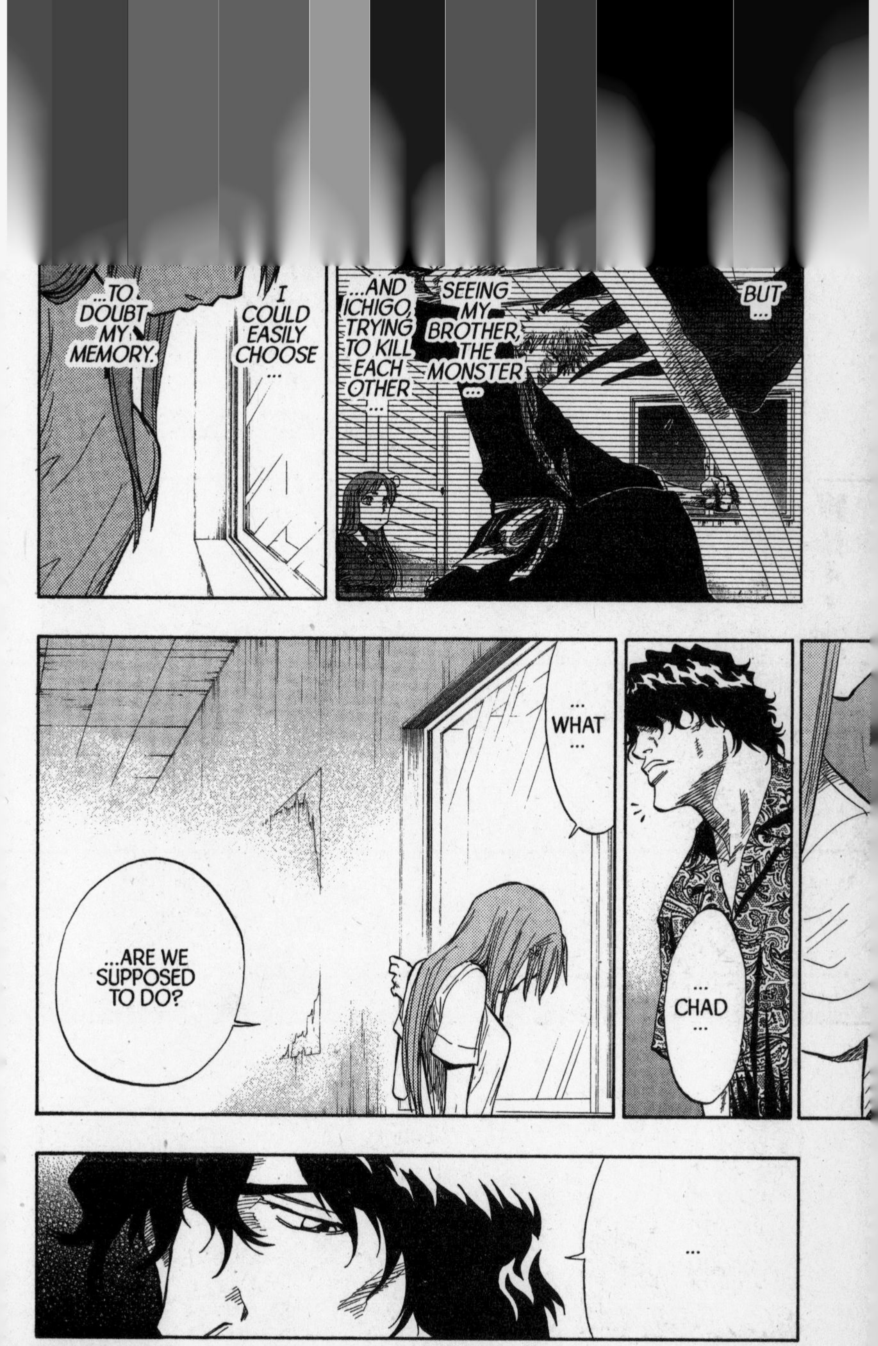
BUT ...
SEEING MY BROTHER, THE MONSTER ...
...AND ICHIGO, TRYING TO KILL EACH OTHER ...
I COULD EASILY CHOOSE ...
...TO DOUBT MY MEMORY.
... CHAD ...
... WHAT ...
...ARE WE SUPPOSED TO DO?
...

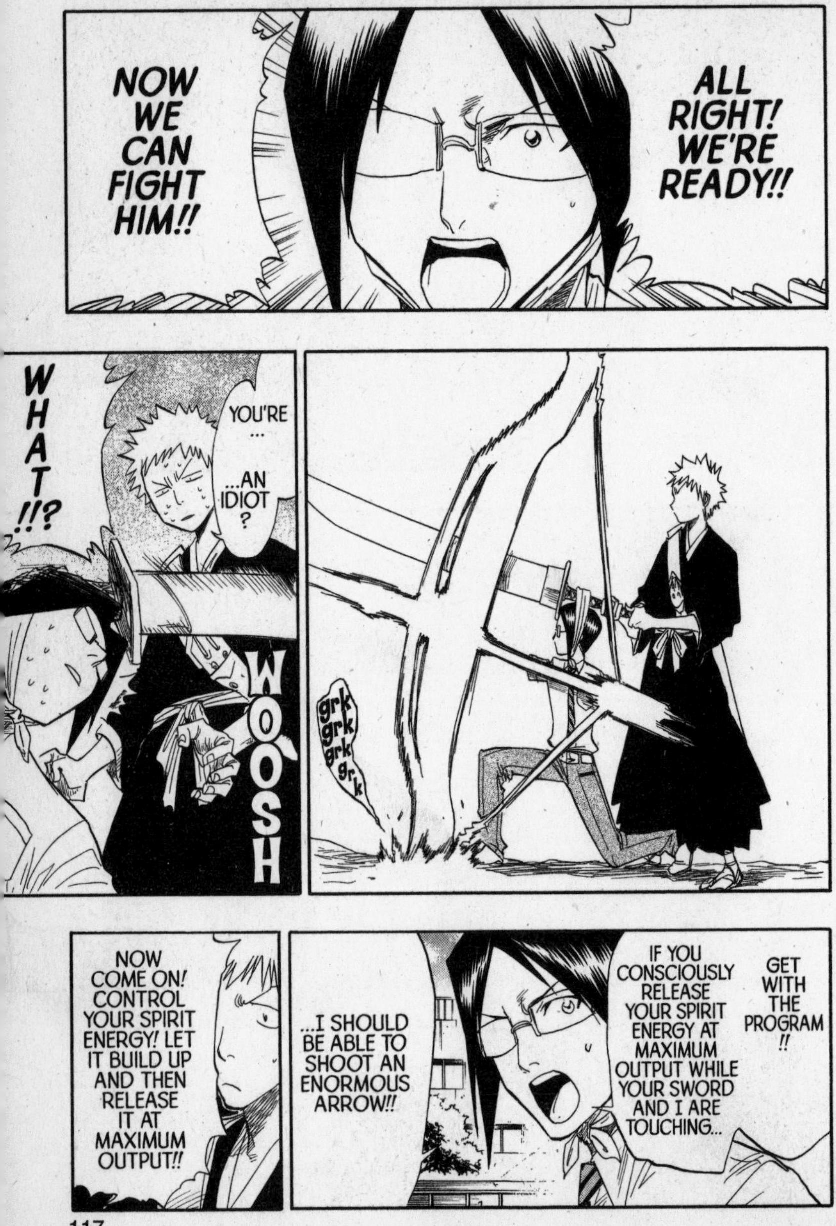
ALL RIGHT! WE'RE READY!!
NOW WE CAN FIGHT HIM!!
grk grk grk grk
YOU'RE ...
...AN IDIOT?
WHAT!!?
WOOSH
GET WITH THE PROGRAM!!
IF YOU CONSCIOUSLY RELEASE YOUR SPIRIT ENERGY AT MAXIMUM OUTPUT WHILE YOUR SWORD AND I ARE TOUCHING...
...I SHOULD BE ABLE TO SHOOT AN ENORMOUS ARROW!!
NOW COME ON! CONTROL YOUR SPIRIT ENERGY! LET IT BUILD UP AND THEN RELEASE IT AT MAXIMUM OUTPUT!!

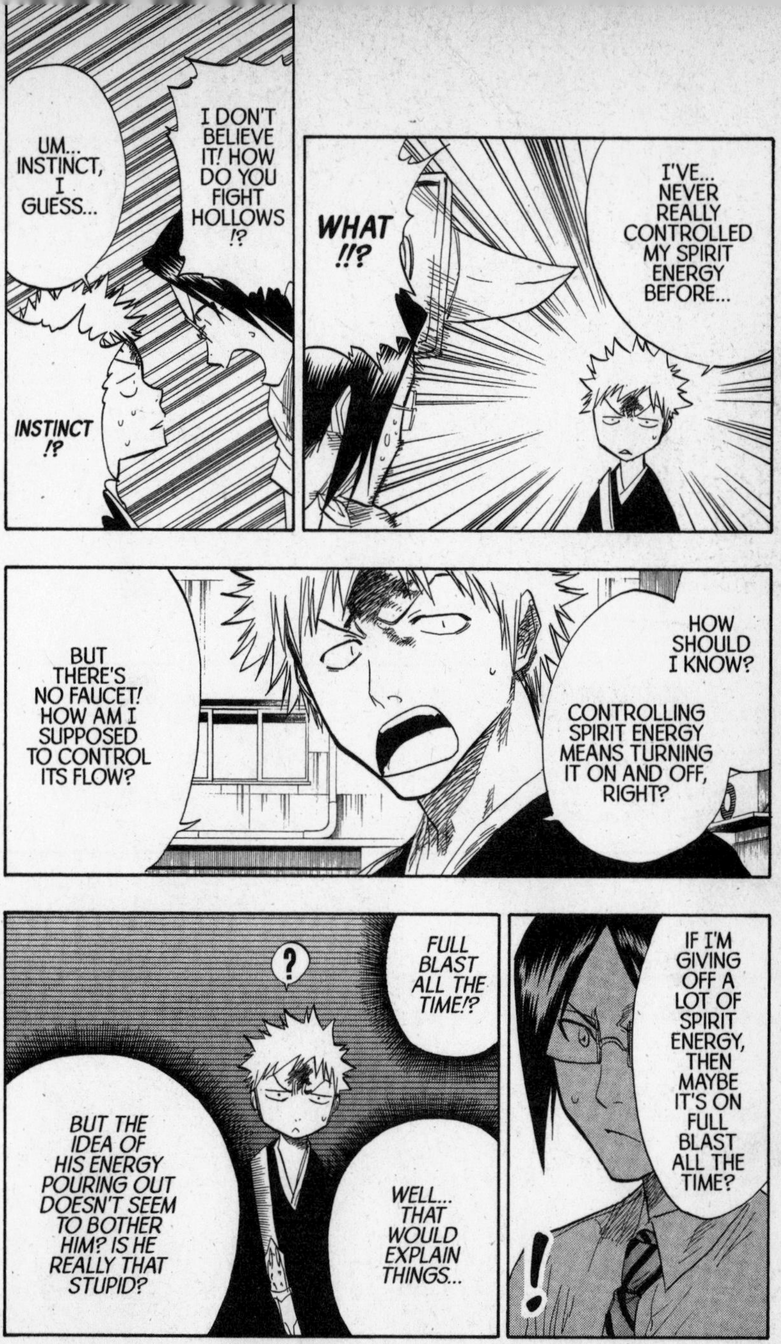

I'VE... NEVER REALLY CONTROLLED MY SPIRIT ENERGY BEFORE...
WHAT!!?
I DON'T BELIEVE IT! HOW DO YOU FIGHT HOLLOWS!?
UM... INSTINCT, I GUESS...
INSTINCT!?
HOW SHOULD I KNOW?
CONTROLLING SPIRIT ENERGY MEANS TURNING IT ON AND OFF, RIGHT?
BUT THERE'S NO FAUCET! HOW AM I SUPPOSED TO CONTROL ITS FLOW?
IF I'M GIVING OFF A LOT OF SPIRIT ENERGY, THEN MAYBE IT'S ON FULL BLAST ALL THE TIME?
!
FULL BLAST ALL THE TIME!?
?
WELL... THAT WOULD EXPLAIN THINGS...
BUT THE IDEA OF HIS ENERGY POURING OUT DOESN'T SEEM TO BOTHER HIM? IS HE REALLY THAT STUPID?

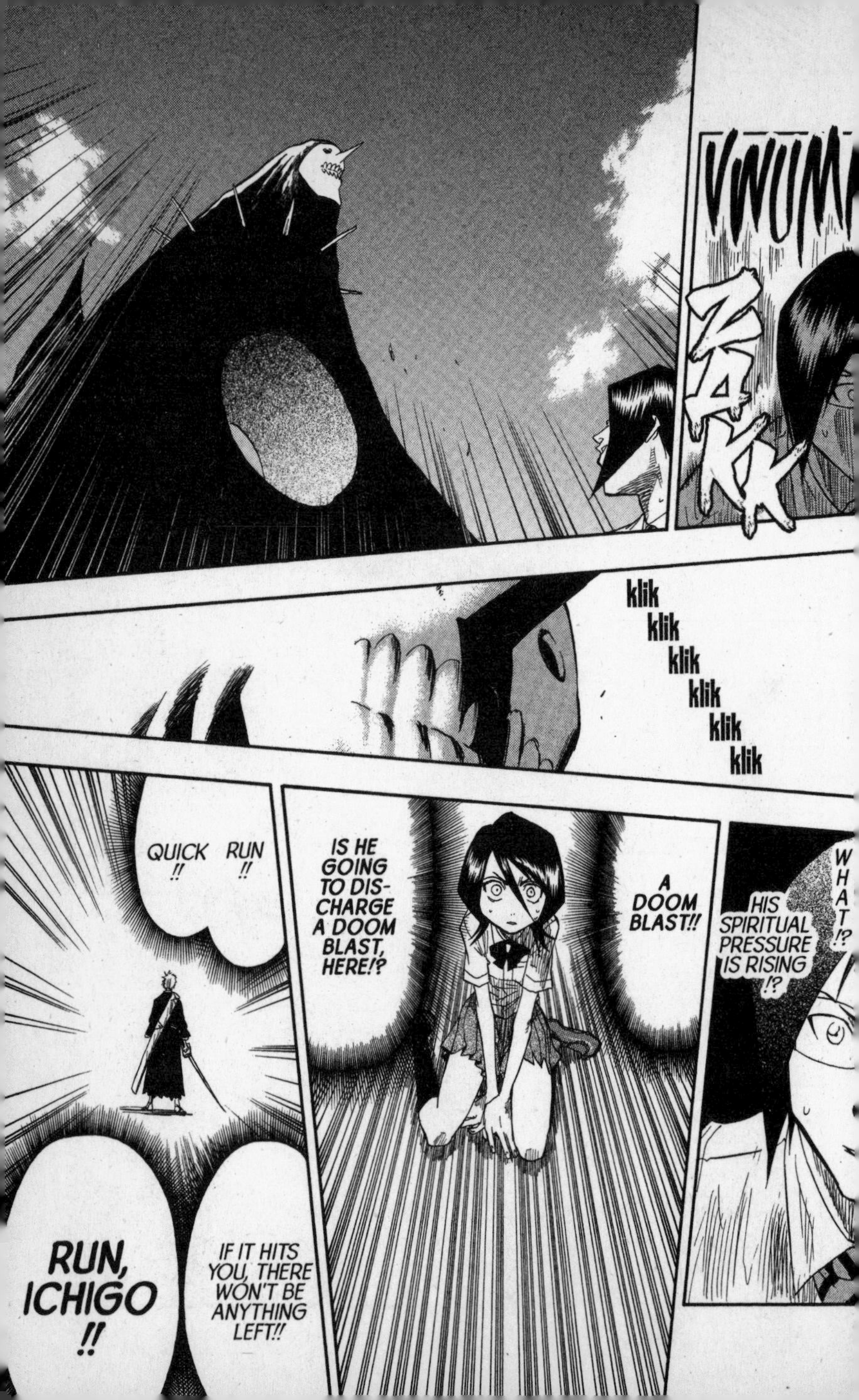
VWUM
ZAK
klik klik klik klik klik klik
WHAT!?
HIS SPIRITUAL PRESSURE IS RISING!?
A DOOM BLAST!!
IS HE GOING TO DIS-CHARGE A DOOM BLAST, HERE!?
QUICK!! RUN!!
IF IT HITS YOU, THERE WON'T BE ANYTHING LEFT!!
RUN, ICHIGO!!

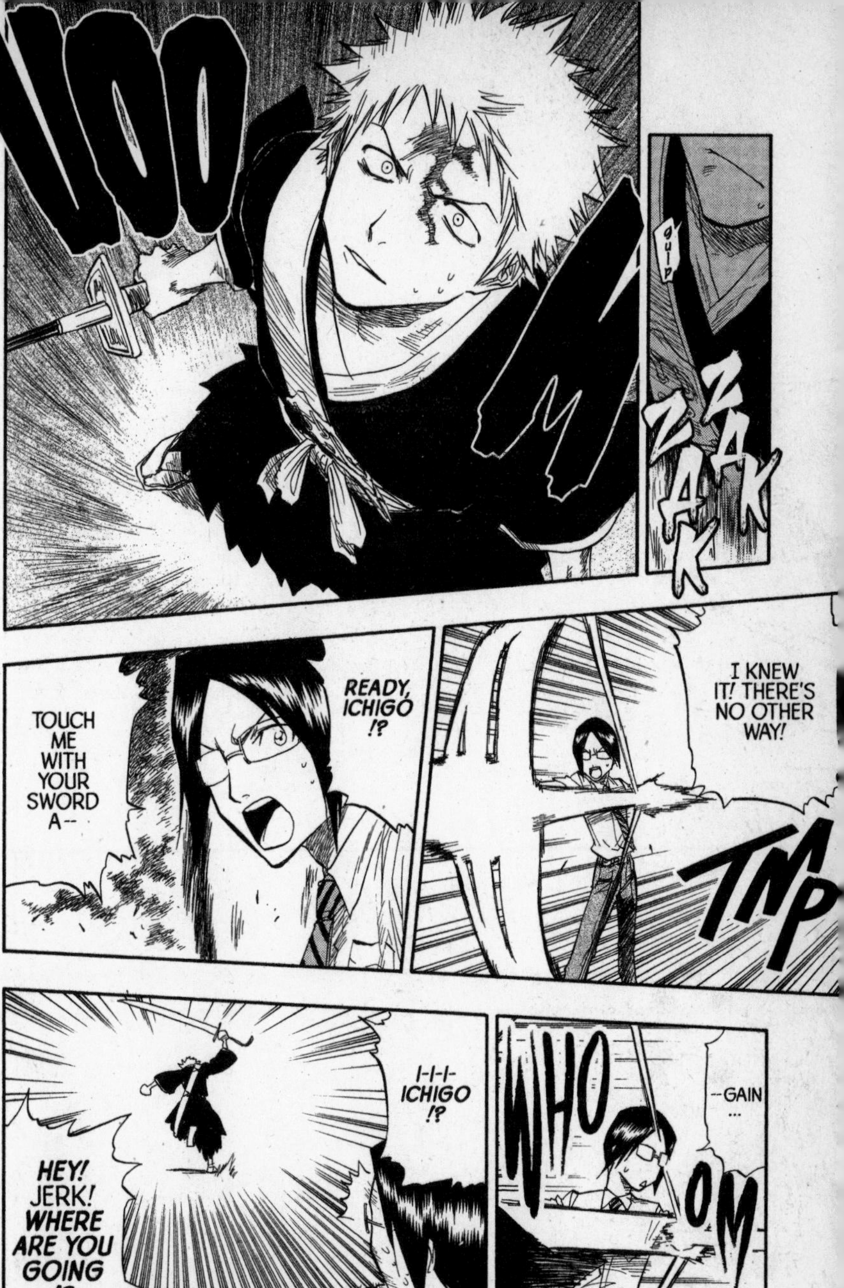
gulp
ZAK ZAK
VOOM
I KNEW IT! THERE'S NO OTHER WAY!
TMP
READY, ICHIGO!?
TOUCH ME WITH YOUR SWORD A--
WHOOM
--GAIN ...
I-I-I-ICHIGO!?
HEY! JERK! WHERE ARE YOU GOING!?

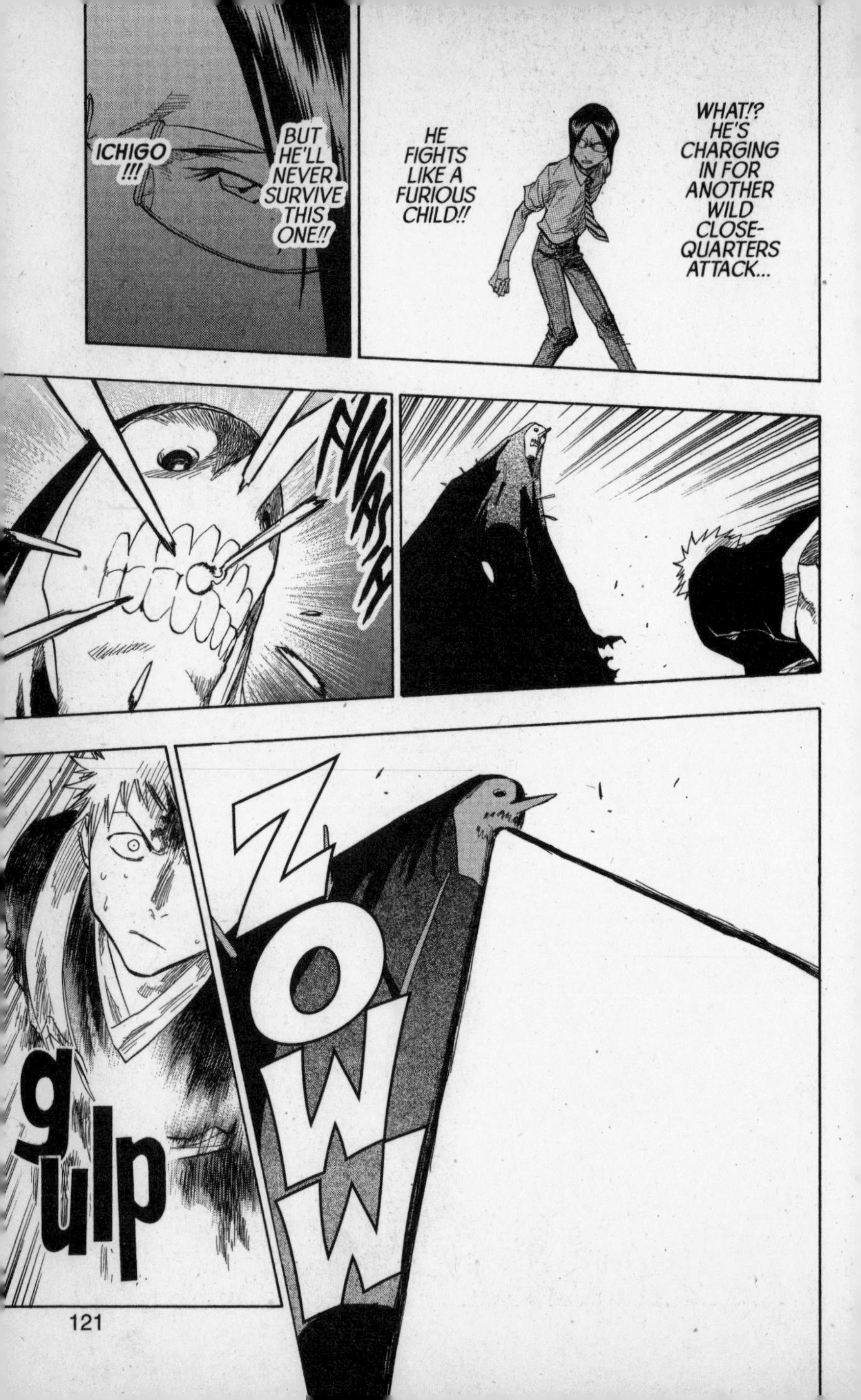
WHAT!? HE'S CHARGING IN FOR ANOTHER WILD CLOSE-QUARTERS ATTACK...
HE FIGHTS LIKE A FURIOUS CHILD!!
BUT HE'LL NEVER SURVIVE THIS ONE!!
ICHIGO !!!
ZOWW
gulp

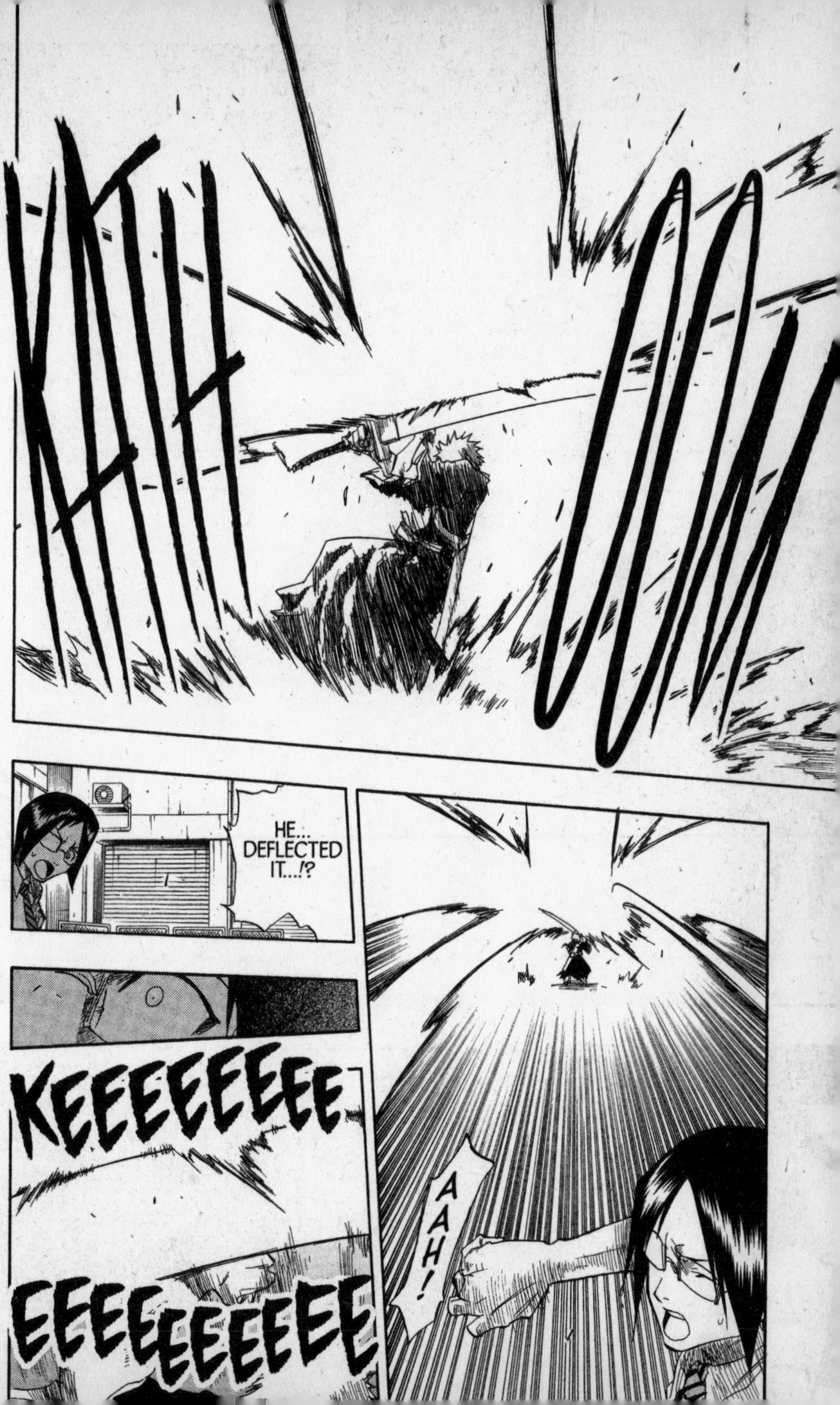
AAH!
HE... DEFLECTED IT...!?
KEEEEEEEEE
EEEEEEEEEEE

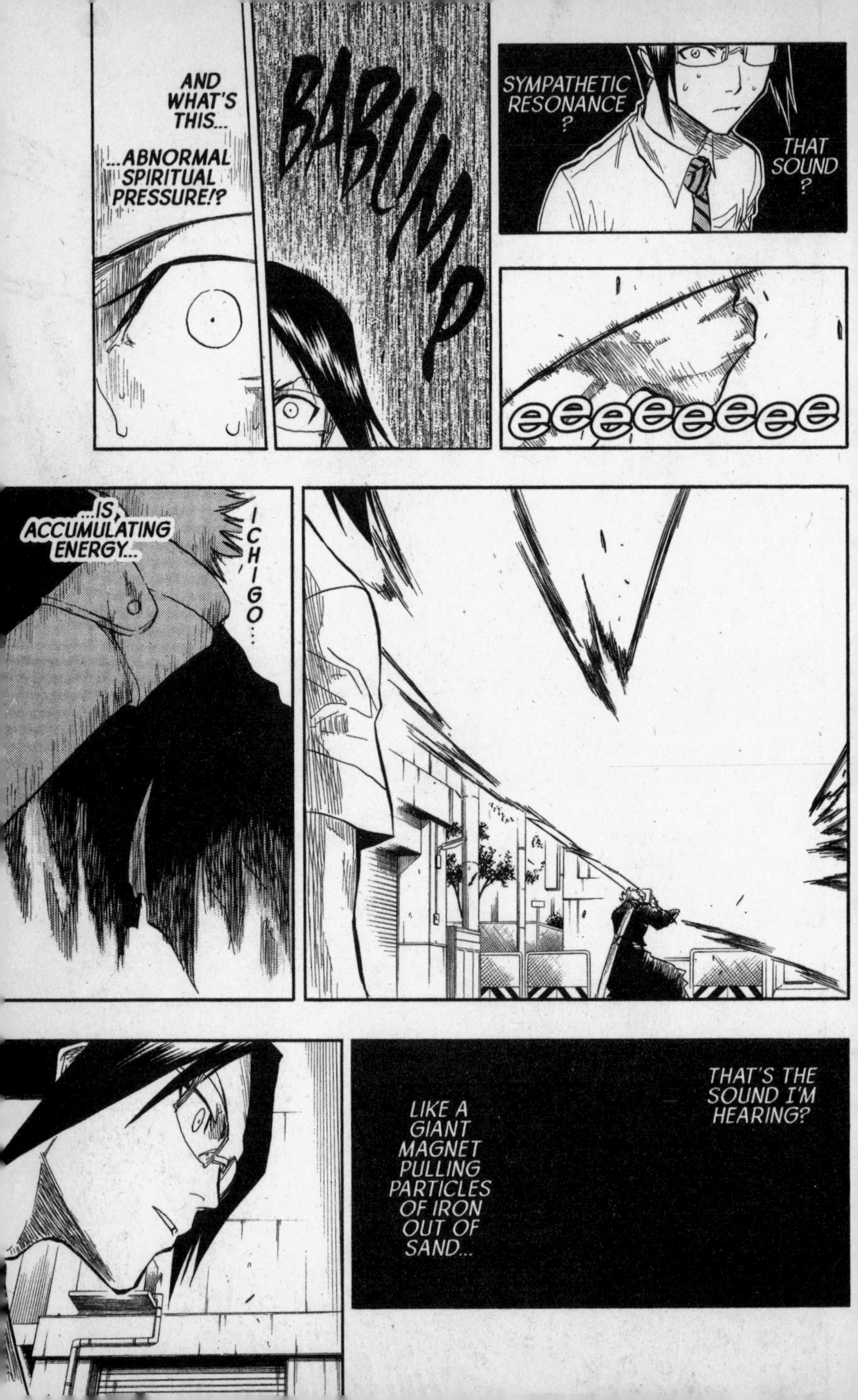
THAT SOUND?
SYMPATHETIC RESONANCE?
eeeeeeeee
BABUMP
AND WHAT'S THIS...
...ABNORMAL SPIRITUAL PRESSURE!?
ICHIGO...
...IS, ACCUMULATING ENERGY...
THAT'S THE SOUND I'M HEARING?
LIKE A GIANT MAGNET PULLING PARTICLES OF IRON OUT OF SAND...

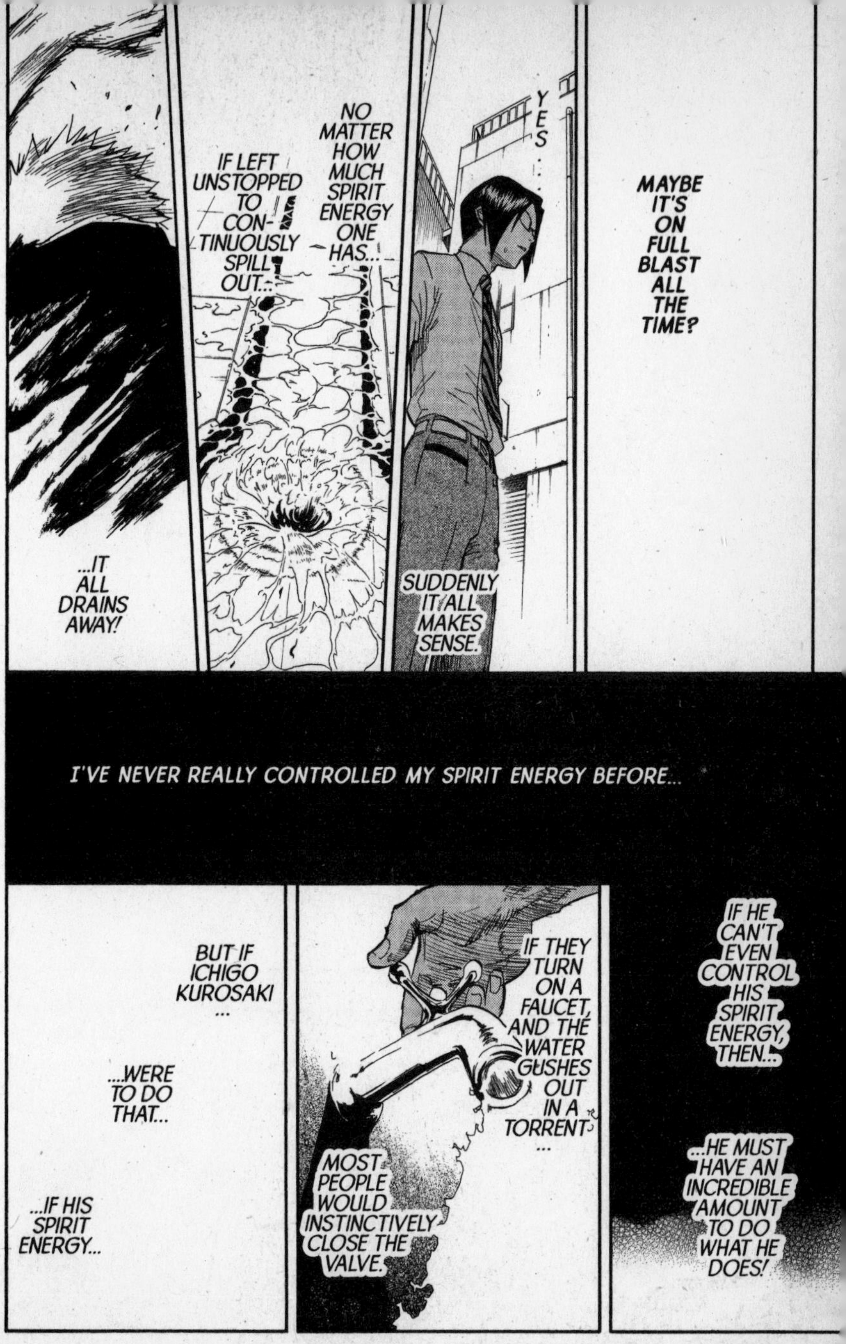
MAYBE IT'S ON FULL BLAST ALL THE TIME?
YES...
SUDDENLY IT ALL MAKES SENSE.
NO MATTER HOW MUCH SPIRIT ENERGY ONE HAS...
IF LEFT UNSTOPPED TO CON-TINUOUSLY SPILL OUT...
...IT ALL DRAINS AWAY!
I'VE NEVER REALLY CONTROLLED MY SPIRIT ENERGY BEFORE...
IF HE CAN'T EVEN CONTROL HIS SPIRIT ENERGY, THEN...
...HE MUST HAVE AN INCREDIBLE AMOUNT TO DO WHAT HE DOES!
IF THEY TURN ON A FAUCET, AND THE WATER GUSHES OUT IN A TORRENT...
MOST PEOPLE WOULD INSTINCTIVELY CLOSE THE VALVE.
BUT IF ICHIGO KUROSAKI...
...WERE TO DO THAT...
...IF HIS SPIRIT ENERGY...

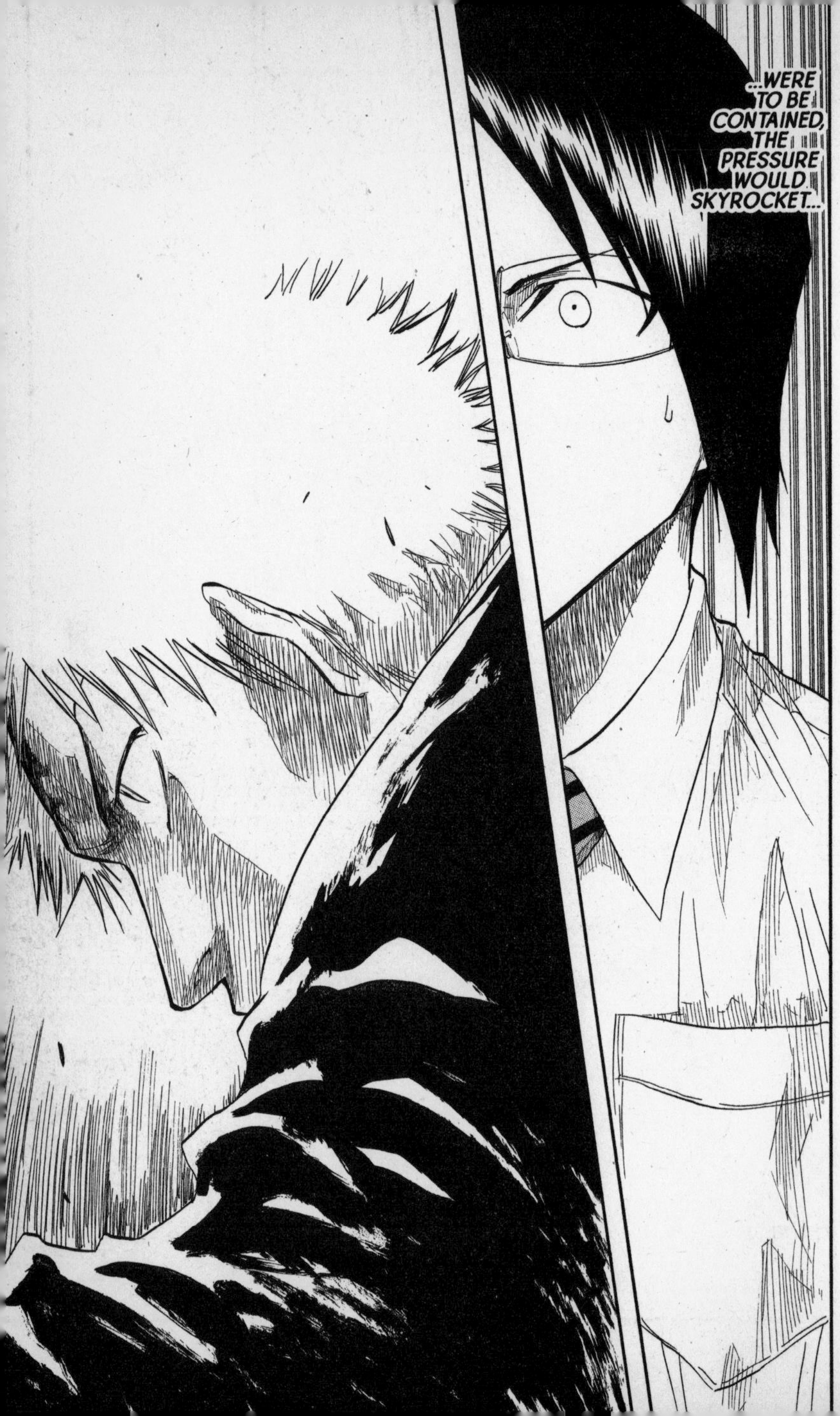
...WERE TO BE CONTAINED, THE PRESSURE WOULD SKYROCKET...

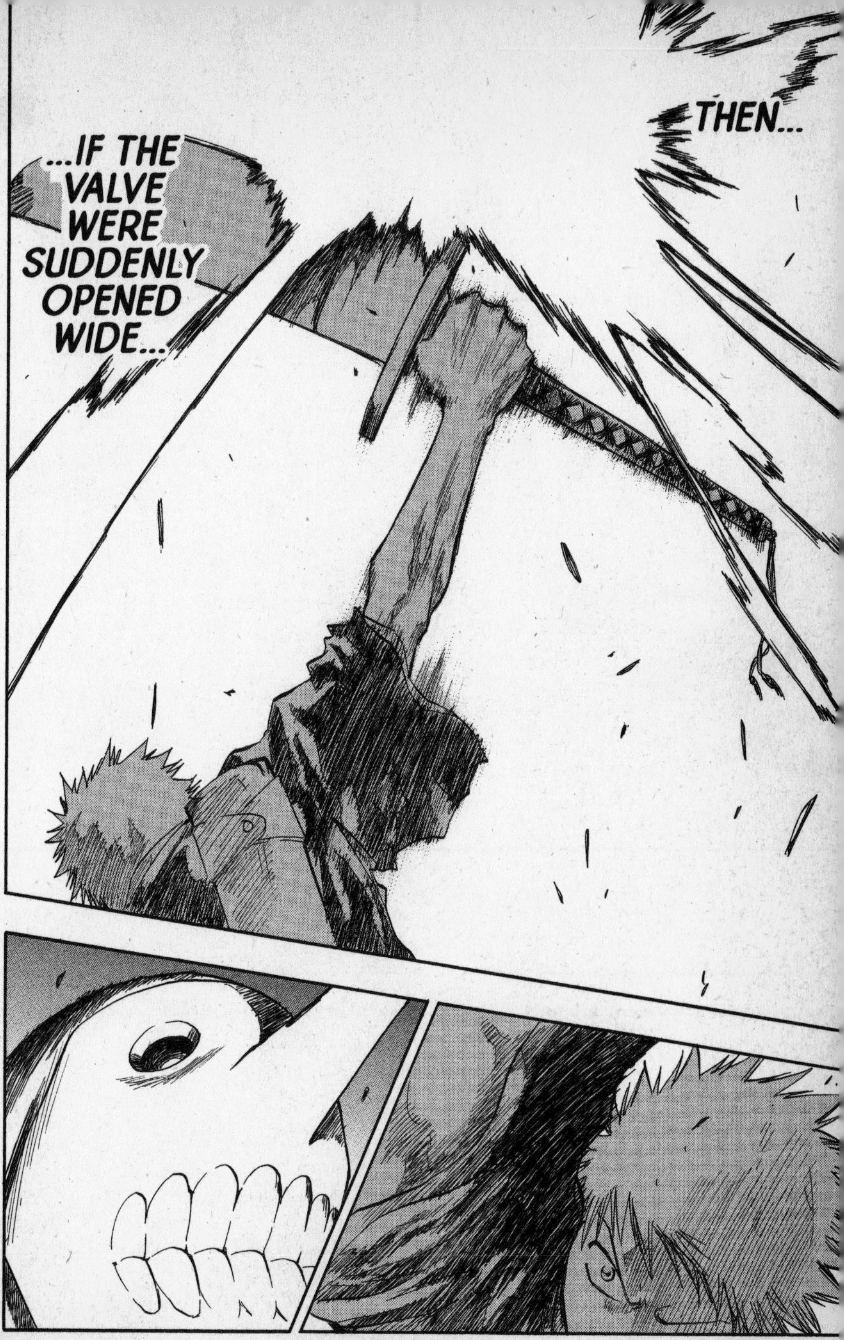
THEN...
...IF THE VALVE WERE SUDDENLY OPENED WIDE...

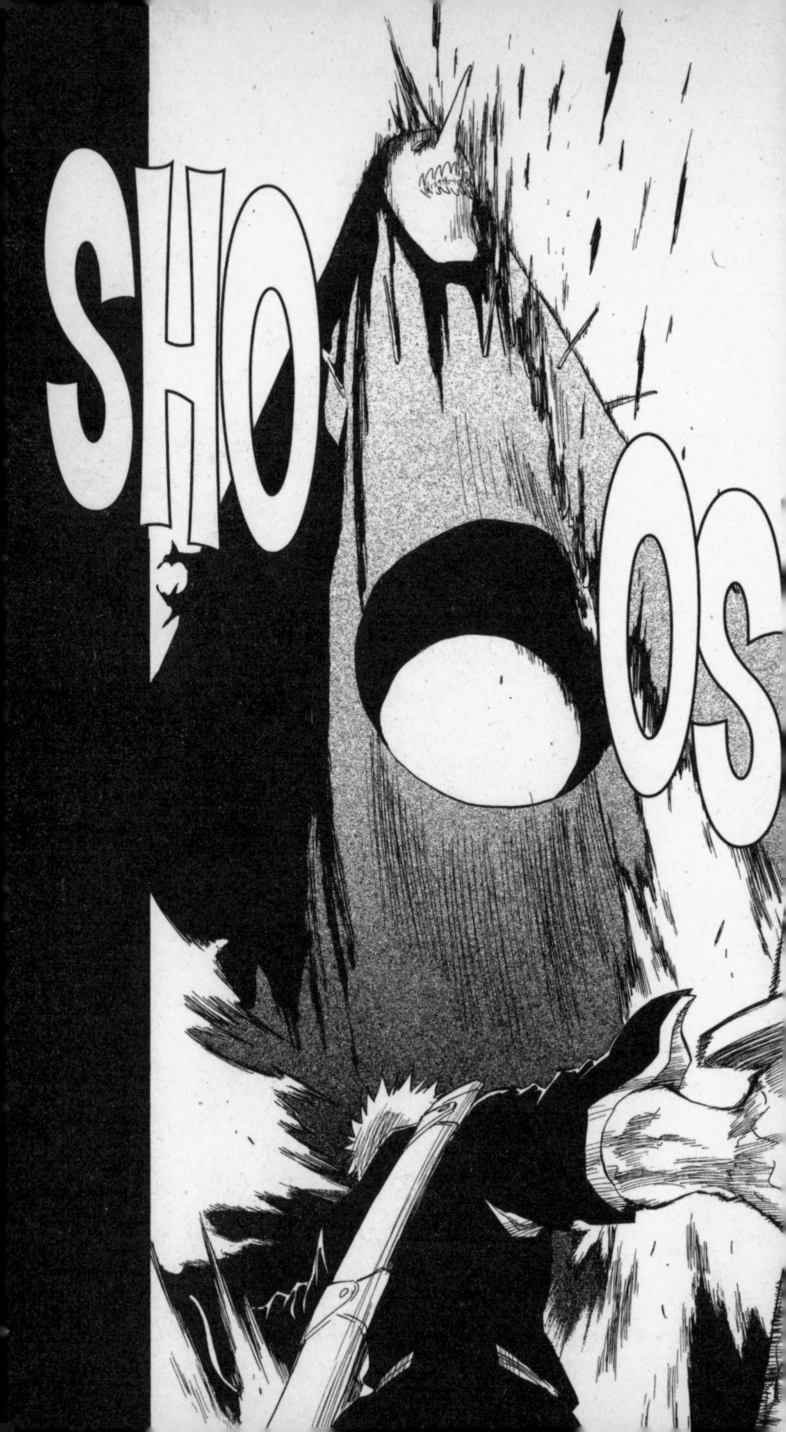
SHO
OS

50. Quincy Archer Hates You Part 2
(Blind but Bleed Mix)

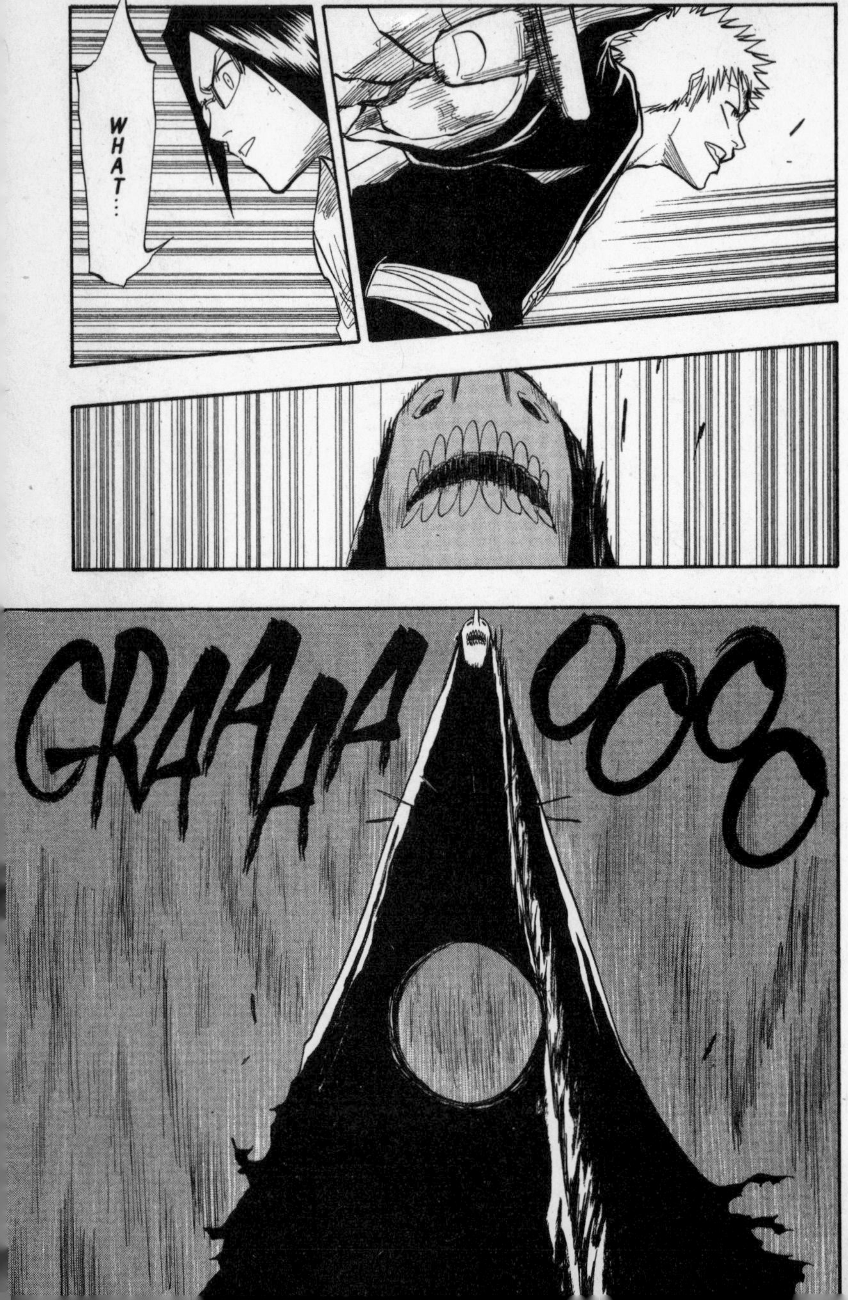
WHAT...
GRAAAAOOOO

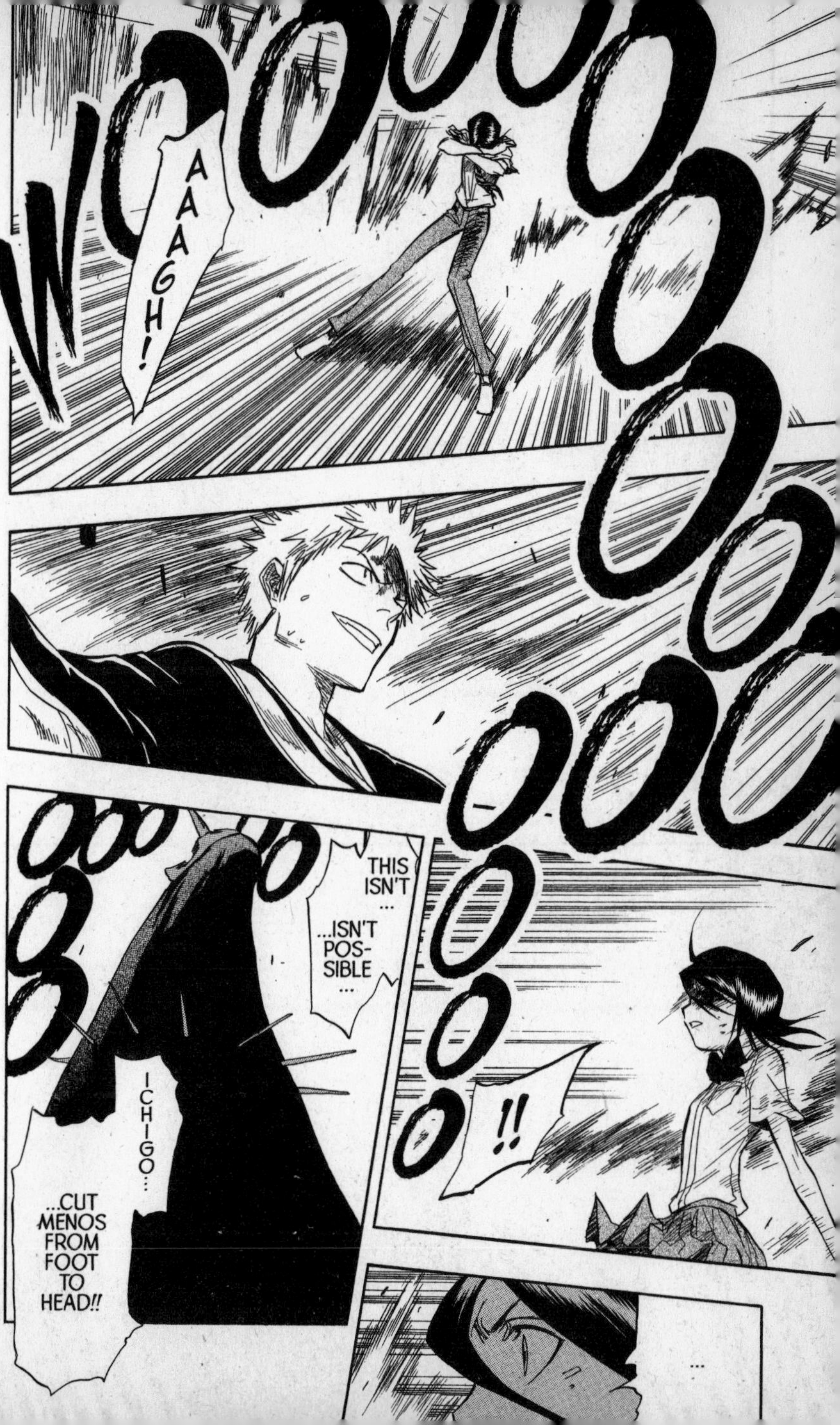
WOOOOOOOOOOOOOOOOOO
AAAGH!
!!
...
THIS ISN'T ... ...ISN'T POSSIBLE ...
ICHIGO... ...CUT MENOS FROM FOOT TO HEAD!!

READ THIS WAY

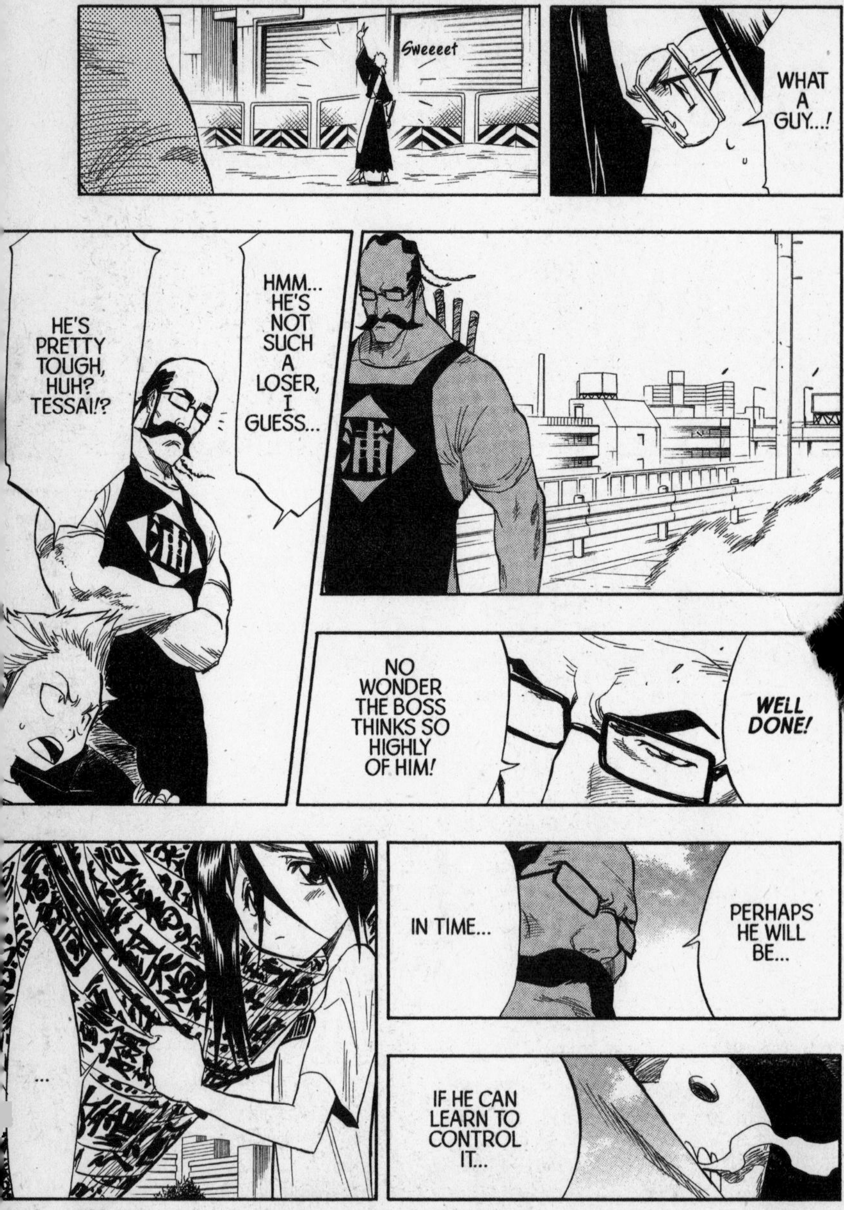
WHAT A GUY...!
Sweeeet
WELL DONE!
NO WONDER THE BOSS THINKS SO HIGHLY OF HIM!
HMM... HE'S NOT SUCH A LOSER, I GUESS...
HE'S PRETTY TOUGH, HUH? TESSAI!?
PERHAPS HE WILL BE...
IN TIME...
IF HE CAN LEARN TO CONTROL IT...
...

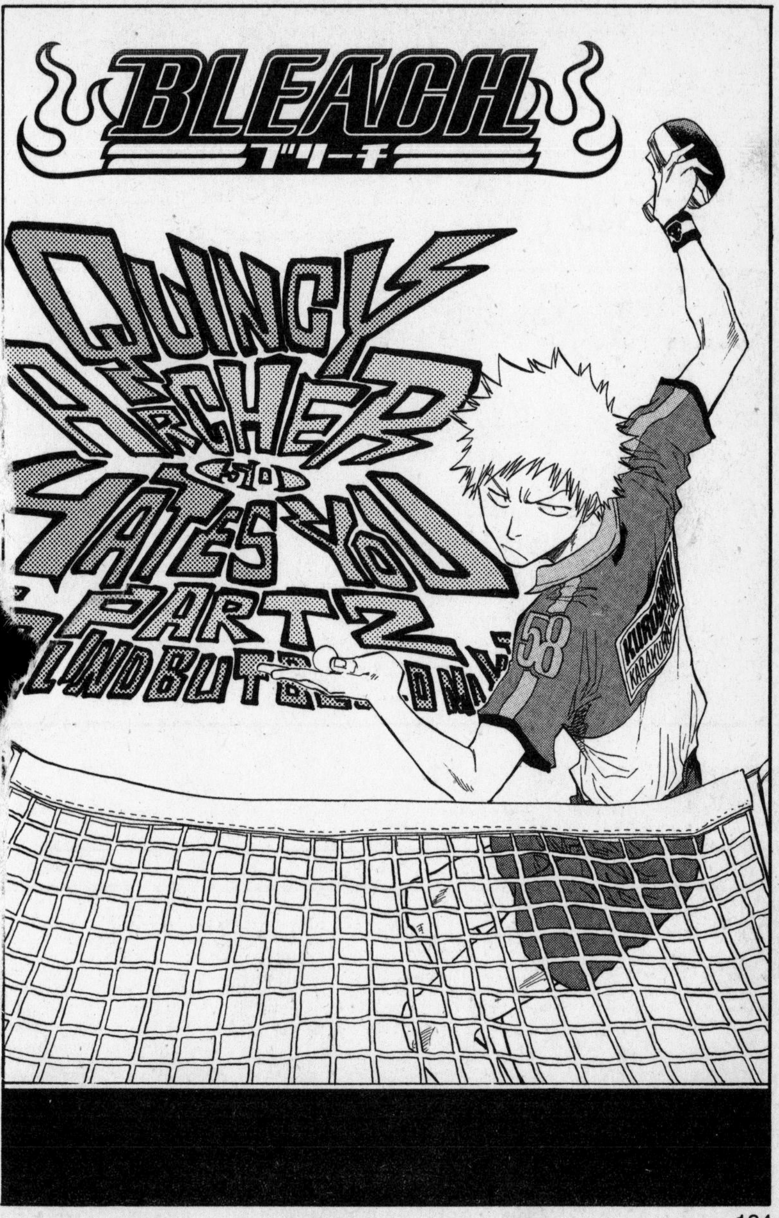
BLEACH
ブリーチ
510
QUINCY ARCHER HATES YOU
PART 2

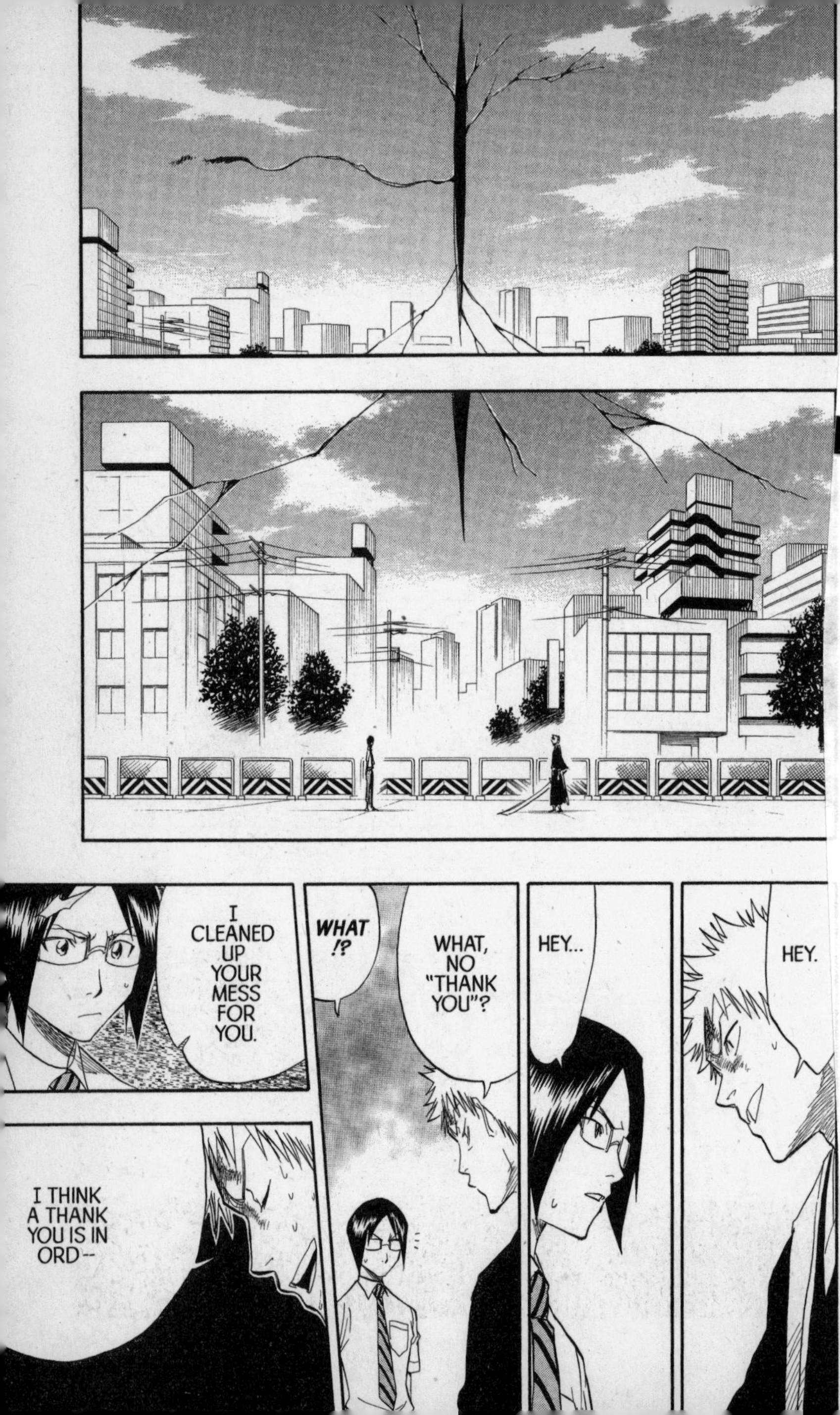
HEY.
HEY...
WHAT, NO "THANK YOU"?
WHAT !?
I CLEANED UP YOUR MESS FOR YOU.
I THINK A THANK YOU IS IN ORD--

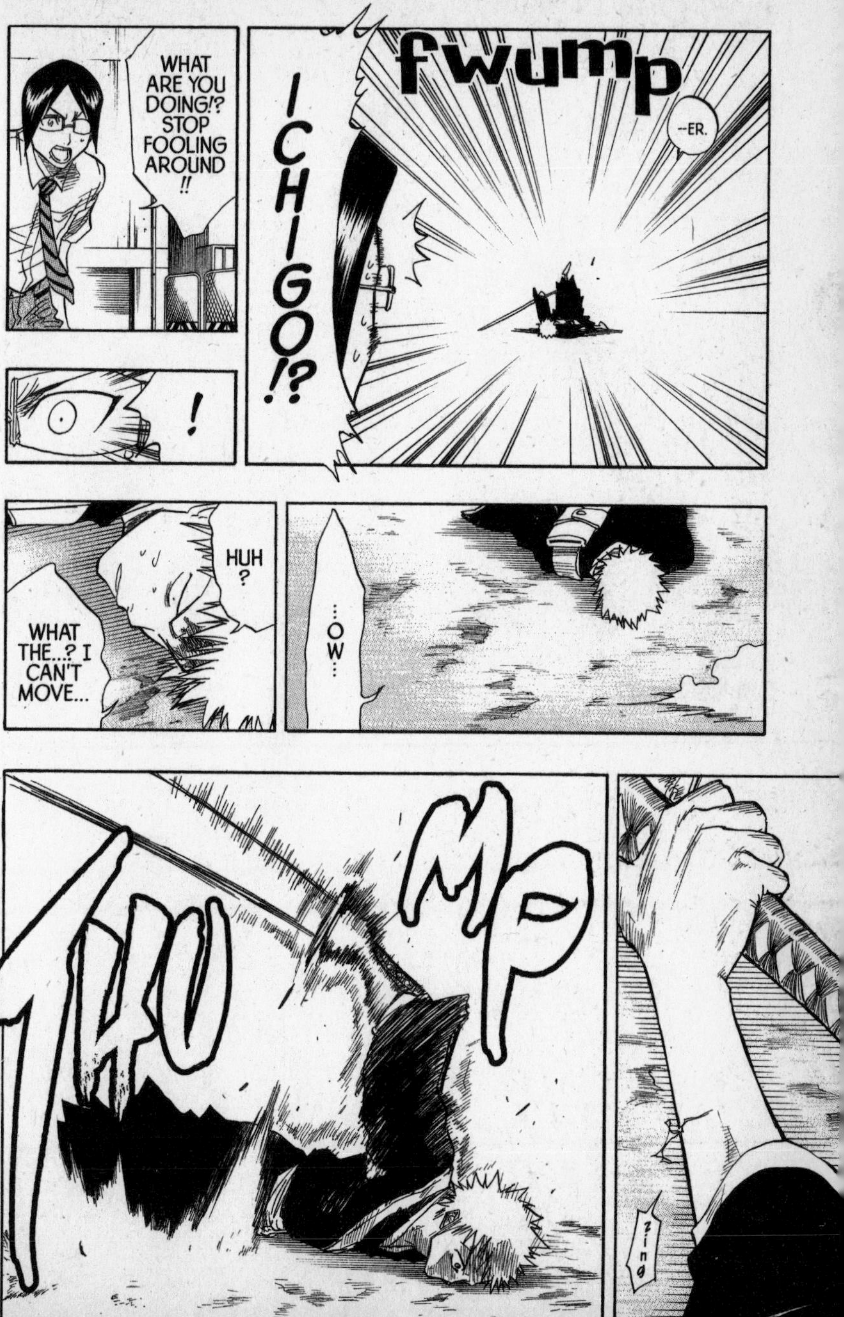
fwump
--ER.
ICHIGO!?
WHAT ARE YOU DOING!? STOP FOOLING AROUND!!
!
...OW...
HUH?
WHAT THE...? I CAN'T MOVE...
zing
THUMP

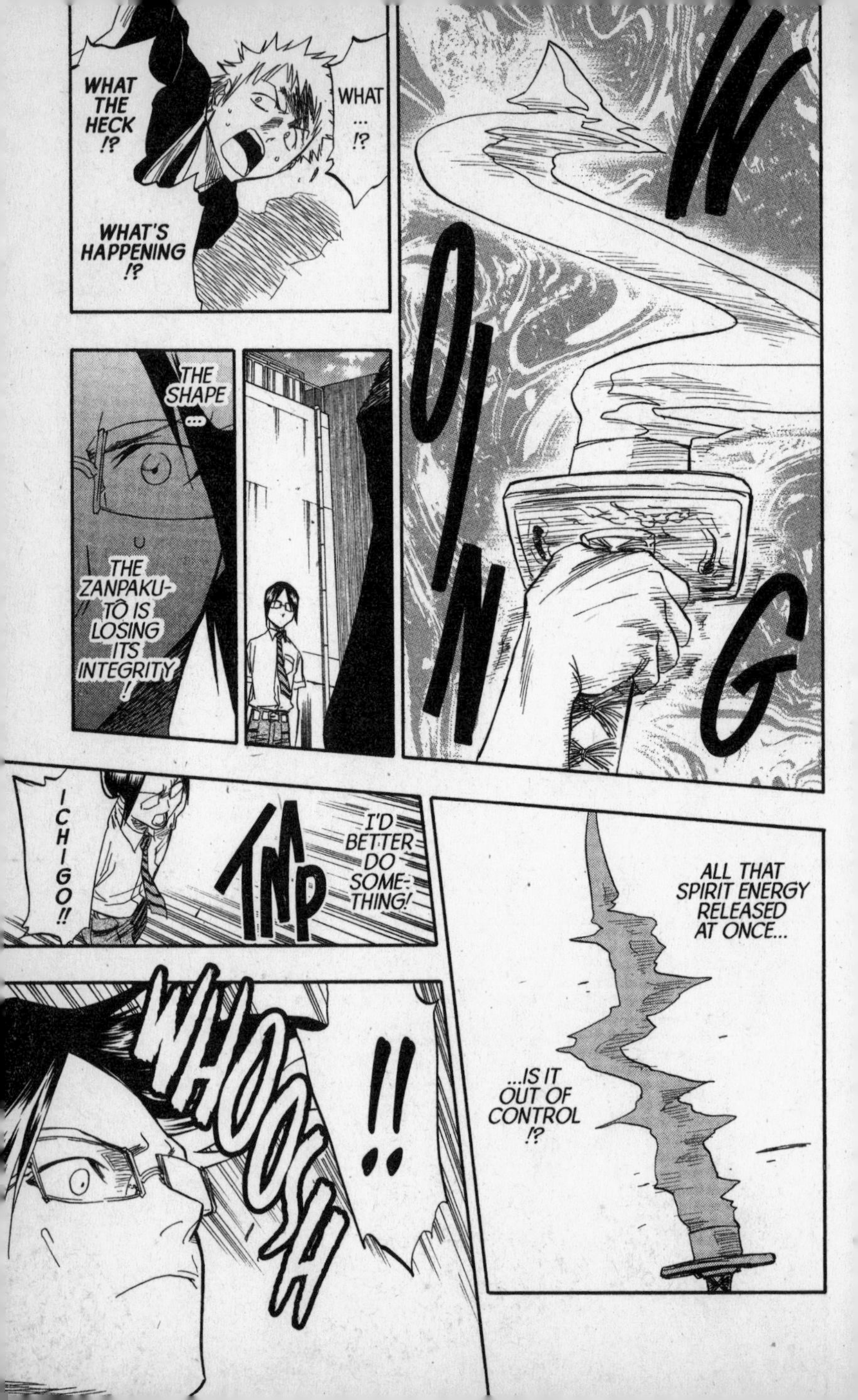
WOING
WHAT ...!?
WHAT THE HECK!?
WHAT'S HAPPENING!?
THE SHAPE...
THE ZANPAKU-TÔ IS LOSING ITS INTEGRITY!
ALL THAT SPIRIT ENERGY RELEASED AT ONCE...
...IS IT OUT OF CONTROL!?
I'D BETTER DO SOME-THING!
TMP
ICHIGO!!
WHOOSH!!

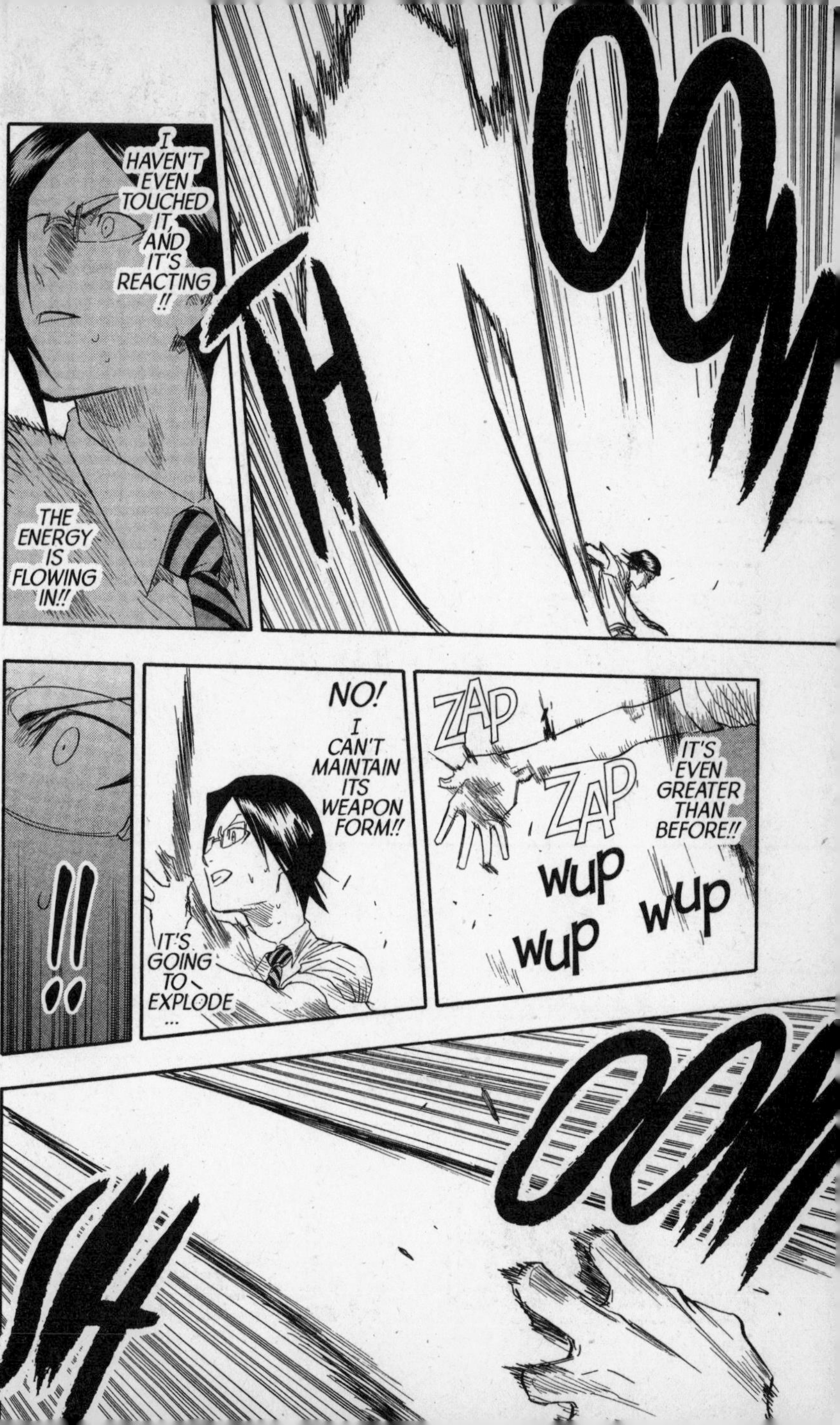
THOOM
I HAVEN'T EVEN TOUCHED IT, AND IT'S REACTING!!
THE ENERGY IS FLOWING IN!!
ZAP
ZAP
IT'S EVEN GREATER THAN BEFORE!!
wup
wup
wup
NO! I CAN'T MAINTAIN ITS WEAPON FORM!!
IT'S GOING TO EXPLODE...
!!

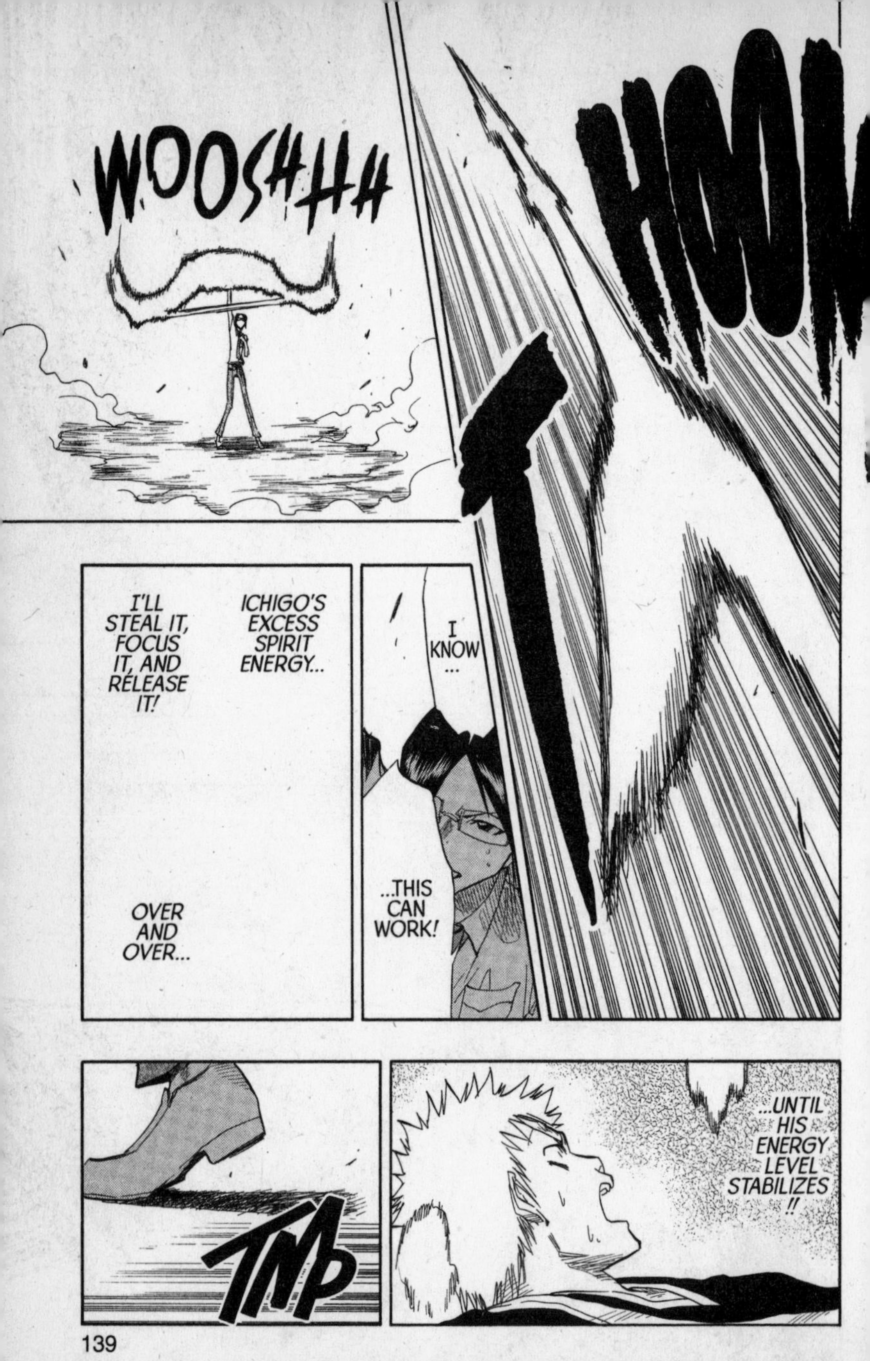
HOOM
WOOSHHH
I KNOW...
...THIS CAN WORK!
ICHIGO'S EXCESS SPIRIT ENERGY...
I'LL STEAL IT, FOCUS IT, AND RELEASE IT!
OVER AND OVER...
...UNTIL HIS ENERGY LEVEL STABILIZES!!
TMP

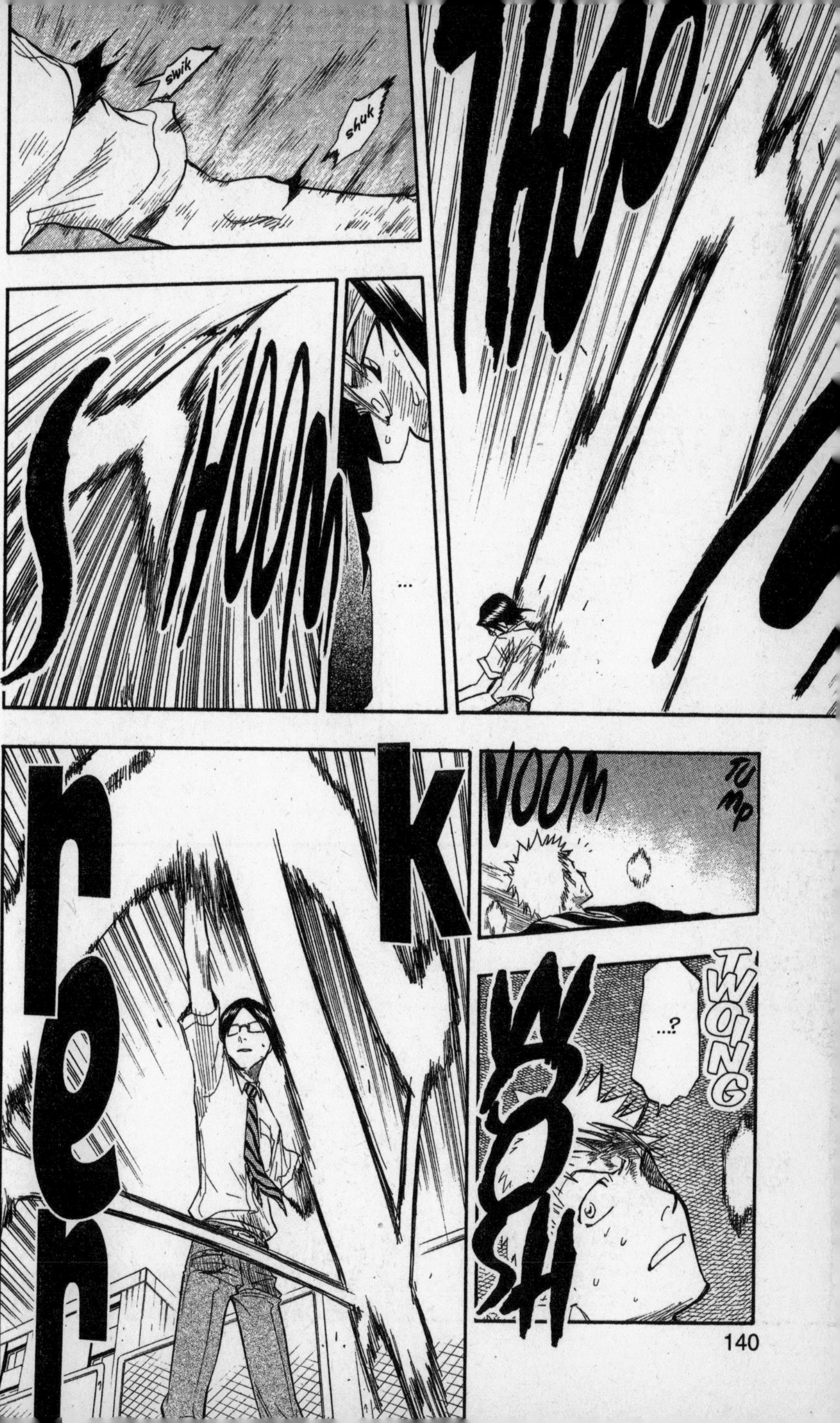
swik
shuk
...
SHUOOM
VOOM
TUMP
TWOING
...?

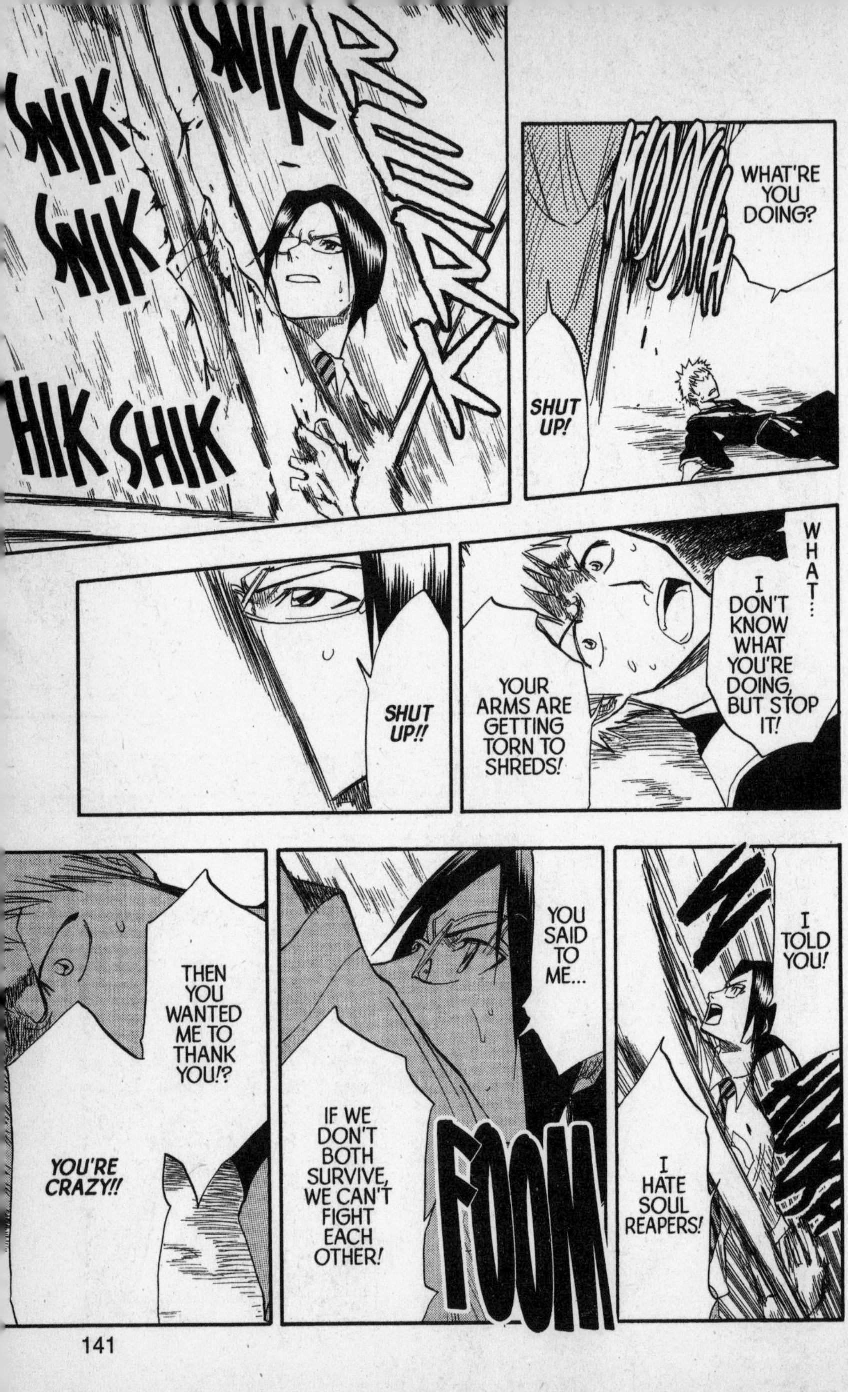
WHAT'RE YOU DOING?
SHUT UP!
SNIK
SNIK
SNIK
HIK SHIK
WHAT...
I DON'T KNOW WHAT YOU'RE DOING, BUT STOP IT!
YOUR ARMS ARE GETTING TORN TO SHREDS!
SHUT UP!!
I TOLD YOU!
I HATE SOUL REAPERS!
YOU SAID TO ME...
IF WE DON'T BOTH SURVIVE, WE CAN'T FIGHT EACH OTHER!
FOOM
THEN YOU WANTED ME TO THANK YOU!?
YOU'RE CRAZY!!

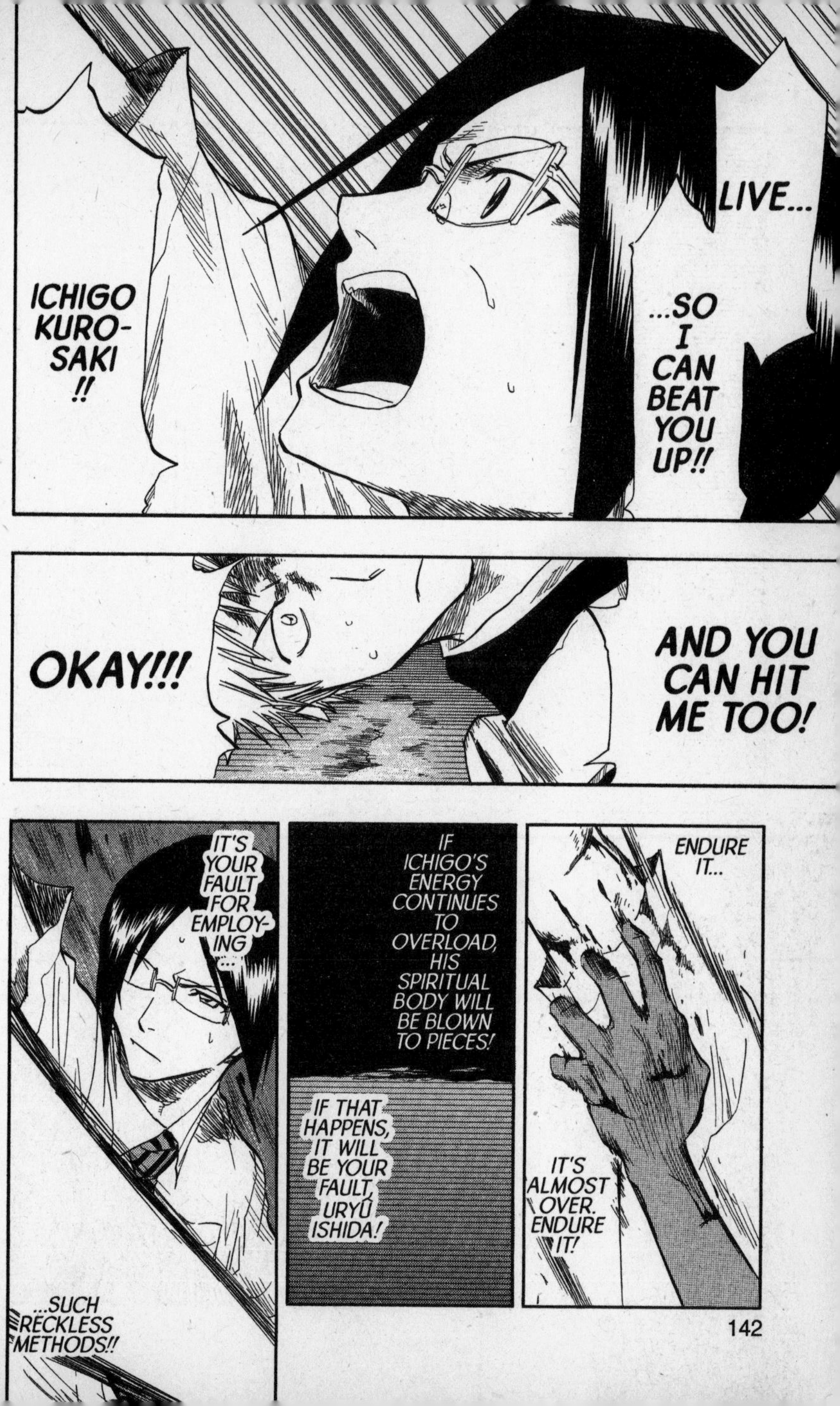

LIVE...
...SO I CAN BEAT YOU UP!!
ICHIGO KUROSAKI!!
AND YOU CAN HIT ME TOO!
OKAY!!!
ENDURE IT...
IT'S ALMOST OVER. ENDURE IT!
IF ICHIGO'S ENERGY CONTINUES TO OVERLOAD, HIS SPIRITUAL BODY WILL BE BLOWN TO PIECES!
IF THAT HAPPENS, IT WILL BE YOUR FAULT, URYŪ ISHIDA!
IT'S YOUR FAULT FOR EMPLOYING...
...SUCH RECKLESS METHODS!!

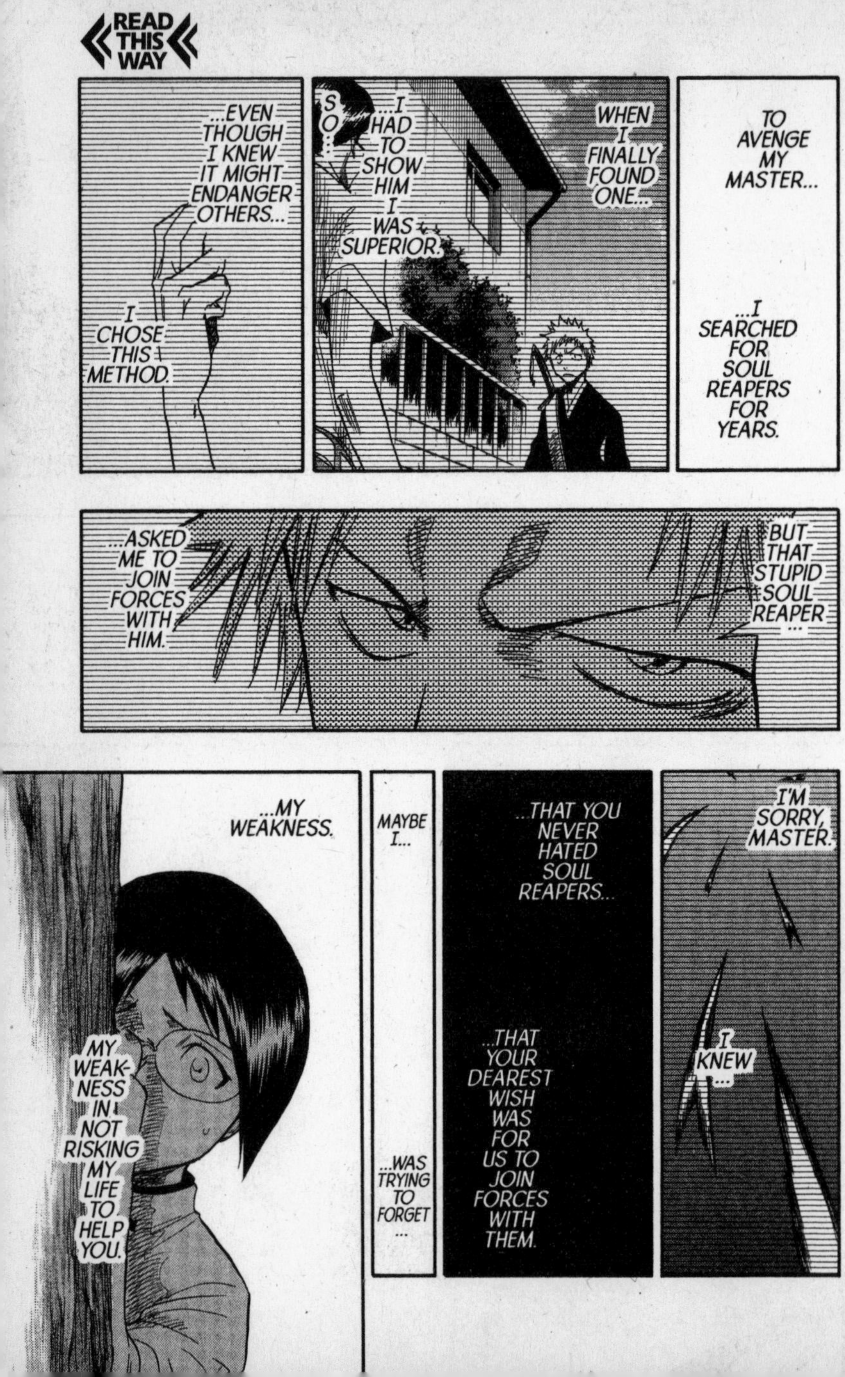
READ THIS WAY
TO AVENGE MY MASTER...
...I SEARCHED FOR SOUL REAPERS FOR YEARS.
WHEN I FINALLY FOUND ONE...
...I HAD TO SHOW HIM I WAS SUPERIOR.
SO...
...EVEN THOUGH I KNEW IT MIGHT ENDANGER OTHERS...
I CHOSE THIS METHOD.
BUT THAT STUPID SOUL REAPER...
...ASKED ME TO JOIN FORCES WITH HIM.
I'M SORRY, MASTER.
I KNEW...
...THAT YOU NEVER HATED SOUL REAPERS...
...THAT YOUR DEAREST WISH WAS FOR US TO JOIN FORCES WITH THEM.
MAYBE I...
...WAS TRYING TO FORGET...
...MY WEAKNESS.
MY WEAKNESS IN NOT RISKING MY LIFE TO HELP YOU.

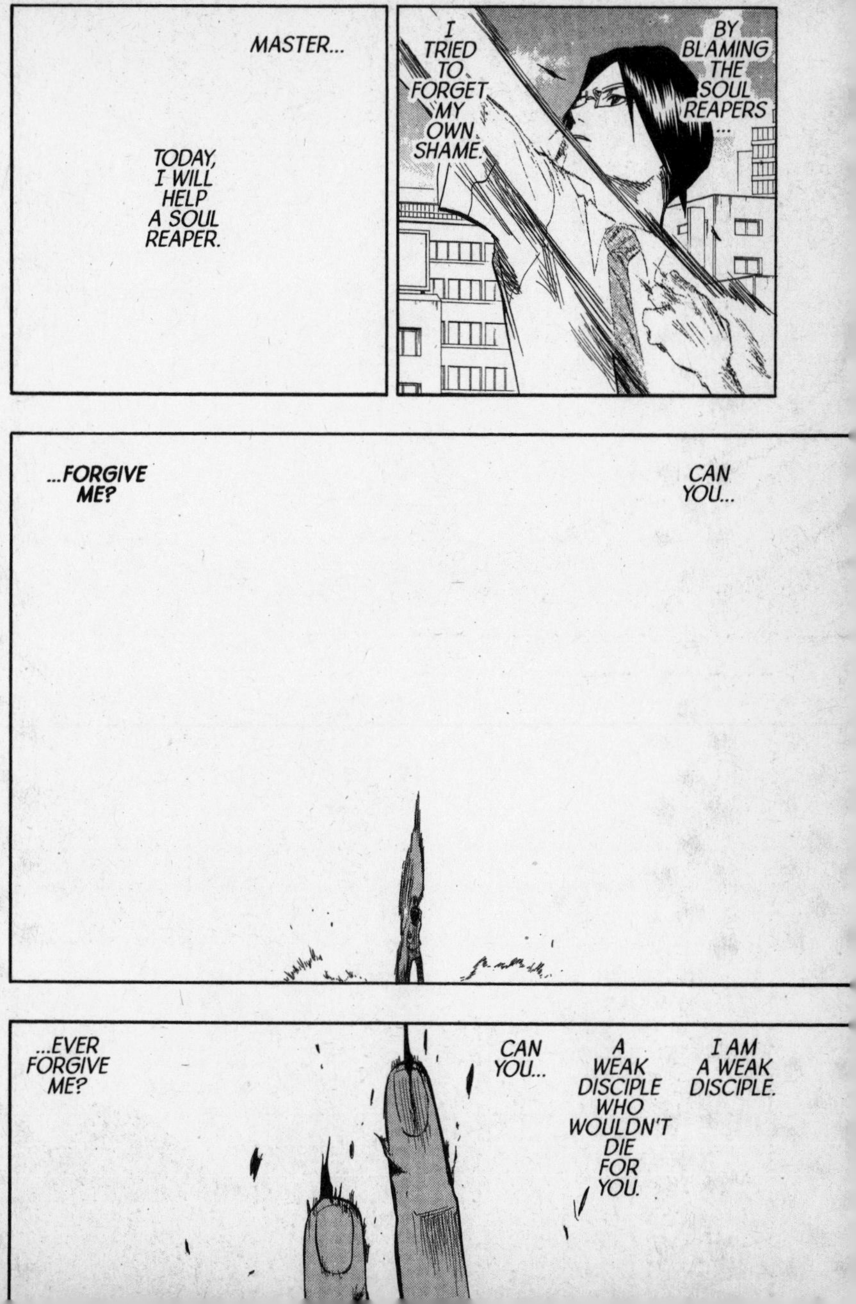
BY BLAMING THE SOUL REAPERS...
I TRIED TO FORGET MY OWN SHAME.
MASTER...
TODAY, I WILL HELP A SOUL REAPER.
CAN YOU...
...FORGIVE ME?
I AM A WEAK DISCIPLE.
A WEAK DISCIPLE WHO WOULDN'T DIE FOR YOU.
CAN YOU...
...EVER FORGIVE ME?

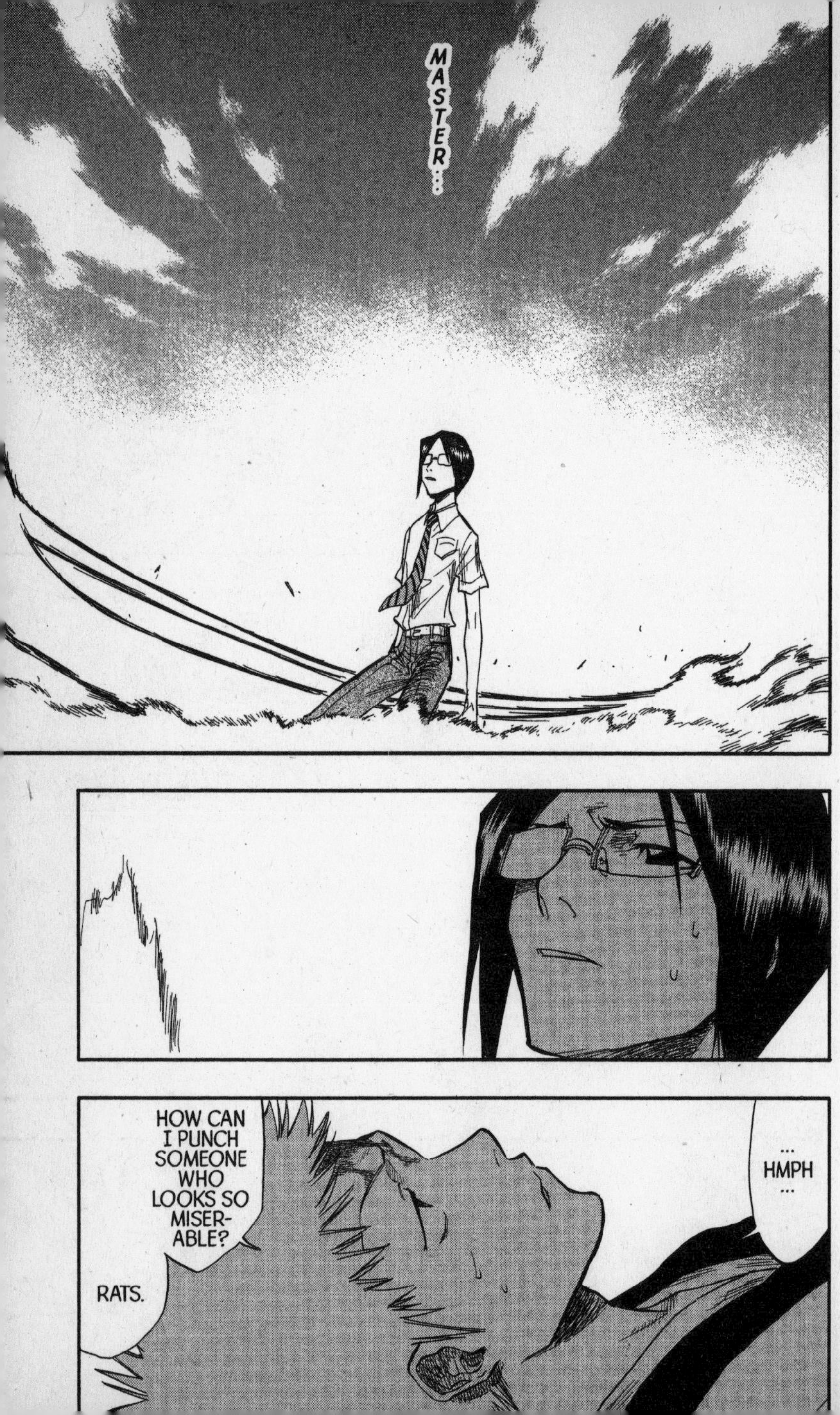
MASTER...
...HMPH...
HOW CAN I PUNCH SOMEONE WHO LOOKS SO MISERABLE?
RATS.

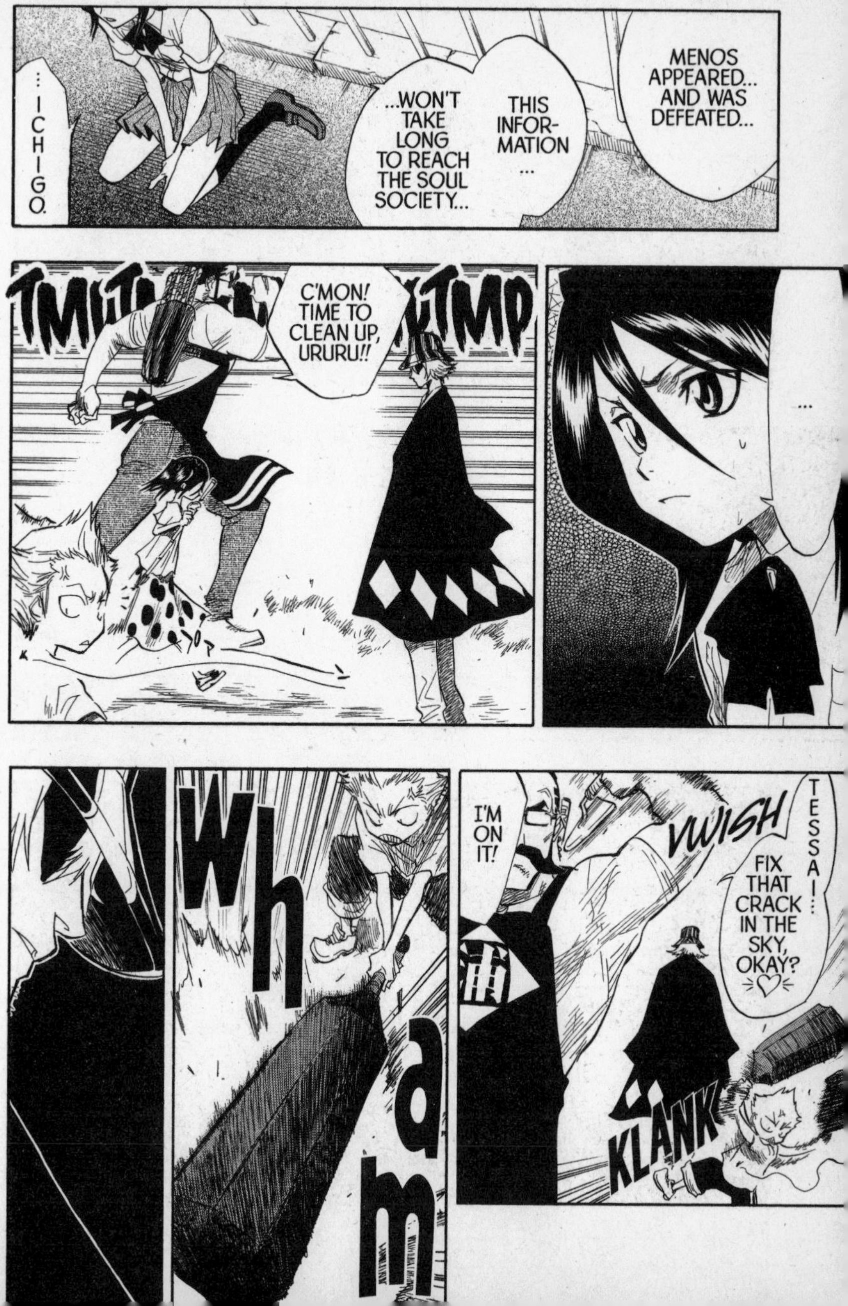
MENOS APPEARED... AND WAS DEFEATED...
THIS INFORMATION ...
...WON'T TAKE LONG TO REACH THE SOUL SOCIETY...
...ICHIGO.
...
C'MON! TIME TO CLEAN UP, URURU!!
TMP
TMP
TESSAI...
FIX THAT CRACK IN THE SKY, OKAY? ♡
VWISH
I'M ON IT!
KLANK
Wham

READ THIS WAY

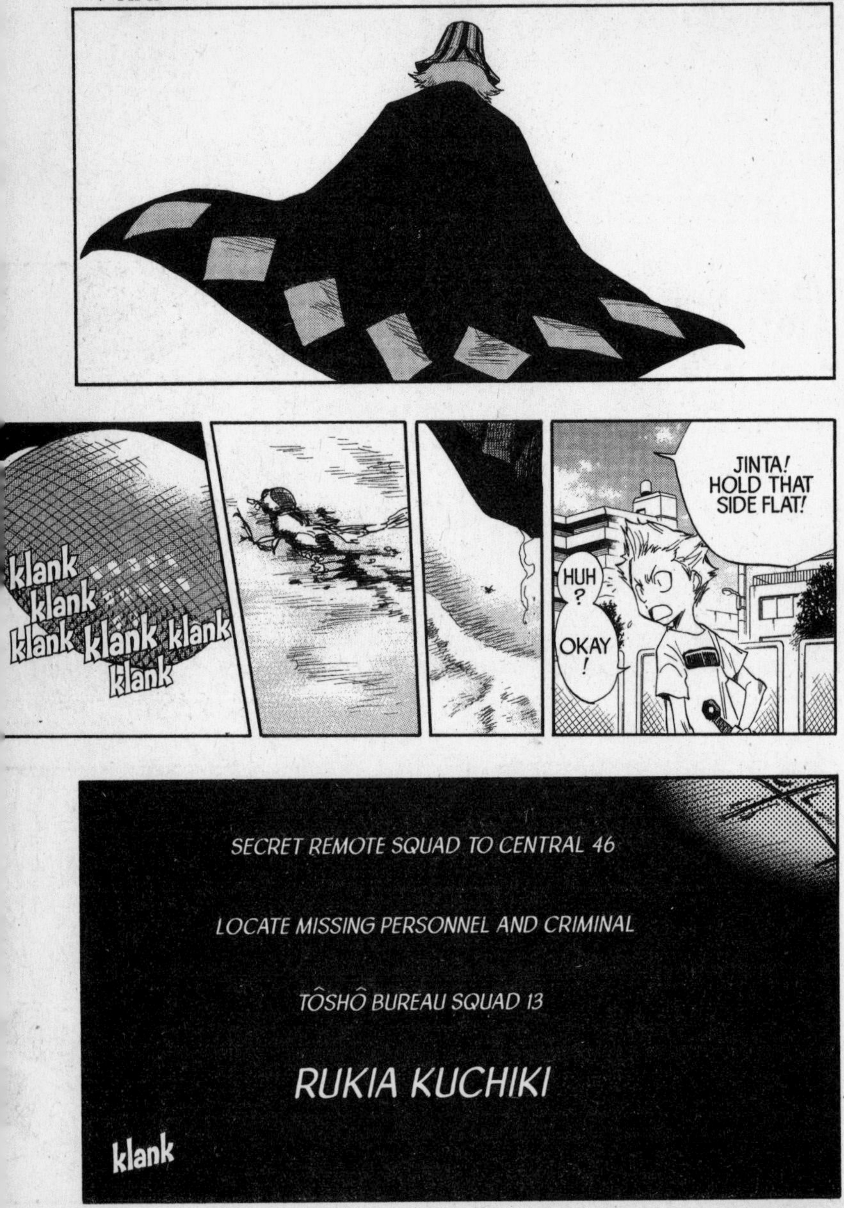
JINTA! HOLD THAT SIDE FLAT!
HUH?
OKAY!
klank klank klank klank klank klank
SECRET REMOTE SQUAD TO CENTRAL 46
LOCATE MISSING PERSONNEL AND CRIMINAL
TÔSHÔ BUREAU SQUAD 13
RUKIA KUCHIKI
klank

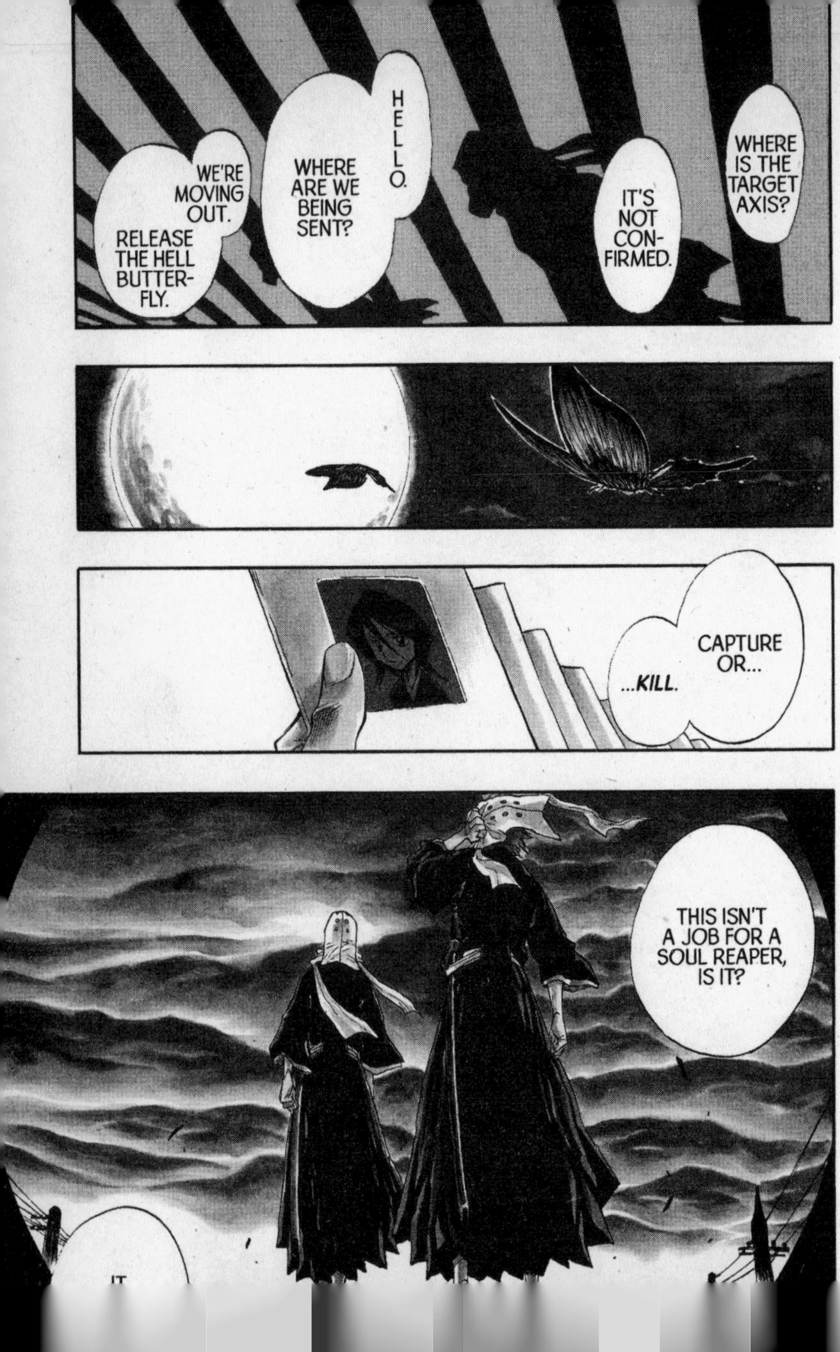
WHERE IS THE TARGET AXIS?
IT'S NOT CONFIRMED.
HELLO.
WHERE ARE WE BEING SENT?
WE'RE MOVING OUT. RELEASE THE HELL BUTTERFLY.
CAPTURE OR... ...KILL.
THIS ISN'T A JOB FOR A SOUL REAPER, IS IT?
IT

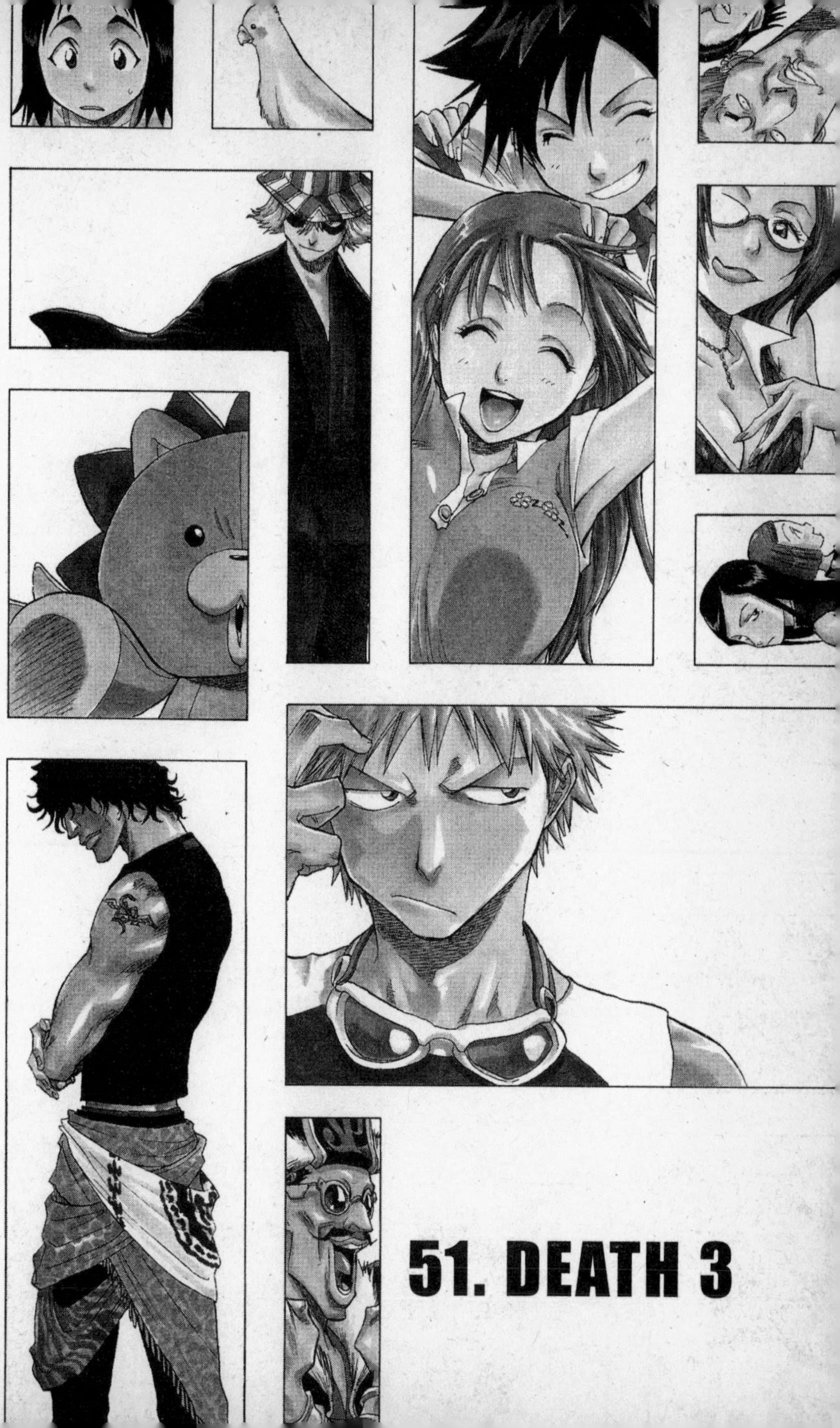

51. DEATH 3

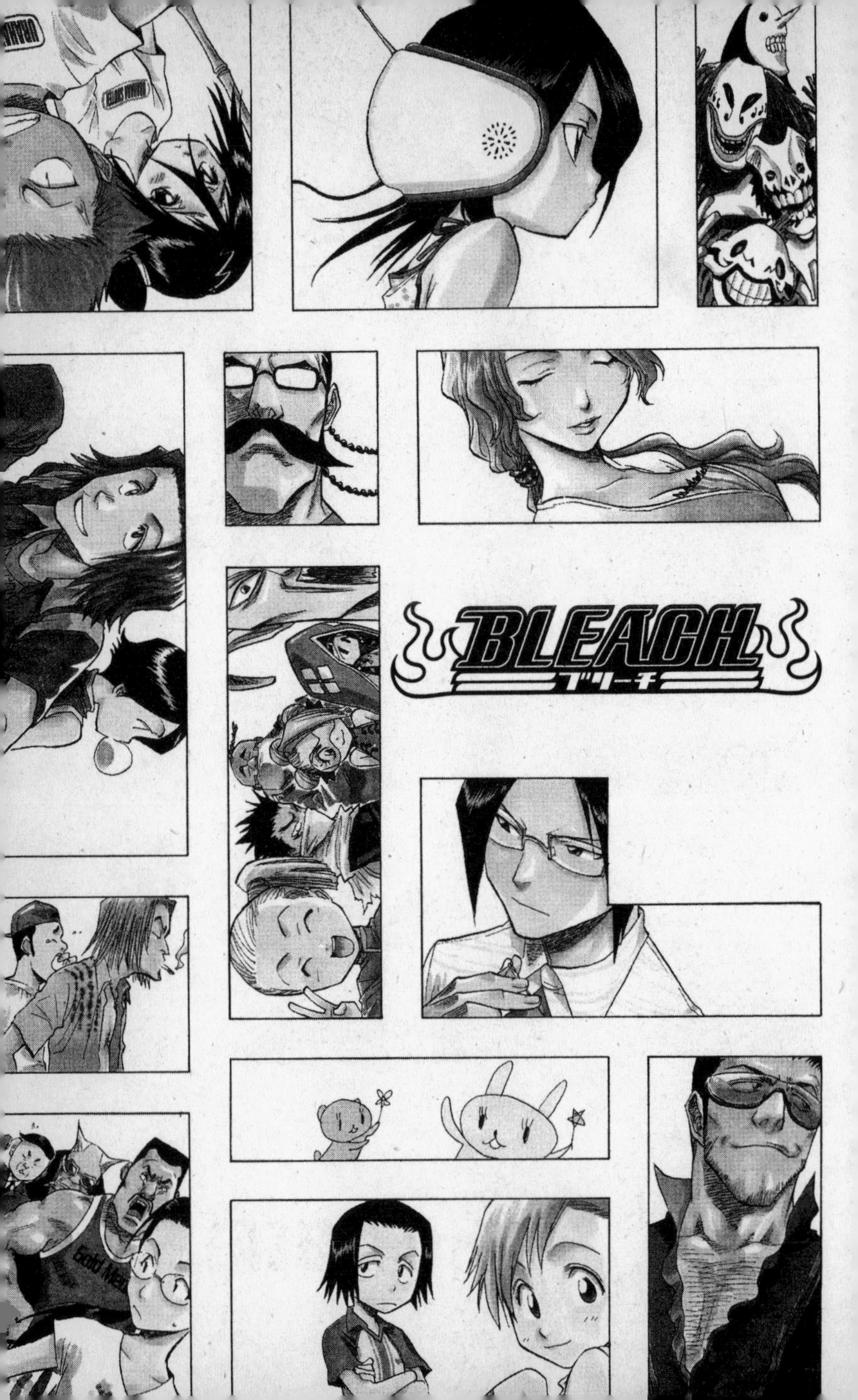
BLEACH
ブリーチ

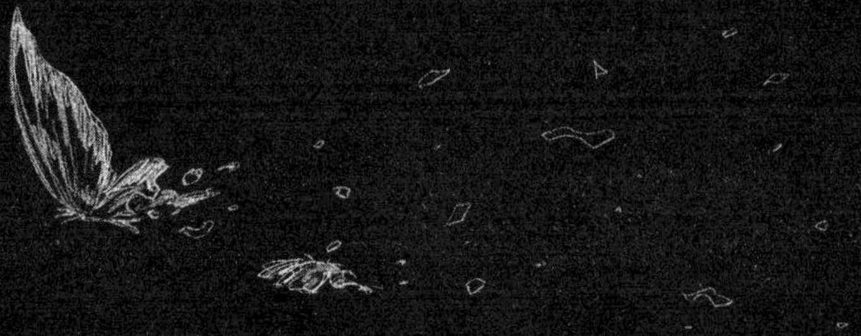

BLEACH
ブリーチ

READ THIS WAY

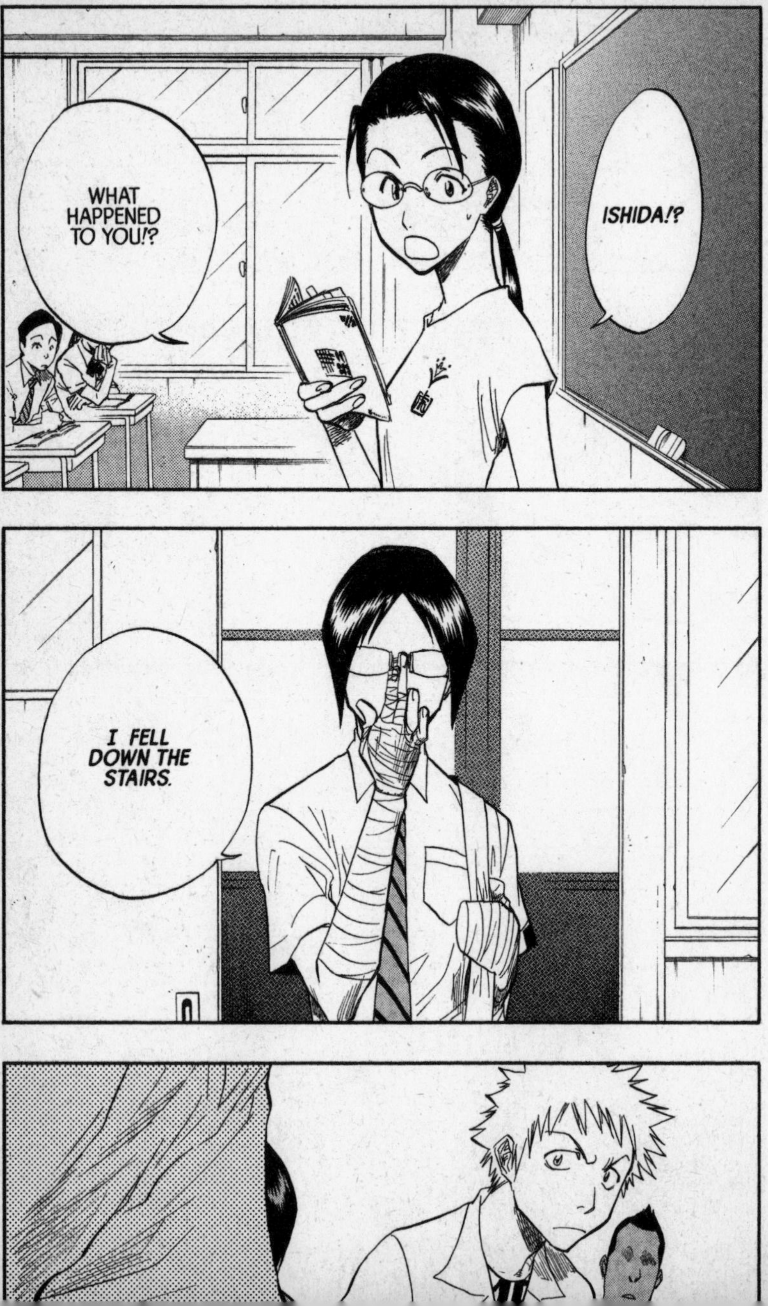
ISHIDA!?
WHAT HAPPENED TO YOU!?
I FELL DOWN THE STAIRS.

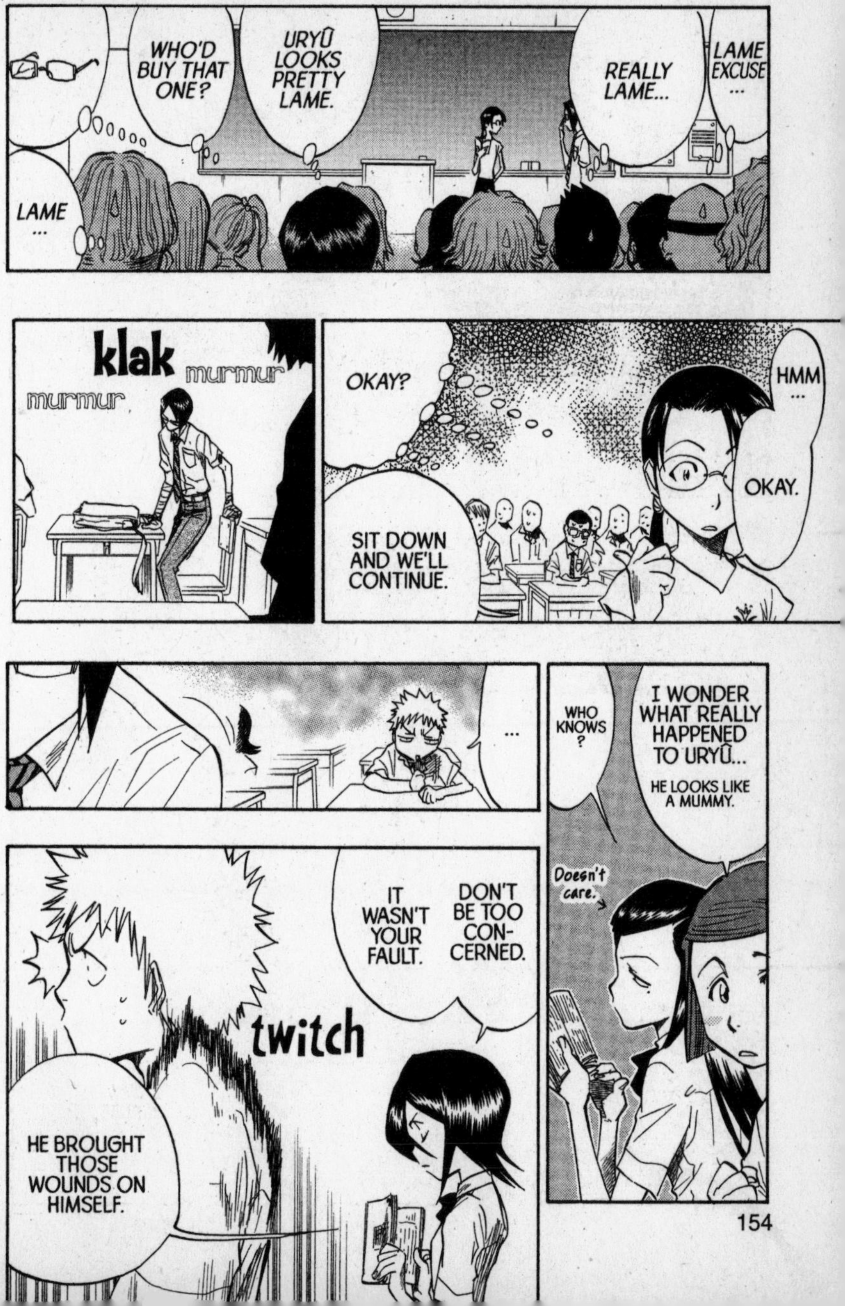

LAME EXCUSE...
REALLY LAME...
URYŪ LOOKS PRETTY LAME.
WHO'D BUY THAT ONE?
LAME...
HMM...
OKAY.
OKAY?
SIT DOWN AND WE'LL CONTINUE.
klak
murmur
murmur
I WONDER WHAT REALLY HAPPENED TO URYŪ...
HE LOOKS LIKE A MUMMY.
WHO KNOWS?
Doesn't care.
...
DON'T BE TOO CON-CERNED.
IT WASN'T YOUR FAULT.
twitch
HE BROUGHT THOSE WOUNDS ON HIMSELF.

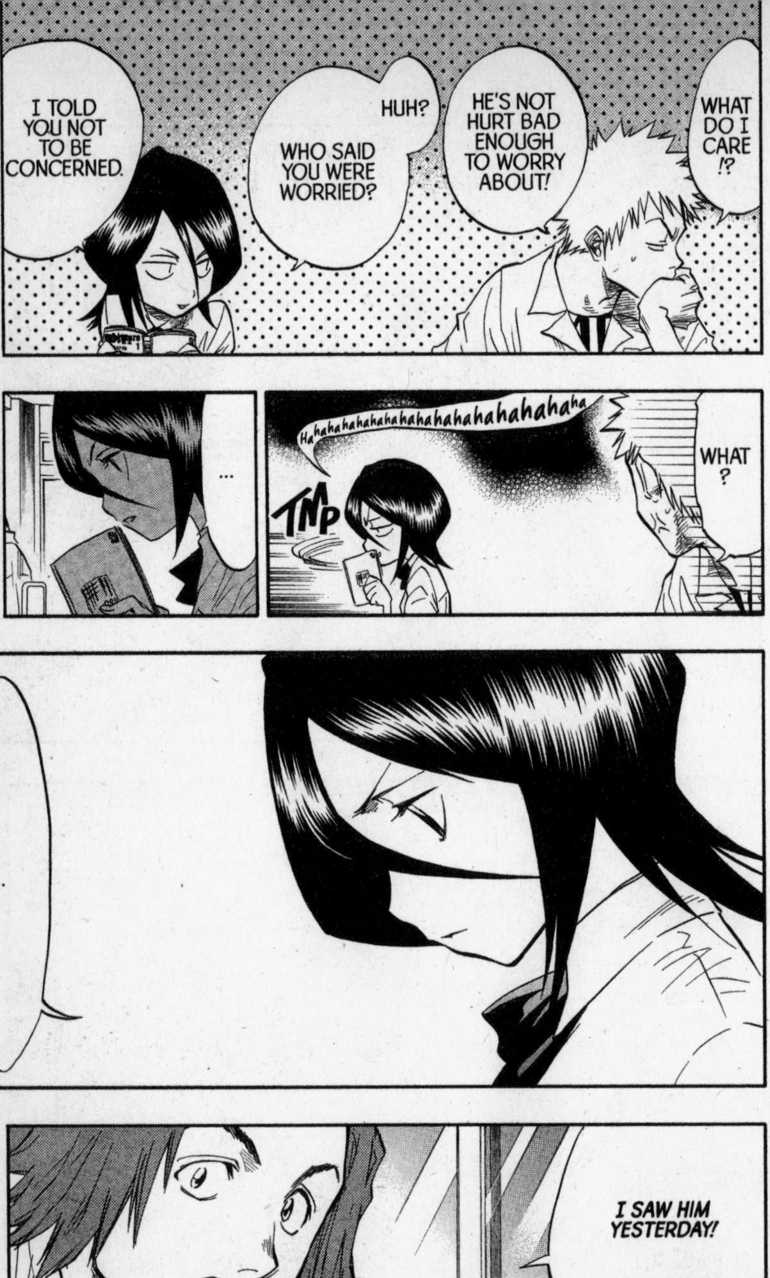
WHAT DO I CARE!?
HE'S NOT HURT BAD ENOUGH TO WORRY ABOUT!
HUH?
WHO SAID YOU WERE WORRIED?
I TOLD YOU NOT TO BE CONCERNED.
WHAT?
Hahahahahahahahahahahahahahahahahaha
TNP
...
...
I SAW HIM YESTERDAY!

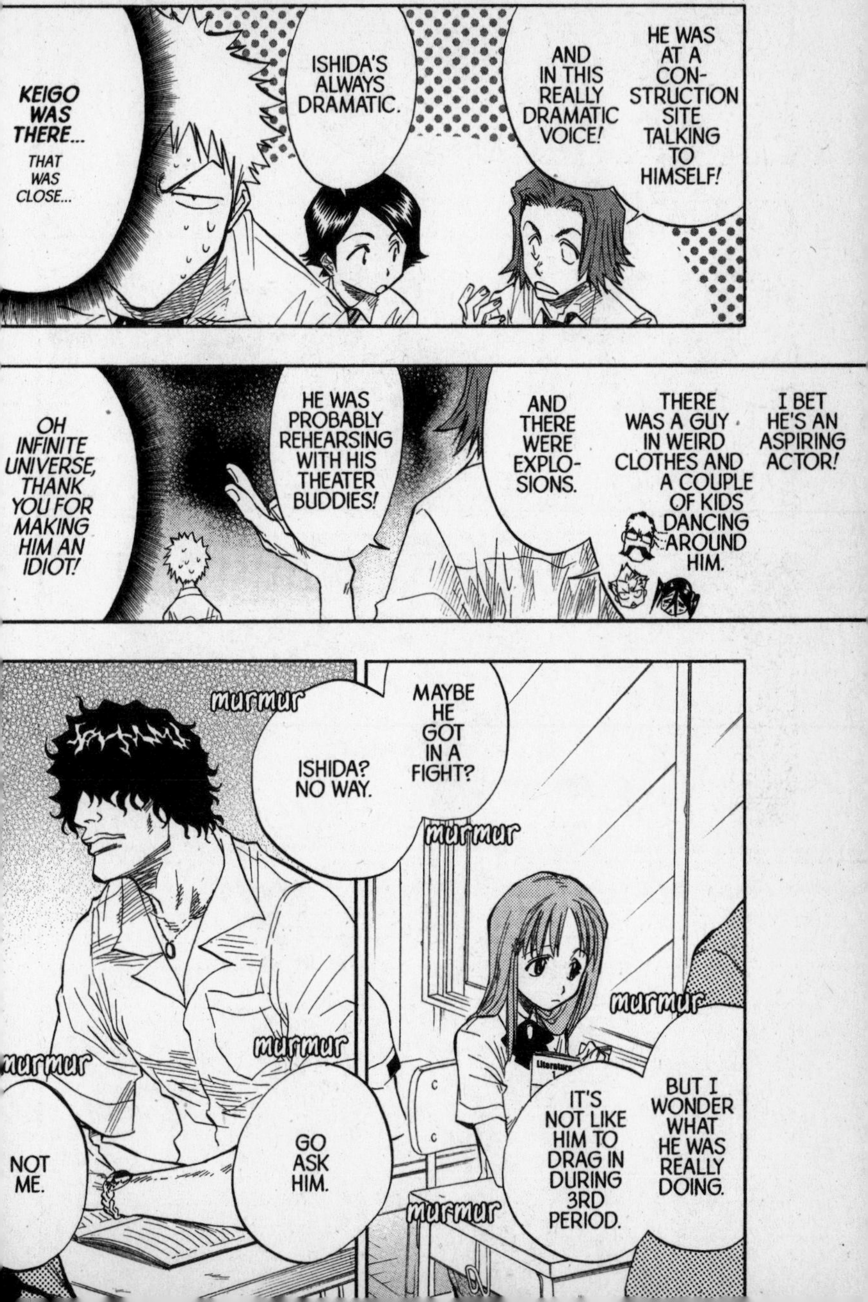
HE WAS AT A CON-STRUCTION SITE TALKING TO HIMSELF!
AND IN THIS REALLY DRAMATIC VOICE!
ISHIDA'S ALWAYS DRAMATIC.
KEIGO WAS THERE...
THAT WAS CLOSE...
I BET HE'S AN ASPIRING ACTOR!
THERE WAS A GUY IN WEIRD CLOTHES AND A COUPLE OF KIDS DANCING AROUND HIM.
AND THERE WERE EXPLO-SIONS.
HE WAS PROBABLY REHEARSING WITH HIS THEATER BUDDIES!
OH INFINITE UNIVERSE, THANK YOU FOR MAKING HIM AN IDIOT!
MAYBE HE GOT IN A FIGHT?
ISHIDA? NO WAY.
murmur
murmur
murmur
BUT I WONDER WHAT HE WAS REALLY DOING.
IT'S NOT LIKE HIM TO DRAG IN DURING 3RD PERIOD.
murmur
murmur
GO ASK HIM.
murmur
NOT ME.

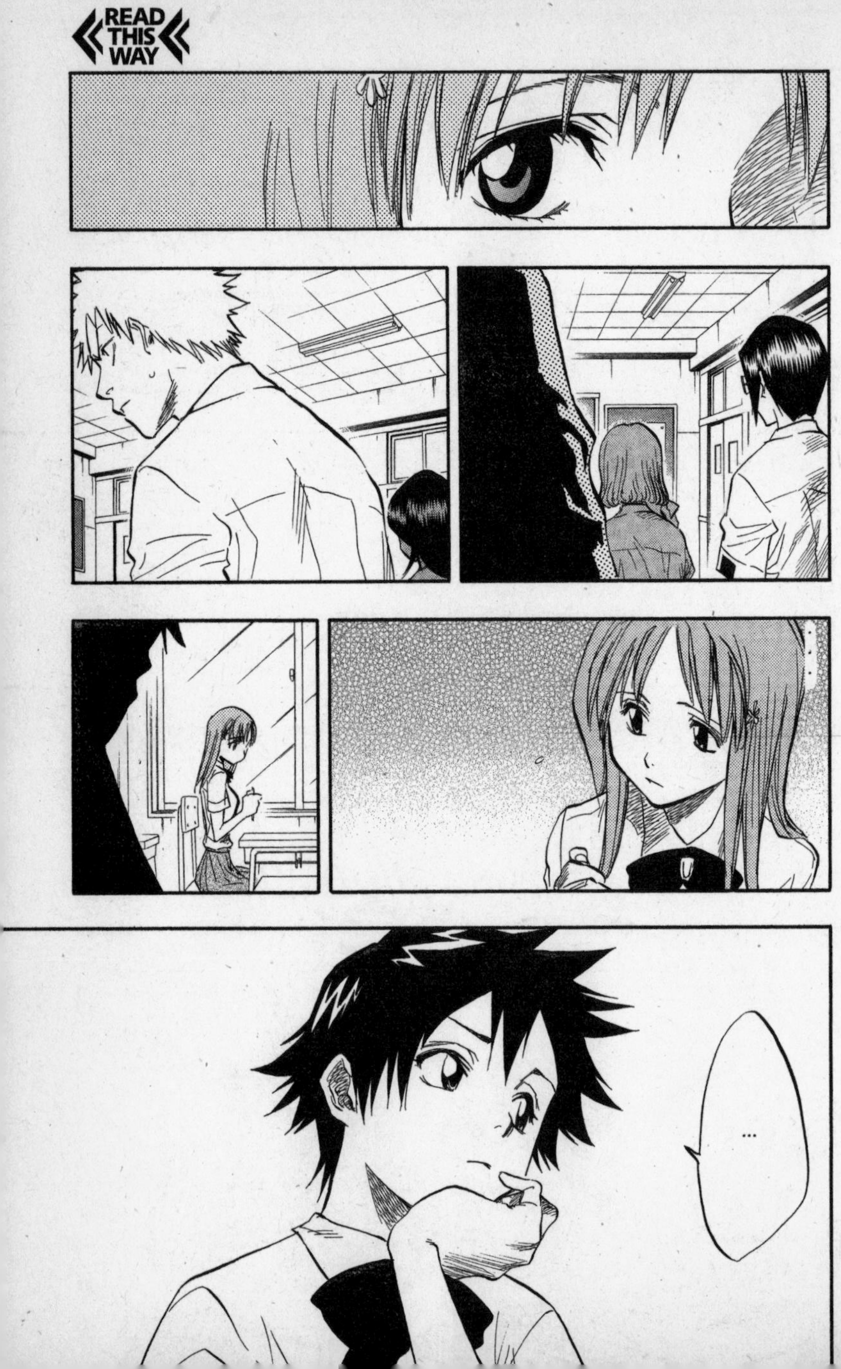
READ THIS WAY
...

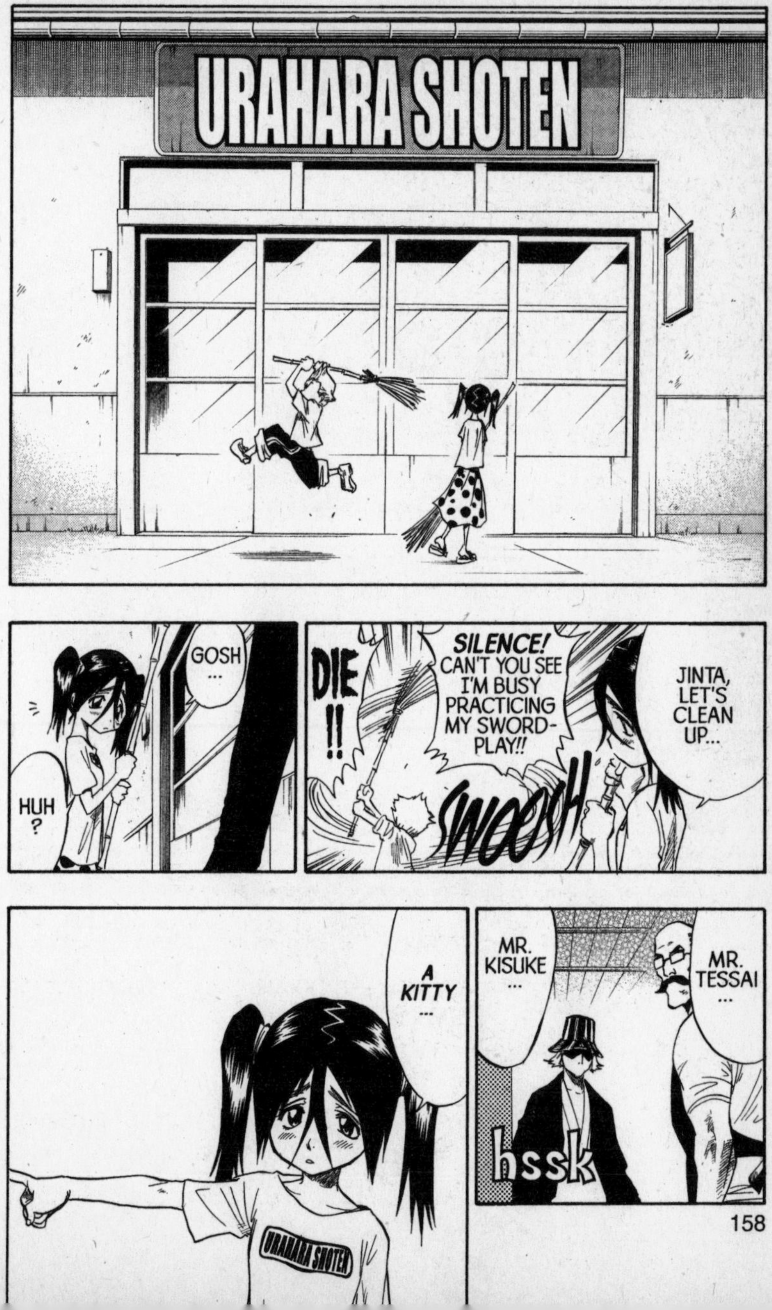
URAHARA SHOTEN
JINTA, LET'S CLEAN UP...
SILENCE! CAN'T YOU SEE I'M BUSY PRACTICING MY SWORD-PLAY!!
DIE!!
SWOOSH
GOSH...
HUH?
MR. TESSAI...
MR. KISUKE...
hssk
A KITTY...
URAHARA SHOTEN

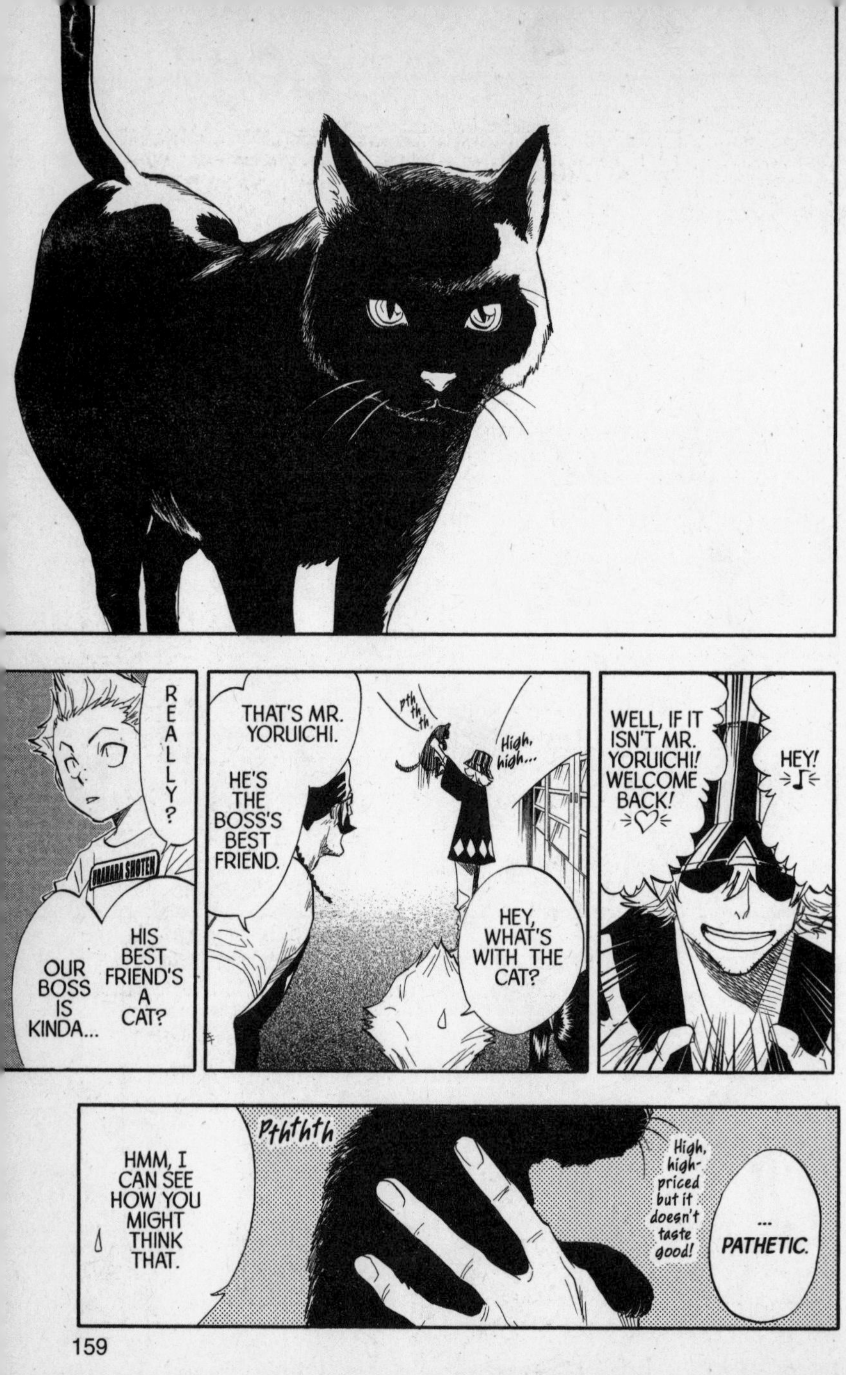
HEY!
WELL, IF IT ISN'T MR. YORUICHI! WELCOME BACK!
High, high...
pth th th
HEY, WHAT'S WITH THE CAT?
THAT'S MR. YORUICHI.
HE'S THE BOSS'S BEST FRIEND.
REALLY?
URAHARA SHOTEN
HIS BEST FRIEND'S A CAT?
OUR BOSS IS KINDA...
...PATHETIC.
High, high-priced but it doesn't taste good!
Pththth
HMM, I CAN SEE HOW YOU MIGHT THINK THAT.

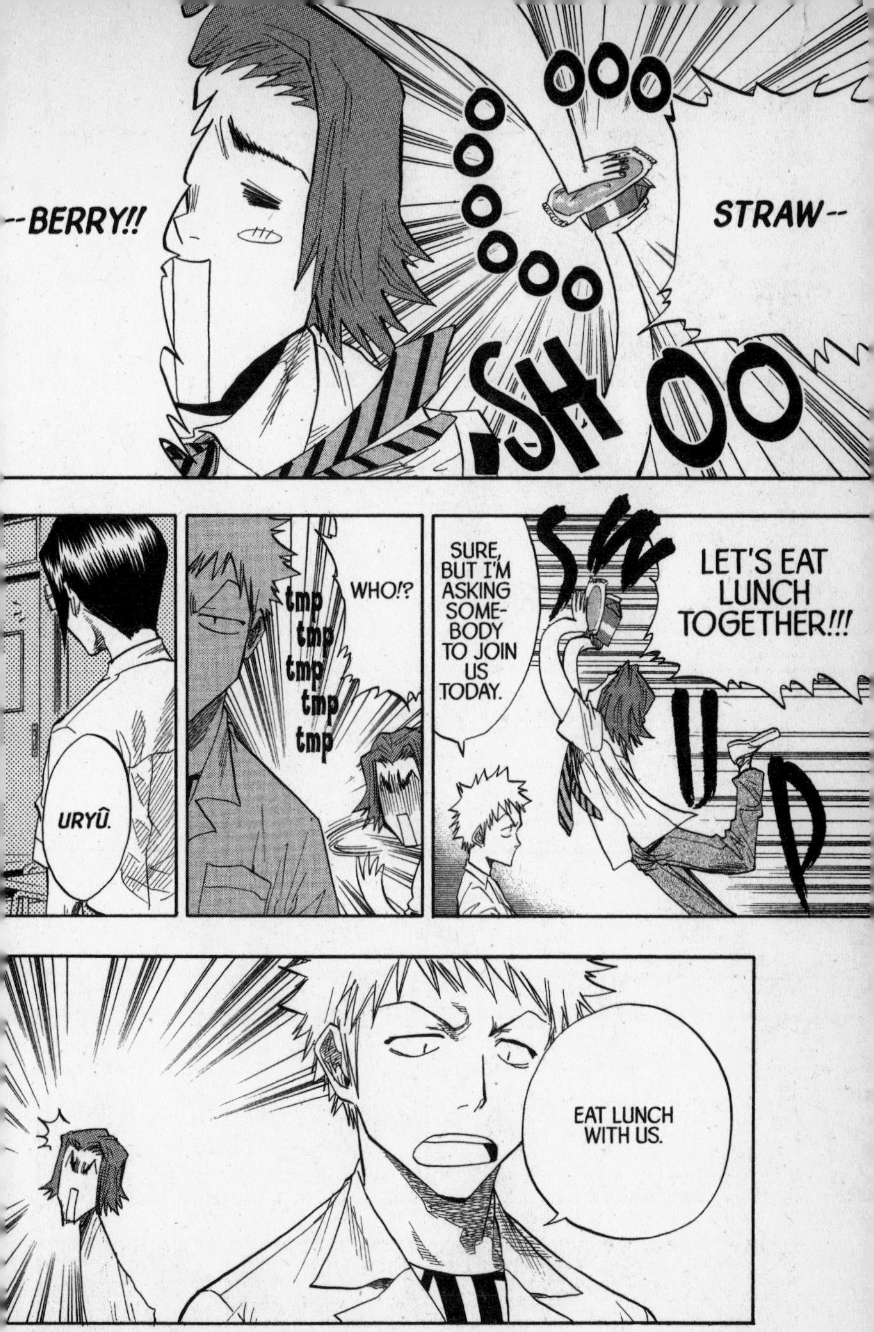
STRAW--
OOOOOOOOOO
SHOO
--BERRY!!
SWUP
LET'S EAT LUNCH TOGETHER!!!
SURE, BUT I'M ASKING SOME-BODY TO JOIN US TODAY.
WHO!?
tmp tmp tmp tmp tmp
URYÛ.
EAT LUNCH WITH US.

READ THIS WAY

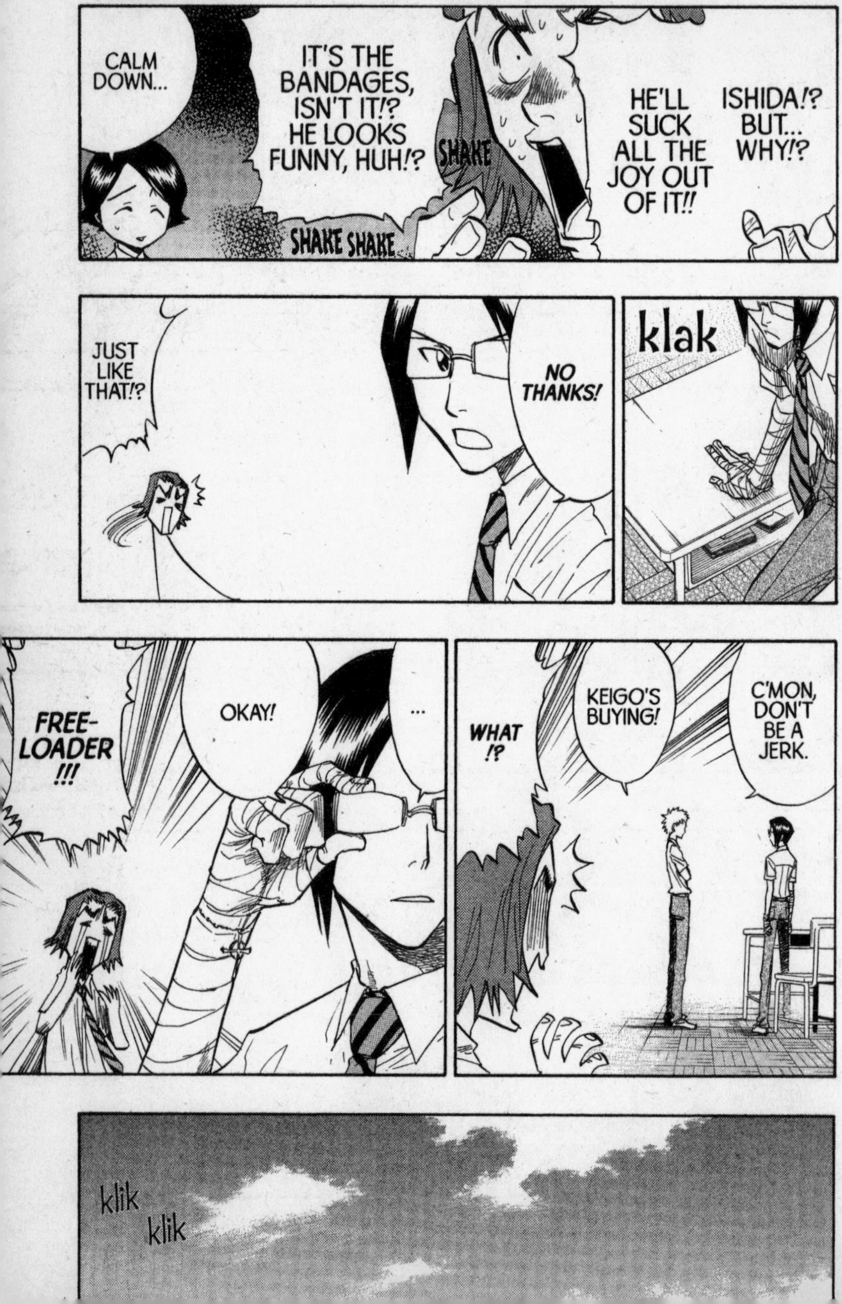
ISHIDA!? BUT... WHY!?
HE'LL SUCK ALL THE JOY OUT OF IT!!
SHAKE
IT'S THE BANDAGES, ISN'T IT!? HE LOOKS FUNNY, HUH!?
SHAKE SHAKE
CALM DOWN...
klak
NO THANKS!
JUST LIKE THAT!?
C'MON, DON'T BE A JERK.
KEIGO'S BUYING!
WHAT!?
...
OKAY!
FREE-LOADER!!!
klik
klik

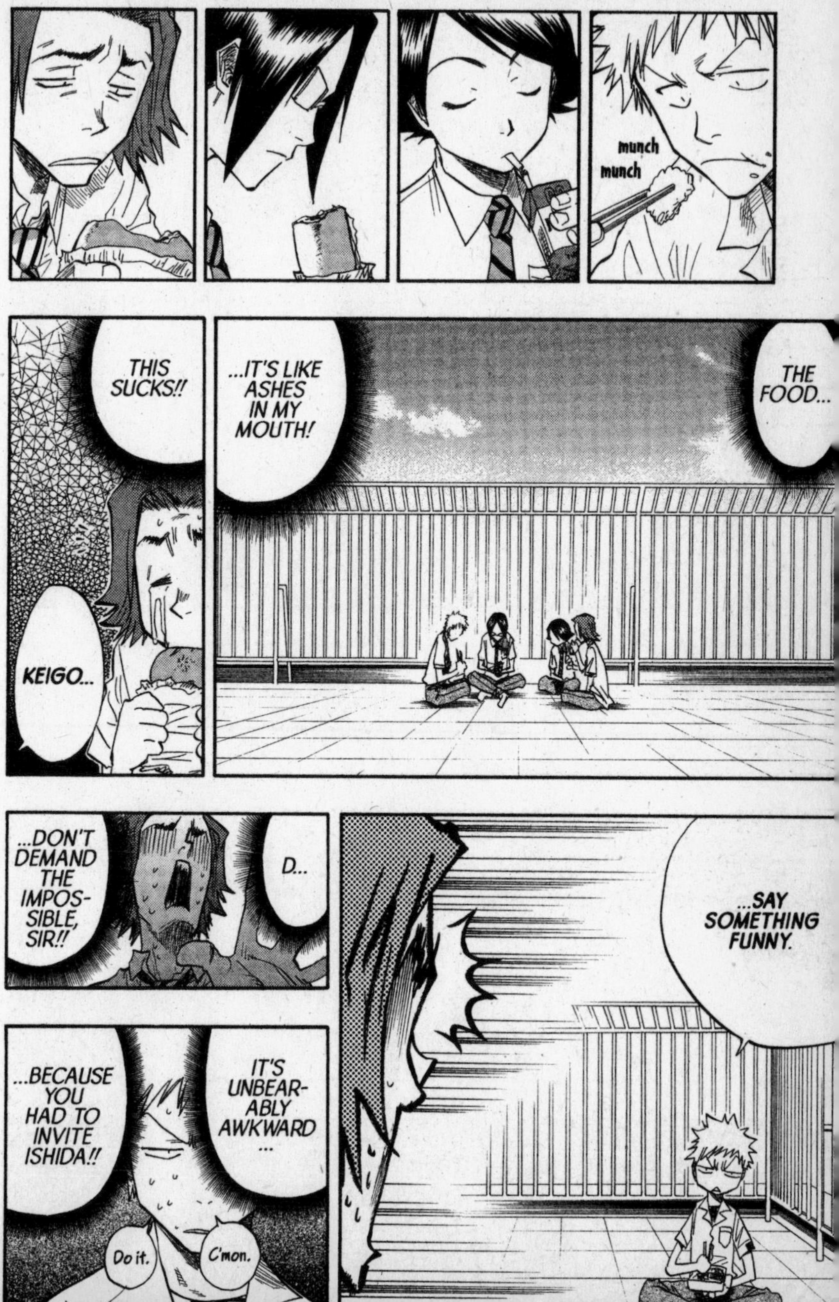
munch
munch
THE FOOD...
...IT'S LIKE ASHES IN MY MOUTH!
THIS SUCKS!!
KEIGO...
...SAY SOMETHING FUNNY.
D...
...DON'T DEMAND THE IMPOSSIBLE, SIR!!
IT'S UNBEARABLY AWKWARD...
...BECAUSE YOU HAD TO INVITE ISHIDA!!
C'mon.
Do it.

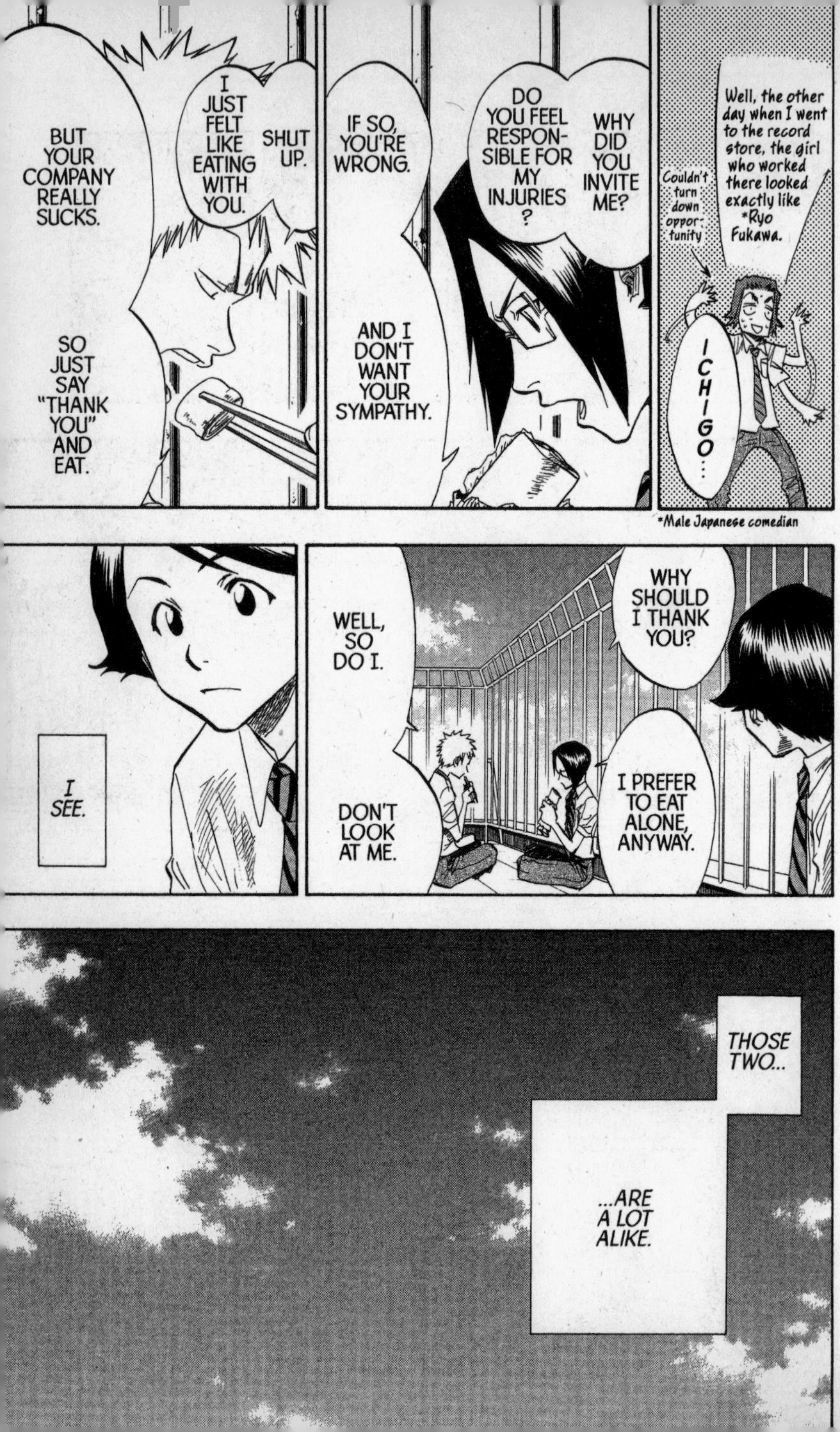
Well, the other day when I went to the record store, the girl who worked there looked exactly like *Ryo Fukawa.
Couldn't turn down oppor-tunity
ICHIGO...
WHY DID YOU INVITE ME?
DO YOU FEEL RESPON-SIBLE FOR MY INJURIES?
IF SO, YOU'RE WRONG.
AND I DON'T WANT YOUR SYMPATHY.
SHUT UP.
I JUST FELT LIKE EATING WITH YOU.
BUT YOUR COMPANY REALLY SUCKS.
SO JUST SAY "THANK YOU" AND EAT.
WHY SHOULD I THANK YOU?
I PREFER TO EAT ALONE, ANYWAY.
WELL, SO DO I.
DON'T LOOK AT ME.
I SEE.
THOSE TWO...
...ARE A LOT ALIKE.

*Male Japanese comedian

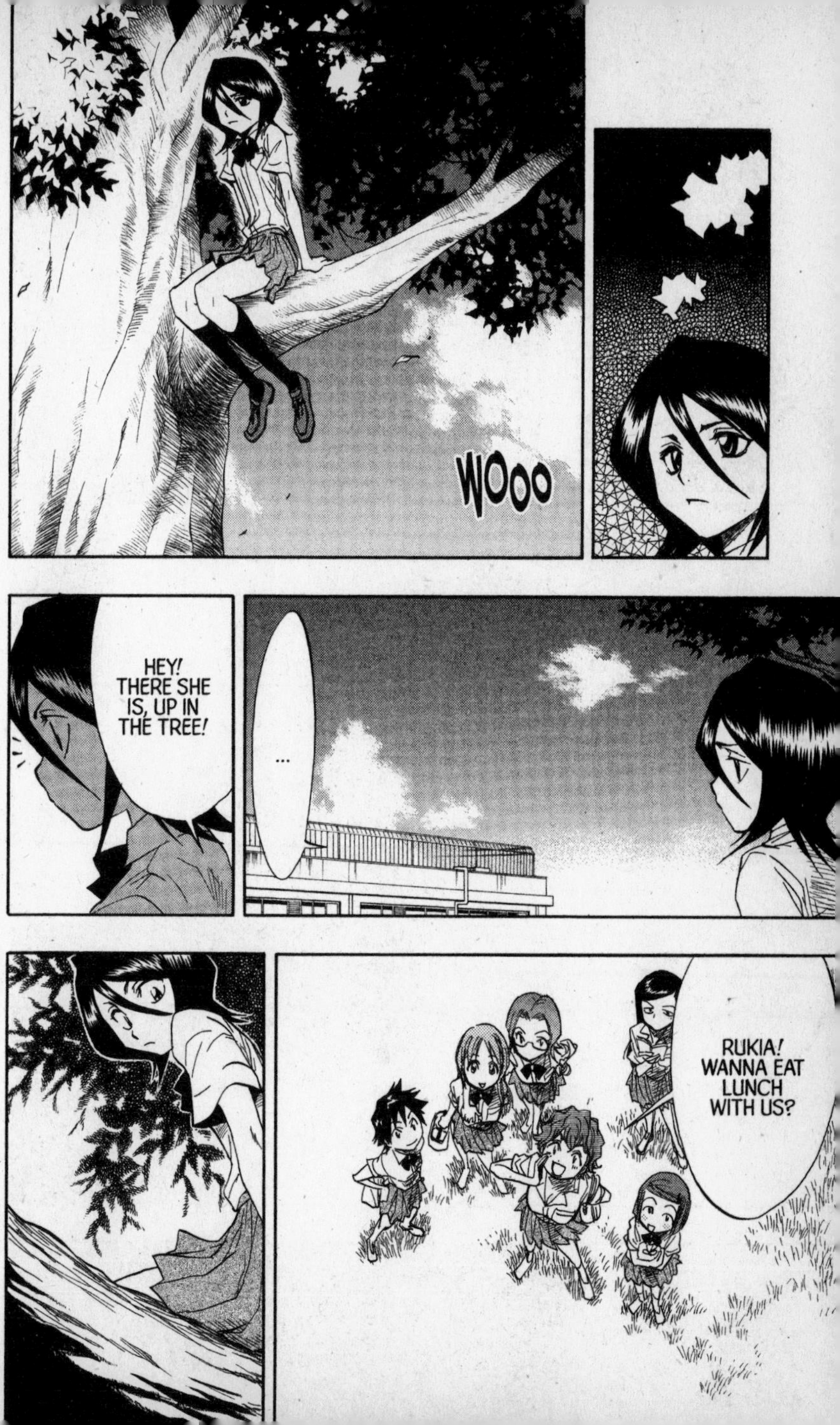
WOOO
...
HEY! THERE SHE IS, UP IN THE TREE!
RUKIA! WANNA EAT LUNCH WITH US?

READ THIS WAY

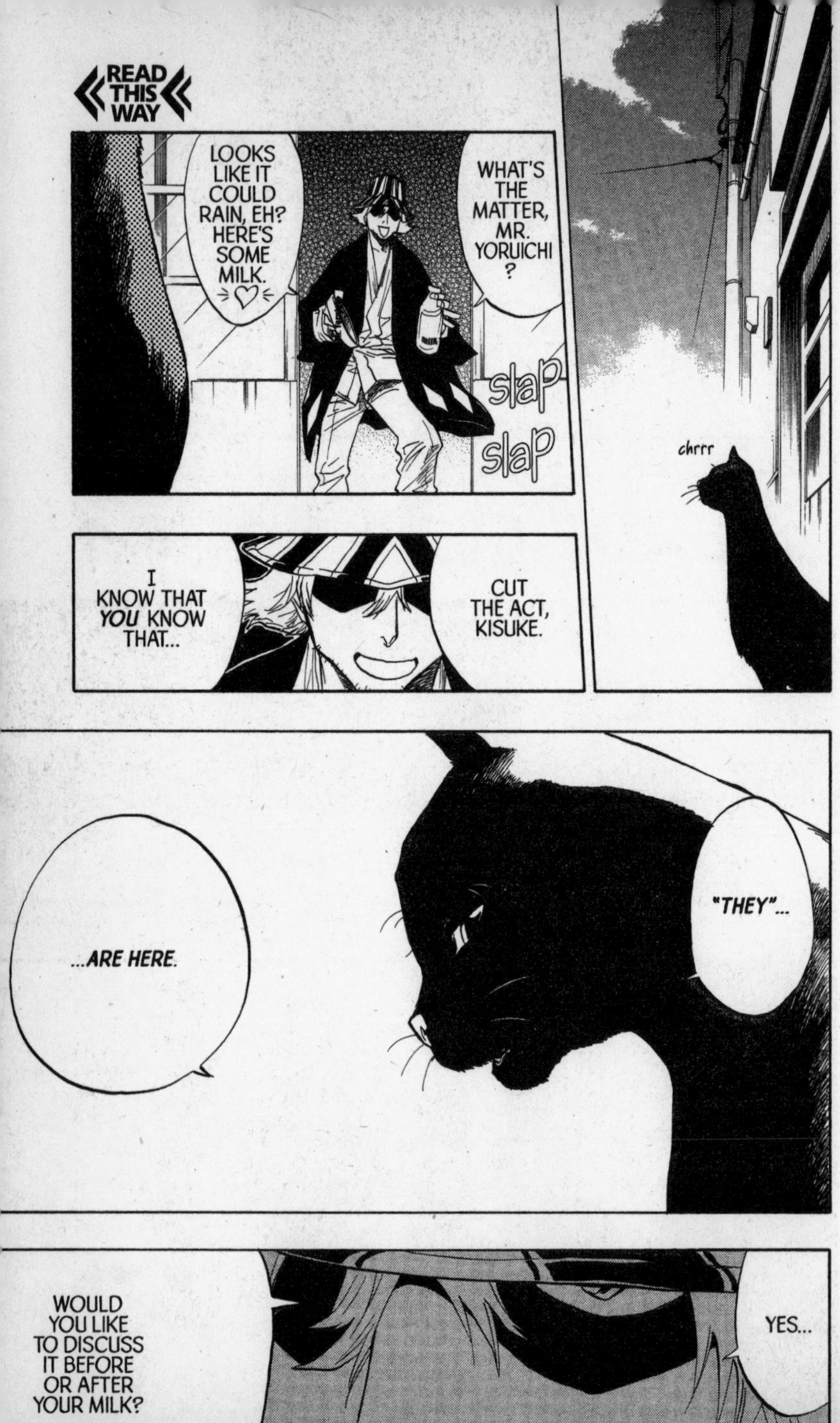
chrrr
WHAT'S THE MATTER, MR. YORUICHI?
LOOKS LIKE IT COULD RAIN, EH? HERE'S SOME MILK. ♡
slap
slap
CUT THE ACT, KISUKE.
I KNOW THAT *YOU* KNOW THAT...
"THEY"...
...ARE HERE.
YES...
WOULD YOU LIKE TO DISCUSS IT BEFORE OR AFTER YOUR MILK?

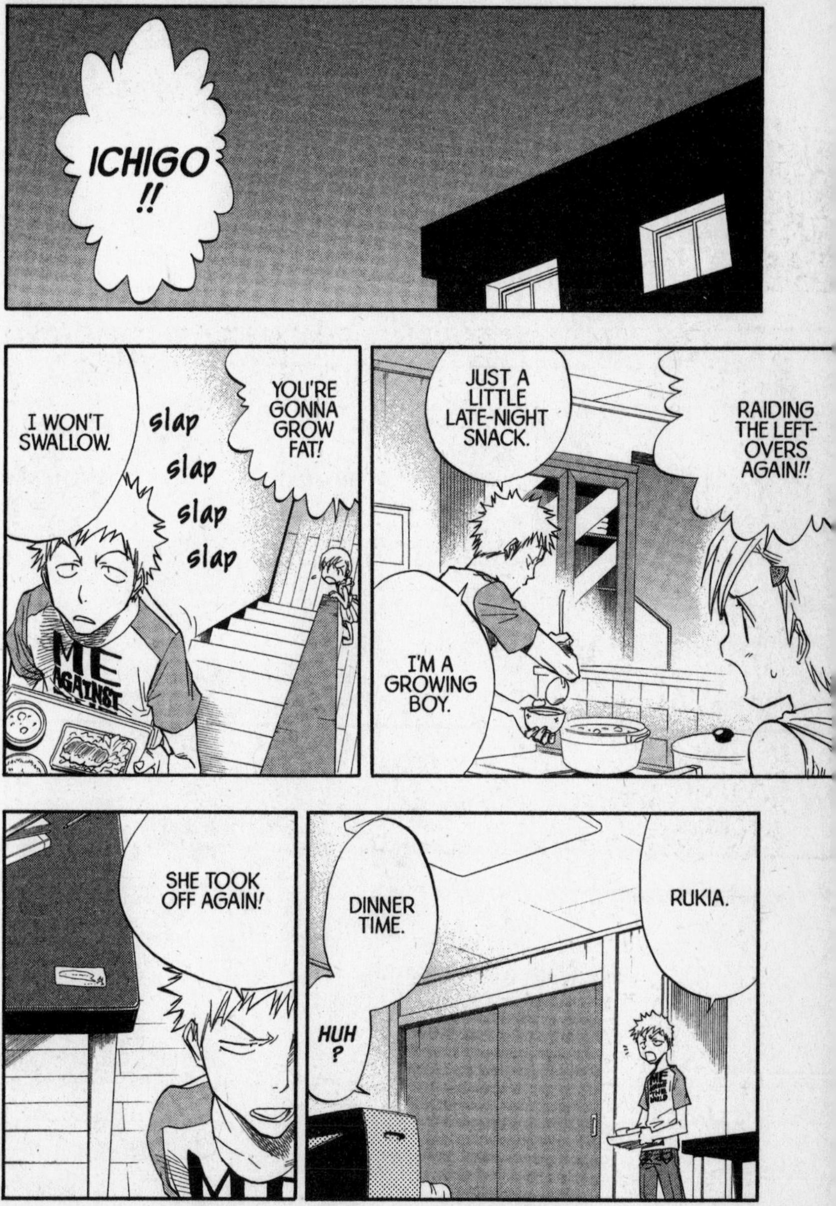
ICHIGO!!
RAIDING THE LEFT-OVERS AGAIN!!
JUST A LITTLE LATE-NIGHT SNACK.
I'M A GROWING BOY.
YOU'RE GONNA GROW FAT!
slap slap slap slap
I WON'T SWALLOW.
RUKIA.
DINNER TIME.
HUH?
SHE TOOK OFF AGAIN!

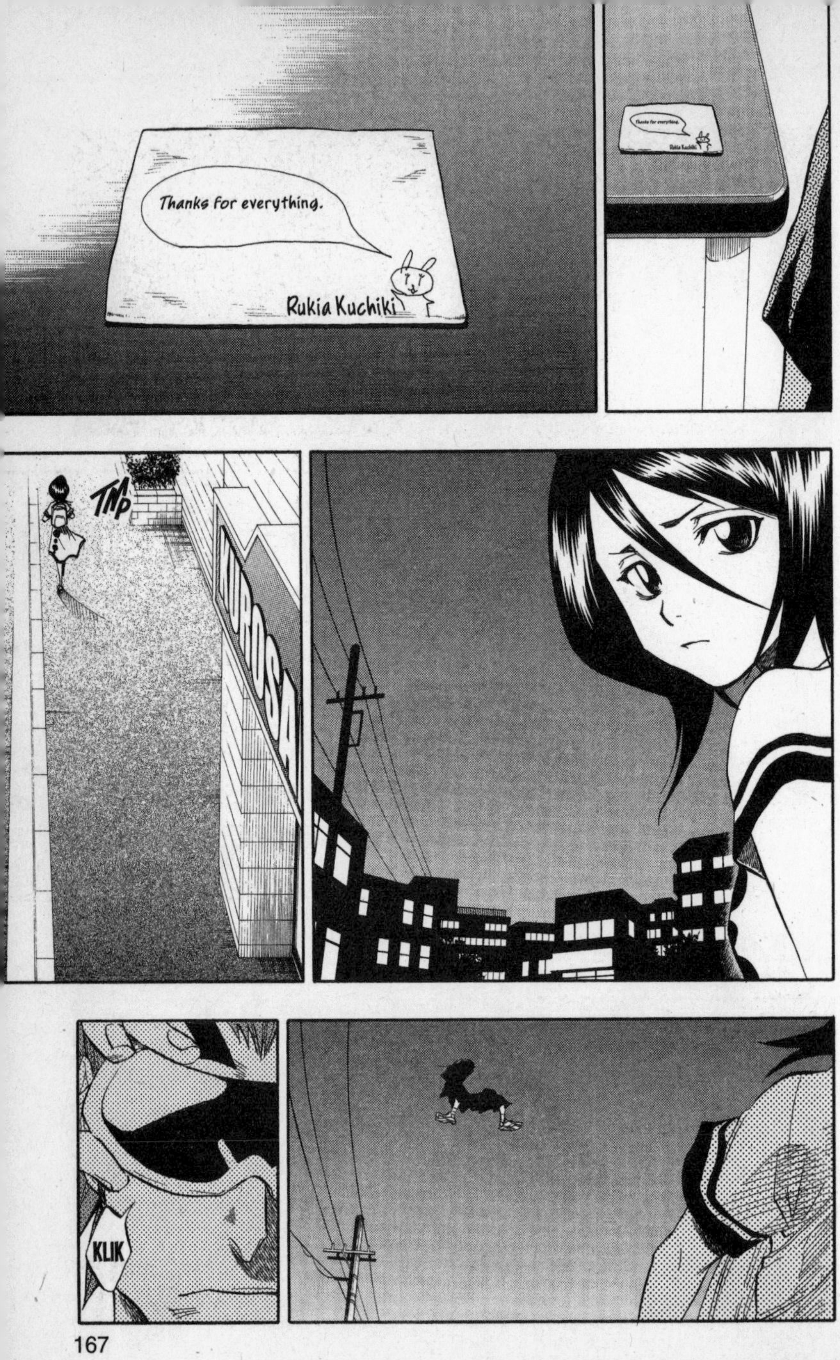
Thanks for everything.
Rukia Kuchiki
Thanks for everything.
Rukia Kuchiki
TMP
KUROSA
KLIK

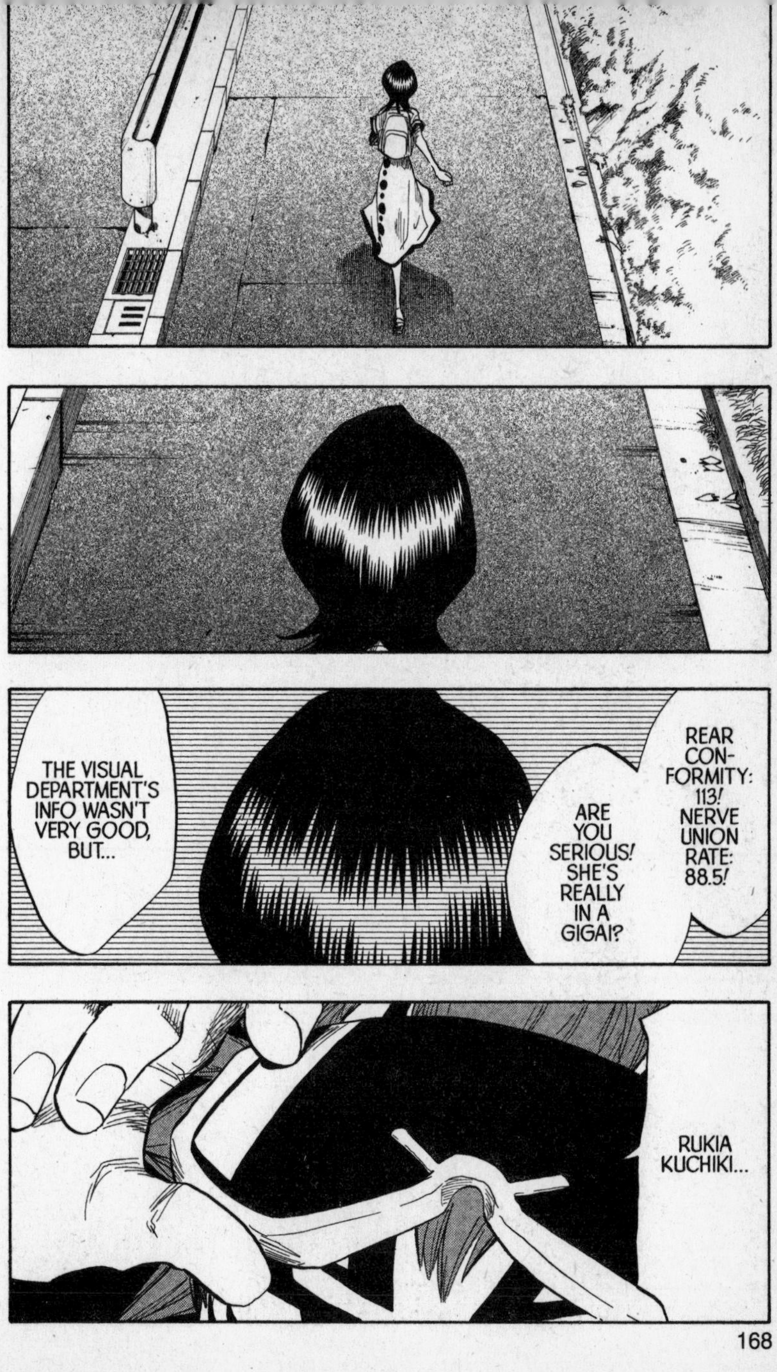
REAR CONFORMITY: 113! NERVE UNION RATE: 88.5!
ARE YOU SERIOUS! SHE'S REALLY IN A GIGAI?
THE VISUAL DEPARTMENT'S INFO WASN'T VERY GOOD, BUT...
RUKIA KUCHIKI...

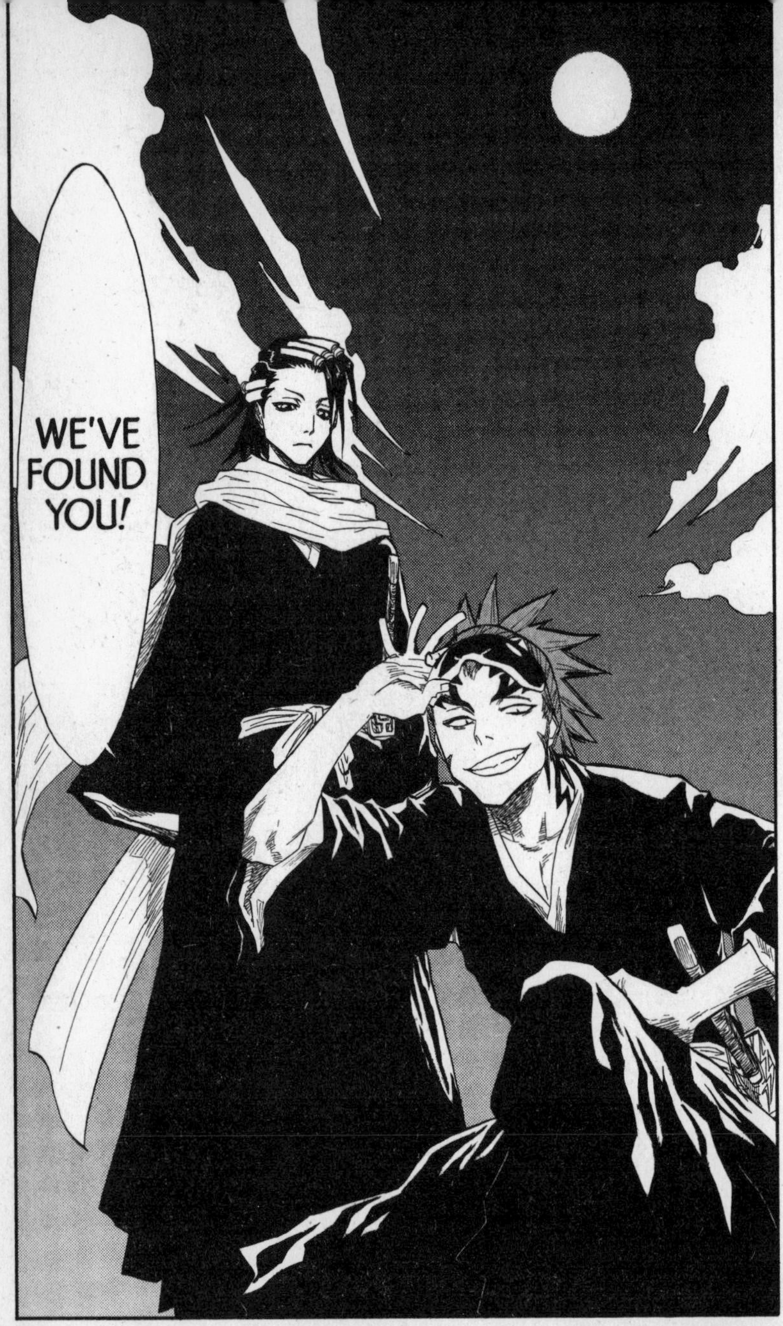
WE'VE FOUND YOU!

52. Needless Emotions

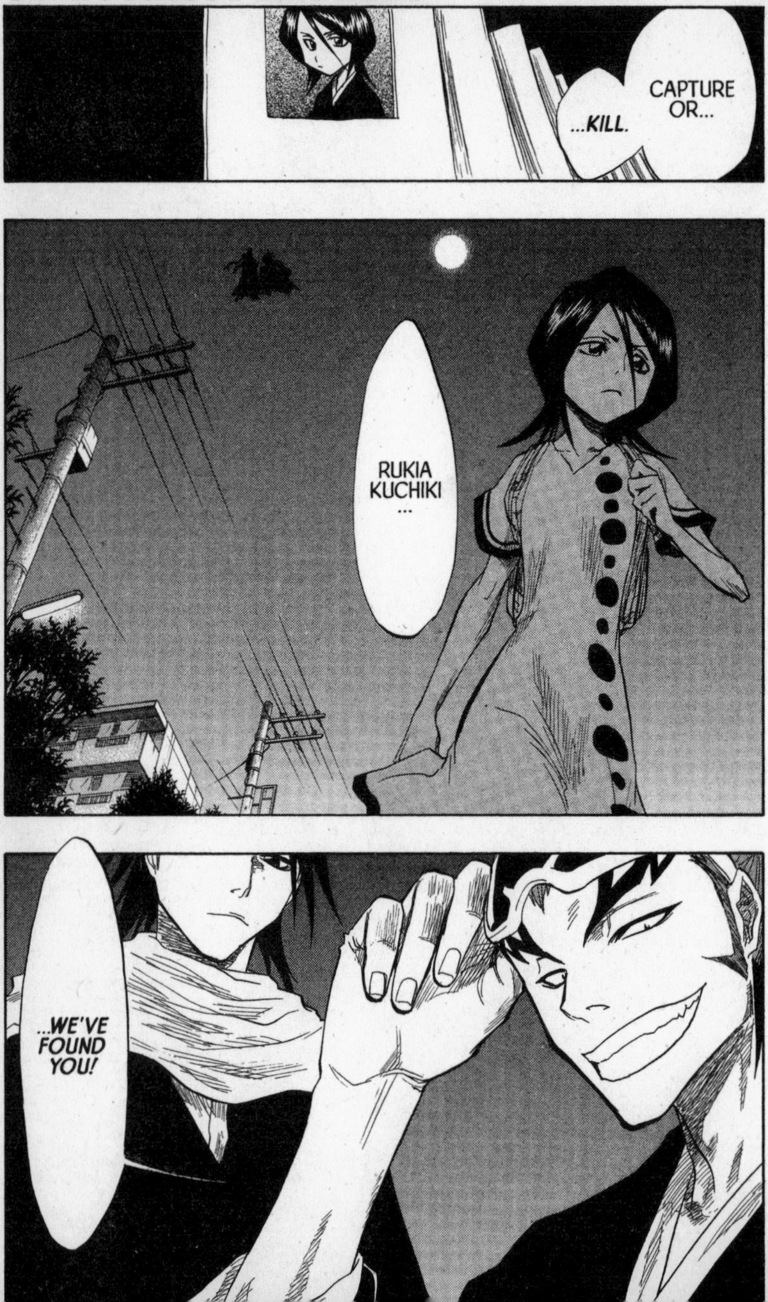
CAPTURE OR...
...KILL.
RUKIA KUCHIKI ...
...WE'VE FOUND YOU!

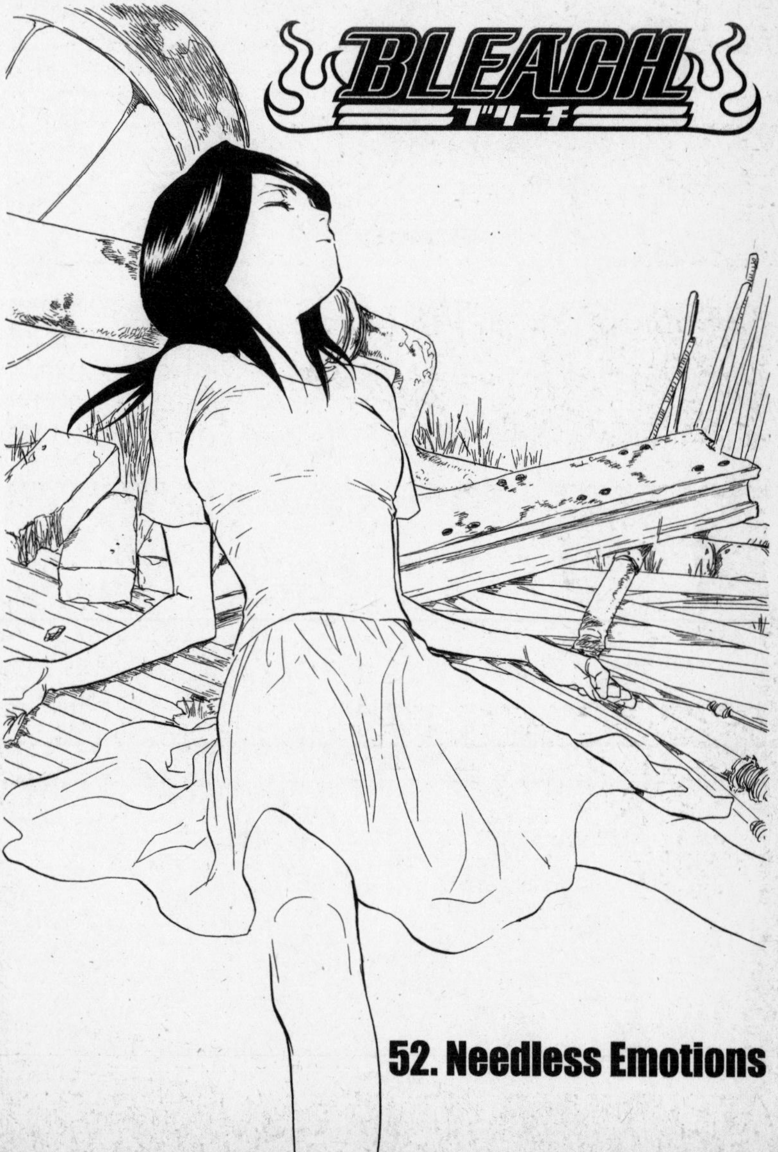
BLEACH
ブリーチ

52. Needless Emotions

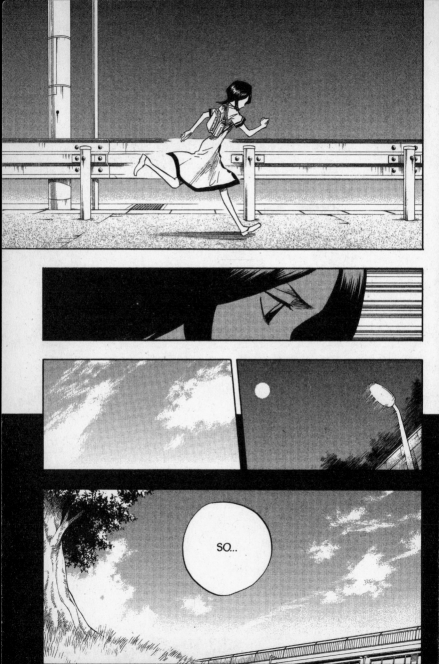

SO...

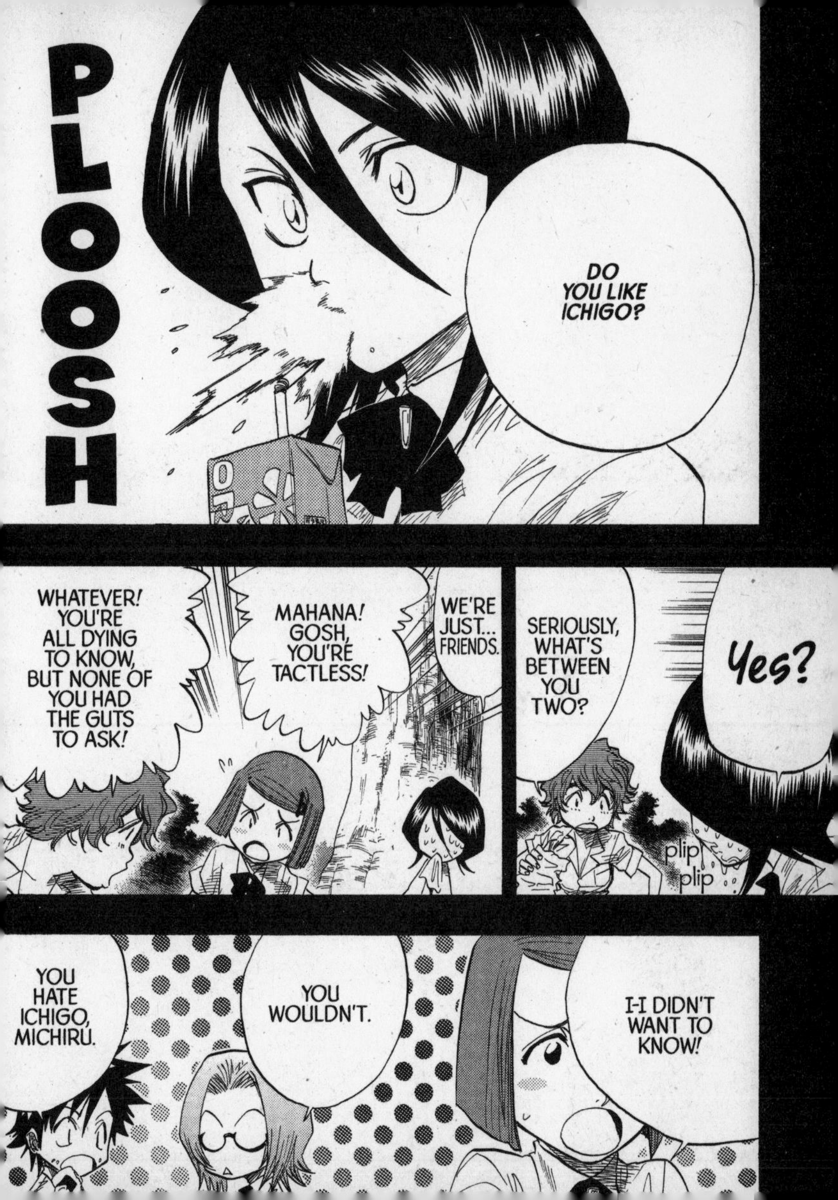
DO YOU LIKE ICHIGO?
PLOOSH
Yes?
SERIOUSLY, WHAT'S BETWEEN YOU TWO?
plip plip
WE'RE JUST... FRIENDS.
MAHANA! GOSH, YOU'RE TACTLESS!
WHATEVER! YOU'RE ALL DYING TO KNOW, BUT NONE OF YOU HAD THE GUTS TO ASK!
I-I DIDN'T WANT TO KNOW!
YOU WOULDN'T.
YOU HATE ICHIGO, MICHIRU.

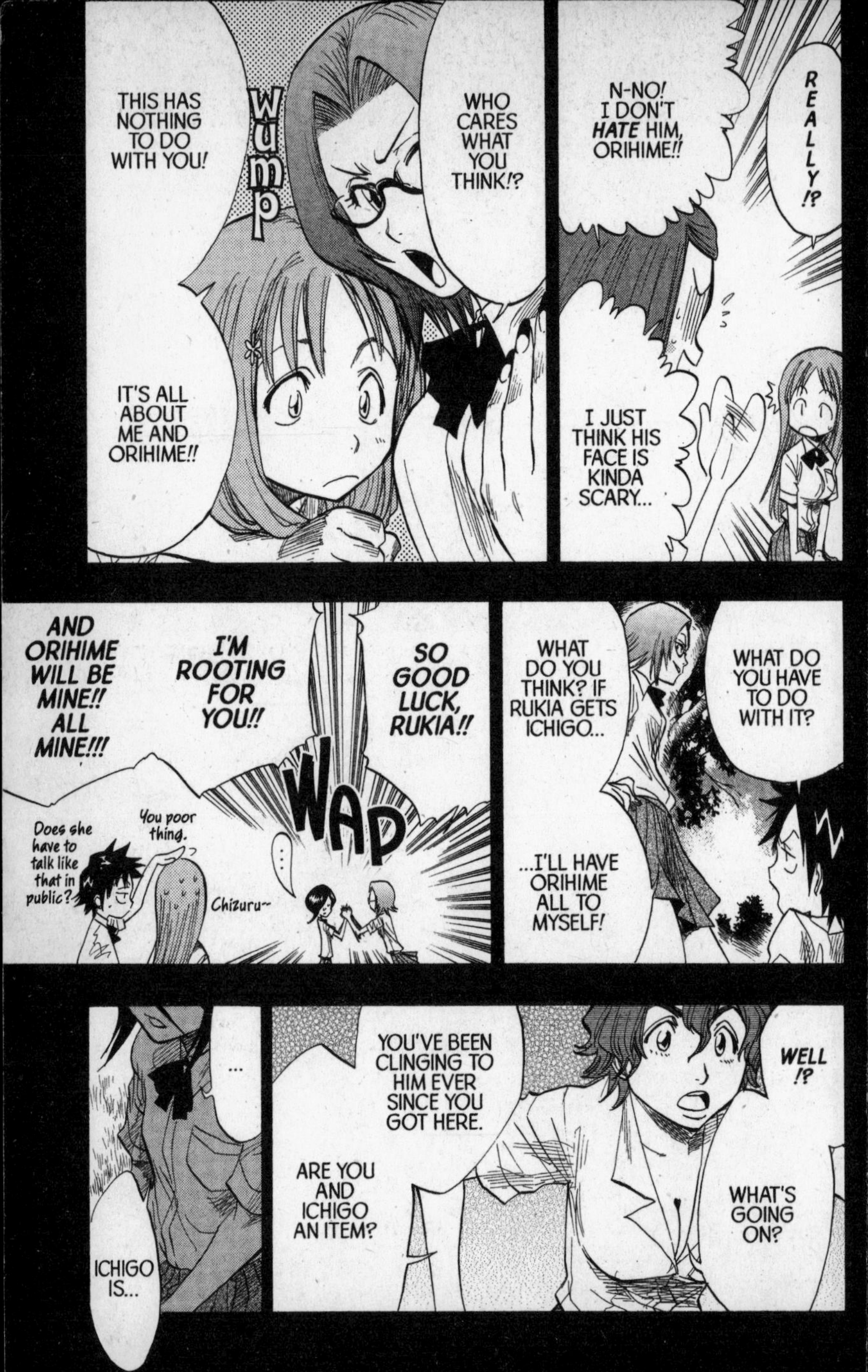
REALLY!?
N-NO! I DON'T *HATE* HIM, ORIHIME!!
I JUST THINK HIS FACE IS KINDA SCARY...
WHO CARES WHAT YOU THINK!?
WUMP
THIS HAS NOTHING TO DO WITH YOU!
IT'S ALL ABOUT ME AND ORIHIME!!
WHAT DO YOU HAVE TO DO WITH IT?
WHAT DO YOU THINK? IF RUKIA GETS ICHIGO...
...I'LL HAVE ORIHIME ALL TO MYSELF!
SO GOOD LUCK, RUKIA!!
I'M ROOTING FOR YOU!!
AND ORIHIME WILL BE MINE!! ALL MINE!!!
WAP
...
You poor thing.
Chizuru~
Does she have to talk like that in public?
WELL!?
WHAT'S GOING ON?
YOU'VE BEEN CLINGING TO HIM EVER SINCE YOU GOT HERE.
ARE YOU AND ICHIGO AN ITEM?
...
ICHIGO IS...

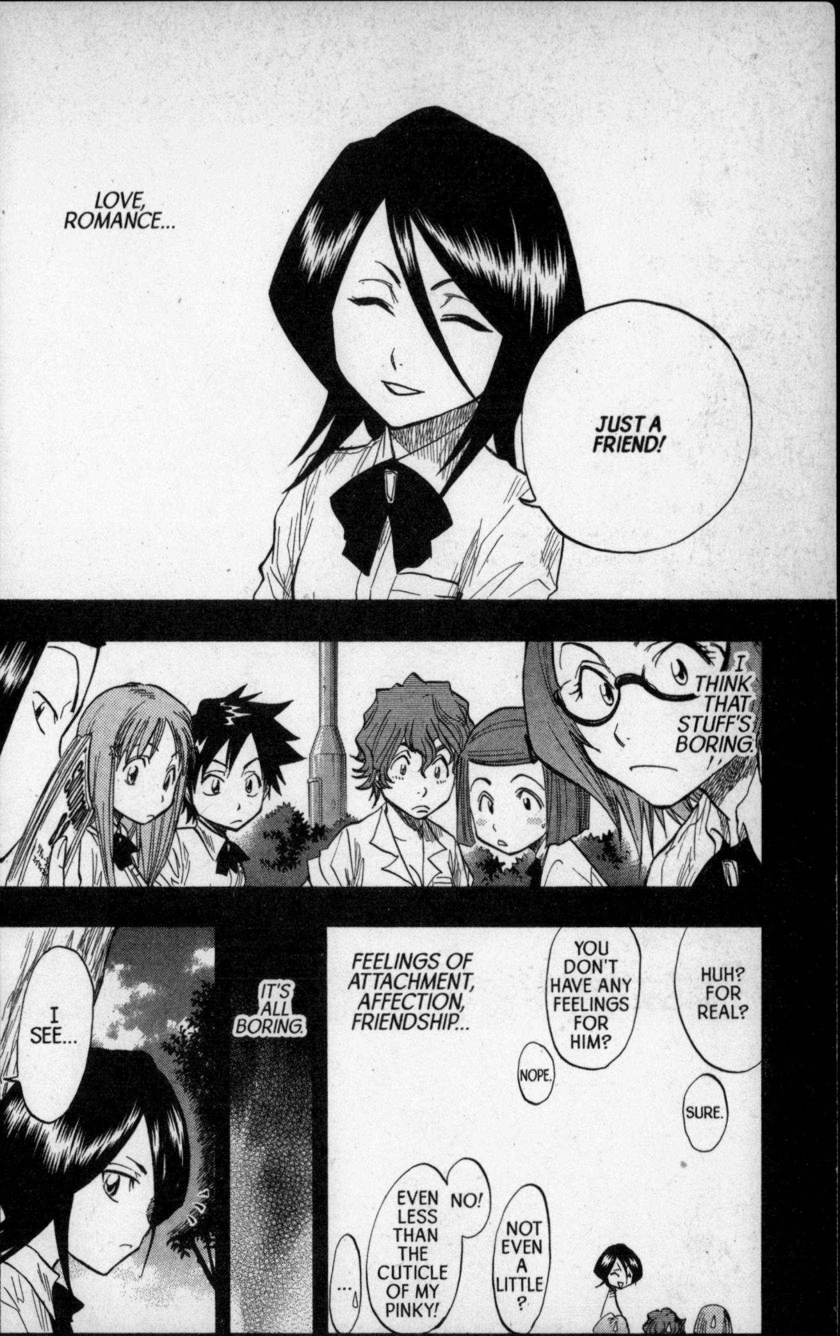

JUST A FRIEND!
LOVE, ROMANCE...
I THINK THAT STUFF'S BORING.
HUH? FOR REAL?
YOU DON'T HAVE ANY FEELINGS FOR HIM?
SURE.
NOPE.
FEELINGS OF ATTACHMENT, AFFECTION, FRIENDSHIP...
NOT EVEN A LITTLE?
NO!
EVEN LESS THAN THE CUTICLE OF MY PINKY!
...
IT'S ALL BORING.
I SEE...

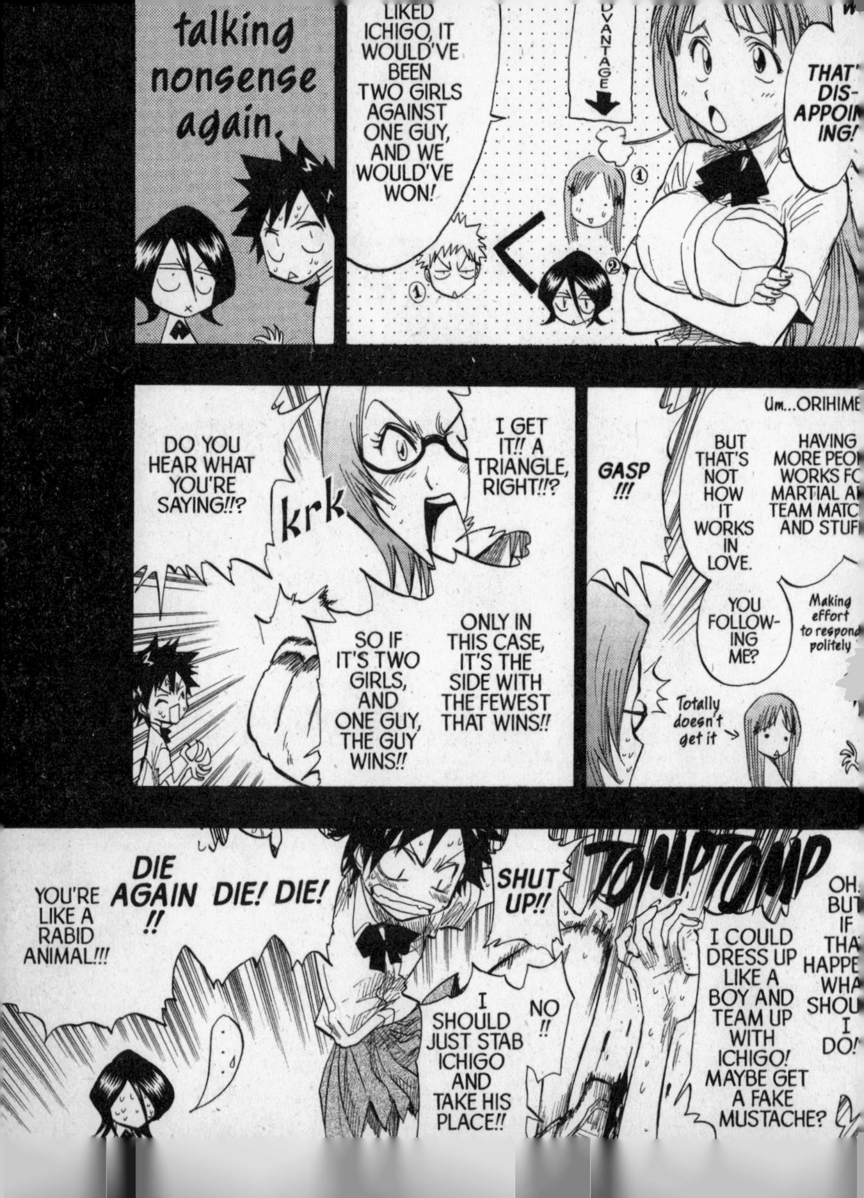
THAT' DIS- APPOIN ING!
DVANTAGE
LIKED ICHIGO, IT WOULD'VE BEEN TWO GIRLS AGAINST ONE GUY, AND WE WOULD'VE WON!
talking nonsense again.
Um...ORIHIME
HAVING MORE PEO WORKS FO MARTIAL A TEAM MATC AND STUF
BUT THAT'S NOT HOW IT WORKS IN LOVE.
GASP!!!
YOU FOLLOWING ME?
Making effort to respond politely
Totally doesn't get it
I GET IT!! A TRIANGLE, RIGHT!!?
DO YOU HEAR WHAT YOU'RE SAYING!!?
krk
ONLY IN THIS CASE, IT'S THE SIDE WITH THE FEWEST THAT WINS!!
SO IF IT'S TWO GIRLS, AND ONE GUY, THE GUY WINS!!
OH, BUT IF THA HAPPE WHA SHOU I DO!
I COULD DRESS UP LIKE A BOY AND TEAM UP WITH ICHIGO! MAYBE GET A FAKE MUSTACHE?
TOMPTOMP
SHUT UP!!
NO!!
I SHOULD JUST STAB ICHIGO AND TAKE HIS PLACE!!
DIE! DIE!
DIE AGAIN!!
YOU'RE LIKE A RABID ANIMAL!!!

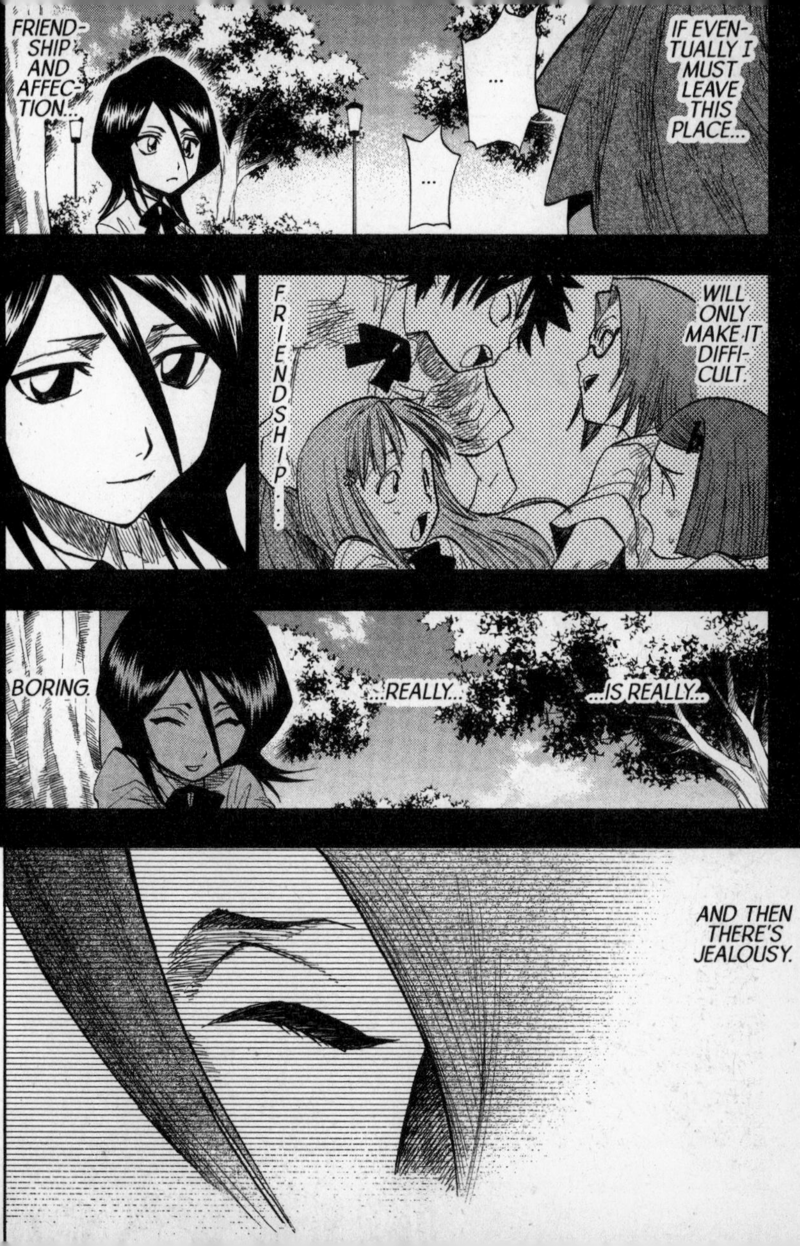
IF EVEN-TUALLY I MUST LEAVE THIS PLACE...
...
...
FRIEND-SHIP AND AFFEC-TION...
WILL ONLY MAKE IT DIFFI-CULT.
FRIENDSHIP...
...IS REALLY...
...REALLY...
BORING.
AND THEN THERE'S JEALOUSY.

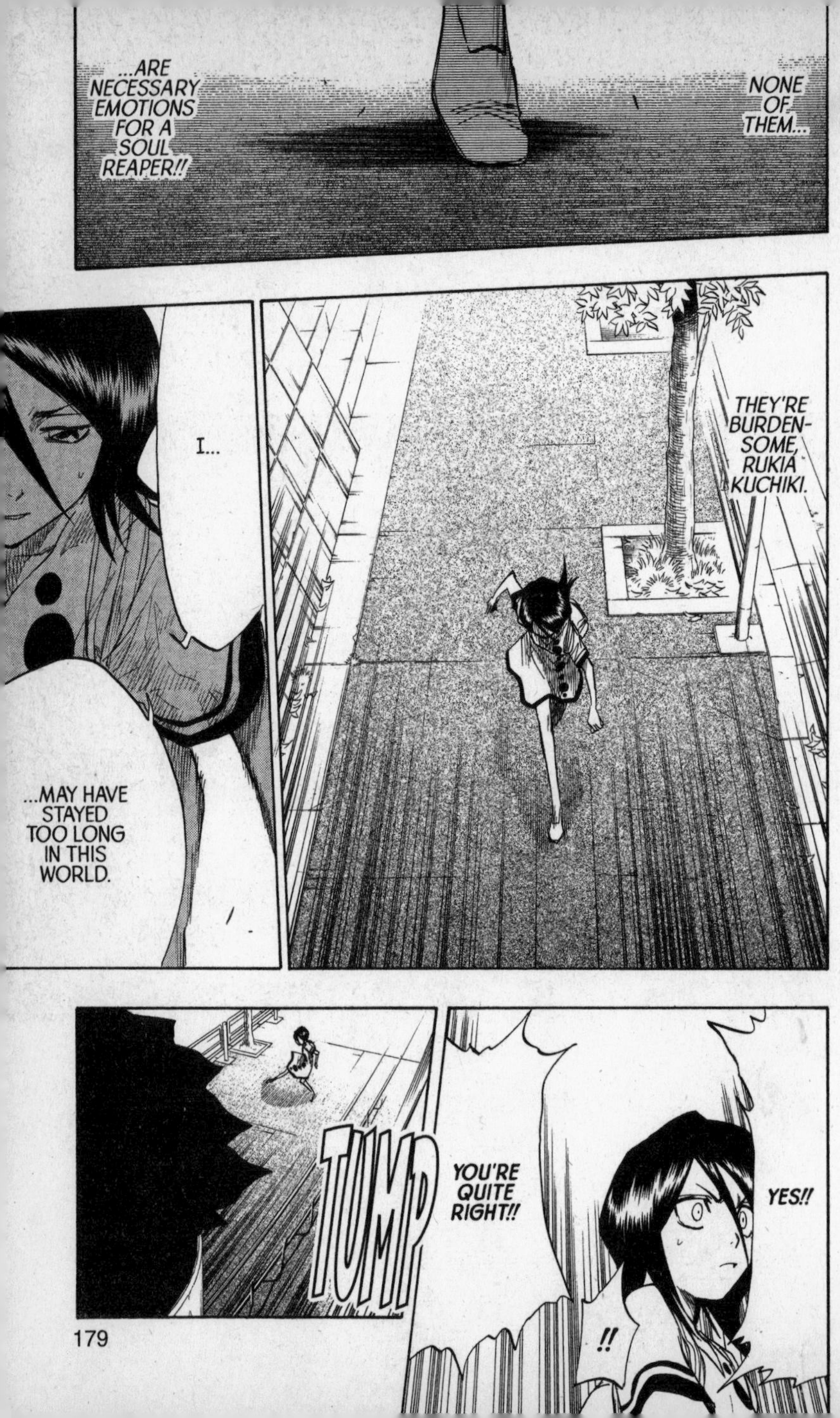
NONE OF THEM...
...ARE NECESSARY EMOTIONS FOR A SOUL REAPER!!
THEY'RE BURDEN-SOME, RUKIA KUCHIKI.
I...
...MAY HAVE STAYED TOO LONG IN THIS WORLD.
YES!!
YOU'RE QUITE RIGHT!!
!!
TUMP

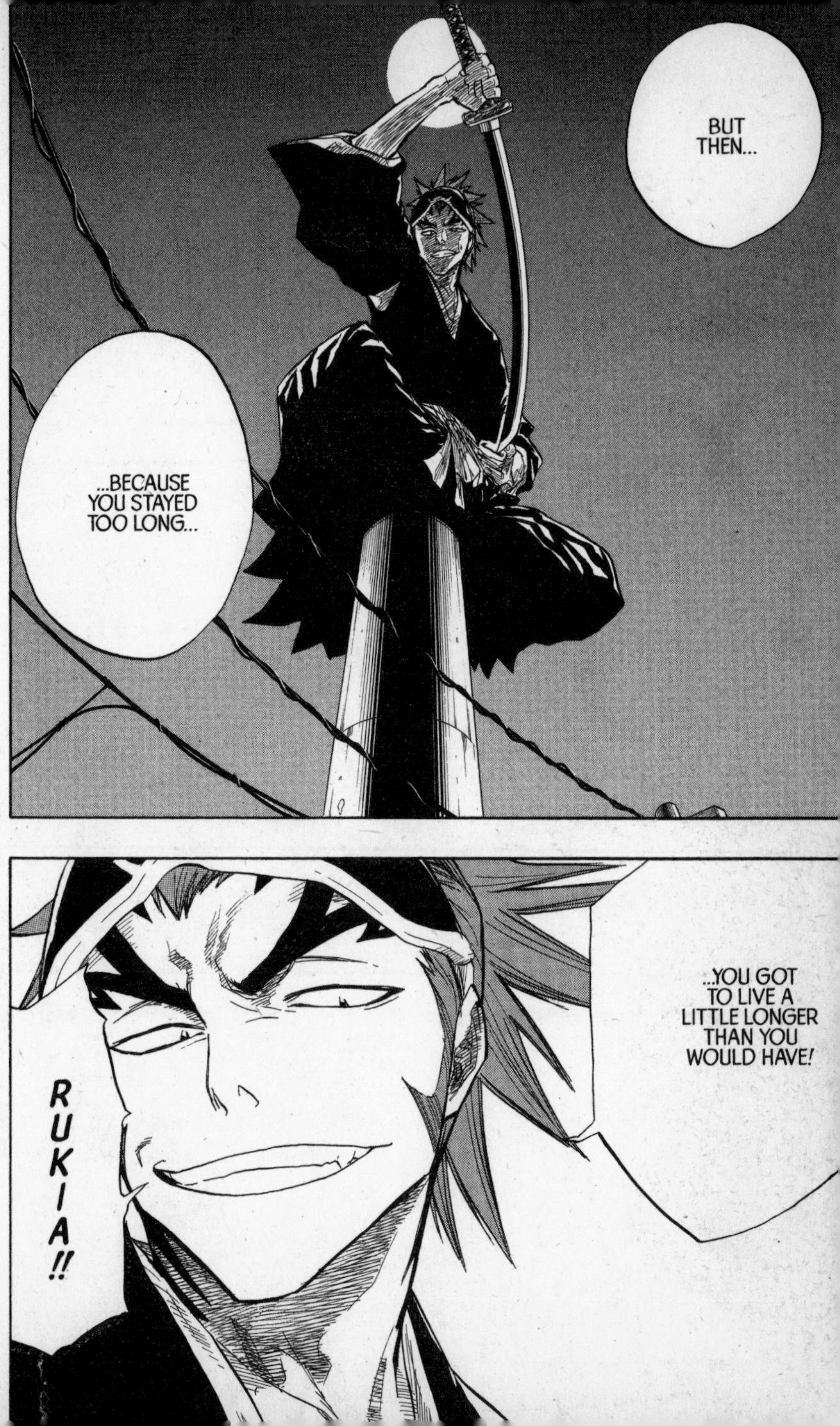
BUT THEN...
...BECAUSE YOU STAYED TOO LONG...
...YOU GOT TO LIVE A LITTLE LONGER THAN YOU WOULD HAVE!
RUKIA!!

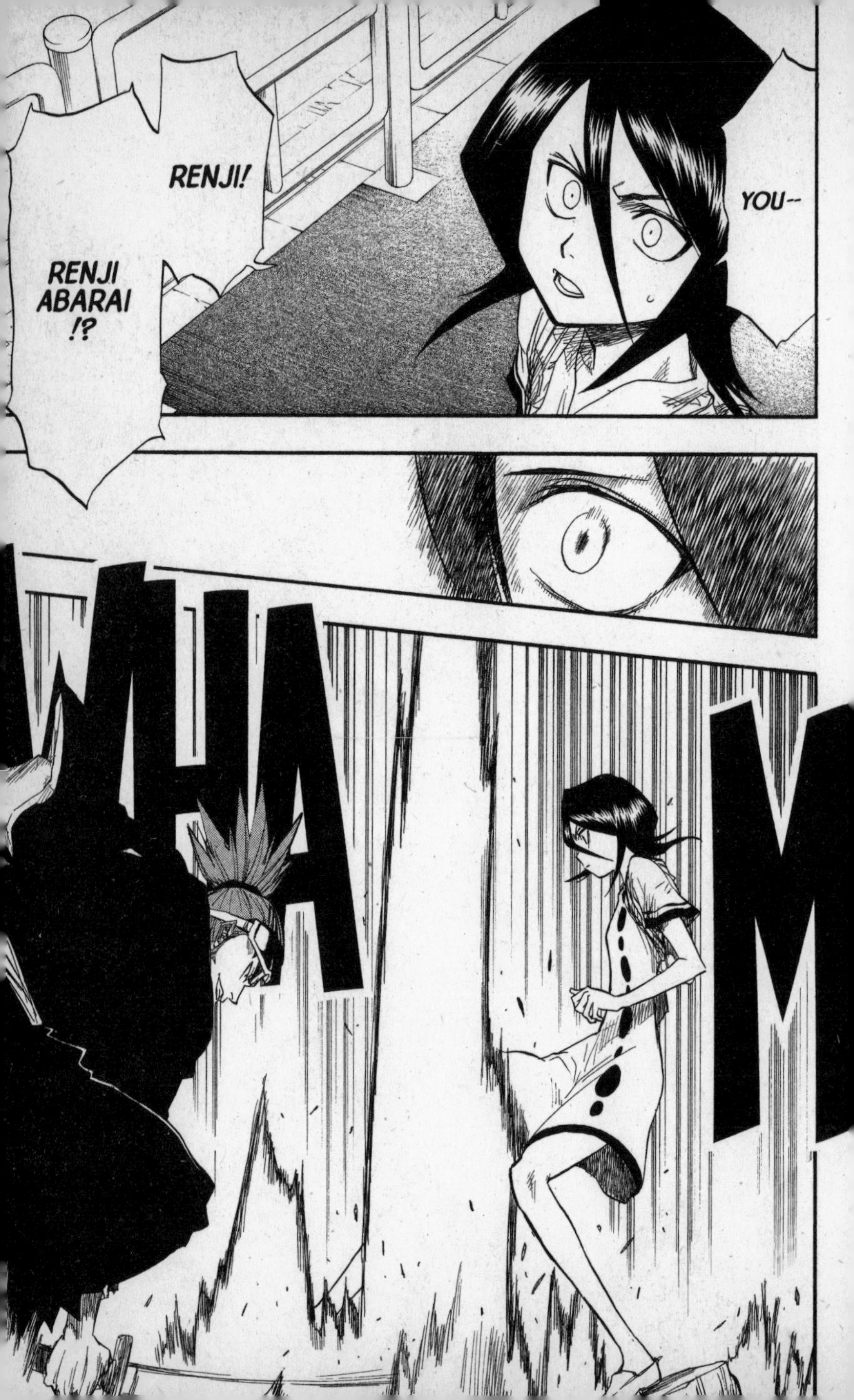
YOU--
RENJI!
RENJI ABARAI !?
WHAM

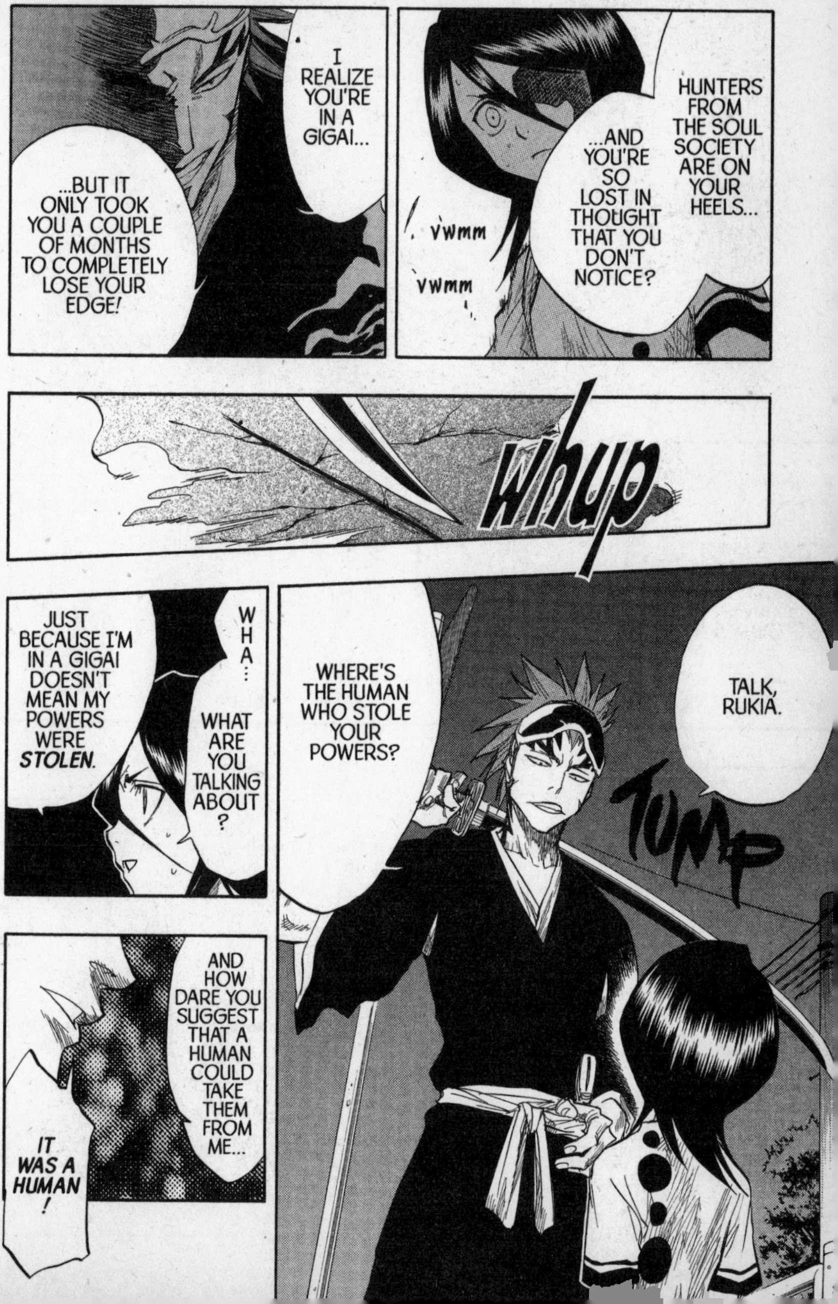
HUNTERS FROM THE SOUL SOCIETY ARE ON YOUR HEELS...
...AND YOU'RE SO LOST IN THOUGHT THAT YOU DON'T NOTICE?
VWMM
VWMM
I REALIZE YOU'RE IN A GIGAI...
...BUT IT ONLY TOOK YOU A COUPLE OF MONTHS TO COMPLETELY LOSE YOUR EDGE!
WHUP
TALK, RUKIA.
TUMP
WHERE'S THE HUMAN WHO STOLE YOUR POWERS?
WHA...
WHAT ARE YOU TALKING ABOUT?
JUST BECAUSE I'M IN A GIGAI DOESN'T MEAN MY POWERS WERE STOLEN.
AND HOW DARE YOU SUGGEST THAT A HUMAN COULD TAKE THEM FROM ME...
IT WAS A HUMAN!

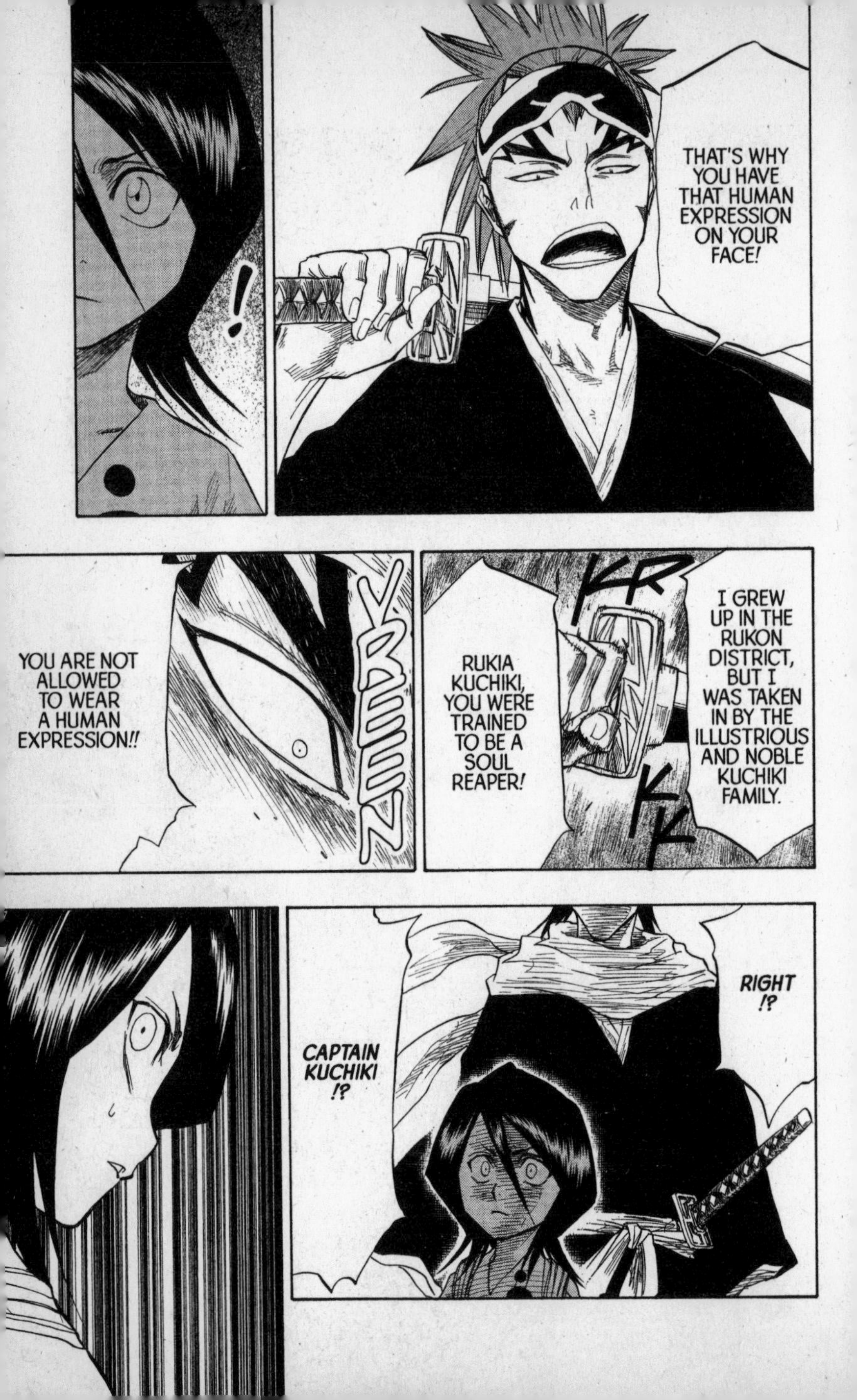
THAT'S WHY YOU HAVE THAT HUMAN EXPRESSION ON YOUR FACE!
!
I GREW UP IN THE RUKON DISTRICT, BUT I WAS TAKEN IN BY THE ILLUSTRIOUS AND NOBLE KUCHIKI FAMILY.
KR
KK
RUKIA KUCHIKI, YOU WERE TRAINED TO BE A SOUL REAPER!
YOU ARE NOT ALLOWED TO WEAR A HUMAN EXPRESSION!!
RIGHT !?
CAPTAIN KUCHIKI !?

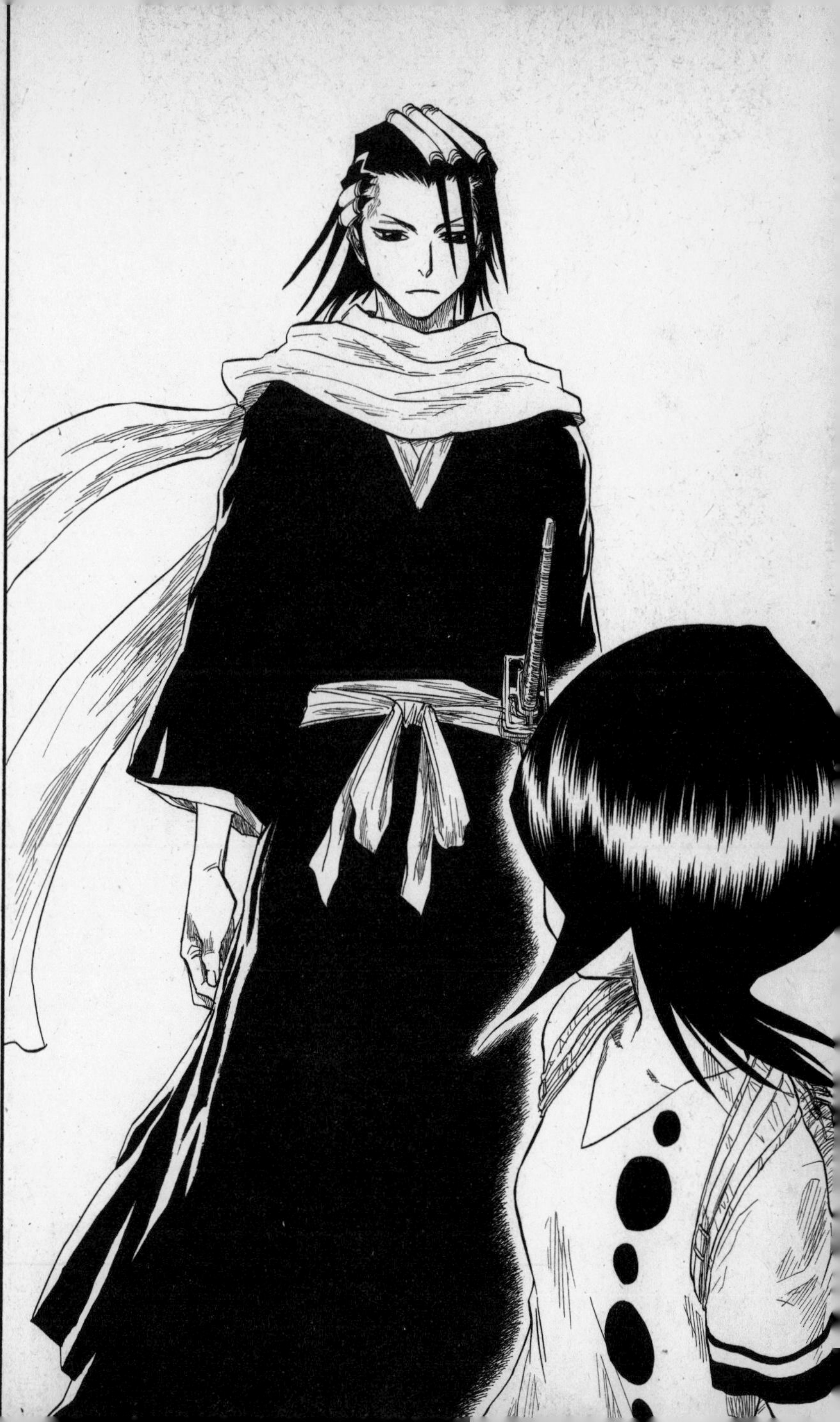

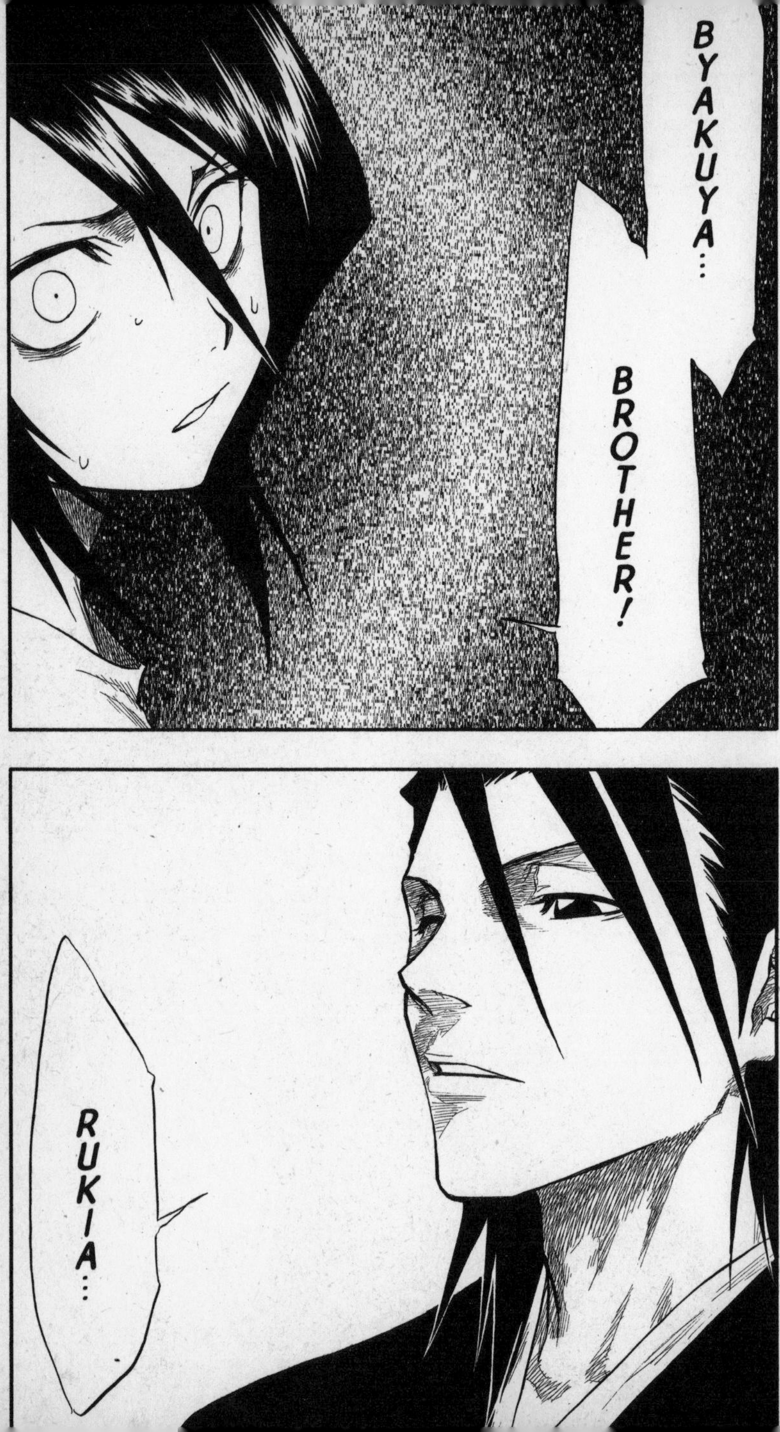
BYAKUYA... BROTHER!
RUKIA...

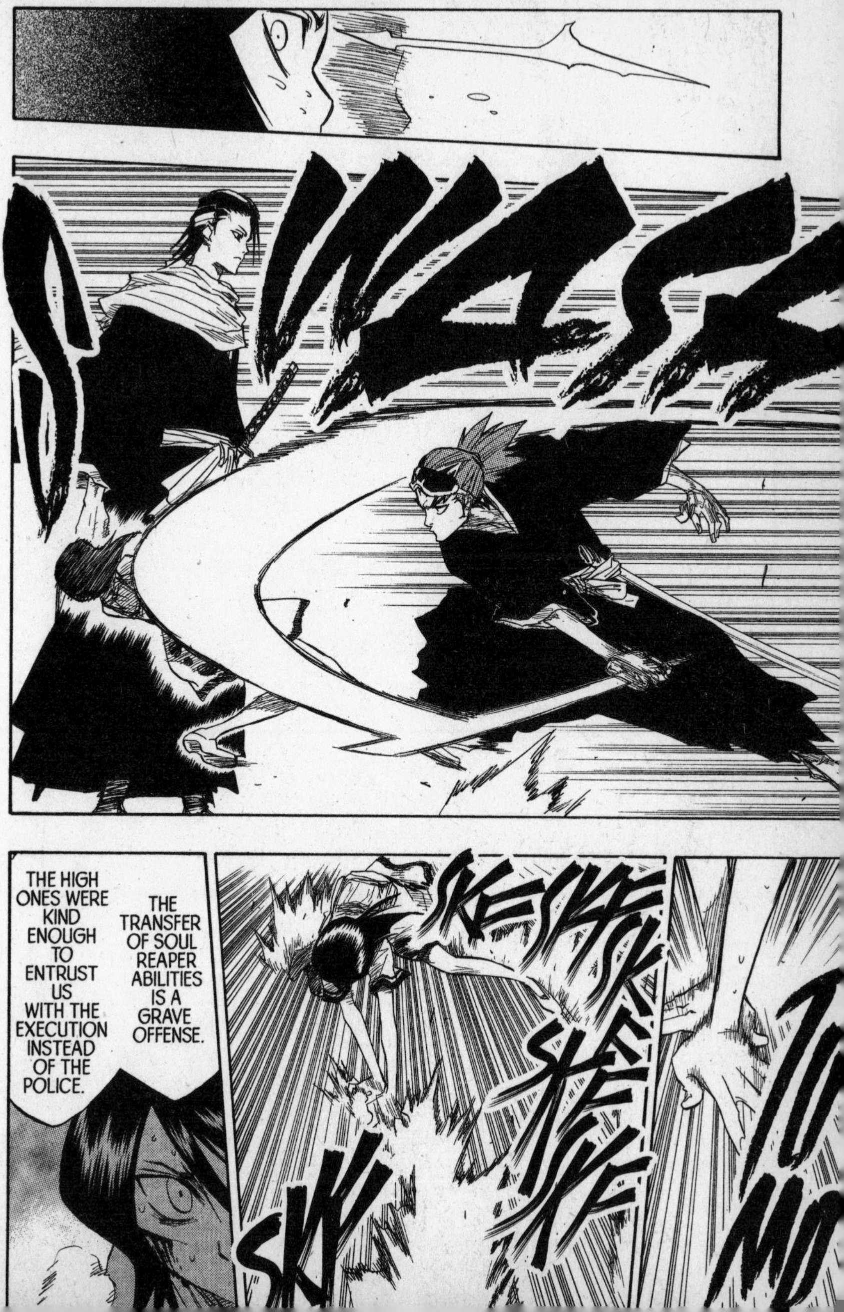
THE TRANSFER OF SOUL REAPER ABILITIES IS A GRAVE OFFENSE.
THE HIGH ONES WERE KIND ENOUGH TO ENTRUST US WITH THE EXECUTION INSTEAD OF THE POLICE.

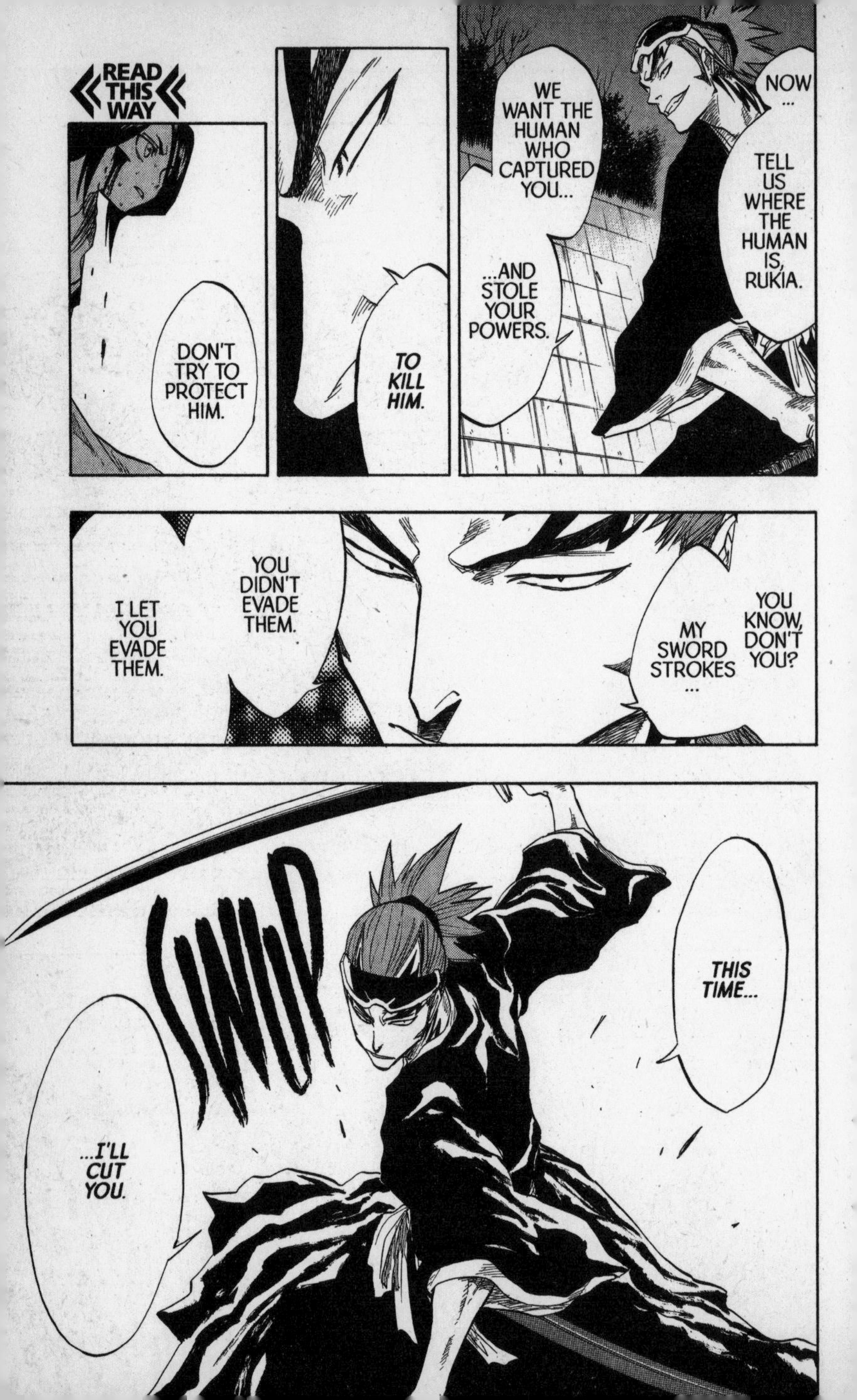
READ THIS WAY
NOW ...
TELL US WHERE THE HUMAN IS, RUKIA.
WE WANT THE HUMAN WHO CAPTURED YOU...
...AND STOLE YOUR POWERS.
TO KILL HIM.
DON'T TRY TO PROTECT HIM.
YOU KNOW, DON'T YOU?
MY SWORD STROKES ...
YOU DIDN'T EVADE THEM.
I LET YOU EVADE THEM.
SWIP
THIS TIME...
...I'LL CUT YOU.

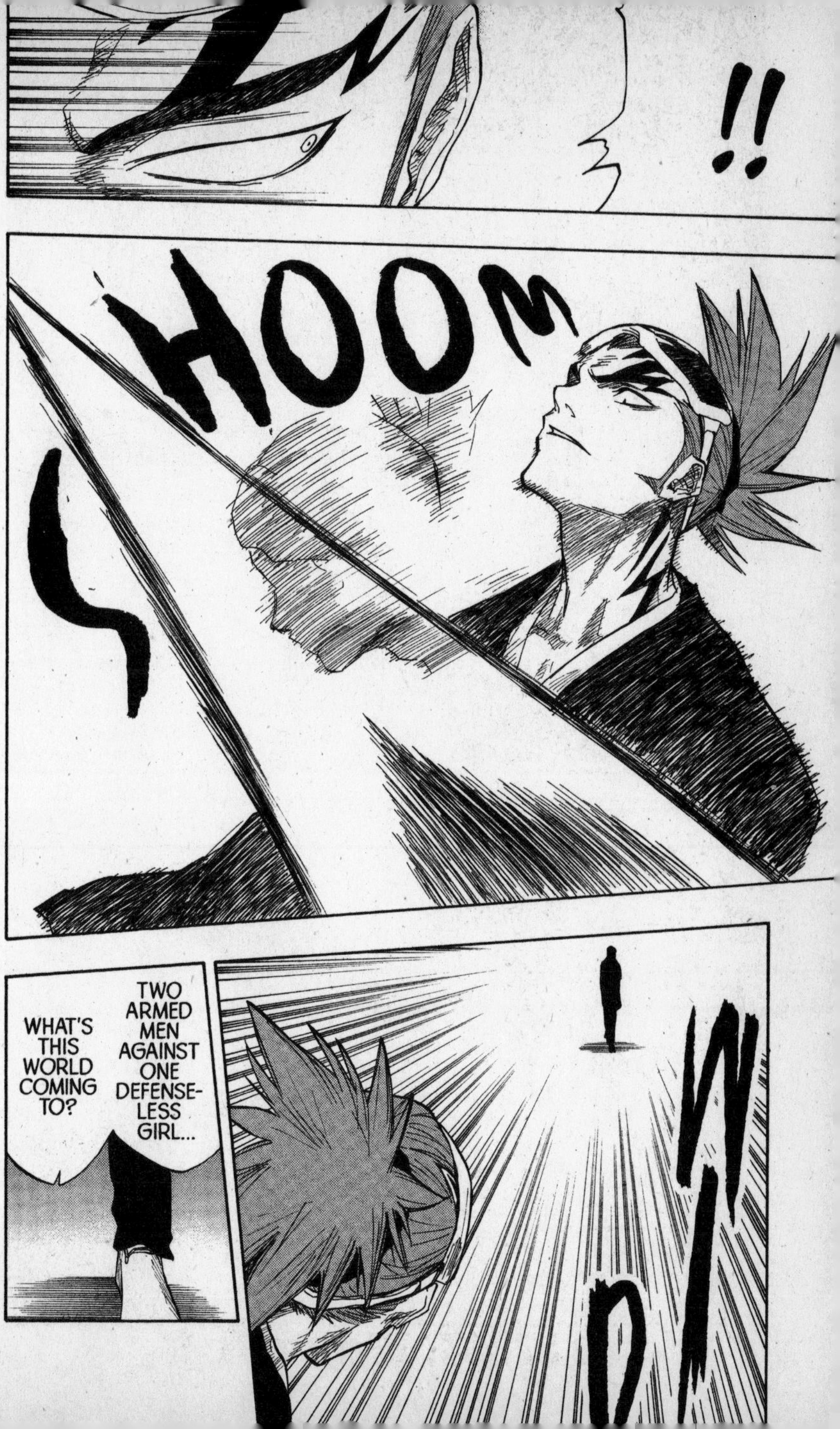
!!
SHOOM
TWO ARMED MEN AGAINST ONE DEFENSE-LESS GIRL...
WHAT'S THIS WORLD COMING TO?

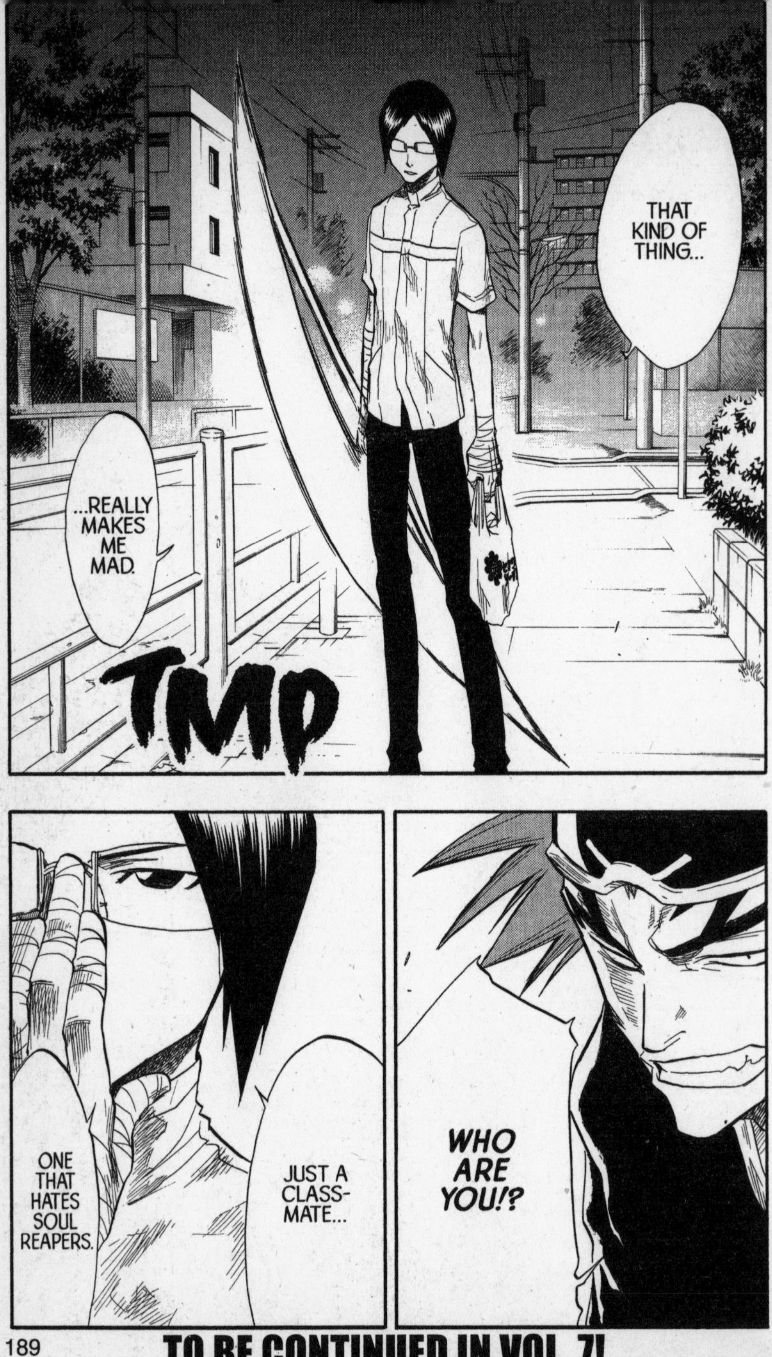
THAT KIND OF THING...
...REALLY MAKES ME MAD.
TMP
WHO ARE YOU!?
JUST A CLASSMATE...
ONE THAT HATES SOUL REAPERS.

TO BE CONTINUED IN VOL. 7!

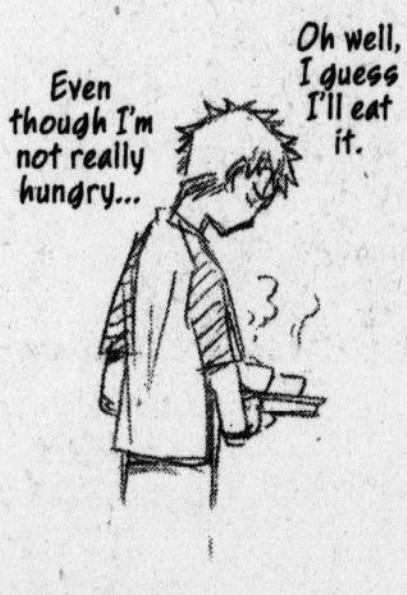
Oh well, I guess I'll eat it.
Even though I'm not really hungry...

RADIO★KON BABY!!

WHAT'S UP, BLEACH FANS!? RADIO-KON BABY IS COMING AT YOU!! THAT'S RIGHT, I'M GETTING MY OWN MANGA VERSION OF A RADIO CALL-IN SHOW! EACH MONTH, YOURS TRULY AND A RANDOMLY SELECTED GUEST CHARACTER WILL ANSWER QUESTIONS SENT IN BY READERS LIKE YOU! COOL, HUH? WELL, IT MAY SOUND SKETCHY NOW, BUT YOU'RE GONNA LOVE IT!! WE'LL ANSWER ANY QUESTION, NO MATTER HOW STUPID OR EMBARRASSING!! SO DON'T MISS IT!

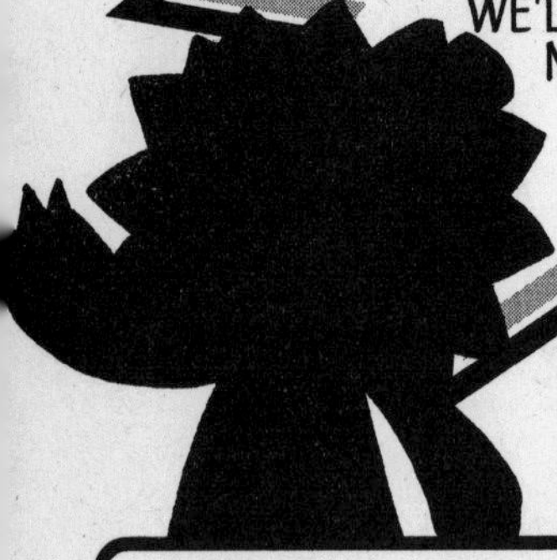

Send your question along with your name, address and age to the address below!!

SHONEN JUMP c/o VIZ, LLC
P.O. Box 77010 • San Francisco, CA 94107
ATTN: RADIO-KON BABY
Email: letters@shonenjump.com

Life in the human world has been a mixed bag of experiences for ex-Soul Reaper Rukia Kuchiki. Now that Menos Grande has been dealt with, Rukia figures that things will be easier on everyone if she stays out of the way. But that's not how the Soul Society sees it—as far as they're concerned, Rukia is a rogue agent, having committed the grand transgression of transferring the powers of a Soul Reaper to a human. Two of the Soul Society's strongest operatives are sent to both retrieve Rukia and permanently neutralize Ichigo. But what will happen when Uyrû, the Quincy, tries to intervene?!

Available in June 2005

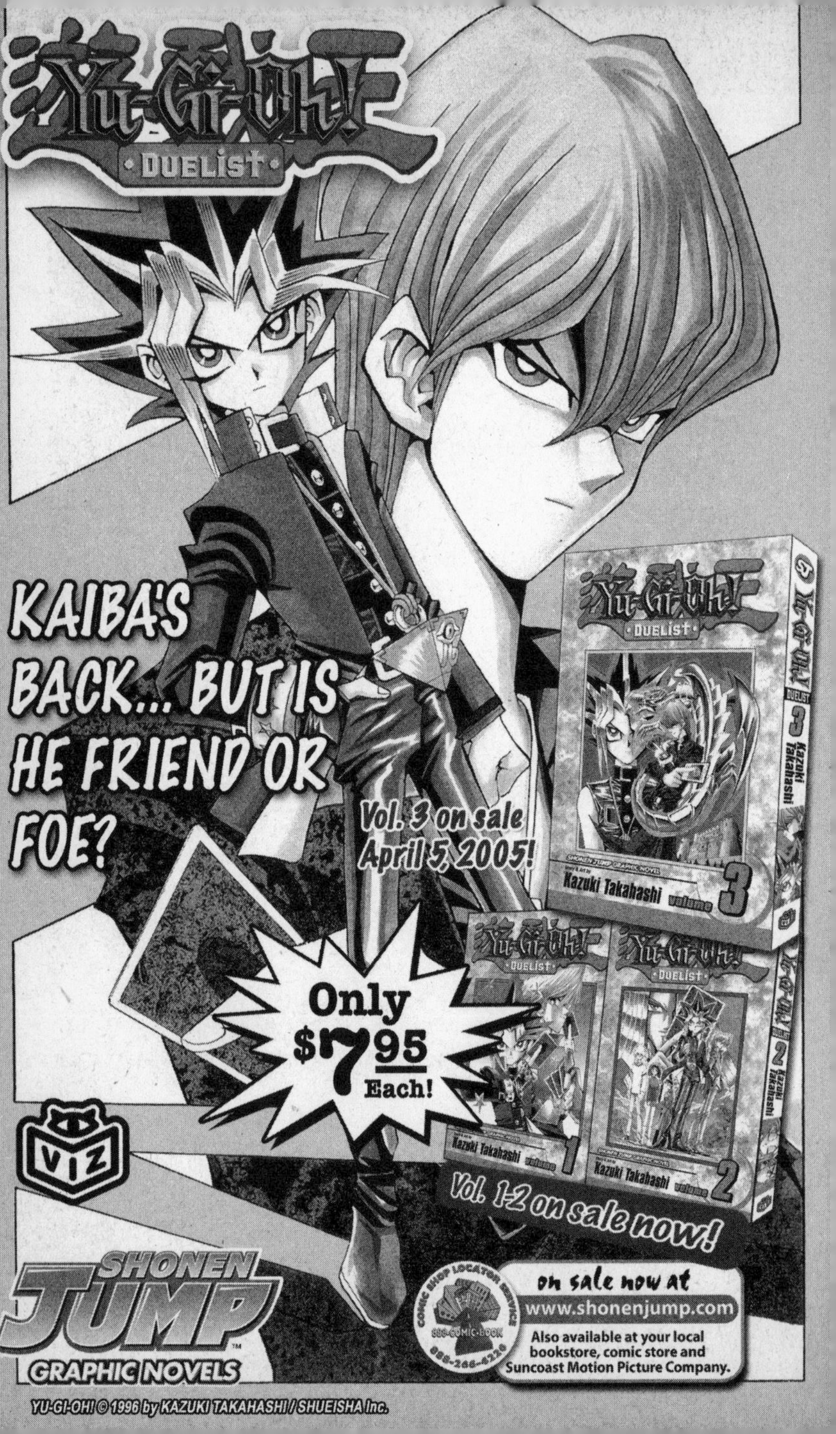
YU-GI-OH! DUELIST
KAIBA'S BACK... BUT IS HE FRIEND OR FOE?
Vol. 3 on sale April 5, 2005!
Kazuki Takahashi volume 3
Only $7.95 Each!
Kazuki Takahashi volume 1
Kazuki Takahashi volume 2
Vol. 1-2 on sale now!
VIZ
SHONEN JUMP GRAPHIC NOVELS
on sale now at
www.shonenjump.com
Also available at your local bookstore, comic store and Suncoast Motion Picture Company.
888-COMIC-BOOK
888-266-4226
YU-GI-OH! © 1996 by KAZUKI TAKAHASHI / SHUEISHA Inc.

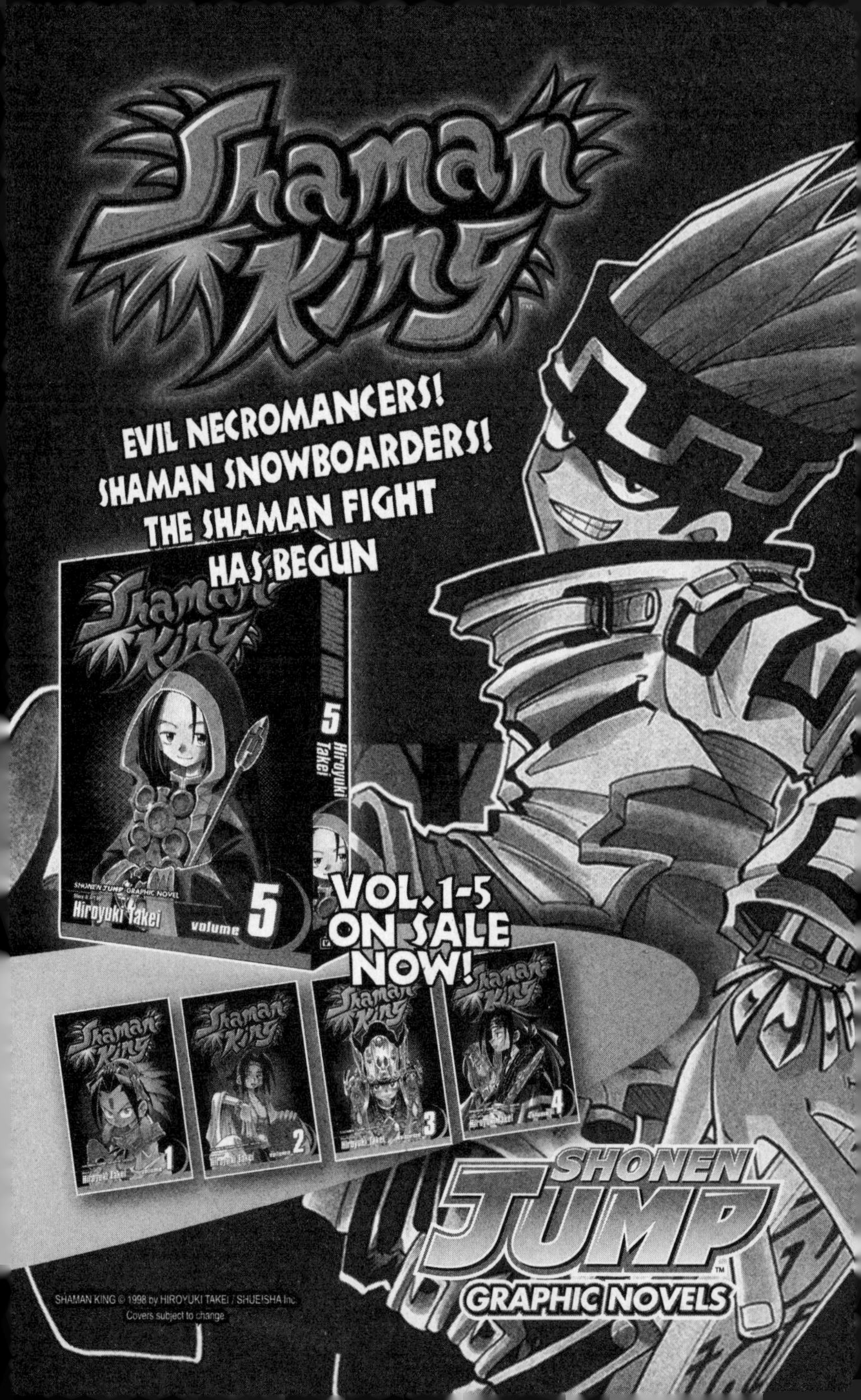
Shaman King
EVIL NECROMANCERS!
SHAMAN SNOWBOARDERS!
THE SHAMAN FIGHT
HAS BEGUN
VOL. 1-5
ON SALE
NOW!
SHONEN JUMP
GRAPHIC NOVELS
SHAMAN KING © 1998 by HIROYUKI TAKEI / SHUEISHA Inc.
Covers subject to change.

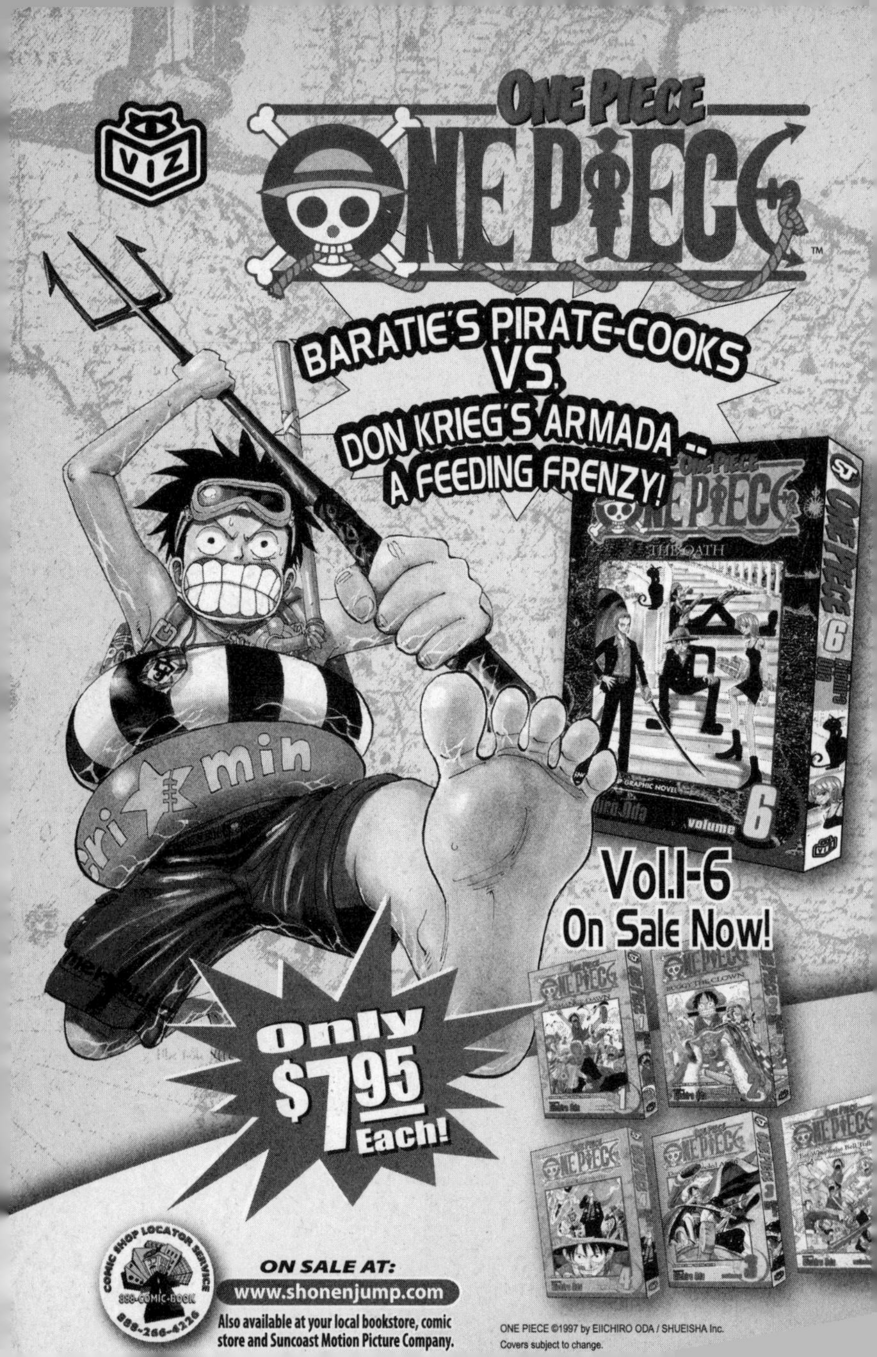

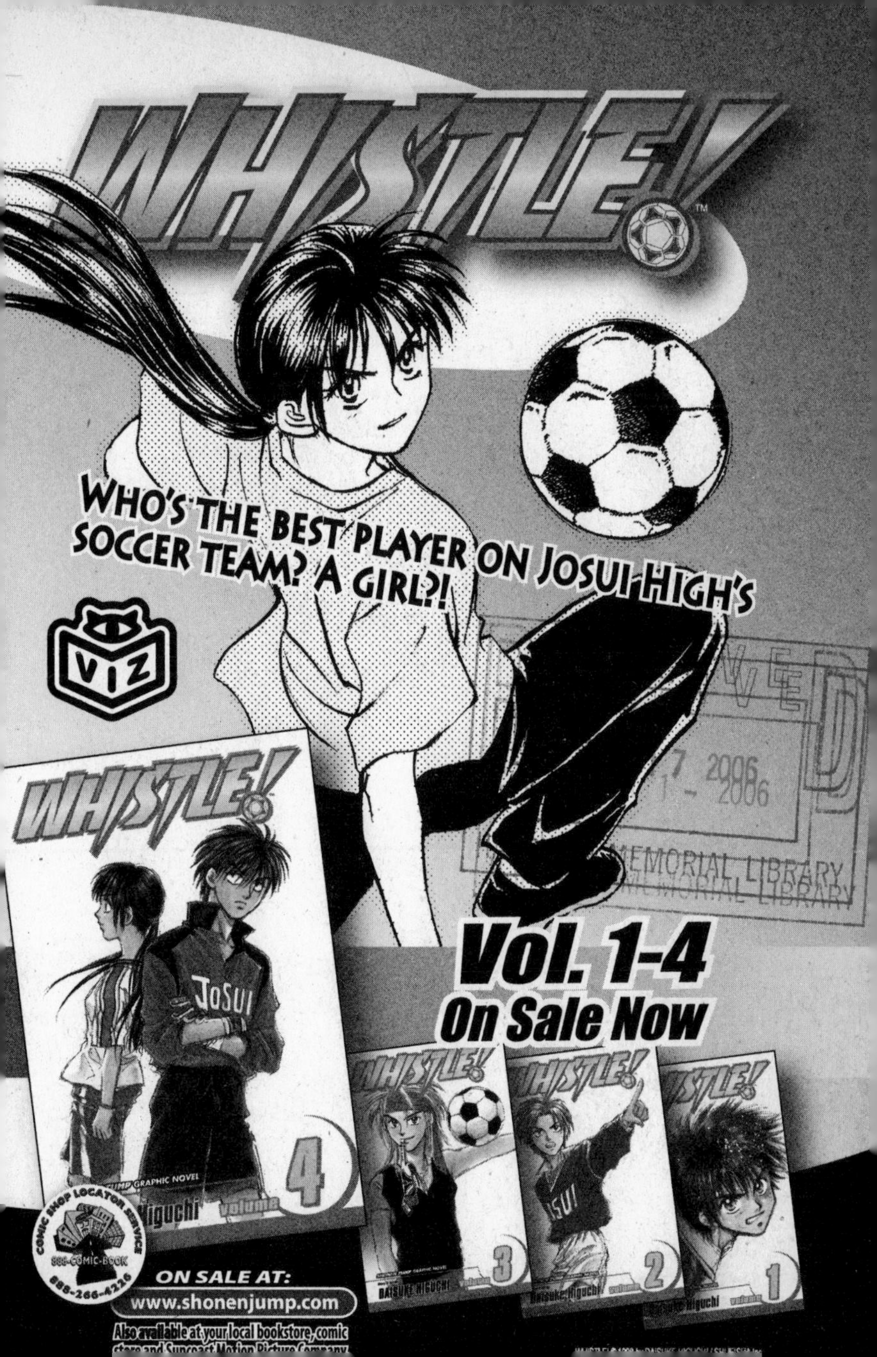
WHISTLE!™
WHO'S THE BEST PLAYER ON JOSUI HIGH'S SOCCER TEAM? A GIRL?!
VIZ
MEMORIAL LIBRARY
WHISTLE!
JOSUI
Higuchi
Vol. 1-4
On Sale Now
DAISUKE HIGUCHI
Daisuke Higuchi
COMIC SHOP LOCATOR SERVICE
888-COMIC-BOOK
888-266-4226
ON SALE AT:
www.shonenjump.com
Also available at your local bookstore, comic

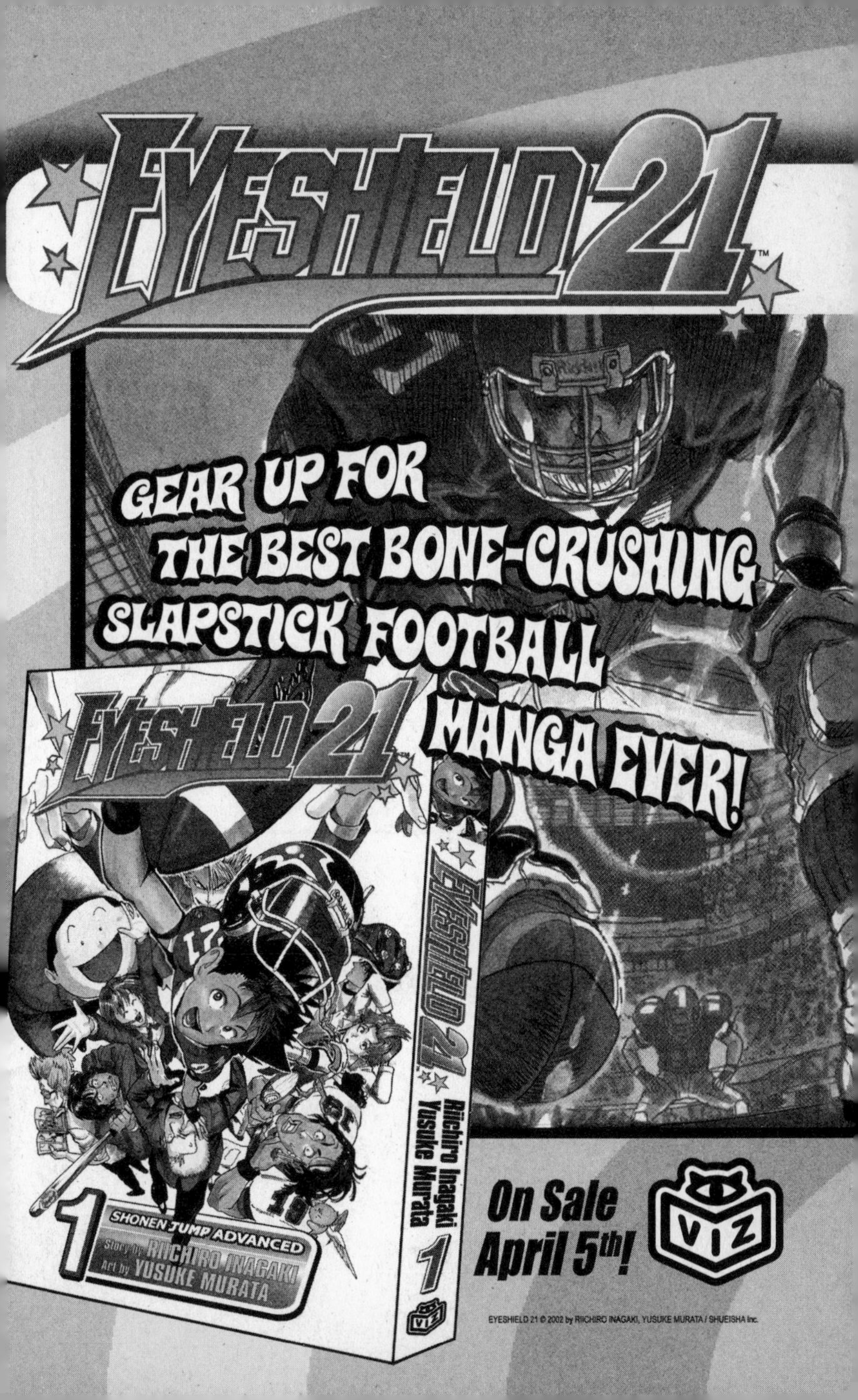
EYESHIELD 21™
GEAR UP FOR
THE BEST BONE-CRUSHING
SLAPSTICK FOOTBALL
MANGA EVER!
EYESHIELD 21
1
SHONEN JUMP ADVANCED
Story by RIICHIRO INAGAKI
Art by YUSUKE MURATA
EYESHIELD 21
Riichiro Inagaki
Yusuke Murata
1
VIZ
On Sale
April 5th!
VIZ
EYESHIELD 21 © 2002 by RIICHIRO INAGAKI, YUSUKE MURATA / SHUEISHA Inc.

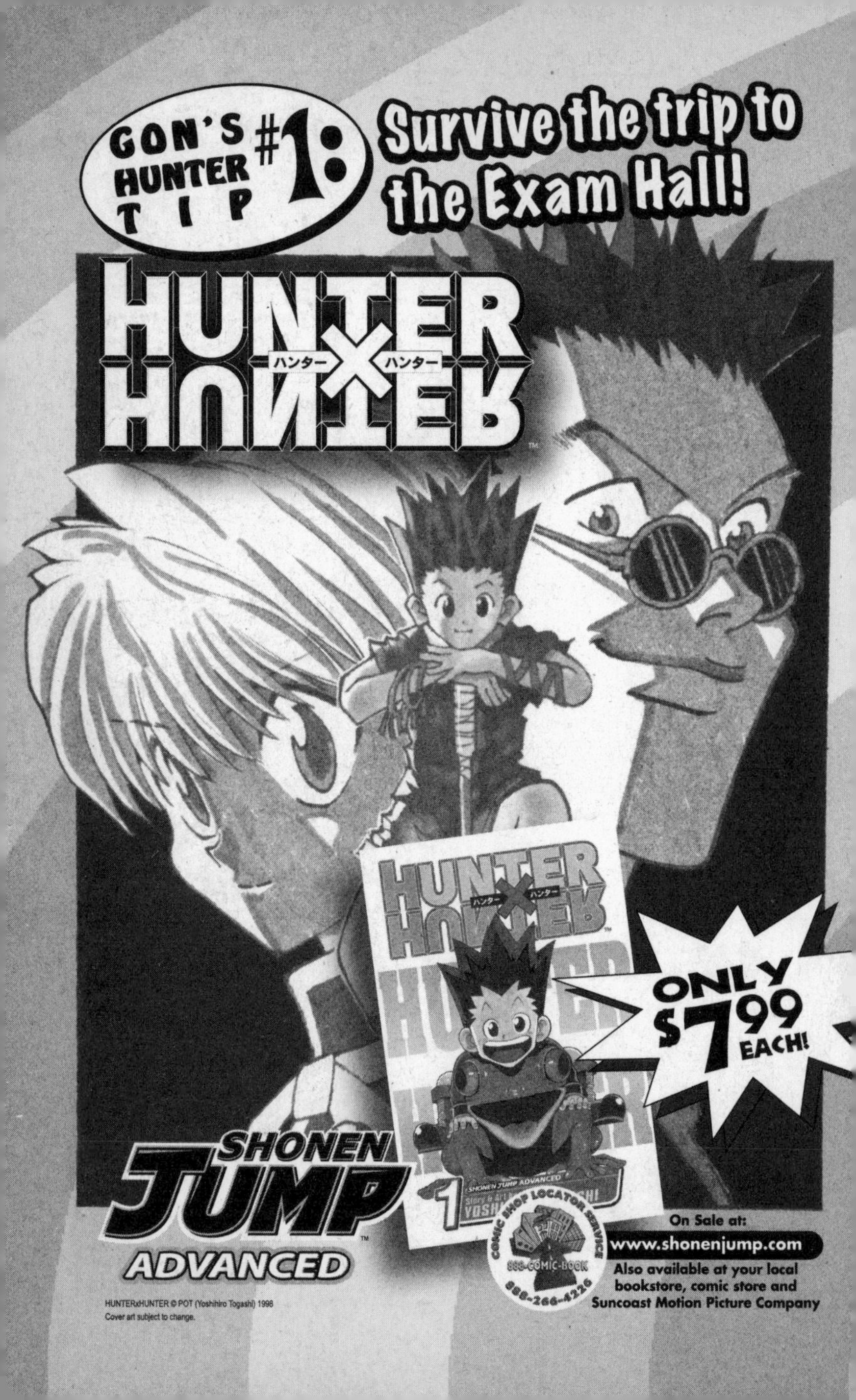

GON'S HUNTER TIP #1:
Survive the trip to the Exam Hall!
HUNTER × HUNTER
ハンター ハンター
ONLY $7.99 EACH!
SHONEN JUMP ADVANCED
On Sale at:
www.shonenjump.com
Also available at your local bookstore, comic store and Suncoast Motion Picture Company
COMIC SHOP LOCATOR SERVICE
888-COMIC-BOOK
888-266-4226
HUNTERxHUNTER © POT (Yoshihiro Togashi) 1998
Cover art subject to change.

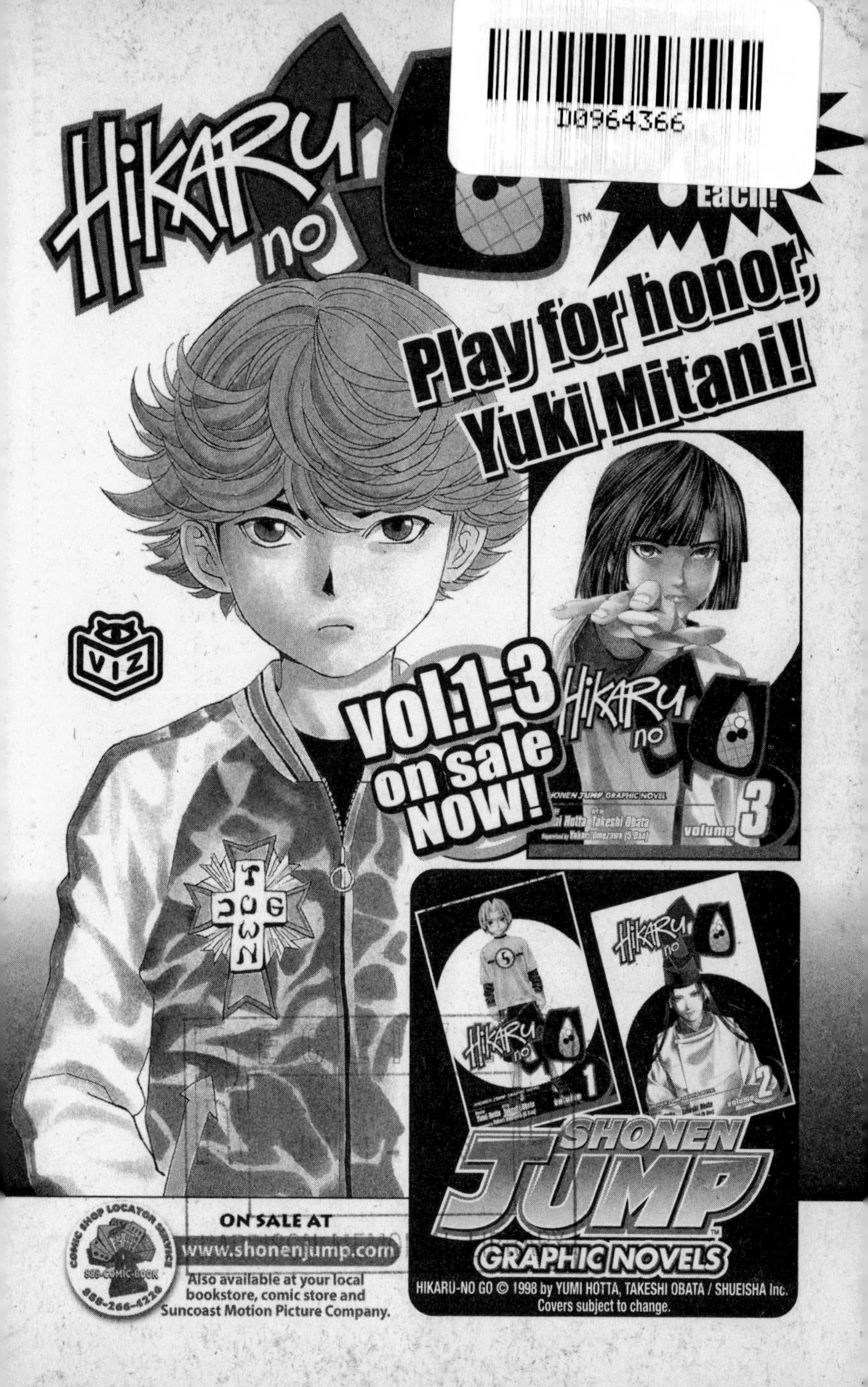

HIKARU no GO
D0964366
Each!
Play for honor, Yuki Mitani!
VIZ
vol.1-3 on sale NOW!
SHONEN JUMP GRAPHIC NOVELS
ON SALE AT
www.shonenjump.com
Also available at your local bookstore, comic store and Suncoast Motion Picture Company.
COMIC SHOP LOCATOR SERVICE
888-COMIC-BOOK
888-266-4226
HIKARU-NO GO © 1998 by YUMI HOTTA, TAKESHI OBATA / SHUEISHA Inc.
Covers subject to change.